MUSICIANS IN ENGLISH SOCIETY

FROM ELIZABETH TO CHARLES I

Da Capo Press Music Reprint Series

GENERAL EDITOR: FREDERICK FREEDMAN
Vassar College

MUSICIANS
IN ENGLISH SOCIETY

from Elizabeth to Charles I

BY WALTER L. WOODFILL

𝄞 DA CAPO PRESS • NEW YORK • 1969

A Da Capo Press Reprint Edition

This Da Capo Press edition of
Musicians in English Society is an
unabridged republication of the first
edition published in 1953. It is
reprinted by special arrangement with
Princeton University Press.

Library of Congress Catalog Card Number 69-12685

Published by Da Capo Press
A Division of Plenum Publishing Corporation
227 West 17th Street
New York, N. Y. 10011

Printed in the United States of America

MUSICIANS IN ENGLISH SOCIETY

FROM ELIZABETH TO CHARLES I

PRINCETON STUDIES IN HISTORY

Volume 9

MUSICIANS
IN ENGLISH SOCIETY,

from Elizabeth to Charles I

BY WALTER L. WOODFILL

PRINCETON, NEW JERSEY

PRINCETON UNIVERSITY PRESS

1953

L.C. CARD 52-8783

PUBLICATION OF THIS BOOK HAS BEEN AIDED BY A GRANT FROM THE
PRINCETON UNIVERSITY RESEARCH FUND

PRINTED IN THE UNITED STATES OF AMERICA BY

PRINCETON UNIVERSITY PRESS, PRINCETON, NEW JERSEY

TO MY

MOTHER

AND

FATHER

CONTENTS

ILLUSTRATIONS

(between pages 48 and 49)

A NOTE ON MONEY

PRECISE sums of money, payments made in the sixteenth and seventeenth centuries, are frequently given in this book, but no precise modern values can be attached to them, of course: the ratios sometimes supplied tend to mislead rather than enlighten. Such sums have most meaning, here at least, if they are considered in relation to each other. Some guidance is given in the text by calling attention to the differences in incomes of various classes of musicians and other persons, and by giving the cost of various commodities and non-musical services to compare with the cost of musical instruments, rewards (gratuities or fees), and so on. A comparative table is given in the conclusion and much further comparable data will be found in the appendices.

The following items may help the reader at the start: in June 1564 the city of Norwich set the maximum price to be charged a gentleman or other traveler by an innkeeper of the city for a dinner or supper consisting of porridge or broth with beef or mutton broiled and "a stroke of some kind of roast," at four pence from Christmas to Easter; in 1596 the town of Ipswich ordered that its jailer be paid thereafter eight pence for each meal he furnished his prisoners; and in 1642 five men, collectors for the earl of Bedford, dined for a total of five shillings. A man obliged, by some strange fate, to pay daily the four-penny rate set by Norwich in 1564 would have spent for his dinners in the course of a year something over six pounds, and at the rate paid in 1642 something over eighteen pounds. (Authorities believe that by about 1650 the price level was three and a half times what it had been in 1500.)

Some readers may find it useful to refer to Judges, "A note on prices in Shakespeare's time," in *A Companion to Shakespeare Studies*, ed. Granville-Barker and Harrison.

ABBREVIATIONS

BM   British Museum, London.

CSPD   *Calendar of State Papers Domestic*

Grove   *Grove's Dictionary of Music and Musicians*, 3d edn., ed. Colles, with Supplementary Volume (1940).

HMC   Historical Manuscripts Commission (reference system recommended in the Commission's *Guide to the Reports*, part I, 1914, pp. 1-15, is used here; thus "HMC *24, Rutland Mss.*, iv, 100" refers, first, to the set of reports numbered "24" on p. 10 of the *Guide*, that is, to those dealing with the papers of the duke of Rutland, next, to the fourth volume of this set, and last, to the page in that volume. In the miscellaneous volumes, except for those officially designated "Various," the name of the owner of the particular collection is given immediately after the volume number).

PRO   Public Record Office, London.

Bibliographical detail omitted in the notes (initials of author or editor, edition, date and place of publication) will be found in the bibliography.

As a rule spelling, capitalization, punctuation, abbreviation (including extension of abbreviations), and numbers in quoted matter have been modernized. Occasionally one or more words as they were originally spelled follow, in square brackets, the modernized version. When the editing, e.g. insertion of a comma, may affect the sense, the possibility is pointed out in a note. Titles of books are frequently abbreviated, but any changes of spelling in them have been unintentional.

Dates are given in accordance with modern usage: 20 March 1578/79 is given as 20 March 1579.

Had [Wagner] been a Sandwich Islander
he could have done nothing.—SHAW

Every public has the Shakespeare it deserves.—GIDE

PREFACE

IN music as in literature England at the end of Elizabeth's reign was enjoying a golden age, the age of Byrd and Dowland as well as of Shakespeare and Donne. This study attempts to contribute to understanding of the place of music in English society in that age, to show, as far as possible, the conditions under which professional musicians worked, and the place of music in the lives of Englishmen generally.

Most of the intensive research has been confined to the years 1558-1640, from the accession of Elizabeth to the calling of the Long Parliament, a unified period in spite of the great changes which took place, gradually, during it. Sometimes the problem at hand has demanded consultation of earlier evidence, notably in the case of the company of musicians of London. It has not seemed necessary, however, to go far back into the Middle Ages in search for origins: while this study illustrates the historical development of institutions over a considerable period, its focal point remains at the end of the reign of Elizabeth and the beginning of the reign of James.

Because of the nature of the problem, because of the character of the records, it is not possible to present a complete description. Many important and interesting questions cannot be answered at all, and for many other questions answers must be half conjecture. The voluminous material gathered for this study is highly suggestive, however, and after absorbing it, and exercising his imagination freely, someone could evoke a detailed picture—essentially a work of the imagination rather than a documented historical reconstruction—of the place of music and musicians in English society. I chose not to create such a picture: my research in this subject started partly in reaction to the statements I often encountered, in sober volumes, to the effect that "every domestic hearth was the scene of musical performance of a very high standard...," and that Thomas Kytson's Hengrave hall was "a typical example of a musical household at this time." I decided to incorporate into my study a large part of the record and thereby to make it possible for each reader, in his own imagination, to sketch in the obscure or blank areas. By selection, by organization, and by comment and suggestion, I attempt to guide the imagination; I suspect that most readers will come to the same conclusions, and hope that these will not be far off the mark.

Comprehensive study of the sources has revealed, more than anything else, extensive information about ordinary, uncelebrated professional musicians. Research seems unlikely to add much, unfortunately, to what the indefatigable labors of E. H. Fellowes and many other scholars have discovered about the famous composers and performers. Information about ordinary professional musicians, however, illuminates the scenes in which the distinguished musicians worked. As Bernard Shaw, Gerald Abraham, and others have discerned, composers write for their times, for consorts of viols if good violists are available, for great choirs if there are great choirs, for masques if someone will stage them—for the organizations, performers and occasions immediately available to them or which they hope can become available. There must be able performers and patronage to stimulate composers, but the number of able singers and players need not be vast, and the patronage prodigal, contrary to what scholars living in an age of mass-production and universal suffrage may unconsciously have assumed. Study of professional musicians, besides giving a setting for the story of the careers of famous musicians and indicating the resources available to them, reveals to some extent the attitudes of society towards music, the place of musical activity in society, and, in general, illustrates the working of many of the institutions and forces of the society. Study of any group in a society, such as the aristocracy, the greater merchants, the drapers, the clergy, apprentices, or the poor, is bound to be illuminating to historians. Musicians, perhaps less a compact group or class than the clergy, having as extremes the gentlemen of the Chapel Royal and vagabond-minstrels, constituted a group, nevertheless, tenuously bound by their art and by the ways society regarded them. Because of the diversity of their social and economic condition, and because they had relations with every social and economic class and with almost all elements of the government, they are in some ways more interesting to study than many groups.[1]

This book starts with the professional musicians of London, the company of London and the waits of London; continues with provincial professional musicians, including household musicians, waits, and independent musicians and minstrels; takes up the church; then the court, including the Chapel Royal and the King's Musick; and concludes with

[1] Abraham, *A Hundred Years of Music*, 13-14, points out how much more circumstance affects musical composition than it does literary composition, how composers cannot communicate directly with their public as novelists can, how they are at the mercy of performers. Elizabethan composers complained of this.

music as the possession of amateur musicians and the general public. No concert, not even for the mind's ear from printed notes, is offered to accompany all this; nor musical analysis: whatever intimate connections there may be between the facts and scenes here presented, and particular musical compositions and styles, are left for others to discuss. As he goes through these pages, however, the reader may well pause occasionally to play a recording of music of the period, or, better still, to convene friends to perform some of it.

Repeating here the whole long roll of my creditor friends and institutions would not discharge my great indebtedness to them. Remembering them all, I shall name only a few, and first of all, G. H. Guttridge of the University of California, Berkeley, and T. E. Mommsen of Princeton University, who always, through the years, responded cheerfully and helpfully to my appeals. I am hardly less obliged to C. C. Gillispie, R. G. Hallwachs, E. H. Harbison, J. R. Strayer, and Oliver Strunk, of Princeton University; Cuthbert Leicester-Warren, Esq., of Tabley house, Cheshire, and the duke of Devonshire, who allowed me to study their manuscripts; F. Thompson, Esq., secretary and librarian to the duke of Devonshire; the Rev. A. Raine, Hon. Archivist to the city of York; A. T. Milne, Esq., secretary and librarian of the Institute of Historical Research, London, who was often helpful and particularly so when I started gathering material for the plates; the corporations of Canterbury, Coventry, London, Nottingham, and York, and their archivists and librarians; the British Museum, the Public Record Office, the libraries of the universities of California, Cambridge, Oxford, and Princeton; the Huntington Library; and the Institute of Historical Research. I have many obligations to the University of California and to Princeton University, and in particular, to the former, for traveling and research fellowships, and to the latter, for generous grants from the University Research Fund, one of which helps publication of this volume. It is a pleasure to join the host of scholars who are indebted to the Princeton University Press; when errors are found in my book I shall be surprised if they can be attributed to the compositors and proofreaders, or to the editor, B. F. Houston, rather than to me. To all of these, and to many more I do not name, I am highly grateful.

Princeton, 1 January 1952

WALTER L. WOODFILL

PART ONE

THE MUSICIANS OF THE CITY OF LONDON

INTRODUCTION

ADORNED with a galaxy of musical organizations including the Chapel Royal, the King's Musick, and the choirs of Westminster Abbey and St. Paul's cathedral, London had two groups of musicians particularly its own, the city waits, and the independent or unretained musicians of the company of musicians of the city of London.

The musicians of these two groups, being neither great nor wealthy, left almost no record of their careers, of how they grew up, of how they fared, of when, where, what, and how they performed. Traces of their struggles remain chiefly in the city records, in brief statements of the troubles that beset the independent musicians of the company, in ordinances passed to help them, in appropriations for increased wages and for new instruments for the waits—traces sufficient to reveal the main outlines of the professional careers of the independent musicians and waits of London, to clarify somewhat the more fragmentary records touching on their provincial counterparts, sufficient, in fact, to make it possible to gain some comprehension of several of the basic elements, such as training by apprenticeship, and basic problems, such as excessive competition, common to the careers of nearly all professional musicians.

CHAPTER I. THE COMPANY OF MUSICIANS
OF LONDON

THE musical profession is not humanitarian or noble in the sense that medicine is, not concerned with morality and ethics in the way the law is, not materially productive as the crafts are, and not obviously useful as merchandising often is. Lacking these evident social virtues, and offering only intangible values, it has always been vulnerable to attack from many quarters. From earliest times some men have regarded music itself as potentially dangerous, a narcotic to be used with caution. Just as long, men have been wary of musicians, surely the first to be corrupted by music's powers. Musicians work in the theatre, play for dancing, in general associate with all that the world tends to suspect. Musicians seem to be idle when other men work, and even when working seem only to amuse themselves: they drink with the wedding guests and take money for an evening's pleasure. They work conspicuously, too, with a result that every musician must behave uncommonly well merely to avoid fastening the general suspicion on himself. Men seldom think music essential: if musicians hunger, let them work at an honest and useful calling. Few musicians have steady jobs bringing them reasonably adequate and dependable incomes; in sixteenth and seventeenth century England this aristocracy included chiefly members of the King's Musick, some waits, and servants in the households of noblemen and gentlemen. As a rule musicians have to depend on casual employment, on an uncertain, irregular succession of odd jobs given to them by many employers. Usually most independent musicians barely subsist, look forward to occasional feasts, and pray for one of the few steady jobs. The unsubstantial nature of their product contributes to the difficulties of good and honest musicians. Men have never found completely satisfactory ways of discriminating between the qualified and unqualified musician: a musician's bad product cannot be confiscated, examined in due course, and destroyed like a weaver's shoddy worsted. Marginal performers, men following primarily other occupations who turn to music to supplement their incomes, often escape control, partly because of the nature of the product, and these marginal performers sometimes lower the reputation as well as the incomes regular professionals try to raise. The particular advantages of the profession, such as the modest capital required, and above all, the pleasure often found in the work it-self, would hardly seem to compensate for its exceptional difficulties.[1]

Affection and respect for the wandering minstrel, a legacy from the Middle Ages, although surviving until the latter part of the sixteenth century, began to weaken long before then, perhaps in the fourteenth century when labor problems, Lollardy, and other considerations caused the governing classes to worry increasingly about vagabondage. Evidence that minstrelsy had begun to arouse apprehension appears in many places, including a patent of Henry VI that required his minstrels to put down the laborers and artificers who wandered about impersonating royal minstrels, and, most conspicuously, in the sixteenth century statutes against vagabondage. As long, however, as most communities welcomed wandering minstrels, the minstrels (or independent musicians) who tried to earn their livings chiefly in one town could hardly enforce a monopoly in their town, or organize a guild or company.[2]

In the sixteenth century the independent musicians of London faced, besides the eternal professional problems, and the hardy but dying tradition of the wandering minstrel, two further difficulties, the great number of outsiders and inadequate governmental support. London sheltered during much of the year the royal musicians, household musicians accompanying their patrons to court, and many of the hungry

[1] Some of the points here mentioned, such as attitudes towards music, and towards musicians, and how far the conduct of musicians seemed to justify the attitudes towards musicians, are considered with respect to the sixteenth and seventeenth centuries in chapters five and nine.

The principal sources for the history of the company are the manuscript Repertory of the Court of Aldermen (1495-1672), the Journal of the Proceedings of the Common Council (1416-1694), and the Letter Books (1275-1688), all preserved in the archives of the city. *The Handbook of the Worshipful Company of Musicians* prints many of the relevant records; its English translation of the patent of 1604, and transcription of the bylaws of 1606 (from a "contemporary copy in the possession of the company") are used here. Hawkins, *A General History of the Science and Practice of Music*, has some material. I have not found a history of the company based on thorough study of these sources but parts of it can be found in the *Handbook*, Hawkins, *Grove*, including the supplement, and Scholes, *Puritans and Music*.

[2] *Calendar of the Patent Rolls . . . 1446-1452*, 262; the patent is here dated 1449. What seems to be the same patent, but dated 1429, is printed in full in Latin and English in *Records of the City of Norwich*, ed. Hudson and Tingey, II, 328-330. Authority given to royal minstrels, and the acts against vagabondage, are discussed in differing connections later in this and following chapters.

minstrels and musical vagabonds of the rest of England and the continent, and most of them competed with London's own citizens. Custom and law allowed the retained musicians to come to London, and the impossibility of forming a strong organization, in large measure because of the deficiencies of the local government, admitted the others. The ability of the city of London to help its musicians gradually declined as the population of the London area spread beyond the city walls and the city's control. This expansion, said to have begun in the fifteenth century, reached important proportions by the 1630s when, it is estimated, the London area had a population of perhaps two hundred and thirty thousand, of whom only some one hundred and thirty thousand lived in the city and under its government. Except for the royal government itself, no one authority controlled the area: the royal government had to depend on local officials, and in the London area divided, obsolescent, political organization failed to provide the fine-meshed control needed for the solution of problems as elusive as those of the musicians.

Of necessity the musicians of the city of London sought the support of the strongest local authority, the city government, and tried to alleviate their problems by forming a guild or company. What is apparently their first recorded complaint, a petition made in 1500 by "the wardens and commonalty of the fellowship of minstrels freemen of the city of London" to the common council of the city, shows that they had begun to unite by the fifteenth century if not earlier. Responding to their protestations of poverty, the council gave them new authority over professional musicians and new articles of organization that served as a constitution or charter, amended but not superseded by later ordinances. The fellowship obtained a second important ordinance in 1518, and others in 1553 and 1574. Then in 1604, evidently seeking broader authority than the city could give, but acting with the consent of the court of aldermen, the fellowship secured royal letters patent of incorporation as the "Master, Wardens and Commonalty of the Art or Science of the Musicians of London," or, the "Company of Musicians." With its jurisdiction extended to include not only the city and its franchises but also the area within three miles of the city, thus including Westminster and more, the new corporation had much the same organization and authority that the old fellowship, sanctioned by the city, had had. Bylaws, confirmed by royal officials in 1606, exempted the king's musicians in ordinary not belonging to the company from its authority, but in spite of this it eventually came into conflict with them and lost its charter.[3]

In about 1635 the king's musicians, suing in the court of chancery, had the 1604 patent voided on the grounds that it had been obtained under false pretenses and to the prejudice of the rights and powers granted by Edward IV in 1469 to his minstrels and their successors, given perpetual authority to govern all minstrels in the kingdom excepting those of Cheshire. The royal minstrels undoubtedly had received the grant in 1469, but had made little if any use of it in the sixteenth century. They can hardly have had strong objection to the fellowship in 1510, for the marshal of the king's musicians then received from the court of aldermen a grant, probably made in answer to his request, of freedom of the city in the "craft of minstrels." In 1521 they seem to have protested to the aldermen that the existence of the city fellowship infringed upon the rights of their fraternity, which a year earlier had procured reconfirmation of its charter of 1469, but for the next century they apparently left the fellowship undisturbed, and in 1604 three of the assistants named in the patent were royal musicians. To all appearances the charter of 1469 had long been forgotten when its powers were reinvoked in the reign of Charles I. Some busy antiquarian may have brought it to the attention of the king's musicians and so given them legal ground for their suit, but the underlying reasons for it were that the city company had "endeavored to exclude the musicians and minstrels entertained into the king's service . . . from teaching and

[3] Ordinance of 1500: Journal, x, folios 183-185, and Letter Book M, folios 22-23; in the Letter Book the word "master" has been added above the line in a different hand and ink, before the word "wardens" when giving the name of the organization; the ordinance takes the form of a petition. 1518: Journal, xi, folios 320-321 verso. 1553: Journal, xvi, folios 253-254. 1574: Journal, xx, i, folios 152-153. Permission to sue for incorporation: Repertory, xxvi, folio 301; 6 March 1604. Charter 1604: Journal, xxxii, folios 102-105 verso, in Latin; *Handbook*, 23-26, in English. Bylaws 1606: *Handbook*, 29-41; the last paragraphs of the bylaws appear after the official confirmation, and may therefore have been added later.

The two city governing agencies mentioned in part one are the court of aldermen and the court of common council. Aldermen, wealthy men and usually members of the twelve greater livery companies, presided over the moot (assembly of freemen) of their wards, saw to most local administration, and with the mayor made up the court of aldermen (almost a closed corporation), the most powerful arm of the city government. The court of common council, consisting of the aldermen and about one hundred and seventy-five other men who were elected (by the end of the sixteenth century) by the citizens in their wardmoots, supervised the general administration of the city and authorized the issuance of ordinances by the mayor.

practicing" music if they would not join the company or "purchase [its] approbation thereunto. . . ," and (probably) that control over professional musicians in London and the rest of the kingdom might be profitable. Having had the 1604 patent voided, the royal musicians then obtained their own in 1635, which made them the sole authority empowered to govern the practice of music in all England, excepting Cheshire but specifically including the city of London. Now the London musicians were worse off than they had been at any time since 1500, being without either royal or municipal authority to control the profession of music, even within the jurisdiction of the city.[4]

Beginning shortly before the appearance of the new patent to the royal musicians, the officers of the old company tried to reestablish themselves under municipal authority. Perhaps the only result of their first petition to the aldermen was negative, a dispersal of the members of the old company among other non-musical companies. The next year, 1636, the "musicians freemen of several companies of this city" complained against the members of the new royal company who were trying "to compel the petitioners to be under their rule and government." Soon they reorganized themselves in fact if not in law as the "master, wardens, and commonalty of minstrels, London," and in 1638 the court of aldermen, recognizing them as "an ancient brotherhood of this city . . . governed by the acts and orders of this honorable court," gave them a new constitutional ordinance. By making it largely a restatement of the ordinance of 1500, the aldermen and musicians apparently tried to emphasize the antiquity of the brotherhood in order to defeat an anticipated argument that its creation violated the monopoly of the new royal company. According to the city records

---

[4] The preamble of the patent granted to the royal musicians 15 July 11 Charles I (1635) tells of the suit to void the patent of 1604: PRO Patent Roll C.66.2692; printed in Hawkins, *History*, 696-698. *Grove*, supplement, 454, states that the proceedings against the 1604 company were taken in 1634.

1469 patent: *Foedera*, ed. Rymer (Hague), v, ii, 169-170; in English in *Handbook*, 19-21. For other references to fifteenth century activities of the royal minstrels see chapter five below.

Admission of the marshal, John Chambre, 1510: Repertory, II, folio 98 verso. Complaint in 1521: Repertory, v, folio 178 (damaged). Reconfirmation of 1469 charter: *Foedera*, vi, i, 179.

Assistants 1604: William Warren, Robert Baker, and Rowland Robedge, royal musicians according to *King's Musick*, ed. Lafontaine, 45, and "Lists of the King's Musicians from the Audit Office Declared Accounts," *Musical Antiquary*, II (1911), 175. City company excluding royal musicians: preamble of 1635 patent, in Hawkins, 697. Extent of authority of 1635 company: patent, in Hawkins, 698.

the reestablished brotherhood remained unmolested until after the Restoration. Except for two or three years about 1635 the city musicians succeeded in maintaining an organization throughout the period under study.[5]

Benefiting from the experience of older companies, the musicians adopted standard forms of organization and procedure. In the sixteenth century, and until they received their royal patent in 1604, they had for officers a master and two wardens, elected at annual meetings of the whole membership from 1500 to 1518, and at biennial meetings thereafter. The patent added thirteen to twenty assistants with life tenure, returned to annual elections, and, in line with the undemocratic tendency then current among the London companies, restricted the vote to the officers themselves. Most of the business of the company seems to have been handled by the officers, who after 1604 could even make bylaws, subject to approval by royal officials. The "common box" received, besides each member's quarterly dues of three pence before 1606 and six pence thereafter: fees paid on presentation of apprentices; and fines levied: for refusing to take office or to pay dues, fees, or fines; for violating any of the company's rules or orders; and for failure to heed summons to attend quarterly meetings or special meetings held for the burial of a brother or sister or for other business. Before 1606 the city had a right to half of the penalties collected, but afterwards the company kept everything.[6]

No doubt poverty and pride, above all, led the independent musicians to form their company. Nevertheless its objectives and functions— religious, fraternal, governmental, educational, and economic—and its

[5] Petition 2 July 1635: Repertory, xlix, folio 253 verso. Petition 24 March 1636: Repertory, l, folio 163 verso. Petition 1638: Repertory, lii, folios 132 verso-133. Ordinance (committee report accepted) 24 July 1638: Repertory, lii, folios 226-227 verso.

On 15 July 1638, just before the aldermen reestablished the city company, the royal charter of 1635 was confirmed, according to a docket in the pro, SP 38/17. In 1665 the royal company brought *quo warranto* action against the city company, which appealed for the help of the city: Repertory, lxx, folio 145 verso.

[6] See ordinances (1500 and 1518 in particular), patent and bylaws (notes 3 and 5 above). The ordinance of 1500 may not originally have provided for a master (note 3 above). Assistants appear in the 1638 ordinance but not in the sixteenth century records. The bylaws authorize the officers to elect liverymen from among the freemen, and they had to accept the dignity and pay one pound or incur a fine of two pounds; the bylaws give liverymen no special rights or duties. The ordinances, patent, and bylaws give many other commonplace details.

methods, like its organization and procedure, conformed to the general tradition of the city.[7]

Neither the religious nor the fraternal aspect stands out in the records, perhaps chiefly because men seldom consciously write of what everyone knows and does: fraternal religious observances and election banquets were so integrally part of guild life that only some failure in them, such as slack attendance or excessive cost, would bring them into the record (musicians' company account books and other records have not survived, apparently). Perhaps the most formal religious note appears in their petition of 1500, when the musicians asked that the articles they submitted be enacted as far as they were reasonable and in "reverence of God and of Saint Anthony their patron to whom they shall continually pray for the prosperous state" of the aldermen and of "this noble city." Their resources probably never allowed them to consider seriously the founding of a chantry. Little more appears about fraternal objectives. The ordinance of 1574 explicitly directed that the company's half of the penalties were to be devoted to the poor of the company, and the bylaws of 1606, in specifying the use to be made of penalties, first named relief of the company's poor, and then general expenses.

The city gave the company, that was in a sense a lesser agency or department of its administration, a considerable amount of governmental, or police, responsibility and authority. First of all the company had to preserve order among all persons performing music for gain, and next it had to do everything it could to see that nothing associated with music contributed to the increase of disorder or immorality among the general public.

By delegating much of their responsibility for the preservation of order among musicians, the common council and court of aldermen relieved themselves of the burden of settling ordinary disputes between musicians and of disciplining them for breaches of order or professional custom, and helped the musicians, who, because of their intimate knowledge of their own customs and problems, could handle their own disputes most quickly, inexpensively, and justly. By settling their minor problems without disturbing the aldermen, the musicians

[7] For the guilds and companies and general tradition see: Lipson, *Economic History of England*, especially I, 308-439, III, 340-342; Unwin, *Gilds and Companies of London*; Clode, *The Early History of the Guild of Merchant Taylors*; Johnson, *History of the Worshipful Company of the Drapers of London*, especially I, 1-59; and other company histories.

could look for more sympathy when a major problem required an appeal.

The ordinance of 1518, strengthening a provision of the first ordinance, laid down the basic rules which remained virtually unchanged thereafter. No freeman of the company should "rebuke or revile with unfitting language or smite" any of his brethren on pain of a fine assessed by the officers according "to the quality and quantity" of the offense. The officers, acting in consultation with the mayor or chamberlain, could "commit . . . unto ward there to abide such punishment as shall be thought reasonable" any of the company who disobeyed or otherwise hindered them in the performance of their duty. Finally, no freeman could sue another freeman of the company in any court of record, on pain of a fine of six shillings eight pence, until the master and wardens had tried to settle the dispute, and, failing, had given him permission. The bylaws of 1606 made only minor changes, and these chiefly in the size of fines authorized, two pounds in the case of "facing, bracing, evil reproaching, or affraying," for example. The absence after 1518 of legislation reinforcing the authority of the master and wardens, and the fact that between 1518 and 1642 the court of aldermen apparently considered only one serious dispute among the members, suggest that the master and wardens succeeded in keeping order within the company.[8]

They did not succeed as well in controlling relations between members of the company and other musicians: men retained by the crown, noblemen, and gentlemen, members of other companies, and amateurs usually could ignore their summons and orders. As a result the city gave the company more and more authority, but never quite enough.

The company always had some authority over some musicians who were not members. The ordinance of 1500 started by giving the com-

---

[8] The provision in the ordinance of 1500 mentioned only verbal offense, not smiting. The bylaw requiring the bringing of disputes to the company officers before taking them to other courts occurs after the confirming paragraph and may therefore be a later addition: see note 3 above.

In 1597 the aldermen settled a dispute between the company and its new master, Robert Streachie or Strachey, who insisted on seeing the company accounts for the preceding year and on having custody of the money held by his predecessor: Repertory, xxiv, folios 72 verso-73. A case almost reached the aldermen in 1594, when the lord keeper wrote to the mayor asking that he see that members of the company no longer prevent the newly elected master from exercising his office: *Analytical Index to the . . . Remembrancia . . . London*, ed. Overall, 92. The master, William Warren, served in the royal Musick from 1594: "Lists," *Musical Antiquary*, ii (1911), 116.

pany the right to see that no person not a freeman of London—"no
manner foreigner of whatsoever condition he be of"—perform minstrelsy, or sing or play on any instrument, on several of the most
profitable occasions. It also exempted from all provisions of the ordinance servants of the royal family and of lords of parliament, who
could continue to perform in the city as they had or ought to have done
before adoption of the ordinance, and so long as they did not live continuously in the city: the most serious competitors could ignore the
company. The ordinance of 1553 opened by forbidding foreigners to
sing or play "in any common hall, inn, alehouse" or similar place;
although the injunction grimly included all foreign minstrels "of what
estate, degree or condition soever he or they be," the exemptions of
1500 must have been understood, so strong was the idea of status. Other
provisions of this ordinance, of the ordinance of 1574, and of the bylaws
of 1606, applied to all persons performing music in the city, including
members of the musicians' company and other companies, and strangers, but probably excluding in actuality musicians with influential
patrons.

Musicians who belonged to other companies caused much trouble.
Sometimes a company admitted a man following the craft of another
company, and sometimes a man, trained in the craft of the company to
which he belonged, forsook his original craft and took up another.
The results both conformed in general to a custom of London that
allowed freemen to work at any craft they knew, and raised jurisdictional problems, beginning with the question of whether such men
should obey the rules of their own companies, or of the companies of
the crafts they engaged in.

Apparently the first case of its kind, involving musicians and recorded in the Repertory of the court of aldermen, arose in 1547. The
weavers, it turned out, had taken in by redemption (by fee) two minstrels who practiced minstrelsy only and retained apprentices contrary to the musicians' ordinances. The aldermen ordered the transfer
of the offenders into the musicians' company, which was to take "but
an easy fine" of one of them and to let him keep two of the apprentices he then had, its "rules to the contrary notwithstanding," and
ordered the weavers in the future to take in "only mere weavers."[9]

In 1562 the aldermen agreed that the lord mayor should call before
him "all such persons as do use and exercise the art and science of

[9] Repertory, XI, folios 392 verso, 395 verso-396.

common minstrels" in the city who were not members of the minstrels' fellowship, and "cause them to be obedient" to its officers and rules. No doubt the lord mayor called these minstrels before him and duly admonished them.[10]

In response to a complaint in 1574 the aldermen agreed on, and the common council passed, an act requiring all minstrels not free of the company of minstrels to obey its laws and orders. The act may have temporarily anesthetized the problem but did not dispose of it.[11]

In 1601 the company complained again of "divers freemen of other companies within this city using their art which take and keep greater numbers of apprentices then in former time they have been accustomed," but the aldermen seem only to have appointed a committee. Later in the year a perfect remedy, rarely applicable, settled one case: the court, with the consent of the masters and wardens concerned, translated a girdler from the girdlers' to the minstrels' company ("which science he now useth") and a freeman of the minstrels' company to the girdlers' company.[12]

Perhaps the musicians hoped that a royal charter, by giving them broader authority, would help them solve the problem. The bylaws provided that anyone, brother of the company or not, using music for his living without the written and sealed consent of its officers, or not obeying their orders, was to be fined not more than two pounds for each offense, and forbade anyone to leave the company and enter another without their permission on pain of fine of ten pounds. Another bylaw ordered all persons getting their living by music but not members of the company to present themselves quarterly and pay six pence, and if they failed, to pay one shilling. The general exemption of royal musicians not belonging to the company applied to these as to the other provisions.

Within a few years the company must have found that it lacked power to enforce these bylaws, for early in 1613, in response to a petition made late in 1612, the court of aldermen decided to recommend to the common council that "all persons living by the profession of music (being free of other companies of the city other then of the musicians) should be translated into the company of musicians." The proposal

---

[10] Anyone objecting was to appear before the aldermen at their next meeting but if anyone did the record fails to mention it: Repertory, xv, folios 142, 144 verso.

[11] Repertory, xviii, folios 179 verso-180; Journal xx, i, folios 152-153.

[12] The committee to consider the complaint was appointed on 23 April 1601: Repertory, xxv, folio 223. The report it was to make in writing had not reached the Repertory by the following 4 February. The reciprocal translations took place on 20 October 1601: Repertory, xxv, folio 293.

seems to have lost out, perhaps because the musicians to be transferred objected to the stricter rules of the musicians' company and prevailed on their companies to block it, perhaps because it would have set precedent in the wider jurisdictional battle long fought by many companies.[13]

Two further cases arose in later years. A musician, freeman in the fletchers' company, complained to the court in 1620 against the musicians' company. Mediation by two aldermen seems to have relieved both the fletcher and the musicians' company. In 1628, at the written request of the earl of Warwick on behalf of "his servant Thomas Butler by profession a musician" who was being "troubled and molested by the company of musicians," the court of aldermen investigated and found that while the company was trying to disenfranchise Butler on the ground that he had married when still an apprentice, its real grievance was that Butler, a member of the company of clothworkers, kept more apprentices than the musicians' company allowed its own members. The court ordered the musicians' company to "surcease" its suit against Butler, and the clothworkers' company to examine him and take "some such order and course for remedy" as it should find "just cause." Perhaps the musicians' company had lost the aldermen's sympathy; perhaps the earl and the clothworkers had more influence: at any rate not the musicians, as in former times, but the clothworkers, had the last word.[14]

The problem of musicians who belonged to other companies could perhaps never reach a final solution. Periodically it disturbed but never threatened to destroy the company: the city always acted in time with remedies adequate for each crisis. Lack of direct control sometimes allowed unfair competition but apparently never defeated the company's efforts to preserve order among professional musicians.

Repeatedly the preambles of ordinances enacted at the request of

[13] Repertory, xxxi, i, folios 6, 85 verso. The Journal, from April through June, does not record passage of the measure. It may have been a similar proposal that the musicians submitted later in the year and that the aldermen referred to a committee to consider whether it was according to the intent and meaning of the report formerly made. Ten days later the committee declared that the proposal agreed with its former report and that it should be passed. The new report was accepted by the court and ordered put in the Repertory; perhaps this signifies that the court of aldermen enacted the proposal without referring it to the common council: Repertory, xxxi, ii, folios 203 verso, 210 verso-211.

[14] 1620: Repertory, xxxiv, folio 433; the Repertory seems to contain no further reference to the mediators, who were to report back if they could not bring the disputants to agreement. 1628: Repertory, xliii, folio 3.

the musicians' company argued that they would help the company arrest the growth of public disorder and immorality. At the end of the reign of Edward VI the desirability of cutting off the great influx of minstrels into London "whereby much disorder, evil rule, vice, and sin doth secretly spring and daily ensue within the said city . . ." was advanced as a justification for increasing the authority of the fellowship. The ordinance of 1574 alleged that the large number of so-called minstrels in London who were not subject to the fellowship were "great occasion of unchaste, wasteful, lewd, and dangerous practices amongst good citizens' children and apprentices." While the musicians may have been less concerned over order and morality than competition, they found the argument useful when they sought general grants of authority. Certainly respectable musicians gained from anything which tended to lessen antipathy towards their profession.

Several regulations enacted at their request seem to have been designed solely in the interest of public order. The ordinance of 1553 prohibited any playing of instruments by anyone except the waits in "the open streets, lanes or alleys . . . from or after ten of the clock in the evening until five of the clock in the morning" and gave the company, which had to enforce the order, authority to assess a fine of ten shillings on offenders. By the time of James so many serenaders seem to have been wandering about the city playing under windows for rewards that they had become a public nuisance; the bylaws of 1606 ordained that no one, "in consort or otherwise," should thereafter play on any instruments in either evening or morning "at or under any nobleman, knight, or gentleman's window or lodging in the street" or at the lodging of anyone else, without the permission of the master, wardens and at least eight assistants of the company, on pain of a fine of three shillings four pence for each offense.[15]

Perhaps "three men's songs" menaced morals as much as order. According to the ordinance of 1553 many craftsmen, such as tailors and "showmakers," "leaving the use and exercise of their crafts and manual occupations and giving themselves wholly to wandering abroad, riot, vice, and idleness, do commonly use now adays to sing songs called three men's songs in the taverns, alehouses, inns, and such other places of this city, and also at weddings and other great feasts made within the

---

[15] One of the later bylaws (see note 3 above) forbade anyone to go or allow his servant to go in the street from house to house with his instrument uncased or uncovered; apparently this was designed to help enforce the rule against unlicensed street playing.

same city to the great loss, prejudice and hindrance" of the minstrels' company. The ordinance required the company to see that no one, whether freeman of the city or not, "using to sing any songs commonly called three men's songs shall from henceforth sing in or at any tavern, inn, alehouse, weddings, feasts, or any other like place . . . any manner of such song or songs (except the same be sung in a common play or interlude)," and provided for forfeiture by offenders, after warning from the master or wardens, of three shillings four pence. In 1606 the bylaws charged the company with the task of seeing that no "person sing any ribaldry, wanton, or lascivious songs or ditties . . . whereby God may be dishonored, or any slander or infamy may arise or be given of or to the said science" of music. Offenders were to pay ten shillings and go to jail "for such convenient time" as the master and wardens thought fit.

Dancing suffered a particularly strong attack in the middle of the sixteenth century. Because music usually accompanied it and teachers of dancing and keepers of dancing schools or halls were usually musicians, much of the task of regulating or suppressing it fell to the musicians' company. The ordinance of 1553, the first of the musicians' ordinances to mention dancing, required them to put down dancing schools altogether. No "minstrel either foreign or freeman or any other person [was] to keep or teach any school of dancing" on pain of a fine of ten pounds (sixty times the fine set in the same ordinance for singing three men's songs). Later in the year, at the beginning of Mary's reign, the aldermen refused to allow two minstrels to keep a dancing school, their petition being "thought by the court not necessary to be granted." The city's action anticipated that of the royal government: in 1555 the lord mayor, on behalf of Philip and Mary, directed the aldermen to see that, amongst other things, there were no "dancing houses" in the city. The demand and rewards must have been great, for less than eight years later the aldermen found it necessary to summon all keepers of dancing schools, and to order the seven who appeared to close their schools or suffer the penalty, a fine of ten pounds, prescribed by the act of 1553. In 1574 the aldermen, apparently concluding that regulation of authorized dancing schools was better than occasional suppression of clandestine schools, appointed a committee "to allow or disallow as many of the company of minstrels" as it thought "meet and expedient to keep dancing schools within this city." The bylaws made under the royal charter of 1604, following this precedent, authorized the company to control all teachers of dancing, who had to be citizens but not necessarily members of the company, and to forbid any of them to teach if they were not well qualified. Persons guilty of causing "any abuse or disorder," refusing to obey the rulings of the company, or failing to appear before its officers for questioning or examination, were subject to a fine of one pound and, in some cases, to imprisonment at their discretion. Moreover, the bylaws forbade even licensed teachers of dancing, and all musicians, to "teach, keep, or play . . . haunt, exercise, or use, any dancing in any school of dancing upon any Sabbath days" on pain of a two pound fine for each offense.[16]

Much, but not all, of the burden in such matters fell on the company. An order of 1555, issued by the mayor in response to royal command, ignored the company while seconding its efforts. Each alderman was to assemble all the keepers of taverns, dancing houses, unlawful games, and the like, and first of all to order them not to permit "any minstrel or minstrels or any other whatsoever person or persons to sing any manner song or songs or to play upon any manner of instrument or to make or play any manner of interlude or play within his or their house," except at marriages and similar festivities. Sixty years later the aldermen again bypassed the company when they established a censorship to prevent blasphemy in foreign languages. They ordered that "no Latin, Italian or French song whatsoever shall be sung [by the musicians of this city or any other] till it be first read in English to the lord mayor . . . and by him allowed." This order is perhaps the only clear indication recorded at any time during the period that the aldermen doubted the company's willingness to do everything it could to guard public morality against infection from musical sources.[17]

While originally developed primarily to serve economic ends, the system of apprenticeship, the means by which guilds and companies discharged their educational function, had taken on independent life of its own by the late Middle Ages, so deeply had its roots grown into the social fabric: many companies tried to maintain the system of apprenticeship long after its economic usefulness to them had disappeared. Musicians found it as valuable in the sixteenth and seventeenth centuries as it had ever been, and the educational function of their company ranked second to none. Besides serving economic ends, the sys-

[16] 2 March 1553: Journal, xvi, folio 254 (the ordinance of 1553). 31 November 1553: Repertory, xiii, i, folio 97 verso. 1555: Journal, xvi, folio 328. 1562: Repertory, xv, folios 142, 144 verso. 1574: Repertory, xviii, folio 232. 1606: *Handbook*, 33-34 (bylaws).

[17] 1555: Journal, xvi, folio 328 (also: Letter Book, S, folios 20-20 verso). 1615: Repertory, xxxii, folio 75 verso.

tem provided the sole school for professional secular musical training, contributed to the preservation of order and morality, and tended to maintain or raise standards of musical performance and professional discipline.

Traditionally apprentices lived with their masters, who were expected to bring them up in religion and good citizenship as well as in the customs and techniques of their trade. Although the intimate relationship between master and apprentice had long been disappearing in many occupations, it probably remained the rule among musicians, perhaps chiefly because they had few apprentices and necessarily worked closely with them.[18]

The custom of London, common sense, and official supervision made it unnecessary that the company's laws include many precepts on the training of apprentices in either common virtue or professional conduct. A prohibition of gambling by apprentices, for example, was not put in the sixteenth century ordinances; that it was in the bylaws probably reflects only the extension of the jurisdiction of the company to areas not governed by the city's laws. Another bylaw, probably adopted after 1606, seems to record old professional customs, perhaps formally enacted at last because recently ignored or challenged. No one should allow "apprentices to serve by themselves with any music . . . , except they do go in . . . the company of two freemen at least well and sufficiently exercised and experienced in . . . music, whereof one to be the master of some one of the said apprentices. . . ." Probably the chief justification for this bylaw is the one it set forth, that apprentices "be the better guided and directed in that science for the laud, honor, and commendation thereof," but it also tended to ensure more strict control over behavior. Musicians' apprentices, if sent out without adult supervision, had even more opportunity to get into mischief than apprentices in general, long notorious for their disorders. The same bylaw also prescribed that the master of one of the apprentices, not an apprentice, should "offer and present the music": the master was to be the active and responsible leader of the group and not merely the ultimate receiver of the money earned or extorted by an unruly band of apprentices. Rules such as these must have been professional custom for centuries among the best minstrels, for only example could efficiently teach where patrons for the evening might be found, how to approach them, how to know which of them might welcome music

[18] On apprenticeship see, besides the works named in note 7 above, Dunlop, *English Apprenticeship and Child Labour.*

but not pay well for it, what kinds of music should be played for each type of person and for each occasion, all the little points apprentices had to know if they were to become respected and successful masters and citizens of London.

Unfortunately, little evidence remains to show how musicians trained their apprentices technically. All apprentices probably practiced on at least one instrument, and nearly all probably practiced singing. Many professional musicians may have picked up entirely by ear the melodies they repeated and elaborated, but the demand for performances of works composed or arranged for the leading organizations, such as the King's Musick and the London waits, by Thomas Morley and others, must have required that most of the best musicians, at least from the middle of the sixteenth century, learn to read music. Good London musicians could hardly have lagged behind the Norwich waits, given a grant in 1533-1534 to help them in "studying on the pricksong."[19] Perhaps few apprentices, other than those who learned instruments that can sound more than one note simultaneously, such as the organ, virginals, lute, and viols, studied musical theory or composition.

The minimum length of time required to prepare an apprentice for his first public appearances depended, as ever, on the ability and diligence of both master and apprentice, the kind of instruments and music studied, and the critical standards of the master and his patrons. To protect apprentices, the system, and the reputation of the profession, the company had to do more than leave the time of first public performance to the discretion of the master, and more than designate a standard minimum period. The ordinance of 1518 strictly forbade any master to allow his apprentice to play his instrument openly or covertly in any employment whatsoever before the apprentice had been "examined and opposed" by the officers and "abled to use his instrument . . . for the honor of this city and honesty of the said mystery." For each offense a master was to forfeit six shillings eight pence. The ordinance of 1574 brought musicians belonging to other companies under this rule, and, "for avoiding partiality" that could beggar a master, provided that if an apprentice of such a master should "not be allowed" by the officers of the musicians' company, the apprentice should then be "apposed" and "allowed or disallowed according to his skill and worthiness" by one of these officers and by some other person, "skilful in music," appointed by the lord mayor. Corresponding provisions in the bylaws of 1606 allowed continuous supervision over ap-

---

[19] Stephen, *Waits of the City of Norwich*, 7-8.

prentices. The master and wardens or their appointees could, as often as they thought necessary, examine and "allow" or "disallow" apprentices according to their "sufficiency and skill." The penalty was now much greater, one pound if the master of the apprentice permitted him to play after being disallowed, and one pound, with imprisonment at the discretion of the officers, if the master failed to see that his apprentice appeared for examination. From 1518 on the company could demand that apprentices attain an arbitrary standard of musicianship before performing in public, and from at least 1606, until about 1635, apparently had continuous licensing authority over them.

The company apparently regarded an examination or equivalent of a masterpiece unnecessary for an apprentice formally ready for freedom. The initial examination, together with the improvement a master would want as the years passed, should have sufficed ordinarily, and certainly the repeated examinations authorized in the bylaws must have fully served the purpose. If the company could have denied freedom to apprentices who had finished their time the temptation to exclude new competitors might sometimes have been too great; it was better that apprentices faced at the last only formal requirements. It was better, too, that by 1606 the company had authority at any time to examine any members of the company or other persons practicing music professionally or teaching it or dancing, and to forbid them to continue their playing or teaching if they showed "insufficiency and want of skill." Anyone who played or taught before being relicensed could be fined one pound, and anyone who refused to appear for examination could be fined one pound and imprisoned at the discretion of the master and wardens, according to the bylaws. The company's educational system did not end at graduation: to keep their degrees masters had to maintain the skill they had acquired in school.

Economic considerations, of at least secondary importance in most of the company's activities, appear undisguised in its attempts to increase employment, to insure fair competitive practices, and to reduce the number of competitors.

The company seems to have adopted only one measure designed primarily and solely to increase employment, a bylaw of 1606 that set the minimum number of musicians to be hired on any engagement. No group "under the number of four, in consort or with violins," was to play at any gathering, on pain of a fine of three shillings four pence for each offender. Musicians' unions now listing the minimum for each restaurant, theatre, and hall follow the same principle. The bylaw, already mentioned as an educational measure, that forbade servants or apprentices to play anywhere except in the company of at least two freemen, also had the effect of setting a minimum.

The attempt to secure fair competitive conditions seems likewise to have required only one general injunction. The ordinance of 1518 ordered that no minstrel "supplant, hire, or get out another minstrel freeman of the same fellowship being hired or spoken to for to serve at . . . any doings whereby any such minstrel should have part of his living," on penalty of a great fine, two pounds, for each offense. The bylaws authorized imprisonment of offenders until they paid their fines. The discretion of the officers and the general custom of London must have taken care of other unfair practices.

In addition to all its efforts to restrict the musical activities of persons not free of London, efforts that tended to lessen competition as well as help maintain order, the company tried to restrict the number of persons who learned music, whether allegedly for pleasure or as apprentices of musicians. Here it cut at the roots of what its members must have regarded as one of their greatest problems, excessive competition.

All guilds tried to confine knowledge of their skills to their members and apprentices. What made the problem of the musicians' company different was that everyone had a virtually inalienable right to perform music. The company could not confiscate musical instruments or jail persons playing on them: the most it could do was to try to control the teaching activities of professional musicians. Several results, all bad from at least the professional point of view, could follow if professional musicians were allowed to teach anyone they chose. An unscrupulous master could avoid the risks involved in taking an apprentice by teaching several boys who claimed that they wanted to learn only for their own pleasure, and then get rid of the poorer ones and bind the best as apprentices, or simply exploit them. If the master were honestly teaching boys only because they professed to enjoy music and could pay for their lessons they might at last leave their proper occupations and turn to music for a living, although perhaps inadequately trained both musically and professionally. If they were apprentices in other companies and became freemen in them they increased the jurisdictional problems of the musicians' company, and if not they enlarged the throng of musical vagabonds. The ordinance of 1500 tried to prevent such difficulties by ordering that "none of the said fellowship . . . teach or inform any other person then his own apprentice in any point of the feat of minstrelsy upon pain of forfeiting of twenty shillings. . . ." Teaching persons who would not become competitors could do no harm, might make them better patrons, and certainly would be immediately profitable; the ordinance continued: "Nonetheless if any gentleman or merchant be disposed for to learn any thing for their pleasure that it be lawful to everyone of that the said craft to inform and teach every such gentleman or merchant." The line between legitimate and illegitimate teaching was hard to see, but it had to be drawn if competition were to be limited, if the system of apprenticeship were to work at all. The bylaws of 1606 dealt with the problem more briefly by providing for the licensing of teachers of music.

None of the other measures undertaken to reduce competition was as enforceable as those limiting the number of apprentices, and none more important. Not only did the number of competing masters depend, in the last analysis, on the number of apprentices: in music, more than in many occupations, apprentices competed with masters. When musicians thought of their collective interests they may sometimes have considered limiting the number of apprentices one of the chief functions of the system of apprenticeship. Ordinarily the master must have thought of apprenticeship above all as a means of getting cheap help without danger that a boy might be enticed from his service just as his investment in the boy's education was beginning to become profitable. The apprentice, or his father, must have seen in the system a safe way of earning an education leading to entrance into a profession. All three aspects of apprenticeship were closely related. Master and apprentice exchanged values, living expenses, education and admission to the profession, in return for a definite period of service. The rules adopted in order to ensure the working of the restrictions on the number of apprentices served also to protect the interests of both masters and apprentices.

The basic regulations that made apprenticeship a way to limit the number of musicians were, first, a definition of the term of apprenticeship, and second, restriction of the number of apprentices that any master might have at one time. Seven years, set "according to the laudable custom of this city" in 1500 as the one authorized term for apprenticeship, had become the minimum term by 1638.[20] This rule

[20] Ordinance of 1500: "Also to ordain that no freeman of the said craft take any servant allowes servant by year or in covenant for any term more or less other wise than by apprenticehood for seven years according to the laudable custom of

was as essential as the second, for the number of musicians would have been much greater if two, rather than seven, years had been considered long enough. Under ordinary circumstances the master gained by keeping an apprentice as long as possible, thereby postponing the costly and more or less tiresome initial training of a new apprentice.

After about a century of effort the company accumulated a reasonably satisfactory set of rules governing the number of apprentices a master could have at one time. Restriction of the number seems to have been becoming part of the general custom of London only towards the end of the fifteenth century, and the musicians' ordinance of 1500 made no limitations specifically although it implied one in the rule "that none of the fellowship [shall] teach . . . any other person then his own apprentice." The ordinance of 1518 definitely forbade any freeman to have more than one apprentice, not only that the apprentice might be "the better learned" but also that he might be "the better . . . set a work." Apparently to compensate present and past masters and wardens for the cost and trouble of office, each could have two apprentices at a time. In spite of the large penalty, two pounds, masters must have disobeyed the order, for in 1553 the ordinance called attention to it by repeating it and adding that masters who, after being admonished "to put away" unauthorized apprentices and paying the fine, continued to keep them would forfeit ten shillings a month for each unauthorized apprentice.

The musicians must have found it even harder to restrain members of other companies, few of which set the limit at one apprentice. The musicians' company based its complaint against the weavers in 1547 partly on the number of apprentices kept by musicians whom they took into their company. To end this unfair competition the common council provided in the ordinance of 1574 that "no person free of this city using the feat of a minstrel shall directly or indirectly have or retain to be brought up in the said art any more prentices at one time then is lawful for a freeman of the said company of minstrels, that shall not have been warden of the said company" except that if the person had "used the said art by the space of fourteen years after his being free of this city" he could have, like a warden, two apprentices.

---

this city upon pain of forfeiture of forty shillings half thereof to remain to the common use of this city and other half to the common box of the said craft." Ordinance of 1638: "And that they may take their apprentices for such terms of years as by the master and apprentice shall be agreed nonobstante any other order so that the same be not for any lesser term then seven years from the date of the indenture."

Equitable rules governing number of apprentices now applied to all freemen, regardless of company, who lived as professional musicians.

The ordinance went further. Expedients violating the spirit of these regulations could no longer be tolerated. No freeman living by the practice of music was to keep "to serve in the said art of minstrels any apprentice then being bound to any other person thereby to defraud the true meaning of this act concerning the excessive number of apprentices in the said art. . . ." The initial fine of two pounds remained, but the monthly penalty decreed in 1553 went up to two pounds, four times what it had been.

Finally, "every such retaining of an apprentice . . . and the indenture therefore . . . and the enrollment thereof . . . shall be void and no warrant to the chamberlain of this city to make any such apprentice free." This may have simplified enforcement of the basic measure, for boys and their parents, knowing that illegal service would not at the end win admission to the company and freedom of the city, had thereafter less temptation to connive with dishonest masters. On the other hand, the chief result may have been only to restrict the number of freemen: boys perhaps continued to serve illegally because of ignorance, need, or a willingness to gamble that an education in the musical profession, even without freedom in the company, would eventually be profitable.

All that legislation could do had been done, and the city records seem to contain no further complaints for over a quarter of a century. No report survives, apparently, from a committee of aldermen appointed in 1601 to consider the petition of the "company of minstrels, touching divers freemen of other companies within this city using their art which take and keep greater numbers of apprentices than in former time they have been accustomed. . . ."[21]

By putting all of the chief elements of the sixteenth century laws restricting the number of apprentices into their bylaws in 1606 and by making no important additions, the members of the company seem to have demonstrated their belief that they had a workable and satisfactory system, or at least that they could think of no substantial improvements. A minor change, made apparently to lessen the troubles of masters losing old and starting new apprentices, allowed any freeman of the company to take a second apprentice in the last half year of the indentured term of service of an old apprentice. The fine for offending against "the true meaning of this act" was reduced to one pound a month. Another change, essentially administrative, provided for the

[21] Repertory, xxv, folio 223.

transfer of the services of apprentices. Instead of simply prohibiting the retention by one master of another's apprentices, as the ordinance of 1574 did, the bylaws authorized any musician to sell his apprentice's remaining years of service to another musician if he first brought the apprentice before the master and wardens and registered in the hall book the "selling and turning over of the said apprentice," and if he paid a "forfeit" of two shillings. The penalty for breaking the rule was a fine of one pound. When entering the sale the officers presumably made sure that the apprentice's new master would not then have too many apprentices. This last provision seems to have been carried over, by implication, into the ordinance of 1638.

The limitations, running counter to the common desire for more than one apprentice, would almost certainly have disappeared during this long period if enforcement had failed badly or if belief had grown general that their effect on competition was negligible.

That the company had, or could have had, a class of journeymen, seems to be recorded only by a few passages in the ordinances and by-laws. The ordinance of 1500, by forbidding a master to hire anyone other than by seven-year contract for apprenticeship, implied that journeymen-musicians could not perform in London, but a phrase in the 1518 ordinance, "any man's servant or apprentice . . . during the time of his retainder or as long as the master and servant be in covenant . . . ," may refer to them. The bylaws of 1606 declared that everyone, "as well masters as journeymen and apprentices" had to be obedient, and the ordinance of 1638 set a journeyman's quarterage at a shilling, half of a freeman's. If a class of journeymen-musicians existed in London at all it probably grew up only towards the end of the sixteenth century, and remained small and unimportant. To set up in music as a master required little capital, and no shop. If sometimes London apprentices found it impossible to take up their freedom immediately, perhaps because of their age, and contracted for a year's service as journeymen, they did not thereby increase competition any more than if they had become masters.

The company's regulations governing the more formal aspects of apprenticeship apparently conformed completely to the custom of London. It prescribed that apprentices be free-born, not receive pay from their masters, give all their earnings to their masters, and not marry during their apprenticeship. Neither general custom nor, apparently, musicians' company rule, set a minimum age for apprentices, but according to an ordinance of 1556 no one could become free of the city until twenty-four years old;[22] since presumably parents wanted their sons to become freemen as soon as they were twenty-four, and since seven years was the minimum term for apprenticeship, seventeen may have been the usual maximum age for the beginning of apprenticeship. A need for boys with treble voices, or simply a feeling that seventeen is too late for the start of training in music, may have led some musicians to take younger apprentices for longer terms. To the usual requirements the musicians added, in the bylaws of 1606, one that was uncommon but not otherwise unknown: apprentices had to be "clean and whole limbed." Shortly after making the contract (the musicians' ordinance of 1500 allowed a month) every master had to present his new apprentice to the officers of his company to give them an opportunity to discover any irregularities and to make the necessary record; and within a year every master had to enroll the contract before the city chamberlain. The musicians included in their ordinance of 1518 a provision, no doubt made in reaction to some recent bitterness, that forbade anyone to "entice, procure, or counsel any man's servant or apprentice" from the service of his master during the time of his retainder, on pain of a fine of one pound, or more or less at the discretion of the officers; the rules of 1574 and 1606 concerning the keeping of other men's apprentices also tended to discourage such theft. When an apprentice completed his term his master had to present him to his company officers, let them satisfy themselves that all conditions had been met, pay a small fee, and have him enrolled as a freeman in the company. Then he had to present the apprentice to the city chamberlain for enrollment as a freeman in the city: this order of presentation may not have been fully accepted as standard, for the musicians' bylaws of 1606 authorized a heavy fine, two pounds, on masters who reversed it.

It is likely that the measures designed primarily and almost solely to fulfill the company's economic function, and particularly those restricting the number of apprentices, were successful in the narrow sense that the company compelled most musicians, freemen of London, to comply with them: the number of apprentices trained in music probably was about what the rules allowed. It is unlikely that these measures were successful in the broad sense that they made the company prosperous. The total effort of the company, exerted in governmental, educational, and economic functions together, seems to have been inadequate to achieve prosperity for musicians. Perhaps they kept

[22] Quoted in Dunlop, *English Apprenticeship*, 52-53.

it going through the sixteenth century and the first half of the seven-teenth because they believed that it helped them, perhaps only because they hoped that someday it would.

Successive generations of aldermen and common councilmen evi-dently placed some credence in the mournful protestations of poverty that the musicians included in their petitions, for most of the petitions became ordinances and the protestations preambles and justifying clauses. "Foreign minstrels daily resorting to this city out of all the countries of England," the ordinance of 1500 alleged, were bringing the "suppliants freemen . . . in such poverty and decay" that they could not "pay lot and scot and do their duty as other freemen do [doon]. . . ." The reason advanced in 1518 for the change to biennial election of officers was that annual elections were "thought to your said orators [the minstrels] right chargeable and not convenient. . . ." The ordi-nance of 1553 charged "diverse and many foreign minstrels from the liberties and freedom of this city" with causing "great loss and hin-drance of the gains and profits of the poor minstrels being freemen of the same city . . . ," and artificers and craftsmen with causing "great loss, prejudice, and hindrance of the said poor fellowship. . . ." In 1574 the common council endorsed the statement that "the company hath of late time not only much decayed but also hath been brought into contempt and hatred by occasion of sundry disorders and enormi-ties used by persons exercising that art being not subject to the good laws and ordinances [governing the company] for that they have been free of other companies of this city. . . ." Although the series of dolor-ous preambles ended in 1574, the musicians' woes probably did not. According to precedent the musicians should have obtained another ordinance, containing another cry of despair, from the city in about 1600. Instead they got a royal charter, and their petitions for it prob-ably again described their misfortunes at least as fully. The laments that must have accompanied the ordinance of 1638 are missing, prob-ably because it took the form of a committee report rather than of a petition as the sixteenth century ordinances had. The musicians were probably no better off in the 1630s than their predecessors had been in 1500, 1553, and 1574.

The company was one of the city's smallest and poorest. Listings of the companies often omitted it, and records of city assessments indicate that it ranked at the bottom. The city assessed the mercers twenty-four pounds, the cooks, basket makers, and minstrels nothing, in 1548-1549; the merchant taylors nine hundred and thirty-six quarters of grain, the grocers eight hundred and seventy-four quarters, several companies including the minstrels' five quarters apiece (the smallest assessment), and several, including the longbow-string makers, nothing, apparently, in 1599; and the grocers £34.19.2, the mercers £32.16.0, the minstrels, bowyers, fletchers, and woolpackers four shillings apiece (the smallest assessment), and several nothing, apparently, in 1603-1604. The musicians' obligation for ceremonies seems to have included only their musical services, and not the furnishing of pageants or cressets.[23]

No documents reveal the gross annual income of independent musicians, and the small payments listed in account books and the clues in contemporary literature suggest only that most of them probably earned less than the waits of London. Henry Walker, "citizen and minstrel of London," who sold the Blackfriars Gate-house to Shakespeare and others in 1613 for one hundred and forty pounds,[24] stands for the few modestly affluent members the company must have had; and he very likely owed his wealth to something besides his musicianship.

That too much competition was a principal cause of their poverty, the musicians seem to have recognized. That some of the competition, such as that from the royal musicians and the servants of noblemen visiting the capital, was untouchable, they recognized. That the heavy competition they faced from provincials and Londoners brought up in many other occupations was to a large extent a result of the involuntary occupational displacement characteristic of their age, they probably could not recognize. Perhaps only the coming of more settled economic and social conditions generally, together with the setting up of centralized and efficient government for the whole London area and effective countrywide administration of social legislation such as the vagrancy laws of 1572 and 1597, could have helped them much.

The work for which they competed did not include playing on the concert stage. Although a few instrumentalists, John Dowland, the lutanist, and John Bull, the organist and virginalist, among them, had international reputations, the age of the prominent soloist who travels from metropolis to metropolis to appear before great public audiences,

---

[23] Clode, *Early History of the Guild of Merchant Taylors*, I, 405-406. Figures for other years appear on the same pages in Clode; *Records . . . Stationers' Company*, ed. Greg, pp. liv-lv; *Records of the Skinners*, ed. Lambert, 392 (compare these figures with Clode's for 1599); Journal, xxxvii, folios 128 verso-129 (list for 1609-1610, appended to 1636 order; compare with data in Clode, 329). Two instances, 1549 and 1605, when the musicians furnished their services, are mentioned in the next chapter.

[24] Chambers, *Shakespeare*, II, 154.

and of the great orchestra dependent on popular support, had not yet come. Concerts for the public were given in London, Norwich, and perhaps elsewhere, but they were by municipal employees and not independent musicians.

The ordinances, charter, and bylaws provide a short list of some of the more important jobs they found. In 1500 they seem to have been most interested in playing in private houses at feasts on "churchehaly-dayes" and church dedication days, at churchings, weddings, and "brotherhedis," that is, the important meetings and banquets of brotherhoods or guilds. "Triumphs, feasts, dinners, suppers, marriages, guilds or brotherhoods [brotherhedes]," and "taverns, hostelries or alehouses" were listed as important occasions or places of employment in 1518. The changes in the church under Henry VIII cost them a good deal of work: fewer church holidays and dedication days meant fewer dinners and other celebrations requiring music. A bylaw, probably added after 1606, names one type of employment, huntsup, not mentioned in the ordinances. Huntsup, probably time-honored by the seventeenth century, was originally music played on horns, presumably, to call out hunters in the morning. The prohibition in the bylaws against playing in the street under the windows of noblemen or others, without the consent of the officers of the company, calls attention to another form of employment. Playing in the street, either by request or on speculation, perhaps somewhat restricted for awhile, still flourished in 1638, as a Frenchman noted when he described the visit to London of the queen mother, Marie de Medici of France: "in all public places, violins, hautbois, and other sorts of instruments [were] so common, for the amusement of particular persons, that at all hours of the day, one [might have his] ears charmed with their sweet melody."[25]

According to nearly every kind of evidence, including household accounts, ordinances, and contemporary literature, "taverns, hostelries or alehouses" universally attracted musicians, and often too many. A passage from Shirley's *The Gamester* (1638) suggests the hostility or contempt that the poorest, sometimes drunken, frequently impor-

[25] The pay of the London waits was increased in 1524 because the change from the celebration of church dedications from many days throughout the year to one day for all churches had decreased the waits' opportunity to earn money, and in 1536 their pay was again increased "in consideration that diverse holidays" had been abrogated: Journal, xii, folio 281, and Repertory, ix, folios 195, 197 verso. Changes which cut waits' incidental income of course cut the income of independent musicians.

1638: Serre, "History of the Entry of Mary de Medicis . . . ," in *Antiquarian Repertory*, iv, 531.

tunate musicians must often have aroused. Hazard, Acreless, Little-
stock, and Sellaway, gamesters, are drinking in a London tavern when
a fiddler enters: "Fiddler: 'Wilt please you, gentlemen, to have a song?'
Hazard: 'You have not wash'd today; go, get clean manners.' (Throws
the wine in his face.) 'You rascal, we have no wenches.' Fiddler: 'I see
nobody, sir, you have wash'd my eyes out.' Hazard: 'It is not necessary
thou shouldst have any: Fill me again.' Acre: 'This fellow would have
t'other cup.' Fiddler: 'I have had a cup too much already, gentlemen.'
(Exit)"[26] Such derelict minstrels brought all musicians into general
contempt, the masters and wardens of the company complained; students in the twentieth century must not fail, as the public may have in
the sixteenth century, to distinguish between them and the respectable
musicians especially hired to play in taverns and elsewhere for weddings and other parties. While it is likely that the better musicians
played and sang all kinds of music, madrigals and fancies as well as
ballads and popular dance music, most alehouse fiddlers probably kept
to ballads, bawdy songs, jigs, and the like. Many of these fiddlers, perhaps most of them in the sixteenth century, were probably interlopers,
members of other London companies, or wanderers from the provinces.

The drama gave employment to independent professional musicians
during part of the period. Before 1574, the date of the foundation of
the first actors' company, and for several years afterwards, the theatre
can seldom have employed independent professional musicians, chiefly
because most of the producers and performers were groups of amateurs who used whatever musicians were most readily available, whether
amateur musicians in a cast of amateur actors, noblemen's household
musicians, members of the King's Musick, or some of the boys in a
cast of choirboys. After 1576, when the first popular theatre was built,
and especially during and after the last decade of Elizabeth's reign,
when most of the theatres were built, the number of independent musicians regularly employed probably increased. It can hardly ever have
been large, however, for not only were few theatres open at one time,
but the companies that presented the most music had musicians among
their members and ordinarily could get along without outside help,
and when they, or the other companies, had to hire musicians, they
were as likely to call in various retained musicians, including waits or
members of the King's Musick, as independent members of the musicians' company.

[26] Shirley: act II, scene ii. King Charles is said to have liked this play better
than any he had seen for seven years. A similar passage occurs in *Love's Cruelty*
(1631), III, i.

According to one estimate, each private theatre with adult rather than juvenile actors usually needed eight to ten musicians, and the public theatres a few less. Some of the musicians seem to have been members and apprentices of members of the companies of actors, trained both in music and acting. Instruments are listed in the inventories of the equipment owned by various companies. Among those of the Admiral's company in 1598 were a treble viol, a bass viol, a bandora, a cittern, and a sackbut. While they may have been needed only as stage properties, some of the members of the companies could probably play them; ordinarily the companies should not have had to furnish instruments to the musicians they hired. The bequest in 1608 by the actor Augustine Philips to his apprentice of a cittern, a bandora, and a lute, and to his "late apprentice" of a bass viol, suggests that all three may have known how to play and sing. Since the actors had no guild or company, analogous to the musicians' company, the connotation of the word apprentice in Philips' will and elsewhere in connection with actors has puzzled students of the theatre; it may signify only that the boys were serving under contract, but it may imply that the master belonged to the musicians' company or other guild and that the boys were therefore apprentices in the more common sense of the word. That for London if not provincial audiences the actors sometimes needed more musicians than their own ranks could supply, is shown by the complaint of the city aldermen in 1613 that when the lord mayor, sheriffs, or aldermen wanted the waits they could not come because they were "then employed at play houses."[27]

Except for the few who won places in the King's Musick or among the city waits, or who got jobs in theatres for a season, most members of the musicians' company had to depend on an uncertain succession of unrelated jobs, the weddings and guild feasts and other occasions already mentioned, engagements at the town or suburban houses of great merchants and gentlemen during Christmas week and at other festival times, and perhaps in the royal palaces or the inns of court when great masques and other fetes required the services of extraor-

[27] Estimate of number of musicians: Cowling, *Music on the Shakespearian Stage*, 84, on the statement of Malone. Inventory: Chambers, *Elizabethan Stage*, II, 541 note 4 (continued on p. 542; why the company had the other instruments listed—trumpets, a drum, a chime of bells, and "tymbrells," can be easily imagined); see also Cowling, 3-4. For Philips' will and discussion of the problem of the employment of boys see Chambers, *Shakespeare*, II, 84-86. Aldermen 1613: Repertory, XXXI, folios 31-31 verso.
Other aspects of music in the theatre are considered in chapter nine below.

dinarily large numbers of musicians. Men who lacked skill, dependability, or advantageous connections can hardly have had better luck at this than their twentieth century descendants, with the consequence that many of them must have been forced to resort to the hazards of alehouse opportunism. Such circumstances, making it difficult or impossible for many to earn a steady, adequate income, help explain why officers of the company repeatedly complained to the aldermen and why musicians longed to exchange their independence for the security offered by municipal or royal employment.[28]

London's great population and great number of visitors made possible the subsistence of enough independent musicians so that they could hope to gain strength through union. The great population also attracted the provincial interlopers. The presence of the court in or near London, a cause for the great population and the many visitors, meant that royal musicians lived there and enjoyed much of the most profitable employment.

The comparatively affluent waits and royal musicians who belonged to the company may have helped it by speaking for it and assuming a relatively large share of unusual expenses, and may also have prevented it from getting strong. Probably members because their careers had started with apprenticeship to freemen of the company, these royal musicians perhaps retained their freedom because it was easier to retain than regain, and perhaps because they hoped that by assuming a leading position in the company they could insure that the independent musicians took no action through the city government that might endanger the privileged position, amounting to complete liberty of action within the city, of the whole body of royal musicians.

The city government acceded to nearly every request the company made of it. But it did not try to exclude royal and noblemen's household musicians, an effort that, without promise of adequate compensation to the greater interests of the city, would have embroiled it with the crown and parliament.

While London had great population and wealth, while the King's Musick flourished in or near it, and while the current economic and social revolution continued, a company of musicians could exist, sustained by hope and a modicum of success, but could never become

[28] For examples of great occasions which probably gave employment to some members of the company see Birch, *Life of Henry Prince of Wales*, 92-94; Chamberlain, *Letters*, I, 425; Inner Temple accounts for the feast week of Christmas 1633 in HMC *8 ii, Gell Mss.*, 390; and chapter nine below.

strong. Most of its freemen would be poor, but they would furnish much of the entertainment of the lower classes, supply recruits to the King's Musick and the city waits, and, because of the competition implicit in their existence as ambitious musicians, impel retained musicians to maintain their standards. The King's Musick, waits, and household musicians were all to disappear; independent musicians, differently organized and often working for new kinds of employers, still exist, complain about many of the same problems, and look for redress in many of the old ways.

CHAPTER II. THE WAITS

OF LONDON

AITS originally seem to have been watchmen or sentinels in camps, castles, and other fortified places, including towns, and to have played some kind of horn as an alarm or signal. By the fifteenth century towns were becoming the characteristic employers of waits, and in some towns waits were coming to be regarded as musicians primarily and watchmen secondarily. By the end of the sixteenth century the transition was general if not complete: waits were then municipal musicians, who had traditional but relatively unimportant guardian functions. Well before this time the waits of London had achieved musical importance because they were, except for the King's Musick, the only permanent, secular musical organization in London, and because they may have been the only organization in England regularly giving public concerts.[1]

The number of musicians playing for the city of London varied considerably, and depended not only on the number of waits employed, but also on how many apprentices the waits could have and whether their training had advanced far enough to qualify them for work alongside their masters. From 1475 until at least the middle of the seventeenth century the city courts considered six the proper number of waits, although there were usually more. Probably restricted to one apprentice apiece, at least from 1502, they asked for and received permission in 1548 to have two apiece thereafter. As a result the maximum number of musicians in the group of waits should have been twelve from 1502 to 1548, and afterwards, eighteen. The profit motive no doubt caused the waits to have their full complement of apprentices ready for public performance most of the time. Beginning in 1570, when the aldermen made an extra place for a foreigner, Segar van Pilkam, numerous special appointments and arrangements kept the number above six continuously until the middle of the seventeenth

---

[1] This chapter is based chiefly on manuscripts in the archives of the city of London: the Repertory of the Court of Aldermen, the Journal of the Proceedings of the Common Council, and the Letter Books. While parts of the record have been printed in various places, no history of the London waits, based on full study of the sources, seems to have been published. On the earlier history of waits in general see *Oxford English Dictionary*; Pulver, *Dictionary of Old English Music*; Bridge, "Town Waits and their Tunes," *Proc. Mus. Assoc.*, 54th session (1928), 63-92; Stephen, *Waits of the City of Norwich*; and chapter four, below.

century. The record of appointments and retirements, practically complete from 1563, shows that from 1571 to 1605 there were seven men and probably twelve or fourteen apprentices, from 1605 eight to ten men and probably fourteen to twenty-one apprentices and boys, and from 1620 to 1635 the greatest number, eleven men and probably about twenty apprentices. It is unlikely that all of these masters and apprentices played together often, if ever, in one band or orchestra of twenty or thirty instruments, but having so many available gave them the advantage of resources ample for almost any engagement.[2]

In the earlier years, until about 1525, they may have played only waits or wait-pipes, as the shawm or hautboy commonly associated with waits was often called. In 1526 the city bought them a sackbut, and others in 1555 and 1559. Important expansion of the instrumentation began in 1561, at the request of the waits, when the court of aldermen ordered purchase of "certain instruments called a set of vialles." A few years later, in 1568, they bought a "whole set of recorders" and six cornetts, in 1576 "certain new instruments," and in 1581 two more sackbuts. The list of city purchases came to a close in 1597 with three sackbuts (one double) and a curtal (like a bassoon). Now the waits had most of the instruments commonly used in purely instrumental music: shawms and a curtal, recorders, cornetts, and sackbuts represented the winds, and viols the strings. Organs and other keyboard instruments, and harps, probably not used ordinarily by the waits, may have been hired or furnished by a wait for special occasions. Flutes, too, may have been provided by the waits themselves if the softer recorder did not satisfy them. What is known of the accomplishments of the waits who served in the last decades before the civil wars indicates that none of the sixteenth century instruments could not be used for want of men qualified on them: appointees included men who played the hautboy, sackbut, double curtal, and unnamed wind instruments, and the bass and other viols. Violinists joined

[2] For record of appointments and references to the manuscripts see Appendix A, below. 1475: Journal, VIII, folio 112. There were nine waits in 1442: Letter Book K, folio 206 verso. In 1588 and 1615, when the numbers of waits were seven and eight respectively, the court of aldermen again stated that the ordinary number of waits was six, and that there should be no more appointments until there were again six: Repertory, XXI, folio 596, XXXII, folio 109 verso.

The waits seem to have been bound by the rules of the musicians' company from at least 1502: see note 9, below. Two apprentices apiece 1548: Repertory, XI, folio 481.

Segar van Pilkam is mentioned again below, including note 6, and in Appendix A.

the waits too in the seventeenth century. Most sixteenth and seventeenth century musicians seem to have played a variety of instruments, some many wind instruments, some several kinds of stringed instruments, and some both.[3]

A major development came with the addition of the lute family of instruments, and of singing. The waits sang, perhaps not regularly, as early as 1555, when Machyn recorded in his diary that "a godly procession [came] from St. Peter's in Cornhill with the fishmongers, and my lord mayor, with a hundred copes, unto Paul's, and there they offered; with the waits playing and singing. . . ." The first official record of it seems to come in 1613 when a section of the waits, later called "the city music of voices," began. In February 1613, five days before Princess Elizabeth married Frederick, elector palatine, and perhaps because of the festivities then, "a man well known to this court [of aldermen] for his rare and excellent skill in singing" was appointed as an extra wait. The next step in a development that went far this year came in April when the singer's appointment was reaffirmed and a committee of aldermen named to arrange for the keeping by the

[3] Sackbuts: 1526: Repertory, vii, folio 137; the entry may indicate that the sackbut was quite new to the city, or merely the backwardness of the secretary, for he had much trouble in writing the name, first, "Hakbush" or "hakbussh," crossed out, then "Sakbutte" above the line; finally, "an Instrument called a Sakbutte." 1555: Repertory, xiii, ii, folio 288 verso. 1559: Repertory, xiv, folio 199 verso.

Viols, 1561: The waits asked for money for a set one week, and exhibited the set they wanted and secured an appropriation the next week: Repertory, xiv, folios 509 verso and 514.

Recorders and cornetts, 1568: Repertory, xvi, folio 407.

1576: Repertory, xix, folio 60 verso. 1581: Repertory, xx, folio 170.

Sackbuts and curtal, 1597: Repertory, xxiv, folios 95 and 145.

Organs: A regals, or portable organ, was hired with two boys to play it and sing, by the merchant taylors, in 1556, for the pageant for the new mayor, and harps and a harper were hired in 1561 for the inauguration of Sir William Harper: Sayle, *Lord Mayors' Pageants of the Merchant Taylors' Company*, 30, 36.

Trumpets, fifes, and drums seem not to have been commonly used in ensemble with other instruments; the city had one or more trumpeters, a fife player, and a drummer who could have been drafted into service with the waits if needed.

Violins: Robert Parker, who served the city from 1619 to 1640, and the royal court, played the "violen" (Repertory, xl, folios 331 verso-332) or "low tenor violin" (*King's Musick*, ed. Lafontaine, 76, 100), perhaps also the treble viol, and certainly hautboys and sackbuts; he was particularly good on the wind instruments. Ambrose Beeland, who served the city from 1631, and the royal court from 1640, played violin (*King's Musick*, 146) and wind instruments (Repertory, xlvii, folio 358). Information as to the instruments the waits played, obtained from records of what some of the same men played in the King's Musick, checks with the incomplete evidence provided by the city records.

waits of a boy "that shall have a special good voice in singing"; by October one of the waits had agreed to keep "two boys to sing with the music of the city." The death, in August, of one of the old waits enabled the court to appoint a lutanist to a regular place in the waits, and it was probably in this year that the unpaid service of a singer and lutanist, nephew of one of the waits, began. The city now had several singers and lutanists by appointment (usually every lutanist was also a singer) and no doubt on occasion the best singers among the other instrumentalists augmented the number of appointed singers. Far from letting "the city music of voices" disappear, the aldermen always kept the extra place of the first appointed singer, filled several places, beginning in 1625, with men known as bass singers as well as instrumentalists, and from 1620 to 1637 hired another extra man who sang and played the orpharion, poliphon (both like lutes, but with wire strings), and the bass viol "which [until 1620] were not used in the consort." From 1568, then, the waits performed all of the principal instruments of the consort, and from at least 1613 included men and boys particularly qualified as singers and players on the lute or analogous instruments.[4]

Their pay, the conditions surrounding their appointments, and their

[4] Machyn, *Diary*, ed. Nichols, 89, 260. "Music of voices": so called in 1637 at the time of the appointment of Symon Ives: Repertory, LI, folios 329-329 verso. Extra wait 1613: Edward Godfrey, appointed 9 February: Repertory, XXXI, folios 44-44 verso. April, October 1613: Repertory, XXXI, folios 102, 175 verso; Richard Ball, who was to keep the boys, served until 1622. August 1613: John Sturt was appointed in the place of John Robson: Repertory, XXXI, folio 150 verso; Sturt was a lutanist, according to the order appointing his successor in 1625: Repertory, XXXIX, folios 86-86 verso. Unpaid singer: In January 1626 Alphonsus Ball was said to have served with the waits twelve years under his uncle Richard Ball (Repertory, XL, folio 83 verso) who died in 1622 (Repertory, XXXVII, folio 21); this would seem to indicate that Alphonsus' service began in 1610. However, in February 1634 he was said to have served the city for twenty years (Repertory, XLVIII, folios 118 verso-119) or since about 1613. All the rest of the evidence suggests that 1613 was the year his service began; he may have been one of the two boys whom his uncle kept for the city from 1613. Alphonsus is known as a singer and musician (musician usually meant instrumentalist) from the Repertory, and more definitely as a lutanist because he was listed as one of the "lutes and voices" of the King's Musick: *King's Musick*, ed. Lafontaine, 66. Bass singers: John Olliver, appointed in 1625, Robert Heardson, serving from 1634 and appointed in 1635, and Symon Ives, appointed to succeed Heardson in 1637, all sang bass and played instruments: Repertory, XL, folio 2 verso, XLVIII, folios 272 verso-273, XLIX, folio 200, LI, folio 347 verso. Extra man 1620: Robert Taylor was first appointed in 1620: Repertory, XXXIV, folio 586; in the King's Musick he was listed among the "lutes and voices" and his son succeeded him as "a musician for the viols and voices": *King's Musick*, 66, 95.

discipline suggest, on rather earthly grounds, that most London waits deserved a high reputation as musicians. Although their wages never exceeded half of what most royal musicians received, the waits were well paid. The record of their pay seems to start in 1475, when the city authorized payment of £1.6.8. a year to each wait. Without an increase for almost half a century, apparently, the waits found it hard to get along. In 1502 the aldermen and common councillors sympathized with them when they complained that action of the company of minstrels, threatening to prevent them from occupying, buying, or selling in the city, was about to force them to leave the city to seek their living elsewhere, and in 1515 they received a bequest, left to them by a former mayor who must have understood their poverty, of ten pounds, to be given to them at the rate of a pound a year for ten years, for the relief of their wages. Then in 1524, because the new practice of celebrating all church dedication days on one day, 3 October, had reduced the number of occasions when waits could earn extra money, the common council voted to increase the wage of each wait by two pounds a year, presumably to £3.6.8. In 1536 they found it necessary again to ask for help "in consideration that diverse holy days," when they had been able to supplement their wages, had been abrogated, and the aldermen granted an increase to six pounds apiece a year. The waits apparently made no further request of the city for over thirty years, and all places were easily filled. Then in less than fifteen years their wages rose three times, in 1568 one-third, to eight pounds apiece, in 1571 to ten pounds, and in 1582 to £11.13.4. For many years after this musicians competed vigorously for waits' places. The greatest increase came early in the reign of James: in answer to their petition, based on "their continual daily and nightly services and small wage," the aldermen almost doubled their pay, setting it at twenty pounds a man. The waits then in office had evidently won particularly high favor, for the grant stipulated that the increase was "not to be drawn to a precedent hereafter for their successors." In spite of this reservation, twenty pounds a year continued as the standard rate. Coincident with the reduction of the service of the waits during the civil wars their pay stopped for a while; in 1644, on petition of seven waits who spoke of their poverty, the aldermen ordered resumption of payments until further notice. General inflation can account for only a small part of this increase, from £1.6.8 in 1475, six pounds in 1536, £11.13.4 in 1582, to twenty pounds in 1605. Perhaps the leading citizens grew more and more interested in good music, and the waits more and more capable of providing it.[5]

The city could retain satisfactory musicians for less than these rates. In 1620 when the musician who played the orpharion, bass viol, and poliphon petitioned for a place the aldermen hired him at half the regular pay for a year's trial and on condition that if they wanted to keep him he should not ask for more. For seventeen years, from 1616 to 1633, two or more musicians held one or more places and divided the wages among them. On the other hand, an extraordinary bonus went to Segar van Pilkam, to whom the aldermen gave an extra place in 1570 at the regular wage of ten pounds a year, paid an extra £6.13.4 a year from 1572 until 1581, the year of his departure to his own country, and then granted a "free gift" of ten pounds.[6]

[5] 1475: Journal, VIII, folio 112; one noble a quarter. 1502: see note 9, below. 1515: Repertory, III, folio 10. 1524: Journal, XII, folio 281. 1536: Repertory, IX, folios 195, 197 verso; "holydayes." 1568: Repertory, XVI, folio 323 verso. 1571: Repertory, XVII, folio 174. 1582: Repertory, XX, folio 290 verso. The raise made in 1571 was inadequate, for in the same year the aldermen decided that they should "at the charging of their ward-mote inquests" exhort the wealthiest inhabitants of the wards "to contribute and give their benevolence and aid towards the relief of the waits of this city": Repertory, XVIII, folio 113. The records do not show the outcome of the exhortations. Five years later the court considered their wages again, but took no action: Repertory, XIX, folio 382 verso.

1605: Repertory, XXVI, ii, folio 520. 1644: Repertory, LVII, ii, folio 27.

[6] 1620: Robert Taylor was hired for one year on condition that if at the end of the year the aldermen wished to continue to employ him, he should not ask for greater pay, and accordingly his pay was again set at ten pounds at the end of the first year; two years later the lord keeper, Bishop John Williams, interceded on his behalf and his pay was raised to twenty pounds: Repertory, XXXIV, folio 568, XXXVI, folio 3, XXXVII, folios 272-272 verso, and note 4, above.

1616-1633: In 1616 the son of a late wait and the apprentice of another were admitted jointly to a wait's place. Two years later a third man was appointed who was to share with them two waits' places. In 1625 another place was divided between two more musicians. Apparently the dissatisfaction of the five—reduced by death to four—men in 1625 resulted in a raise of pay, to fifteen pounds apiece, and by 1633 to twenty pounds. The whole complicated story is in the Repertory, XXXII, folio 356, XXXIII, folios 323 verso-324, 326, XXXIV, folios 205-205 verso, XXXVIII, folios 148 verso-149, XXXIX, folios 86-86 verso, XL, folios 2 verso-3, 16 verso, 383 verso, XLIII, folio 37, XLV, folio 216 verso, XLVII, folios 358, 372 verso.

Two other cases of smaller than normal pay are worth notice. An apprentice, Robert Baker, of a wait who had been granted five pounds a year in 1583 to help defray the cost of bringing up the apprentice, served with the waits but without a regular place, at five pounds a year, then at ten pounds a year, before his pay was raised to £11.13.4, what the other waits were getting; Repertory, XX, folio 453, XXI, folios 417, 596. A wait appointed to an extra place in 1611 was receiving only £11.13.4, instead of twenty pounds, in 1615 when he requested that his pay be made equal to that of the others. He seems to have served without pay since

Sometimes special awards augmented the wages. In 1625, at the suit of the waits, the aldermen voted to pay them for their service at King Charles' going to Whitehall "as formerly they have received." Other grants included the profit to be gained from making men free of the city by redemption, and several times men received their pay in advance. Although no regular pension system provided for aged or sick waits, all who retired after long service seem to have received help in some way, in the later years by grant of partial or full pay for life.[7]

Annual livery may have preceded the wages. In 1442 the waits, alleging the example of other towns, petitioned successfully for yearly "livery and clothing." From 1502, if not earlier, this included two sets, winter and summer. Besides the blue gowns and red caps of their livery, each wait was entrusted with a silver "Coller of Essys" (collar or chain of ss) and a badge of the arms of the city, weighing together in 1582 about thirteen ounces and valued at £3.7.6. As symbols of

---

1605, as a reversion holder, and at low pay from 1611: Repertory, xxvii, folios 66-67, xxx, folio 121, xxxii, folio 179 verso.

Segar van der (?) Pilkam, or Pilkin Segar: Repertory, xvii, folios 63, 423 verso, xx, folio 185.

[7] 1625: Repertory, xxxix, folio 244 verso.

Redemption: In 1613 a wait was granted the profit to be gained each year from one of the twenty made free of the city annually by redemption, in consideration of his keeping two singing boys: Repertory, xxxi, folio 175 verso. The profit from one redemption was awarded in 1634 to a wait "in regard of his charge in breeding up a son to perfection in voice, song, and music for the city's service": Repertory, xlviii, folio 485. In 1629 the same reward was given to a musician who had served fifteen years without a place; he presented a man to be made free in the company of cooks: Repertory, xliv, folios 71, 79.

Advances: One musician was advanced a year's pay in 1617, was presented with £13.6.8 in 1622, and in 1623 was advanced three years' wages: Repertory, xxxiii, folio 201, xxxvi, folio 37, xxxvii, folios 112-112 verso, 142-142 verso. In 1633 John Wilson, perhaps the famous singer and lutanist, was loaned ten pounds: Repertory, xlvii, folios 90 verso-91.

Pension: Places in an alms house were granted in 1495, 1506, and 1518: Repertory, i, folio 12, ii, folio 3, iii, folio 237. In 1555 an aged wait who resigned was granted £2.13.4 for life in place of his wage of six pounds: Repertory, xiii, i, folio 255 verso. In 1569 a wait was granted four pounds a year—half pay—for life: Repertory, xvi, folio 484 verso. In 1597 full pay, £11.13.4, without livery, was given for life to two waits in consideration "of their old ages, long honest and painful services done" for the city: Repertory, xxiv, folio 53 verso. A wait who had served forty years and was "unfitting to supply the place" was permitted to retire on full pay in 1616, but his successor had to serve without pay until the old wait died: Repertory, xxxii, folios 247-247 verso. These are probably all the cases in which waits were retired because of age or sickness; most waits died in office.

office certifying dignity and prestige they probably increased the waits' private employment and the rate of pay for it.[8]

The waits had two great privileges. The first, by which a wait, on appointment, automatically gained the right to become a freeman of the city in the company of musicians, without any charge, was of great advantage as the company tried to make its control more strict and exclusive. The second great privilege, granted in 1548, gave each wait the right, previously enjoyed only by officers or former officers of the company, to keep two apprentices at a time.[9]

Other variable sources of income helped the waits. When they were performing the duties for which they were paid by the city, their auditors often rewarded them. It is apparent, from various indications in the city records, that the waits, together or separately, were much in demand for private affairs. In a codification of rules for the waits in 1625 it was ordered that when they or any of them should be appointed to play on any extraordinary occasion, someone employed for the purpose by the waits, or one of the youngest of them, should enquire concerning the business and inform all of them in order that they should be ready with "such variety of music, as shall be required at the time and place. . . ." The lord mayor, sheriffs, and aldermen habitually

[8] 1442: Letter Book K, folio 206 verso. In 1502 they were granted "their summer clothing": Journal, x, folio 251. In the terms of their appointments waits were granted livery; that this meant summer and winter liveries is indicated by a 1623 grant, whereby a wait had his pay increased to twenty pounds and "two liveries as other of the city waits do receive": Repertory, xxxvii, folios 272-272 verso.

Insignia: The collar was first mentioned in 1518, when a new wait was given the collar of his deceased predecessor; eight years later all of the collars were made over in a new "good fashion." In 1582 the weight and value were recorded when a wait had to pay for the one he had lost. In 1625 the city was said to have lost four pounds because a recently deceased wait had pawned his collar; to safeguard the city thereafter, waits were to put up security for their collars and badges before any more wages were to be paid to them. Repertory, iii, folio 235 verso, vii, folio 100 verso, xvii, folio 174, xx, folio 314 verso, xl, folios 20 verso-21. (See illustration of chain and badge of the Norwich waits in this book.)

[9] Freedom: Granted by the common council in 1502, in answer to the request of the waits who stated that whereas from time out of mind they had been reputed and taken as freemen of the city in virtue of their services, they were now prohibited by the fellowship of minstrels to occupy, buy, and sell in the city unless they were first admitted freemen of the city in the minstrels' "craft," and that because the waits were not wealthy enough to buy their freedom, they would be forced to seek their living elsewhere, unless the council should order that they be admitted freemen of the fellowship without any charge: Journal, x, folios 250 verso-251.

Apprentices: Repertory xi, folio 481. Upon completion of their service these apprentices presumably became freemen in the musicians' company.

called the waits to perform privately for them; the marriage of a daughter was mentioned as an example in the record of their complaint in 1613 that when sent for by the magistrates the waits could not come because of their employment at playhouses. The theatres probably paid better, for the complaint continued that "when they come to any magistrate's house of the city they demand unreasonable for their pains." Companies also hired them. The skinners' accounts for 1503-1504 show payments for hats of crimson and tippets of black tartaran "for the trumpeters and the waits to wait upon Mr. Thomas Graunger, our sheriff," when he went to Westminster. The merchant tailors seem to have had a standing arrangement with them. Their books show payment of ten shillings in 1434-1435 "To the waits of London attending upon the company at the feast of St. John. . ."; forty shillings "to John Scryven for himself and the rest of the waits of the city his fellows" for playing for the mayor's pageant (Sir William Harper, a merchant tailor) and on other occasions, and for caps for them, in 1561; and in 1602 that the company increased its annual fee: "Upon the humble petition of the waits or musicians of the city of London, shewing that their service to this company is extraordinary and more then to any company in London, and cannot be performed without six in number on the election day, it hath pleased the company to increase their fee from thirty-three shillings four pence to forty shillings." They also played for private persons such as Lord Willoughby and Thomas Kytson, who gave them large rewards in the earlier years of Elizabeth's reign. These earnings came to so much that collection and distribution had to be carefully regulated, and evidently made it worth while for able musicians to serve for many years with low pay, and for others to serve without any, in anticipation of the time when they could claim all of the profits of a full wait's place.[10]

[10] Rewards when performing duties: In 1634 the court stated that a musician who was substituting for a sick wait, doing "his service in the night watches [should] receive an equal part with [the other waits] of such benefit and offerings as do thereby accrue": Repertory, XLVIII, folios 484-485.

1625: Repertory, XXXIX, folios 175 verso-176. 1613: Repertory, XXXI, folios 44-44 verso. Skinners: *Records of the Skinners of London*, ed. Lambert, 140. Taylors: Clode, *Early History . . . Merchant Taylors*, I, 7, II, 269; *Memorials of the Guild of Merchant Taylors*, ed. Clode, 540.

Richard Bertie, Lord Willoughby, gave them five shillings in 1561: HMC 66, *Ancaster Mss.*, 465. Thomas Kytson, London merchant and musical patron of musicians, of Hengrave, Suffolk, gave them six shillings for playing at his house in London in 1573: Gage, *History . . . of Hengrave*, 197.

Regulation: The rules of 1625 ordered that the extraordinary profits gained by one or more of them should be paid to the waits in rotation; the collector should

Altogether, the waits enjoyed excellent incomes and a position much more favored than that of unattached professionals. They had a fixed minimum income of wages and livery on which they could subsist, if not more, in hard times, and hope of special awards from the city and pensions in their old age; they could enter the musicians' company without charge and could keep two apprentices apiece in spite of the company's rules; they collected substantial sums while performing for the city and private employers; and they benefited from the prestige of their official positions, advertised by their gowns and insignia.

Musicians often competed hotly for vacant places, and the aldermen, expediently as well as properly, always seem to have let musicianship rather than sponsorship rule their judgment. The earl of Leicester's candidate in 1582, Sir Walter Mildmay's candidate (Nicholas Yonge, editor of two famous collections of Italian madrigals) in 1585, the candidate of the queen's attorney-general and the gentlemen of the inns of court in 1634, were not appointed. John Wilson, candidate of Viscount Mandeville and the great marquis of Buckingham, and perhaps the musician later famous as lutanist and composer, received a place in 1622 only "upon trial had of that his sufficiency and judgment." The aldermen sometimes prescribed competitive examinations. The examiners, in the only instance in which their names are known, were three members of the famous Anglo-Italian musical family of Bassano, all Queen Elizabeth's musicians; they or two of them were to "try and examine" which of two candidates was "the more skilful and efficient musician in all manner of musical instruments." Grants of reversions went ordinarily only to men who had shown their ability in service with the waits, sometimes as their apprentices. Even the holder of a reversion might be passed over for some musical reason. A violinist, loser in a competition for a place in 1619 but of "approved skill and knowledge in music," secured a reversion in 1624 after five years of service without pay and then, in 1625, lost the next vacancy because another musician was a better lutanist and therefore better qualified

---

divide these funds within six days of receipt among all of the waits except those who had failed to appear for duty after proper notification. If the collector did not make the payments the city chamberlain was to withhold the amounts from the collector's next quarterly wage installment: Repertory, xxxix, folios 175 verso-177.

Apparently extra waits did not share in the private employment and rewards as a matter of course; in 1615 the court gave an extra wait, appointed the year before, this privilege, saying that he "shall go with the rest in consort at private meetings or otherwise and to share with them": Repertory, xxxii, folio 79.

to replace the deceased wait. Both the competition for appointments and the attention given to them by the aldermen should have contributed to the maintenance of high standards.[11]

Evidently well aware that perpetuation of their favored position depended largely on close attention to duty and orderly self-government, the waits gave the aldermen occasion to discipline them only twice, according to the records, once in 1558 when an unprotesting wait was discharged for negligence, and once in 1637, almost eighty years later, when their pay was stopped for some months because they sent substitutes instead of appearing themselves on festival days. About 1625 they came close to losing their self-government: the aldermen had learned "that through the contentions and ill dispositions of some particular persons of this society [of waits] the whole company suffereth often in their credits and reputations by uncivil and retorting of bitter and

[11] 1582: *Analytical Index to the . . . Remembrancia,* ed. Overall, 275, gives the earl's letter, requesting appointment of John Dower, the earl's "servant," in the room of the late "Mr. Baker." Repertory, xx, folio 376 verso states that Edward Blancq was appointed to John Baker's place.

1585: Repertory, xxi, folio 137 verso; Yonge's volumes, *Musica Transalpina,* appeared in 1588 and 1597.

1634: In choosing between the two candidates, Heardson (attorney general, inns) and Alphonsus Ball (twenty years service with the waits, and in King's Musick), the aldermen decided to appoint the one that should be adjudged better in a competition in singing bass. They probably wanted to appoint Ball, because of his long service, and did when the king wrote in his favor, but they also liked Heardson's voice, and appointed him later. Repertory, xlviii, folios 118 verso-119, 272 verso-273.

1622: Repertory, xxxvii, folio 21; see articles "Wilson," in *Grove* and in Pulver, *Biographical Dictionary* (references in both), and note 13 below.

Bassano: Andrew (Andrea), Arthur and "Jeronomye" "Bassanye gentes professing musicke" were appointed to give the examination in August 1601, and the place was granted in September: Repertory, xxv, folios 271 verso, 274 verso. They had all been in the King's Musick from at least 1590: *Returns of Aliens,* ed. Kirk, ii, 427.

Reversions: The earliest grant in reversion seems to have been made in 1583 to an apprentice of one of the waits, who was training him for service with the waits and receiving five pounds a year therefore: Repertory, xx, folio 453. The second grant, 1605, was made to the son of a wait, for the place of a seventh wait: Repertory, xxvii, folios 66 verso-67. In 1635 one of the waits often had a substitute serve for him in the waits because he had to serve in the King's Musick; the substitute was granted a reversion, which he later had transferred to his brother, who had also served with the waits: Repertory, xlix, folios 331 verso-332, lii, folios 254-254 verso. The regular substitute of a chronically ill wait was granted a reversion in 1634 and appointed in 1641: Repertory, xlviii, folios 484 verso-485, lv, folio 63 verso.

Violinist: Repertory, xxxiv, folios 205-205 verso, xxxviii, folios 148 verso-149, xxxix, folios 86-86 verso.

unsavory jests and calumnious aspersions upon one or other of them; which only nourish the discord and confusion amongst them with continual quarreling and heartburning yea especially in the times of their service to this honorable city. . . ." The waits agreed in time, perhaps just in time, and got the court of aldermen to enact a set of rules they had drawn up. Probably reflecting on the whole old customs, and to some extent also problems exaggerated by the swollen number of waits, the rules authorized them to assess two-shilling fines to go to the common fund, and directed "the ancientest" wait to report any improper speech, causing quarreling, to the city chamberlain for the information of the court of aldermen, which would mete out severe punishment. With the enactment of these rules the crisis seems to have ended.[12]

Two of the rules that are primarily disciplinary have wider implications. The seventh rule provided that the government of the waits "in the disposing, ordering, and directing of their music" for the city was reserved "to the ancientest of their society only." Obviously responsibility for arranging meetings and direction of affairs in general fell upon the senior musician, and perhaps also responsibility for consort functions corresponding to those of the modern orchestra conductor. The first rule directed the waits to assemble at eight o'clock every Monday morning "to continue their practice upon several sorts of instruments ["Musicke" written first, then crossed out] until noon." To prevent further quarreling over these meetings, which may have resembled modern orchestral rehearsals, the rule provided that if the waits could not agree on a convenient place the city chamberlain should name it.

Several less material considerations suggest that the waits had earned a reputation for good musicianship. Ten or more of them seem to have served in the King's Musick. Robert Baker, for example, received his training as the apprentice of a wait, had an extra wait's place created for him by 1588, and in 1594 resigned to serve Queen Elizabeth. Three of the waits seem to have been composers with published works—John Adson, John Wilson, and Symon Ives—and it is possible that two others—Edward Blanck and Robert Tailor—also published music, although the identifications are more conjectural. Other indi-

[12] 1558: Repertory, xiv, folio 63 verso. 1637: Repertory, li, folios 329-329 verso, lii, folios 47-47 verso, 53.

Rules of 1625: Repertory, xxxix, folios 175 verso-177; the quotation comes from the final paragraph of the rules.

cations of their superiority, such as great demand for their services, appear at various places in this chapter, and further evidence is, perhaps, superfluous in the light of the dedication, to the lord mayor and aldermen, of *The First Booke of Consort Lessons*, in which Thomas Morley, after mentioning the city's "excellent and expert musicians . . . your lordships' waits," recommends the pieces to their "careful and skilful handling: that the wants of exquisite harmony apparent [in the pieces] may be excused by their melodious additions. . . ."[13]

Their duties fall roughly into two classes, marching duties, including night watches, and concert, or purely musical, duties.

In 1454 the common council adopted, among various measures designed to maintain the peace, an order that the waits were to perambulate each night for the recreation of the people and to prevent robberies.[14] The fact that the first-named object of perambulation was to entertain is a foreshadowing of the development of the watch kept by the waits. The constabulary appointed at the wardmoots must have done far more to keep order than the musicians, whose playing must have warned housebreakers and brawlers of their approach. The waits, instead of weapons, carried valuable instruments and insignia easily lost, damaged, or even stolen in a scuffle. Musicianship, not strength

[13] Baker: see note 6, above; successor appointed: Repertory, xxiii, folio 296. The identification of the following waits with men of the same name and time in the King's Musick is definitely proved in some cases and quite probable in others: Robert Baker, Alphonsus Ball, John Adson, Robert Parker, Robert Tailor, John Wilson, Ambrose Beeland, Edward Strong, and William Saunders. Theophilus flitz and Robert Strong were applicants for a wait's place in 1650, and presumably one was appointed. Some of these men were not appointed to the Musick until the Restoration. Some served in both organizations concurrently.

Chambers, *Elizabethan Stage*, ii, 349, doubts the identification of the wait Wilson with the composer Wilson. John Adson served 1614-1640: Repertory, xxxi, ii, folio 336, liv, folio 238 verso. John Wilson served from 1622 (Repertory, xxxvii, folio 21), was still in service in 1638 (Repertory, lii, folio 53), and had had no successor appointed by 1644, although his name does not appear on a list of the waits then (Repertory, lvii, ii, folio 27). Symon Ives served from 1637 and was still in service in 1645: Repertory, li, folio 347 verso, lvii, ii, folio 115 verso.

Edward Blanck, wait 1582-1594 (Repertory, xx, folio 376 verso, xxiii, folio 319 verso) may be the Edward Blancks who wrote sacred music in late Elizabethan times and of whose biography nothing is known. Robert Tailor, extra wait 1620-1637 (Repertory, xxxiv, folio 586, lii, folio 11 verso) may be the Robert Tailour who wrote the music for *Sacred Hymns* (1615). These are set "to be sung in five parts, as also to the viol, and lute or orph-arion"; the wait, Tailor, played or-pharion, poliphon, and bass viol.

The first edition of Morley's *Consort Lessons*, from which this passage is quoted, signature A2, was published in 1599, and the second in 1611.

[14] Journal, v, folio 145 verso.

or agility, was the principal quality required of a candidate, at least from about 1550. Although originally waits may have been hired chiefly to look out for robbers and fires, in London by 1454 musical entertainment was becoming the more prominent part of their watch and, by the sixteenth century, completely predominant.

In 1553 an order forbidding anyone to play any instrument in the open streets of London between ten at night and five in the morning specifically exempted the waits in terms which suggest that "keeping watch" and "playing" were equivalents: the act was not to be prejudicial to the waits "in playing or keeping their accustomed watch as they at their accustomed times and hours use and heretofore have used. . . ." The subordination of patrol to musical interests appeared incidentally, again, in 1560, when a wait asked that he "be clearly discharged" from his service because he was "not able to watch in the night season." He was apparently an able musician, for the court of aldermen seems to have been gratified when he indicated willingness to suspend his resignation if he were excused from the watch portion of his duties: "And yet he agreed to serve the city until Allhallowe'entide next and longer if he may which his request the court did grant unto him." If the patrol had been more important than the music, certainly a strong man could have been found to take his place, in the unlikely event that no musician was immediately available. What seems to be the next reference in the city records comes as the fourth of the rules of 1625. Every wait "during the times anciently accustomed to watch and walk in the nights through the streets of this honorable city (that is to say) from the Monday next following after Allhallows day until the week before Christmas; and from the first Monday in . . . Lent until our Lady-day, shall be ready and meet at . . . eleven of the clock, at the furthest [of] the places heretofore usual and accustomed." The waits served as watchmen only about three months a year, and not during such critical times as Christmas; neither they nor the city can have regarded their watch as very important. Another piece of information about it appears in the record for 1634. A wait suffering from a chronic ailment received permission to send a substitute to do his service "in the night watches" as he had hitherto done with a designated group of three other waits. Since only four waits seem to have gone out together, and since there were more than eight waits at this time, they may have alternated in groups of four, or served in different parts of the city. Another provision of the same order, that the substitute should receive an equal part with the other three men of "such benefit and offerings" as they might receive during their watches, again seems to throw emphasis on the musical aspect of the watch, for it seems likely that the offerings were the gifts of the people who heard them play. The waits evidently continued to perform their ancient watch at certain seasons of the year, but its principal function had become to entertain, rather than to protect.[15]

By watch Tudor Londoners also meant a periodic march that combined the functions of a modern military review and lord mayor's pageant. Although the last of the great marching watches seems to have taken place in 1548, talk of reviving it arose a time or two later in the century. According to a manuscript book presented to the aldermen for their guidance in 1585, the waits had a conspicuous part in the old midsummer marching watches: they ("noise of music as the waits of London") should march near the head of the column behind the mayor's party, and after them other city officials, grave persons, ensigns, players, morris ("morishe") dancers, twenty-five drums, thirteen fifes, and two more groups of musicians.[16]

Other processions, similar to the marching watches, gave the waits further opportunity to help glorify the city and to entertain everyone. In the greatest of these, the annual ceremonies inaugurating the lord mayor, the waits were always the principal band of musicians. In 1556 the music included, besides the waits, who played at Westminster when the mayor took his oath and "at other accustomed times" when the mayor went to St. Paul's, also twenty-four royal trumpeters, the city drummer and two flutists, and two boys who sang and played on regals (portable organ) hired for the occasion. In 1561 at the inauguration of Sir William Harper five harps, hired for the famous harpists,

[15] 1553: Journal, xvi, folios 253 verso-254 (from the ordinance for the company of musicians). 1560: Repertory, xiv, folio 346 verso; Jeffrey ffostei surrendered his place, and his successor was appointed, within a year: Repertory, xiv, folio 448 verso. 1625: Repertory, xxxix, folios 176-176 verso. 1634: Repertory, xl, folios 484 verso-485. On the watch see also chapter four, below.

[16] On the great marching watch see Palmer, *English Social History*, 114-131. Elizabeth planned to revive it in 1585: Journal, xxi, folio 421 verso. Mountegomerye, "A booke contayning the manner and orrder of a watche . . . ," is in the city archives. Another copy, from which quotation is made, is in Cambridge University Library, Ms. Ll.iv.4. In 1573 Mountegomerye had presented a similar book to the court of aldermen, and had received for it a reward of £6.13.4 (Repertory, xviii, folio 29 verso), but according to his 1585 book, the marches had not been held and therefore his book not used. Apparently his new book was not used either, for Stow, *A Survey of London*, ed. Kingsford (edition of 1603), i, 103, although mentioning the book, states that the old marching watch had not been used since 1548.

including Orpheus and Arion, portrayed in the pageant, added to the music furnished by the waits, by trumpets, a drum, and flutes, by regals again, and by the children of the choir of "the late monastery of Westminster." A citizen wrote a description of the ceremony of 1575, fairly typical of them all. After going by water to Westminster with the companies all in barges, taking his oath, and returning by water, the lord mayor, with the aldermen, mounted to ride along the ranks of liverymen on Cheapside. The procession was led by devils and other fantastically dressed men who cleared the way, and by great standards, two drums, a flute, an ensign of the city, and seventy or eighty poor men in blue gowns with red sleeves and armed with pikes and targets. "Then a set of hautboys playing, . . . certain wifflers [young freemen with staves] in velvet coats, and chains of gold, . . . then the pageant of Triumph richly decked . . . sixteen trumpeters . . . sixteen trumpeters more . . . the drum and flute of the city . . . and after, the waits of the city in blue gowns, red sleeves and caps, every one having his silver collar about his neck." Various city officers, including the sword bearer and the common crier with his great mace, and, finally, the two sheriffs, followed. After dinner at the Guildhall the day ended with evening prayer at St. Paul's cathedral. In the seventeenth century the waits frequently, perhaps always, gave up their place in the procession and did all their playing at one station, in 1605 on the porch of St. Peter's parish church in Cheapside, and there again in 1624 and 1630 "as in former years"; viols and lutes are instruments better played seated than on the march. In 1612 when the pageant *Troia-Nova Triumphans* by Thomas Dekker complimented Frederick, elector palatine, and the new lord mayor, the waits probably performed in a room near the action of the pageant, rather than on the street or a porch, for a song was sung with "the music being quaintly conveyed in a private room, and not a person discovered."[17]

[17] The waits provided the principal or only music in 1568, 1602, 1610, 1612, 1624, 1630, and perhaps other years. In 1546 they were the only real "consort" of music; the only others were "the whole blast of the king's trumpeters." The waits were always rewarded for their services: Sayle, *Lord Mayors' Pageants of the Merchant Taylors' Company*, 48-52, 65-69, 90-93, 97-102, 110-115; 14-15.

1556: Sayle, 16-17. 1561: Sayle, 36-41; "Mr. More," probably the well known royal harper, William More, rented the harps and furnished "his child" to play one of them, and John Holt, "momer," attended the children. 1575: William Smythe "citezen and haberdasher of London," *A breffe description of the Royall Citie of London . . .*, in Sayle, 2-3.

Fixed post: Sayle, 73-83, 93, 115, 121; Sayle writes only of the years in which the new lord mayor was a merchant taylor.

LADY MARY WROTH AND HER ARCHLUTE
Courtesy Lord De L'Isle and Dudley
from photograph supplied by National Portrait Gallery, London

SHAWMS
All in Mason Collection, Museum of Fine Arts, Boston. For details see Bessaraboff, *Ancient Musical Instruments*. Photograph courtesy Museum of Fine Arts, Boston.

CHAIN AND BADGE
OF THE NORWICH WAITS
Photographs by Jarrolds' Ltd., Norwich, furnished courtesy P. Hepworth, Esq., City Librarian, Norwich.

MATTHEW GODWIN, BACHELOR OF MUSIC

Organist of Exeter Cathedral, at the time of his death in January "1586" (i.e. 1587). The instruments represented seem to be organ, trumpet, two lutes or related instruments, and (on right) cornett. Esdaile, *English Church Monuments*, p. 108, names the string instruments as lute and theorbo. Photograph reproduced by permission of the National Buildings Record, London.

DETAIL FROM THE UNTON MURAL

PORTRAIT OF SIR HENRY UNTON

Sir Henry Unton, 1557?-1596, of Wadley near Faringdon, Berkshire, related through his mother to Edward Seymour, duke of Somerset, was educated at Oriel College, Oxford, the Middle Temple in London, and by travel in France and Italy. He served the queen as a soldier abroad, as a member of the House of Commons, and twice as ambassador to Henry IV of France, who became his good friend. While on the embassies Sir Henry accompanied the king to various sieges, and fell sick and died at the siege of La Fère.

This portrait, painted by an unknown artist, apparently for Sir Henry's widow, shows the chief episodes of his life—his birth, foreign cities he visited, progress of a masque celebrating his wedding, his death, and his funeral monument in Faringdon church.

Two consorts of musicians are shown in the detail on the opposite page. Galpin, *Old English Instruments*, p. 279, and Plate LIV, identified the consort for the masque as "treble violon, flute, cittern, pandore (?), lute, and bass viol. On one side a drum." The consort on the left seems to include viols (note how the bows are held) and lutes or similar instruments, and some players seem to be singing.

Reproduced by permission of the National Portrait Gallery, London

Children of the Chappell.

Gentlemen of the Chappell.

GENTLEMEN AND CHILDREN OF THE CHAPEL ROYAL IN THE FUNERAL PROCESSION FOR QUEEN ELIZABETH, 1603
BM Add Ms 35324, folio 21v, reproduced courtesy of the Trustees of the British Museum

TREBLE LUTE

An Italian instrument of the seventeenth century. One of the instruments collected by the Rev. F. W. Galpin, and now in the Leslie Lindsey Mason Collection at the Museum of Fine Arts, Boston. See Bessaraboff, *Ancient Musical Instruments*, pp. 233, 234. Photograph courtesy Museum of Fine Arts, Boston.

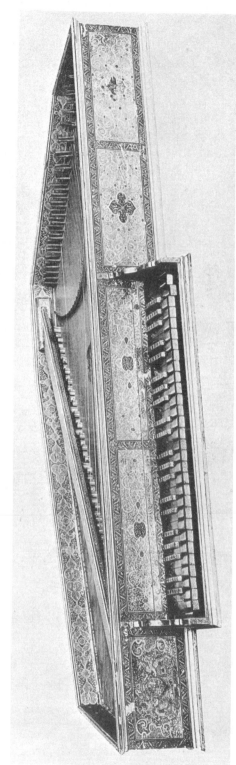

VIRGINALS

Commonly called "Queen Elizabeth's Virginals" because of the royal arms included in the decoration. The instrument is a spinet and evidently of Italian origin (see James, *Early Keyboard Instruments*, plate xix). Photograph courtesy Victoria and Albert Museum, London.

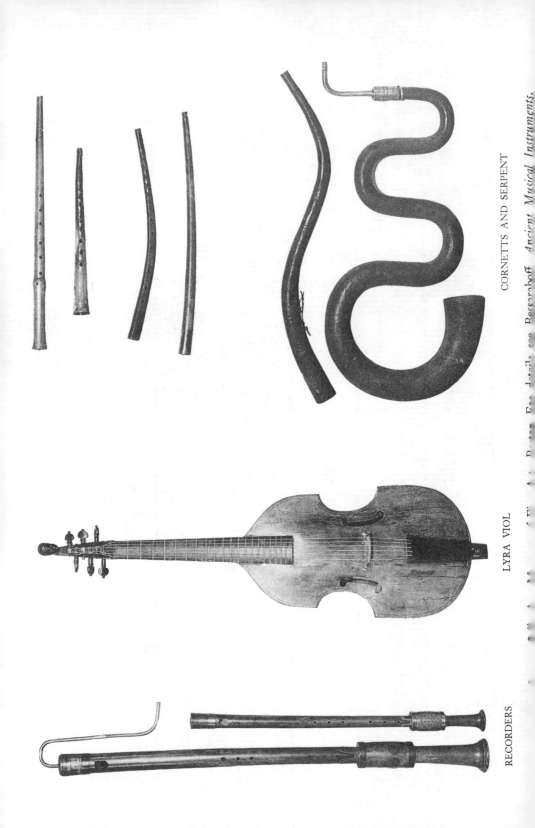

CORNETTS AND SERPENT

LYRA VIOL

RECORDERS

For detail see Besaraboff *Ancient Musical Instruments.*

Sometimes the waits alone furnished the music when the city honored the sovereigns passing through, as in 1554 when they helped welcome Philip and Mary, and in 1625 when the new king, Charles, went to Whitehall. Occasionally the musical arrangements were much more elaborate. In 1549 the waits, all of the brethren of the musicians' company divided into eight bands, all of the fellowship of parish clerks divided into seven choruses, and the children of St. Paul's, who were to play and sing at designated points—a total of seventeen groups of musicians—helped welcome young King Edward. Music greeted Queen Anne, wife of James, at almost every turn in her trip from the Tower to Whitehall palace in 1604. Four "noises" of music played at pageants—one of them sounding "an heavenly melody"—and a "noise of trumpets" rejoiced at another point. Farther on the queen encountered in their customary position on the church porch "the waits of the city, which did give a pleasant noise with their instruments. . . ." At still another place another "noise of instruments" played, and finally, as the queen left the city at Temple Bar, she heard "a noise of singing children. . . ." At least once the aldermen sent the waits out into the country to entertain the sovereign: in 1587, at a cost of over a pound, they hired a wagon and four horses to carry the waits out to Sir Nicholas Bacon's house at Gorhambury, Hertfordshire, where Queen Elizabeth was spending part of the summer.[18]

For an idea of the more ordinary and regular duties of the waits it is necessary again to rely on casual hints and references in records written by clerks who intended to set down only the special or new.

They had to play at the great festival seasons before the houses of the mayor and sheriffs, and to be available for any special call from them or the aldermen. The aldermen named two of the regular occasions in 1557 when they directed the waits to play annually for the mayor and sheriffs at Candlemas (2 February) just as they had always done at Christmas, any previous prohibition or contrary usage notwithstanding. Such days particularly called for the wearing of livery, as various notations in the Repertory state. This duty counted heavily with the city's governors throughout the period; in 1629 the aldermen granted a wait's request in consideration of his past services "in song and music at the houses of the lord mayor and sheriff upon festival days," and in 1637 the reason they gave for the pay stoppage was that

---

[18] 1554: Repertory, xiii, i, folio 191. 1625: Repertory, xxxix, folio 244 verso. 1549: Repertory, xii, i, folios 156-156 verso. 1604: S. S[tafford], *The Royal Passage of her Majesty*, sig. Di versio. 1587: Repertory, xix, folio 275.

some of the waits were "oft times absent upon solemn and festival days kept by the lord mayor and sheriffs" for the honor of the city.[19]

The waits also gave a regular series of public concerts. In 1571 the court of aldermen ordered them to "play upon their instruments upon the turret at the Royal Exchange every Sunday and holiday towards the evening" every year from Lady-day (25 March) to Michaelmas. This order evidently marked the beginning of these regular concerts, for it was made in consideration of an increase in pay granted at the same time. Moreover, the magnificent Exchange, completed only the year before, gave place and occasion for such an innovation. The next spring the aldermen ordered the waits to hold the concerts, "as before this time they have been used," every Sunday and holiday evening until Pentecost from seven till eight in the evening. Then, as the days became longer and warmer, they were to play from eight until nine. As before, the season was to end on 29 September. Although this order may have been drawn up only to set the hours of performance, its issuance three weeks after the concerts should have begun suggests that the waits themselves, unwilling to let this new duty become an established custom, intentionally neglected to start the concerts on Lady-day as the previous year's order had required. Whatever the waits may have wanted in 1572, it is certain that the concerts became a regular duty. The rules of 1625 stated that they should attend at the Exchange at five o'clock "upon such days and at such times as have been anciently observed (that is to say) from our Lady-day until Michaelmas. . . ." In 1642, when sabbatarian feeling prevailed in London, the aldermen ordered the waits to "cease to play at the Royal Exchange London on Sundays as heretofore hath been accustomed" and to continue on "every holy day hereafter" as usual. This duty is perhaps of more interest to historians of English music than any other, for one reason because it places the earliest public concerts in England a century before the concerts begun by John Banister in 1672, the accepted date for the first public concerts in England. Banister's concerts stand as the first commercial venture of the kind in London, but take second place to the waits' concerts for antiquity and continuity of existence.[20]

In short, the waits' chief functions were to glorify the city and to entertain its citizens by performing music on their night watches, at

[19] Repertory, XIII, ii, folio 474 verso, XIV, folio 353 verso, XXXIX, folio 176 verso, XLIV, folio 71, LI, folios 329-329 verso.

[20] Repertory, XVII, folio 174, XVII, folio 300, XXXIX, folio 176 verso, LV, folio 450 (21 June 1642). German *Turm-musik*, tower music, may have had an influence here.

great processions, and in concert before the houses of the mayor and sheriff and at the Royal Exchange.

Some towns had traditional wait-tunes, simple airs suitable for playing on wait-pipes "with very cold fingers" during night watches, but it is wrong to infer that the repertoire of waits extended little beyond such tunes, particularly in the case of the London waits during the reigns of Elizabeth, James, and Charles. What the London waits played is suggested chiefly by their capabilities: highly qualified on many instruments and in singing, they could play music for sets of shawms, recorders, sackbuts, violins, and viols, for viols and voices, lutes and similar instruments and voices, and for "broken consorts" of mixed instruments and voices. Perhaps most of the music they played, including theatre and masque music and some specially written for them to perform in concert or pageant, existed only in manuscripts now lost, but its characteristics remain in what survives. Much of the music, including madrigals, printed in Elizabethan and early Stuart England, was "apt for viols and voices," or "apt for viols or voices," according to the title pages, and suited their skills. At least twenty-three collections published in England between 1590 and 1638 provided material specifically written for various consorts. They include *Courtly Masking Ayres for violins, consorts and cornets* by John Adson (probably a wait), published in 1611 and again in 1621, "framed only for instruments; of which kind, these are the first that have been ever printed." The first eighteen pieces are in five parts for unspecified instruments, the next in five parts for cornetts and sackbuts, and the last ten for six unspecified instruments. The famous lutanist, John Dowland, published *Lacrimae, or Seaven Teares Figured in Seaven Passionate Pavans, with divers other pavans, galiards, and almands, set forth for the lute, viols, or violens, in five parts* in about 1605; this dance and concert music achieved great popularity. Michael East published many books of instrumental music, one of them almost entirely devoted to music for the viols—duets, trios, and four part "ayerie fancies." Thomas Forde's *Musicke of Sundrie Kindes*, 1607, contained songs for four voices to the lute, orpharion, or bass viol, a dialogue for two voices with two bass viols, and many duets for viols without voices. The popularity of Orlando Gibbons's *Fantazies in Three Parts* for viols or other instruments called for editions in 1606, 1610, and perhaps two in 1630. Anthony Holborne's *Pavans, Galliards, Almaines, and Other Short Æires*, published in 1599, contained sixty-five short pieces in five parts "for viols, violins, or other musical wind instruments." *Captaine* [Tobias] *Humes Poeticall Musicke*, 1607, contained music that could be played by many combinations of instruments, including two bass viols, three bass viols, two tenor viols and a bass viol, two orpharions and a bass viol, and tenor and bass viols, orpharions, and virginals or a wind instrument and voice. A number of publications suitable for the London waits were written by Robert Jones; one of them, *Ultimum Vale*, 1608, contained music for combinations of lute, voices and viols. Morley's *First Booke of Consort Lessons*, 1599 (second edition, 1611), mentioned already, was of course just the thing for the waits: for treble lute, pandora, cittern, bass viol, flute, and treble viol. Ten years after this first appeared, a similar work, arranged by Philip Rosseter, was published: *Lessons for Consort . . . set to sixe severall instruments: namely, the treble lute, treble violl, base violl, bandora, citterne, and the flute* (1609). Besides the English music in these and other volumes and in manuscript, the waits could exploit the vast resources, published and unpublished, of the continent.[21]

The apparent indifference with which instrumentation was indicated on the title pages of many books published in this period may reflect the eagerness of publishers and composers to make sales no matter what the potential customers played. Bacon noted another explanation for the apparent indifference: "In that music which we call broken music or consort music, some consorts of instruments are sweeter than others (a thing not sufficiently yet observed); as the Irish harp and bass viol agree well; the recorder and stringed music agree well; . . . but the virginals and lute, . . . agree not so well. But for the melioration of music there is yet much left (in this point of exquisite consorts) to try and enquire." The waits of London and the King's Musick gave English composers almost their only laboratories—fairly

[21] On cold fingers and town tunes see Bridge, "Town Waits and their Tunes," *Proc. Mus. Assoc.*, 54th session (1928), 63-92.

Adson: quotation from the dedication to the marquis of Buckingham.

East: *The Seventh Set of Bookes, wherein are duos for two base viols, so composed, though there be but two parts in the eye, yet there is often three or foure in the eare. Also fancies of 3. parts for two treble viols, and a base violl: so made, as they must be plaid and not sung. Lastly, ayerie fancies of 4 parts, that may be as well sung as plaid* (1638).

Forde: *Musicke of Sundrie Kindes, set forth in two bookes. The first whereof are, Aries for 4. voices to the lute, orphorion, or basse-viol, with a dialogue for two voices, and two basse viols in parts, tunde the lute way. The second are pavens, galiards, almaines, toies, jigges, thumpes and such like, for two basse-viols, the lieraway, so made as the greatest number may serve to play alone, very easy to be performde. No. 18 in the second book is named "A pill to purge Malancholie."*

large and permanent groups of all instruments—and much of the steady demand for music, which they needed.[22]

The London waits also helped form public taste. Morley's *First Booke of Consort Lessons* was known to a few gentlemen before it was published, of course; one gentleman, who presumably had heard the music, paid the printing costs in order to have the parts "for his private pleasure, and for divers others his friends which delight in music." Morley may have thought of a wider audience and a wider sale of the book when he recommended it to the waits' "careful and skilful handling." What their audiences, including persons of influence and taste from the provinces as well as London, heard and liked, must soon have become the fashion throughout the country.[23]

Whatever their influence, their music must have been one of London's more delightful attractions. C. Desainliens (translated C. Hollyband) suggested its flavor in *The French Schoolemaister, wherein is ... shewed, the true ... way of pronouncinge the French tongue, without any helpe of Maister*, published in 1573. A polite inquiry about the night's rest brings the reply that "I could not sleep all the night. . . ." "Why?" "What, have you not heard the minstrels and players of instruments, which did play so sweetly before the city's storehouse, from midnight even unto the breaking of the day?" [Who were they?] "I cannot tell truly: except perchance they were the minstrels of the town, with those of the queen, mingled with the voices of Italians and Englishmen, which did sing very harmoniously." "Would to God I had heard them, and it had cost me a quart of wine." "I would you had for your sake: for it would seem unto you to be ravished in an earthly paradise. . . ."[24]

---

[22] *Sylva Sylvarum*, Cent. III; my attention was drawn to this passage by Galpin, *Old English Instruments*, 277.

[23] The first quotation is from the title page of the *Consort Lessons*, and the second from the dedication, sig. A2.

[24] Desainliens, *The French Schoolemaister*, 68-70. "Queen" is "Queenes" in the original. The dialogue is in both English and French.

PART TWO

PROVINCIAL PROFESSIONAL MUSICIANS

INTRODUCTION

Travel was still so integrally part of the way of life of minstrels and musicians in the provinces in the sixteenth century that the statutes against vagabondage concerned them all in one way or another.

Harassed sixteenth century authorities could see no end to the increase in the number of the unfortunate and homeless poor, the wandering peddlers, the sturdy beggars, the shifty entertainers, and plain vagabonds and rogues, and tended to regard them all both as a menace to order and as recalcitrants who wandered because they hated work. Before Elizabeth's reign the lawmakers relied on punishment as the chief remedy and provided little central supervision over enforcement. A law passed in the first year of the reign of Edward VI (1 Edward VI, chapter 3) defined a vagabond as any able-bodied person without an income from lands or other sources sufficient to maintain him, who was found, "either like a serving man wanting a master or like a beggar," lurking or wandering and "not applying [him]self to some honest and allowed art, science, service or labor . . . for three days or more together," and who refused to work. A minstrel could be a man following an "allowed art," or a vagabond, as justices of the peace saw fit to decide. The failure of this law, apparent within three years, led to the revival (by 3 and 4 Edward VI, chapter 16) of 22 Henry VIII, chapter 12, which remained the basic vagrancy law until 1572. Although the reason given for repealing the first Edwardian statute had been the harshness of the penalties it prescribed, branding with a "V" and enslaving for two years, the revived act ordered whipping until bloody, pillory, loss of ears, and work—unpleasant alternatives for minstrels down on their luck.

The statute of 1572 (14 Elizabeth, chapter 5) was the first to include minstrels specifically among those liable to punishment as vagabonds. Not all minstrels, however: fencers, bearwards, "common players in interludes," and minstrels, "belonging to any baron of this realm or towards any other honorable personage of greater degree," could travel unmindful of the statute; and, even without such patronage, all these, and jugglers, peddlers, tinkers, and petty chapmen, could "wander abroad" if they had license of two justices of the peace of the particular shire in which they wandered. Minstrels and the rest who had neither an adequate patron nor a "passport," as a license was sometimes called, risked being "grievously whipped, and burnt through the gristle of the right ear with a hot iron of the compass of an inch about . . ." upon first conviction, and death upon third conviction.

The next, and definitive, statute against vagabondage, that of 1597 (39 Elizabeth, chapter 4) omitted, except for the players of interludes, the privileges extended in 1572 to servants of noblemen, made no provision for licensing minstrels or the others, and provided that offenders be whipped until bloody and then returned to the place of their birth or last residence or put into a house of correction for a year unless sooner employed. The exception favoring players disappeared at the beginning of the next reign (1 James I, chapter 7).[1]

None of the statutes mentions musicians. At the beginning of the sixteenth century "minstrel" seems to have been used to designate all kinds of public entertainers, and more particularly those who acted and performed music, but as the century wore on the tendency seems to have grown steadily stronger to confine use of the word to wandering ballad singers who often played some instrument and perhaps mimed or acted, and danced; it became, increasingly, a derogatory term. "Musician," especially from about the middle of the century, became the term used to designate more respectable men who ordinarily specialized in music alone. By including minstrels in the statute of 1572 the lawmakers in effect recognized the dubious connotation the word had come to have, and probably hastened its complete dis-

---

[1] One of the licensing justices had to be of the quorum (specially designated justice of the peace having superior knowledge of the law) of the shire wherein the licensee wandered. Later statutes, before 39 Elizabeth, modified 14 Elizabeth in various details.

For brief discussions of origins of the problem of vagabondage, and of related topics, see Aydelotte, *Elizabethan Rogues and Vagabonds*, chapter one; Judges, *The Elizabethan Underworld*, introduction; and Leonard, *The Early History of English Poor Relief*, chapter two.

In general, the manuscripts and printed source materials on which part two is based include municipal records, court records, parish records, household accounts, and contemporary literature. The manuscripts of the duke of Devonshire (Cavendish and Clifford families particularly) and of the corporations of Canterbury, Coventry, Nottingham, and York; the publications of the Historical Manuscripts Commission (e.g. HMC 24, *Duke of Rutland Mss.*, iv); *Records of the Borough of Leicester*, ed. Bateson; *Oxford Council Acts*, ed. Salter; *The Court Leet Records of the Manor of Manchester*, ed. Earwaker; *Quarter Session Records for the County of Somerset*, ed. Harbin, are examples of the more useful collections. Some works that do not appear either in the footnotes or in the bibliography have been useful because they have provided corroborative detail, or, in some cases, because the absence of reference to music and musicians has been suggestive.

Modern works throwing light on some of the problems discussed include Aydelotte, *Elizabethan Rogues*; Chambers, *The Mediaeval Stage*; Lipson, *Economic History*; Webb, *English Local Government*.

crediting: it is probably more than coincidence that in the Nottingham chamberlains' accounts for 1567-1568 (Book No. 1611), and earlier accounts, privately retained practitioners of music are almost invariably called minstrels, and that in the next surviving accounts, for 1571-1572 (the year of the statute of 14 Elizabeth), and in later accounts, they are almost invariably called musicians. (The appendices below of extracts from household and municipal accounts give further illustration of how the meaning and use of the word "minstrel" changed and how in the last decade of the sixteenth century "poor" usually qualified it.) The distinction did not make musicians, formerly minstrels, immune to prosecution under the statutes: musicians stood in the same relation to the statutes after 1572 as minstrels had before. John Gyrlynge of King's Lynn discovered this in 1580. The Norwich court book records that he, "calling himself a musician," was "found in this city exercising the idle trade of minstrelsy," and that the court ordered him thereafter not "to use the same within this city under pain to be punished according to the tenor of the statute against such roguing [roagyng] minstrelsy lately made and provided." To be fully safe with respect to the statute between 1572 and 1597 a musician had to regard himself as a minstrel and to secure either an adequate patron or passport. Or he could instead take the risk of traveling without these guarantees, no longer available in any case after 1597, and hope that he (or his employer if he had one) was so well known that no official would regard him as a minstrel. The statutes should have discouraged both musicians and minstrels from traveling, and particularly from going outside neighborhoods in which they were well known.[2]

The lawmakers obviously intended to discourage wandering by all but the upper classes. The records indicate that vagabondage, in general, did decrease in the reigns of James and Charles, and suggest that musicians, in particular, also traveled less. Part two describes the state of the musical profession in the provinces under these modified conditions. The distinctions made in part one between retained and independent musicians are again employed, more because they are convenient than because they represent actual categories or well defined classes. One of the retained musicians of chapter three ("Belonging to Any Baron") might once have been and have become again, one of the retained musicians of chapter four (Provincial Waits) and, even more likely, one of the independent musicians of chapter five.

[2] Gyrlynge: *Records of . . . Norwich*, ed. Hudson and Tingey, II, 188.

Thomas Sharp, writing in about 1825, in *A Dissertation on the Pageants . . . at Coventry*, 213, noted that soon after 1570 "musicians" replaced "minstrels" in the records.

CHAPTER III. "BELONGING
TO ANY BARON"

THE belief, widely held since at least the latter part of the nineteenth century, that many Elizabethan composers found happy homes as the resident professional musicians of noblemen and gentlemen, seems to be supported by little definite, positive evidence.

Of well-known composers John Wilbye (1574-1638) is perhaps the only one who was without question a professional musician and in domestic service most of his life. When about twenty-one years old he entered the service of Sir Thomas Kytson at Hengrave hall, near Bury St. Edmunds, Suffolk, and in 1628, on the death of Sir Thomas's widow, retired to the Colchester house of Sir Thomas's younger daughter, Lady Rivers. Edward Johnson, another composer, may also have been living in the Kytson household about 1600. Earlier, about 1575, one Johnson, perhaps John Johnson, lutanist and composer, seems to have been in residence at Hengrave, although he may have served the Kytsons only occasionally.[1]

Similar uncertainty characterizes the biographies of the other composers of the age who did not hold court or church positions most of their lives. When George Kirbye wrote, in the dedication of his *First Set of English Madrigals*, 1597, to Anne and Frances Jermyn, that his madrigals were their "own, being no strangers, but home bred . . . for [their] delight and contentments . . . ," he may have referred to previous or continuing residence as a professional musician in the household of the young ladies' father, Sir Robert Jermyn of Rushbrooke, near Bury St. Edmunds, or merely to services as their teacher. John Attey's case is parallel. In dedicating his *First Booke of Ayres*, 1622, to the earl and countess of Bridgewater, he wrote that "the best part thereof were composed under your roof, while I had the happiness to attend the

---

[1] Wilbye: see Fellowes, "Wilbye," in *Grove*.

Edward Johnson: see Fellowes, *English Madrigal*, 13-14. Robert Johnson, composer, also named here, was evidently not a Kytson employee, as Arkwright points out in *Grove*, ii, 783.

John Johnson: Entries in the Kytson accounts, printed in Gage, *History . . . of Hengrave*, 190, 205, show that "Johnson" served the Kytsons at least from time to time. Arkwright, in *Grove*, ii, 783, and others suggest that this Johnson may have been John the composer, who entered the King's Musick in 1579 ("Lists of the King's Musicians from the Audit Office Declared Accounts," *Musical Antiquary*, i [1910], 249).

service of . . . your daughters . . . ," and on the title page he was designated "gentleman, and practitioner in music." The daughter-in-law of
Sir Henry Fanshawe (died 1616) of London and Ware Park, Hertfordshire, wrote in 1676 that he was "a great lover of music, and kept
many gentlemen that were perfectly well qualified both in that and in
the Italian tongue . . ."; John Ward, a distinguished writer of madrigals, was certainly one of these gentlemen, but he may have been an
amateur rather than professional musician and servant. Henry Lichfield, whose *First Set of Madrigals* was published in 1613, may have
been a professional musician in the service of Lady Cheyney or Cheney
of Toddington house, Bedfordshire, to whom the work was dedicated,
but it is more likely that he was household steward and like Ward an
amateur musician. Richard Alison, in dedicating his *An Howres Recreation in Musicke*, 1606, to Sir John Scudamore, was a good deal more
specific than most: "Receive therefore (most honored knight and my
worthiest patron) the fruits of your bounties and the effects of those
quiet days, which by your goodness I have enjoyed. . . ." The title page,
however, suggests that Alison was not a professional musician in residence, for it defined him as "gentleman and practitioner in this art,"
and in the title described the music as "framed for the delight of gentlemen and others which are well affected to that quality, all for the most
part with two trebles, necessary for such as teach in private families. . . ."
Alison had already dedicated another work, *The Psalmes of David in
Meter*, 1599, to the countess of Warwick, whose husband had been
"sometimes my good lord and master." Thomas Bateson, dedicating
The Second Set of Madrigales, 1618, to Lord Chichester, lord high
treasurer of Ireland, wrote that he was anxious to have the songs take
sanctuary under the lord "First, because they were solely intended for
your honor's private recreation. . . . Secondly, it is not the least of your
honor's favors conferred upon me, to grace me with your honorable
service, and to call me to a more immediate dependency upon your
lordship. . . ." The title page described Bateson as "bachelor of music,
organist, and master of the children of the cathedral . . . Dublin," which
he had served since 1609.[2]

[2] Kirbye: see dedication, and "Kirbye," in *Grove*.
Sir Henry Fanshawe: Lady Anne Fanshawe, *Memoirs* (1829), 13-14, as quoted
in Mathew, *Jacobean Age*, 81.
Ward: The dedication of Ward's *First Set of English Madrigals* (1613) indicates a close connection. Additional evidence of this is given by Squire in *Grove*, v,
627. Fellowes, *Grove*, III, 192, asserts that he was an amateur musician.
Lichfield: see the dedication, and Fellowes's article in *Grove*.

While the biographical material for these and the other composers who did not spend much of their lives in royal or ecclesiastical service is inconclusive, it is hardly likely that of all the Elizabethan composers only Wilbye found a career as a professional musician in a private household: love of music, and vanity too, should have led more than one gentleman and nobleman to maintain a composer as a servant. Some of the composers may have been born and raised as gentlemen, lived on their own incomes or as gentlemen retainers in wealthy households, and practiced music and composed as amateurs. Others may have earned their livings in non-musical capacities, as estate managers for example, and also have been amateur musicians. And still others perhaps lived primarily as professional teachers and performers of music but not usually as resident retainers: one of these might have been the recipient, in about 1620, of the ten pounds paid by Endymion Porter, at the command of his lord the marquis of Buckingham, to a musician who presented a set of books. All of these possibilities and others are compatible with the evidence. Now that scholars have searched for a century for biographical detail it is unlikely that positive evidence will come to light to sustain the belief that many composers lived as professional musicians in residence in private households.[3]

Often associated with this belief, and no better supported by definite, positive evidence, is another, that many ordinary professional musicians who were not composers found their livelihoods as the resident retainers of gentlemen and noblemen.

Entries in household accounts showing payment of wages to musicians at regular intervals would be the best evidence, but they have not been brought forth heretofore, and have seldom appeared in the manuscript and printed accounts examined during research for this study;

[3] Buckingham: csPD *1580-1625*, 631.
Instances in which dedications imply more than hope of patronage but which seem to indicate at most that the composers had taught members of the family (which does not necessarily mean that the teacher lived with the family as a salaried retainer) include: John Bartlet (*fl.* 1610; earl of Hertford); John Dowland (1563-1626; lutanist to Lord Walden, eldest son of the earl of Suffolk, for a time before 1612, according to preface to his *A Pilgrimes Solace*); Thomas Greaves ("Lutenist to Sir Henrie Pierrepont" according to the title page of his *Songs of Sundrie Kindes*, published in 1604); Thomas Robinson ("sometimes Servant unto . . . Thomas Earle of Excester" according to the dedication of his *New Citharen Lessons*, published in 1609); Thomas Weelkes (in the service of Edward Darcye, groom of the Privy Chamber, for a time about 1598, according to the dedication of his *Balletts and Madrigals to Five Voyces*); Henry Youll (taught four sons of Edward Bacon before 1608, according to the dedication of his *Canzonets*).

these same accounts often show occasional payments of one kind or another for music. The wage accounts for Christmas 1573 of Sir Francis Willoughby of Wollaton hall, Nottinghamshire, show payment of five pounds to "the musician"; the list of servants paid at Christmas 1574 does not again include the musician. In December 1599, Sir William Cavendish of Derbyshire, whose accounts of wages paid for the year then ending do not include payment to musicians, hired in London a French lutanist whom he took back to Derbyshire with him. The Frenchman, who was to be paid six pounds a year, had left his service by September 1600. Francis Clifford, fourth earl of Cumberland, had a musician in attendance in 1611. His accounts of servants' wages paid at Londsborough on 23 June 1611 include £3.6.8 to George Mason for the half year ending at midsummer. Mason may have continued in the earl's service at least six more years, for he was one of the composers of *The Ayres that were sung and played, at Brougham Castle in Westmerland*, when the earl entertained King James in 1617. Other similar records must exist and many more undoubtedly have disappeared.[4]

Ambiguous evidence is more common. Margaret, countess of Rutland, gave "my lord's [presumably the earl of Rutland's] musicians" a reward of forty shillings on 18 March 1558; but it is doubtful that the earl had professional musicians in residence, for the printed excerpts from the Rutland manuscripts fail to show payment of wages to them. In January the countess had rewarded "Weston" for teaching the lute to Richard, her page, and in April he was again rewarded, this time for teaching "my lord's page to play on the lute." Weston appeared once again in the printed record, on 4 January 1559, when he was given six shillings eight pence, evidently as a New Year's gift. The printed record does not show whether Weston was a musical gentleman, living as a retainer with the family, a music teacher who came to give lessons, a servant of some kind who also happened to be able to teach the lute, or whether he was a professional musician in residence. According to the evidence of the printed records the earls of Rutland did not maintain any musicians in their households from this time on, although they did have music teachers and even musicians

[4] Willoughby: HMC *69, Middleton Mss.*, 439-440, 449-450. Earlier in 1573 (24 October) payment was made for "glass for the musicians chamber" (no indication of singular or plural possessive; the same, p. 434).

Cavendish: Mss. of the duke of Devonshire, Cavendish Ms. 23, folios 26 verso, 24, 35; Ms. 10A, accounts for December 1599.

Clifford: Mss. of the duke of Devonshire, Bolton Ms. 94, folios 73 verso and following.

called "the earl of Rutland's." Peter Lupo, a "violin" player in the King's Musick from 1567 to 1608, is said to have first found employment in England with the earl of Leicester but of what kind and for how long is unknown. The earl of Leicester was interested in music and it is quite possible that he maintained professional musicians in his household. The register of aliens resident in London for 1568 lists James Dennys, born in Flanders, as "a musician, and, as he sayeth, servant to the lord marquis of Northampton"; that he lived with his family in a rented "chamber room" rather than in the household of the marquis does not mean necessarily that he could not have served in daily attendance. The register for 1571 notes that William de Man (probably William Daman, later known as a composer and as one of Queen Elizabeth's musicians) had been brought to England six years previously "by my Lord Buckhurst," and that he was "servant to the same." "de Man" was apparently one of the musicians, "some for the voice and some for the instrument," "the most curious he could have," whom Sir Thomas Sackville, Lord Buckhurst, later first earl of Dorset, is said to have employed. A contemporary account of the death in 1576 of the earl of Essex indicates that he had a musician in his household but of course fails to say whether or not the musician was a professional in residence: the night before he died the earl "willed William Hayes his musician to play on the virginals, and to sing. 'Play,' said he, 'my song, and I will sing it myself.' And so he did most joyfully. . . ." When King Charles inspected the navy at Portsmouth in 1627 it was reported that dinner was as pleasant as Sir Robert Deall, the king's fool Archie, and the duke of Buckingham's musicians could make it. Specific reference to the duke's musicians, rather than to musicians, suggests that he may have employed them frequently, and even that they may have worn his livery, but does not necessarily mean that they attended him daily as regular household servants. More information is needed, too, about the earl of Warwick's "servant, Thomas Butler, by profession a musician," on whose behalf the earl intervened in 1628 when Butler was being "troubled and molested by the company of musicians" for keeping too many apprentices. That the household accounts for 1635 of the dowager countess of Derby show payment of twenty shillings to Mr. Jones, Mr. Allen, and Mr. Cotton "to find their viols with strings" for half a year, could indicate that she kept musicians in her establishment at Harefield, Middlesex. She and her family showed much interest in music and literature. She presented Milton's *Arcades*, with music by Henry Lawes, at Harefield; her stepson, the earl of Bridgewater, presented *Comus,* also with music by Lawes; and her grandchildren, at least some of whom studied music under Lawes, took part in both. These bits of evidence and others like them, while more plentiful than the positive items from wage accounts, do little to strengthen the foundations for the belief that many households maintained professional musicians in residence.[5]

Perhaps the principal source for this belief is the multitude of entries in household and municipal account books recording payment of rewards to visiting minstrels and musicians said to be the servants of various lords and gentlemen. The Nottingham chamberlains' accounts for 1577-1578, for example, show payment of rewards to musicians said to belong to the earl of Warwick ("the Earle of Warwycke musyssyans and plears [players]"), Mr. Marcham, Sir Thomas Venable (venabylles), Mr. Sacheverell (sachaveryll), Sir Thomas Stanhope, Mr. Powtryll, Mr. Bradlay, Sir William Hollys, Lord Willoughby (wyllobe), Lord Dudley, the earl of Essex, Lord Stafford, Mr. "few Wyllyams," Mr. Ratlyfe, Sir George Turpyn (?), Lord Mounteagle, and Lord Darcy (darsy). In some years the number of rewards was less, in some more, but this year is fairly representative of most of the years of Elizabeth's reign. The similar entries in the extracts from accounts of the earls of Rutland, printed in the fourth volume of the report of the Historical Manuscripts Commission on the papers of the duke of Rut-

---

[5] Rutland, 1558: HMC *24, Rutland Mss.,* iv, 380. The earls of Rutland had minstrels in their regular pay earlier; two are on the roll of servants for 1540, for example (the same, p. 308). Weston: the same, 383, 386.

Lupo: for service in the King's Musick see "Lists . . . ," *Musical Antiquary,* I (1910), 121ff., II (1911), 51ff., 235. His service with the earl of Leicester is mentioned in the *Dictionary of National Biography.*

Dennys: *Returns of Aliens,* ed. Kirk, III, 380.

de Man: the same, II, 39.

Sackville: two different sources, quoted in West, *Knole and the Sackvilles,* 38.

Essex: account by the earl's secretary, in *Devereux Papers,* ed. Maldon, 9.

Buckingham: CSPD *1627-28,* 212.

Butler: see chapter one, above.

Derby: HMC *78, Hastings Mss.,* i, 377-378. Payment on 26 March, till Michaelmas, for viol strings. Alice Spencer (of Althorp, Northamptonshire) married Ferdinando Stanley, fifth earl of Derby, who died in 1594, and Thomas Egerton, Viscount Brackley (the lord chancellor) who died in 1617. One of her daughters, Frances Stanley, married a son of Viscount Brackley by his first marriage, John Egerton, who became second Viscount Brackley and first earl of Bridgewater in 1617. On further family connections of musical interest see below.

Lawes speaks of himself as teacher of the daughters of the earl of Bridgewater in the dedication of his *Ayres and Dialogues* (quoted in Pulver, *Biographical Dictionary,* 291). He was a gentleman of the Chapel Royal from 1626.

land, are the data most commonly cited; and further entries, from household and municipal accounts, appear below in appendices. Unsupported by other evidence, these indicate no more than that many minstrels and musicians passed as the men of certain lords and gentlemen and received rewards from other lords and gentlemen and from towns.[6]

The discrepancy between the number of these entries and the number of entries showing payment of regular wages to resident household musicians may reflect, not reality, but only a distortion caused by deficiencies in the available record. Another and more probable explanation is that most of the rewarded visitors were only nominally the servants of these lords and gentlemen, that although deficient, the available record reflects a society in which nominal retainers far outnumbered domestic musicians.

Continuing a medieval custom, apparently, in the sixteenth and seventeenth centuries minstrels or musicians who served some nobleman or gentleman at more or less regular intervals and who were paid each time for their service, were often recognized by him as his "servants." Except for this occasional service they were at liberty, as far as the master was concerned, to spend their time wandering about the country earning rewards where they could.

Actors often followed this custom. A letter written on behalf of one of their companies in the middle of Elizabeth's reign explains most clearly the nature of the agreement between lord and "servant," whether actor or musician. These actors, fearing that their master, the earl of Leicester, might sever his connection with them because of a proclamation against great numbers of retainers, asked him to continue to retain them as his "household servants and daily waiters . . ."; they did "not mean to crave any further stipend or benefit" but liveries as they had had heretofore, and also the earl's "license to certify" that they were his "household servants" when they had "occasion to travel [travayle]" as they usually did once a year and as other noblemen's players were doing and had done in the past. About 1580 a writer, perhaps

[6] Mss. of the Corp. of Nottingham, Nottingham Chamberlains' Accounts, Book No. 1617, pp. 3-6.

Chambers, *Mediaeval Stage*, I, 51, pointed out that established minstrels were not always in constant attendance. He was of course writing about medieval minstrels. From at least 1558 the royal musicians seem rarely, if ever, to have left the court to wander as their minstrel predecessors had done. See also Aydelotte, *Elizabethan Rogues*, 45.

Note that in many of the ambiguous cases presented in the first paragraphs of this chapter the musician could have been a nominal retainer.

Anthony Munday, wrote against the noblemen who "restrain the magistrates from executing their office . . . by permitting their servants . . . whom for nearness they will not maintain, to live at the devotion or alms of other men, passing . . . from one gentleman's house to another, offering their service, which is a kind of beggary. . . . For commonly the goodwill men bear to their lords, makes them draw the strings of their purses to extend their liberality to them; where otherwise they would not." In Shirley's play, *The Witty Fair One*, licensed in 1628, Worthy, while describing the heroine's father, refers to the usage (he erred if he implied that it was new): "Her father is a man who, though he write himself but knight, keeps a warm house i' the country, amongst his tenants, takes no lordly pride to travel with a footman and a page to London; humbly rides [in] the old fashion, with half a dozen wholesome liveries, to whom he gives Christian wages, and not countenance alone to live on. . . ."[7]

Records showing clearly and unmistakably the existence of this relationship are rare, as they should be if it was quite common and simple and required formal and permanent memoranda only when difficulties arose. The court book of the mayor of Norwich provides one instance dated 13 November 1594: "The same day certain musicians who brought Sir Arthur Hevingham's letter to Mr. mayor and his brethren were demanded how long they had served him, and one of them confessed he was his retainer and wore his livery. And the rest confessed they were retained with him but yesterday, being the twelfth of this month." The musicians had presented themselves with their letter to the mayor with the expectation of being allowed to perform, and, whether or not they performed, of being rewarded from the city treasury, by the listeners, or by both, according to local practice. Instead, they were questioned, perhaps because one man wore livery and the others did not. (If events had gone as the musicians expected official records would either ignore their visit, or show in the chamberlains' books payment of a reward, in form such as "Sir Arthur Hevingham's musicians, six pence.") In 1595 Lord Dudley gave a warrant to Francis Coffyn and Richard Bradshaw, "his servants to travel in the

---

[7] Leicester: Given by Murray, *English Dramatic Companies*, ii, 119-120, from *Notes and Queries*, 3d series, xi, 350, from manuscripts of the marquis of Bath. Undated; probably about May 1574, according to Murray.

Munday (?): Anglo-Phile Eutheo, *A Second and Third Blast of Retrait from Plaies and Theaters* (London, 1580), 75-76. (Attention drawn to this passage by Chambers, *Elizabethan Stage*, i, 266).

Shirley, *The Witty Fair One*, Act i, scene ii.

quality of playing and to use music in all cities, towns, and corporations. . . ." Chester records note, "They came 20 November 1602."[8]

Musicians' passports are seldom mentioned in the records, probably because authorities did not ask for them unless the musicians were strangers to the neighborhood. The gentlemen named as masters of musicians rewarded in Nottingham between 1570 and 1590 seem almost invariably to have frequented Nottingham a good deal and to have been well known to the writer of the municipal accounts; the entry of 1588, "Item given in reward to one Mr. Ambrose musicians," is an exception. (Master and musician seldom if ever seem to have been in Nottingham at the same time, as they probably would if the musicians had been fully retained household servants.)[9]

From the 1590s on the number of privately retained musicians declined gradually, if the available record of rewards given to them is not misleading. Several motives could have led musicians to abandon the tradition of the wandering minstrel. Legally their status as travelers became less secure after passage of the statute of 1572, and still worse after 1597, when they all were technically at the mercy of any officials who might choose to call them minstrels; at the same time the decline of vagabondage in general made traveling musicians more conspicuous. The governing classes had, as the statutes themselves and the increasing vigor with which they were enforced indicate, a declining interest in wanderers as sources of entertainment: throughout this period musicians must have found themselves received with decreasing enthusiasm and generosity at castle, manor house, and town hall. The old tradition of hospitality, of keeping great country houses fully staffed and open to all who came by, was passing: less often resident in the provinces, noblemen and gentlemen began to form the habit of sending for entertainers when they wanted them. With good reason

[8] Norwich: Quoted in Murray, *English Dramatic Companies*, II, 337.
Dudley: Murray, II, 234, from Harleian Mss. 2173, 81, quoted in Morris, *Chester in the Plantagenet and Tudor Reigns*, 353n.
[9] Mr. Ambrose: Nottingham Chamberlains' Accounts, Book No. 1627, p. 16. Similarly the musician of an unnamed nobleman was given a reward at Coventry in 1587-1588: Coventry Corp. Mss., Chamberlains' and Wardens' Accounts 1574-1636, p. 172.
The Nottingham chamberlains rewarded Mr. Candishe's, or Cavdishe's (probably Cavendish) musicians "having a passport" in 1587-1588: Nottingham Chamberlains' Accounts, Book No. 1627, p. 9. Mr. Candidge's, or Cavdidge's, musicians were rewarded in October 1586 and after August 1587 (the same, Book No. 1626, pp. 7 and 23), and Mr. Henry Candish's, or Cavdish's late in 1588 or early in 1589; all of these may refer to the same persons, but only the once is a passport mentioned.

for abandoning speculative tours and nominal patronage, musicians turned to other connections and other ways that were more safe and profitable.

It is clear that the nobility and gentry retained musicians throughout the period, although perhaps less and less commonly as the decades went on; and it is likely, although not demonstrable statistically, that in most cases the relationship was virtually nominal.

It is not surprising that little is known of the life of fully retained household musicians. According to general custom their compensation should usually have included livery, board, and room. The Willoughby and Kytson musicians had chambers of their own in the family dwelling; if the marquis of Northampton's servant, who lived in a rented room, belonged to this category, he may stand as representative of some of the married musicians. As for money payments, evidence such as that given towards the beginning of the chapter suggests that an anonymous church musician of the early seventeenth century had the amount about right when he wrote that musicians gladly "betake themselves to the service of gentlemen for meat and drink and four or five pounds a year." Other masters besides Wilbye's may have esteemed their musicians so highly that they treated them almost as members of the family and gave them substantial gifts and bequests. In such cases service probably lasted many years, as Wilbye's did; often it must have ended shortly, as the Cavendish Frenchman's did.[10]

Most household musicians had probably been educated as professional apprentices in the usual way, some in the church as the anonymous writer just quoted complained, and a few in the households of noblemen and gentlemen. The last, although perhaps comparatively uncommon, may have been important, not only because boys kept in households may have served as substitutes for adult professional musicians, but also because the training given was in all likelihood well above average in some cases.

The indenturing on 29 March 1596 of Robert Johnson, later lutanist in the King's Musick and a composer, to Sir George Carey, is the best-known instance of this practice. Robert Johnson, "son of John Johnson, late of the queen's musicians," was to serve as an "allows or covenant servant" for seven years, and in return to be taught music, boarded,

[10] Willoughby: see note 4, above.
Wilbye: see the following, all by Fellowes: "Wilbye," *Grove; English Madrigal Composers*; "John Wilbye," *Proc. Mus. Assoc.*, 41st session (1915), 55-86.
Anonymous: BM Royal Ms. 18Bxix, folio 15: see chapter six, below.

lodged, and clothed, and to receive a penny a year. The Careys were notable patrons of music and letters. In 1589 William Byrd dedicated his *Songs of Sundrie Natures* to Sir George's father, the first Baron Hunsdon (died 1596), and in 1597 John Dowland dedicated his *First Book of Songes*, and Morley his *Canzonets or Little Short Aers*, to Sir George, now second Baron Hunsdon. His wife, Elizabeth Spencer, friend and patron of Edmund Spenser, was a granddaughter of Sir Thomas Kytson, the father of the Sir Thomas Kytson who was Wilbye's master; and sister of the countess of Derby, already mentioned, who patronized Henry Lawes and Milton. If the Careys did not keep a professional musician in residence, the teaching of young Johnson may have been entrusted to one or more of the musicians, who included Morley, Byrd, and Dowland, at court.[11]

The earl of Salisbury seems to have indentured Nicholas Lanier, later famous as lutanist, master of the King's Musick, composer, and artistic adviser to Charles I. In 1605 Nicholas Lanier's father wrote to the earl requesting that he secure for Nicholas a reversion of "old Piero Gaye's place as one of his majesty's musicians for the flute," and declaring that the reversion would not prejudice the earl's rights to Nicholas' services because during the remaining years for which Nicholas was bound to the earl he (the father) would continue, as he had for twenty years, to serve in Gaye's place. The letter indicates that the earl had a servant of some kind, perhaps a professional musician, able to report on Nicholas' "sufficiency for the flute."[12]

Sir John Harpar of Swarkeston, Derbyshire, may have indentured more than one boy at a time, and perhaps kept a band of musicians as well. In 1610 the earl of Huntington gave Sir John's musicians a large reward, one pound, at Swarkeston, and in 1622 Sir John wrote to the earl that, "Upon the great desire" of the master (apparently) of the school at Repton, Derbyshire, "to have a boy to teach others to sing" he had placed one with him. The two boy musicians apparently in the

[11] Contract preserved at Berkeley castle, published in "Mr. Jeayes' Catalogue of Lord Fitzhardinge's Muniments" according to W. B. S[quire] in "John Dowland," *Musical Times*, xxxviii (1897), 92. On the Derby connection see note 5, above.

[12] See HMC 9, *Marquess of Salisbury Mss.*, xvii, 297, and chapter eight, below. Nicholas apparently did not get the reversion, for the first place he seems to have held was a lutanist's (1616; "Lists. . . ," *Musical Antiquary*, iii [1912], 55), and Piero Guy seems to have died in 1606 ("Lists. . . ," *Musical Antiquary*, ii [1911], 177; *King's Musick*, ed. Lafontaine, 47). It is possible that the servant, "Mr. Cormack," may be identified with a musician named Cormock or Gormock McDermott; see chapter eight, below.

Kytson household in 1573, and a boy who played lute in the earl of Cumberland's household in 1614, may have been other exemplars of the system. An instance of the sale of a boy's services, perhaps the remaining years due to some gentleman, appears in a passage in the *Life of the Duke of Newcastle* (William Cavendish, 1592-1676), by Margaret, duchess of Newcastle: "My lord had bought a singing-boy for fifty pounds, a horse for fifty pounds and a dog for two pounds. . . ." Whether any of these boys later achieved prominence is unknown.[13]

The education for which several composers thanked noblemen and gentlemen may have been provided under this arrangement. Robert Dowland, dedicating his *Varietie of Lute-lessons*, 1610, to Sir Thomas Monson, wrote, "Sir, the grateful remembrance of your bounty to me, in part of my education, whilst my father was absent from England, hath emboldened me to present these my first labors to your worthiness. . . ." Perhaps William and Henry Lawes, said to have been taught by Giovanni Coperario (John Cooper) through the favor of the earl of Hertford, were indentured to the earl; Aubrey described him as "the great patron of musicians," and John Bartlet wrote in his *A Book of Ayres*, 1606, dedicated to the earl, of "the many benefits, and infinite favors your honorable bounty hath conferred on the professors of that faculty. . . ." The teachers may have been the master of the household or some gentleman or lady in it, a professional musician of the neighborhood, or a resident household musician; whoever they were, if several composers indeed owed much of their education to this arrangement it deserves notice in the history of music.[14]

Nominally retained musicians probably expected little from their patron but the use of his name and, when they served him occasionally, a reward and perhaps food and lodging for a day or so. The patron may have given greater rewards to his own men than they could expect from other persons. The account book kept for Sir Henry Sidney, lord president of the council for the Marches of Wales, shows payment of

---

[13] HMC 78, *Hastings Mss.*, i, 369, ii, 60; the letter is not in quotation marks in the HMC volume. It is possible that the boy Sir John sent was his son, of course.

Kytson: Gage, *Hengrave*, 200. Cumberland: Mss. of the duke of Devonshire, Bolton Ms. 95, folio 242. Newcastle: Everyman's Library edition, p. 134.

[14] Lawes: see Robertson, *Sarum Close*, 169, and *Musical Antiquary*, 1 (1910), 108 (quotation from Fuller). John Bartlet's dedication of his *A Book of Ayres* (1606) makes Aubrey's description of the earl, "the great patron of musicians," seem apt; Bartlet wrote that it is hard to know whether music is more graced by the earl's "singular skill and exquisite knowledge . . . both in the speculation and practice thereof: or by the many benefits, and infinite favors your honorable bounty hath conferred on the professors of that faculty. . . ."

£6.13.4 to musicians, apparently only nominally retained, who played for him at Christmas in 1571, no doubt for several days. The earl of Rutland's musicians also received £6.13.4 "for Christmas music *anno* 1617," and the earl of Huntington's, ten shillings, for an unspecified occasion in June 1607. Payments by a patron to his own musicians appear in the accounts much less often than payments to other musicians. Sometimes the patron furnished clothing or badges. Sir Henry Sidney's accounts note payment of one pound for liveries for musicians on 25 March 1572; musicians otherwise unnoticed in the printed accounts of the earl of Rutland seem to have received badges in 1624: "Paid to Ryley, the embroiderer, for badges for musicians, 25 June 1624, thirty-six shillings"; and one of Sir Arthur Hevingham's unfortunate musicians was wearing his livery in Norwich in 1594. Some may have traveled with only a letter to indicate their status as servants of a baron or personage of greater degree: the Nottingham accounts for 1586 record, "to the bishop of York his musicians that came with his letter to Mr. mayor. . . ," but do not indicate whether they also wore livery. A contribution made by some other patrons, below the rank of baron, could have been helping their musicians get passports; many of the patrons must have been justices of the peace themselves. Perhaps the musicians ordinarily carried no sign of their relationship, unnecessary in their own neighborhood. The most important contribution any nominal patron made was countenance, giving a measure of protection and almost a right to a reward: "For commonly the goodwill men bear to their lords, makes them draw the strings of their purses . . . where otherwise they would not."[15]

They did not open their purses wide, normally, as the appendices make clear. Although once in a while a band serving for several days might receive a substantial sum, rewards usually were a matter of pence. Often the account books may show only a part of a musician's takings for the day: other listeners besides the gentleman of the house may have contributed, and the mayor and burgesses perhaps added individually to the six pence the chamberlain handed out and recorded. Moreover, favorable reception by town officials sometimes amounted to

[15] Sidney: 1571: "Wages of servants in the household there as cooks, brewer, baker, catur and such like, for one whole year ended 25th March 1572, with £6.13.4 to the musicians in Christmas, £46.13.0": HMC 77, *De l'Isle and Dudley Mss.*, i, 359; livery 1572: the same.
  Rutland: 1617: HMC 24, *Rutland Mss.*, iv, 514; 1624: the same, p. 526.
  Huntington: HMC 78, *Hastings Mss.*, i, 366.
  York: Nottingham Chamberlains' Accounts, Book No. 1626, p. 9.

license to play elsewhere in the town for further rewards (occasionally magistrates rewarded entertainers and asked them not to perform in the town). What the rewards added up to in the course of a year probably not even the musicians themselves ever knew, but perhaps on the average it was to a sum not much more or less than the annual allowance of household musicians, and almost certainly it added up to enough to allow them to dress presentably, for they had to help constables understand that they were not poor minstrels, to make sure of their welcome at castles and council chambers, and to give their patron satisfaction in knowing that they were advertising his name and dignity throughout the region.

Not many signs point to their musical characteristics. Some of them, called minstrels, may have been as much actor, juggler, and ballad singer, as musician. A "blind harper, which was my Lord Derby's man, and played here upon his harp" in 1612 carried on the old tradition. The close alliance between music and other entertainment, even when the day of the minstrel had passed, is brought out by the differing identifications of Sir George Hasting's men in two sets of accounts for 1587-1588: in the Nottingham chamberlains' accounts they are called "musicians and players," and in the Coventry wardens' accounts simply "players." A number of times throughout the period the records identify retainers as waits, that is, players of wait-pipes or shawms: Sir Francis Willoughby rewarded "Mr. Stanhope's waits" in 1573 and 1574, the chamberlains of Nottingham "Sir Thomas Stanhope's waits" (called musicians earlier and later in the same accounts) in 1589, Lord William Howard "Sir H. Curwen's three waits" in 1612, and the wardens of Coventry the "lord deputy's wait players" in 1636-1637 and "the Lord Cavendish's waits" in 1639-1640. While they may also have played viols and sung madrigals and have been educated and versatile musicians, the chances are that they were usually rustic, even if skillful, musicians with a small repertoire of traditional country airs, better played at the castle gates, or along with the noise of a banquet in a great hall, than in a music chamber. The probability that some of them played more delicate instruments and knew more subtle music finds a little support in the records. Richard Bertie's accounts for 1562 mention "my lord of Rutland's man which played upon the lute" and the earl of Rutland's accounts for 1602 "my lord of Northumberland his men playing upon cornetts." Some of them must have matched the quality of any of the musicians of the provinces. A member of the military company in

Norwich, Lieutenant Hammond, who recorded his impressions of tours he made in England in 1634 and 1635, wrote of the waits of Lichfield: "The musicians (for fiddlers I must not call them) were the gentlemen waits of the town, that wore the badge of a noble brave lord [earl of Essex] and they were of that garb, and skill, as they were fitting to play to the nicest ears."[16]

Musicians belonging to any baron or other private patron made up a relatively small, and probably declining, part of the provincial professional class. Their average standard of living seems to have been mediocre, probably comparable to that of the singing-men of most cathedrals. The retainers who were resident household servants were probably not numerous, but good musicians, some of them celebrated composers. The retainers who received from their patrons chiefly blessings probably outnumbered the others, and were likely as a rule to have less musical education. They were a decaying relic of the customs and conditions of earlier centuries, a relic the privy council and justices of the peace were glad, at least in principle, to see disintegrating.

[16] Derby: Mss. of the duke of Devonshire, Bolton Ms. 94, folio 96b verso.

Hastings: Nottingham Chamberlains' Accounts, Book No. 1627, p. 13; Coventry Chamberlains' and Wardens' Accounts 1574-1636, p. 172. It is possible, of course, that the players and musicians had separated, but more likely that the group was small and that some or all of the men were both players and musicians.

Stanhope: HMC 69, *Middleton Mss.*, 433 and 442 (spelled "weates"; Stanhope was a neighbor); Nottingham Chamberlains' Accounts, Book No. 1629, p. 21 (compare same accounts, p. 15, and Book No. 1630, p. 25, for 1589).

Curwen: *Selections from the Household Books of Lord William Howard (of Naworth Castle)*, ed. Ornsby, 27.

Coventry: Coventry Chamberlains' and Wardens' Accounts 1636-1711, pp. 29 and 69. On the use of the word "waits" for the instrument, see above; these are examples of further extension of the word.

Bertie: HMC 66, *Ancaster Mss.*, 467; the item does not say, of course, that the lutanist was a professional musician or nominal retainer.

Rutland: HMC 24, *Rutland Mss.*, iv, 437; the remark after the preceding reference pertains here too.

[Hammond], *A Relation of a Short Survey of 26 Counties Observed in a Seven Weeks Journey Begun on August 11, 1634. . .* , ed. Legg, 59. A similar account appears in [Hammond], *A Relation of a Short Survey of the Western Counties . . . in 1635*, ed. Legg (*Camden Misc.*, xvi). These are referred to hereafter as Hammond, *Relation 1634* and *Relation 1635*.

CHAPTER IV. WAITS

HUMMING gnats [are] all the town music they have. . . ,"
Lieutenant Hammond reported of Crowland, near Ely, in
1635. Except for such hamlets, probably owing their arrested
musical development only to their petty size, nearly every
town in England would seem to have kept at least one wait, as
the incomplete list, given in an appendix, of over seventy towns that
did, suggests: Ashbourne, Barnstaple, Barton-upon-Humber, Bath, Beverley, Bewley, Blyth, it runs, and on to Westminster, Worcester, and
York.[1]

In many of the larger provincial towns, as in London, the waits had
apparently become so preoccupied with musical activity by Queen Elizabeth's time that the old night watch was no longer their most important
duty and its character no longer primarily protective. That this may
have been true nearly everywhere is indicated principally by the fact
that most towns let their waits go on the road now and then; detailed
evidence in such matters seldom appears in the available records of the
smaller towns.

The vestiges of a watch that had lost much of its original function
can be seen most clearly in the case of Coventry. According to a memorandum, said to have been written in the reign of Elizabeth or within a
few years after, "The usual manner for the playing of the waits in this
city was thus. . . :" going out during half of each quarter of the year, in
the first quarter they played from the first week in Lent to Easter, in the
second from 1 May to midsummer (24 June), in the third from Lammas (1 August) to Michaelmas, and in the fourth from Allhallows to
Christmas; during the first three quarters "they divided the city into
four parts, and played four several mornings. . . ," Monday through
Thursday, beginning at two o'clock, and in the fourth quarter "they
were to play . . . five days in every week throughout the town . . ."
(every day but Thursday and Sunday), and "they usually began at
twelve of the clock at midnight, and continued till four in the morning."
The schedule, with hours from midnight until four in November and
December and from two in the other quarters, suggests that the watch
had an ancestry going back to a patrol intended to discover fires and
prowlers. It also shows that this watch actually contributed relatively

[1] Hammond, *Relation 1635*, ed. Legg, 90. Hammond, further identified at the
end of the preceding chapter, invoked rhetoric to complain of "Crowland sacke"
and gnats.

little to the safety of the city: the waits marched during the year a total of only about one hundred and twenty-five days and on only about thirty-five of these days in more than one quarter of the city on any one night; and they left the city unguarded, as far as they were concerned, during many of the dangerous hours even on the nights when they marched through all the sections. The memorandum, which describes "the manner for the playing" as something formerly done, may have been written about 1615 in connection with a contemplated reestablishment of the waits. The annual payments to them do not appear in the chamber accounts for 1614, nor in either the chamber or wardens' accounts for 1615, and in August 1615 the council appointed a group of waits who were to play "about the city according to the ancient custom" and at certain other times. The former waits must have offended somehow, perhaps by neglecting their night watch over a long period, and various groups of their successors gave so little satisfaction that the council found itself able to dispense with them for several periods each lasting many years. In 1678 the council, once again appointing a group of waits, recalled the vestige of the ancient watch by defining their duties as "to play through the whole city every morning (except Sundays) from Michaelmas till the 22 of April yearly and are to begin to play on their instruments of music at two of the clock till break of day. . . ."[2]

The records for Ipswich also show a relic of the old watch. The order appointing John Betts and his company in 1597-1598, repeating substantially an order of 1587, prescribes that they "shall walk about the town with their waits from Michaelmas until our Lady-day . . ." and "shall go thereabout nightly from two of the clock until they have gone throughout the town. And further that they shall be at the demandment of the town during the whole year for further [orders] in their music. . . ." In 1601 the town paid Betts and his company for "their painstaking in walking about the town and playing with their waits," but whether they continued this watch in prescribed form for many more years the printed record does not say.[3]

To justify discharging the waits in October 1620 the Manchester jury

[2] Sharp, *A Dissertation on the Pageants . . . at Coventry* (Coventry, 1825), 211, dates the memorandum "the reign of Elizabeth, or early in that of James I." Coventry Corp. Mss., Chamberlains' and Wardens' Accounts 1574-1636, pp. 537-568; Council Book 1556-1641, p. 394. 1678: Sharp, 211.

[3] 40 Elizabeth: Wodderspoon, *Memorials of the ancient town of Ipswich*, 182-183. 1587: Bacon, *The Annalls of Ipswiche*, ed. Richardson, 350. 1601: HMC 8, *Ipswich Mss.*, 251.

alleged that they had failed to "perform their duties by their respective care and pains which they ought to take in the winter season, by their walking and going abroad in the night whereby they might discover many dangers and misdemeanors which may happen to fall out in the night. . . ." To justify the appointing of waits again in October 1647 the jury declared that "there hath been formerly allowed a certain number of waits to go through the town in the dead time of night whereby hath been prevented many dangers not only of night walkers and robberies but also great danger of fire discovered and prevented and other general benefits accruing thereby to many. . . ." How long before 1620 the waits had been neglecting their responsibilities with respect to the "dangers . . . in the night" is uncertain, but it may have been many years. In October 1567 the jury appointed two men as waits on condition that "they from time to time do their duties in playing morning and evening together as others have been heretofore accustomed to do . . ." and on condition "that they do not absent themselves without license of the steward" and two other designated persons. Again in 1600 it ordered that "our waits in Manchester" "shall not absent themselves at any time from playing about the town evening and morning without a very reasonable cause made acquainted to some two or three of the jury. . . ." Both orders speak of evening and morning and say nothing of "the dead time of night," or of "night walkers and robberies," and both use the word "playing," which the later orders do not. Perhaps the justification given in 1620 was a convenient legalism concealing a desire to end what had come to be regarded as an unprofitable luxury. Manchester had other persons to guard it, and managed to get along without waits for over a quarter of a century. When the jury wanted them once more it again found it convenient to hark back to ancient custom. Whether the men appointed in 1647 actually served as real watchmen does not appear in the record but an order of 1669, that the waits "according to the ancient custom shall play through this town every Thursday in the evening," suggests an emphasis on music rather than on patroling in the dead time of night, every night. The memory of the ancient watch seems to have survived long after the waits' steady performance of it.[4]

---

[4] *The Court Leet Records . . . Manchester*, ed. Earwaker, III, 32, IV, 8, I, 115, II, 163, V, 99 (see also p. 166). "The Town-Musick" took a conspicuous place in the ceremonies celebrating the restoration of Charles in 1660: the same, IV, 284. According to Earwaker, in note 1, I, 83, "it has been stated that they acted as night watchmen, but this is very doubtful."

Waits

Orders for the waits of Lincoln, Leicester, Nottingham, Carlisle, and York seem to be kin to the sixteenth century Manchester orders. In October 1560 the Lincoln common council ordered that the waits go according to custom from the feast of Allhallows to Candlemas, and in October 1561, from the morning after the first leet court following Michaelmas to the Annunciation. In November 1582 the Leicester council ordered that the waits "play every night and morning orderly, both winter and summer. . . ." The following February it put out a new order, of which the relevant part reads "playing about the town both evening and morning, continually and orderly at reasonable and seasonable times." Here, in addition to "playing" and "evening and morning," is a new phrase, "at reasonable and seasonable times": apparently the waits were to play at hours not disturbing to the town (and the waits?) and perhaps also when the waits' fingers were not numb with cold; in other words, not during the hours when watchmen are most needed. At Nottingham in 1628 the common council made an order for the waits' pay conditional on their doing "their duties and services according to their oaths, in walking and playing with their instruments assigned thereunto, as well in the day as in the night, for the credit and worship of the town, as hath been anciently used and accustomed." Here safety clearly yielded precedence to music and entertainment, and to the "credit and worship of the town." The court leet rolls of Carlisle for 23 October 1633, specifying the winter season as Lincoln and other orders do, require adherence to "former custom" with one exception that may reflect the puritan spirit of the day: the waits should be "commanded to play beginning presently and so continue until Candlemas and to play both at Christmas and at all other times according to former custom except only the Sabbath days. . . ." It is doubtful that in Carlisle fewer dangers fell out in the night on the Sabbath than on weekdays.[5]

[5] HMC 37, *Lincoln Corp. Mss.*, 52, 53.
Records of . . . Leicester, ed. Bateson, III, 192, 192-193.
Records of . . . Nottingham, ed. Stevenson, V, 129-130. See also in the same, IV, 335, presentments at sessions, 1615: the waits were presented "for that they do not go their watch in the daytime on Tuesdays, Thursdays and Saturdays as their predecessors have used. . . ."
Some Municipal Records . . . Carlisle, ed. Ferguson and Nanson, 286.
It is possible that the time of waits' watches had earlier been adjusted with relation to the watching time prescribed by the statute of Winchester (1285, repealed under James I), from Ascension to Michaelmas, i.e. spring and summer; waits may have taken up the watch when the statutory watch left off at Michael-

An order, issued in 1570 by the common council of York, that the waits should thereafter "use and keep their morning watch with their instruments accustomed every day in the week except only Sundays in the morning and the time of Christmas only excepted," any previous usage notwithstanding, is among the several indications that in York the waits' watch was no longer an important part of the police system. The story of what happened when the plague came demonstrates the point more strikingly. At the first rumor that it had afflicted London or a nearer town, York adopted precautions and doubled them when it came close: men could not gather at alehouses; the regular watches by wards and especially at the bars (the gates in the walls) were greatly strengthened; no one could enter the city, not even citizens of York who lived in the sections outside the walls. This last particularly affected the waits in 1599, when the inhabitants outside the walls would not make their customary payments for the "last winter watch" because the waits, "by reason the bars were shut," had been unable "to go forth to play by night" for them. In 1632 "in regard of the times of danger now being within this city and suburbs thereof" the council ordered the waits not to "play as formerly...," although it allowed them to go about to collect money as usual. After three weeks the worst had passed: "And now the waits are permitted to go their night watch as they formerly have done." The relationship between the waits of York and the public guard was inverse: when the times required maximum vigilance the council ordered the waits to stop their night watch.[6]

In several of these towns and others the watch, now a matter of play-

---

mas. In Leicester there seems to have been no connection; see introduction to *Records of . . . Leicester*, ed. Bateson, III, p. xxix, and references there.

[6] 1570: *York Civic Records*, ed. Raine, VII, 18. 1599: York Corp. Mss., House Book 27, folio 262; see also folio 38. 3 and 24 October 1632: House Book 35, folios 128 verso, 134.

A provision of the 1578 ordinance of the York minstrels' fellowship, repeated from the 1561 ordinance, exempts the waits from a prohibition against hiring any person except by apprenticeship: "Provided that this act do not extend to the waits of the city of York . . . to hire any man to help them in their watch." The exemption may be a survival of custom important when the waits were real watchmen, but by 1561 and 1578 it could be taken to give them permission to hire help for their musical perambulations. In 1580 the council appropriated ten shillings to be divided among the waits "for the payment of the piper they hired this year for the watch," but it apparently did not make the appropriation in other years. York Corp. Mss., Book 22, folio 143; House Book 27, folio 262.

HMC *31*, *Rye Mss.*, 29, reports the appointment in 1574 of a drummer and a fifer (probably not waits) to go abroad in the winter nights for the watches of Rye.

ing about the town evening and morning, had evidently become a pleasant device informing everyone of the arrival of bedtime or rising time. On Sunday mornings and at Christmas time, when almost everyone could sleep later, and in the spring and summer when the longer daylight hours made signals less necessary, towns could do without the watch for the time being, and when they fell upon hard times or simply came to regard the music as an extravagance, or when the waits misbehaved, they could easily do away with it altogether, as Manchester did. Even brief and extremely intermittent watches like London's could yield this service as a seasonal luxury. It may have helped some men, inclined to be slugabeds, for energetic Elizabethans got up early. At Gloucester in the earlier part of the seventeenth century the waits played in the chief streets at four in the morning, and at Rochester in 1640 two musicians promised to "play through the city every morning upon their loud music called the waits between Hallowtide and Candlemas as is usually done in the city of London and Canterbury." Lieutenant Hammond and his friends arrived late at the *Crow* in Chester in 1634, and were aroused early the next morning by "the city waits, whose absence we had rather desired, not for the charge, but for our rest. . . ."[7]

As an institution the waits' watch seems generally, in the course of decades or generations, to have lost most of its protective character and to have become primarily musical and secondarily useful in other ways, at the same time that the waits, devoting more and more of their attention to music, became better musicians and found themselves increasingly in demand for musical service at public and private gatherings.

Waits had long helped welcome distinguished visitors. The Gloucester records for 1573-1574 show a reward to the Shrewsbury waits "for playing about the city every morning as long as the queen's grace was here," and in Norwich its waits were prominent when the queen came in 1578. The York magistrates, in a flurry as King James approached the city on his way to London after Elizabeth's death, made elaborate

[7] Willcox, *Gloucestershire*, 232. Burtt, "On the Archives of Rochester," *Archaeologia Cantiana*, VI (1866), 112. Hammond, *Relation 1634*, ed. Legg, 48-49.

Perhaps with special reference to the forthcoming visit of the lord president and council, in December 1579 the Shrewsbury council voted to give "the wait-men" new coats "in respect of their painstaking to play every morning": HMC 47, *Shrewsbury Corp. Mss.*, 21. An order of 1673 required the Beverley waits to play their morning watch from 25 October to 1 March every year: *Beverley Borough Records, 1575-1821*, ed. Dennett, 157.

preparations to welcome him, cleaning up the streets, repairing and painting everywhere, deciding on appropriate gifts and, with much hesitation and bargaining, on a large loan, and, of course, working out a program of entertainment in which the waits had a considerable share. They were first to play at the gate where the king was to be received into the city, and then to hurry over the river to "Applebye's house" and "Bowthome Barr," where there was to be a scaffold for them to play on. Canterbury, both because of its geographical position and its ecclesiastical eminence, had many opportunities to welcome the great. In 1613 the city rewarded the five waits "for playing the loud music, on the top of All Saint's church, at the coming, into the city by Westgate, of the Prince [Charles], his sister the Lady Elizabeth, and the palsgrave her husband"; the books for 1624-1625 show rewards to the musicians for playing when the king entered the city, and to the person who carried a ladder to St. George's gate for the waits when the French ambassador came.[8]

Among the holidays that the waits had to help celebrate, the monarch's accession day took a leading place. Records of their participation survive for Canterbury 1578 and 1602, Nottingham 1588 ("the day of rejoicing for her majesty"), Oxford 1590, and Norwich 1618 (coronation day). Lincoln had a custom of "Crying Christmas" for many years in Elizabeth's reign and perhaps after. In 1569 Nottingham brought in May with the help of its waits, dancers, gunners and gunpowder; no doubt waits throughout the country officiated at this same ceremony that year and many other years. The news of the defeat of the Armada seems to have been the occasion for bell ringing and music at bonfires in Nottingham in 1588.[9]

Everywhere the waits seem to have been at "the demandment of the

---

[8] HMC 27, *Gloucester Corp. Mss.*, 470-471. Stephen, *Waits of Norwich*, 10-12.
York House Book 32, folios 255 verso-256; 11 April 1603. On 7 April a sackbut was bought for the waits for eight pounds, evidently in anticipation of the king's visit: the same, folio 254.
Ancient Canterbury. The Records of Alderman Bunce. Republished from the Kentish Gazette of 1800-01, 17. HMC 8, *Canterbury Corp. Mss.*, 163.
[9] HMC 8, *Canterbury Corp. Mss.*, 157; Canterbury Corp. Mss., Chamberlains' Accounts, Book 17, folio 21 verso ("for their attendance and music bestowed upon Mr. mayor's deputy and such as dined with him at the Swan on the queen's holiday five shillings"). *Records of . . . Nottingham*, ed. Stevenson, IV, 225 (1588), 133 (1569), 217 ("bone fiers"). *Oxford Council Acts, 1583-1626*, ed. Salter, 367: see also *Oxford Council Acts, 1626-1665*, ed. Hobson and Salter, 48, 416, both for 1633. Norwich Public Library, Mann Mss., Norwich Musical Events, VIII, folio 75. HMC 37, *Lincoln Corp. Mss.*, 58-60, 65, 67.

town" for service at all public ceremonies. The great portmoot of Liverpool agreed in October 1562 that "the water bailie, the sergeant, the keeper of the common warehouse, and the wait, shall every of them give their attendance on master mayor every festival day and market day, every of them bearing a handsome and comely bill meet for such purpose etc." A general order in 1615 required the Coventry waits "to play at all solemn feasts, at Mr. mayor's command," and shortly afterwards they were rewarded by the city for performing at "Allhallows dinner." The York council decreed in 1580 that the waits "yearly from henceforth the day of the swearing of the new lord mayor play on their instruments before him and his brethren etc. from the common hall to his dwelling place and sword bearer to wear the hat of maintenance. . . ." They were also supposed to play at the aldermen's "beef breakfasts," apparently traditional festivities held at the expense of each alderman. The Nottingham waits played before the mayor and burgesses on Michaelmas (the day the new officials took office), before the justices, and for the "mayor's dinner . . . at the sitting of the commission"; the Oxford waits attended the mayor as a rule when he rode the franchises (made a circuit of the boundaries of the city); the Canterbury waits played at the mayor's dinner, at a buck dinner, and at quarter sessions dinners: the variety of occasions was almost endless. The Liverpool portmoot even decreed, in 1583, that the wait "shall play at every man's door that hath borne office" and a year later found him liable to a fine for not doing it.[10]

Only Norwich may have required its waits to give concerts regularly as London did. On 3 May 1553 the mayor's court of Norwich agreed "that the waits of the city shall have liberty and license every Sunday

[10] *Liverpool Town Books*, ed. Twemlow, I, 197, II, 461, 478. The wait or waits had to accompany the mayor and other officers when they went around the confines of their fair: the same, II, 314n. Coventry Council Book 1556-1641, p. 394; Coventry Chamberlains' and Wardens' Accounts 1574-1636, p. 575 ("Allholland").

York House Book 27, folio 218. Beef breakfasts: House Book 32, folio 126; this item, 1600, refers to difficulties the waits were having with an old obligation. The York waits received "accustomed fees of the sheriff" when the justices met for a jail delivery in 1555: Mss. of the duke of Devonshire, Cumberland Mss., Bolton 12A, folio 12.

Records of . . . Nottingham, ed. Stevenson, IV, 117 (1557); before the justices: HMC 69, *Lord Middleton Mss.*, 424 (1573); Nottingham Corp. Mss., Chamberlains' Accounts, Book No. 1629, folio 37 (1588-1589). *Oxford Council Acts, 1583-1626*, ed. Salter, pp. xxxviii-xxxix, 393, 412-414; for other events at Oxford requiring music see in the same pp. 359, 371, 382, 392, 409. Canterbury Chamberlains' Accounts, Book 16, folios 35 verso, 39 (1598-1599 accounts); Book 17, folios 22, 25, 26 verso, 28 (1602-1603).

at night and other holidays at night betwixt this and Michaelmas next coming to come to the guildhall, and upon the nether leads of the same hall next the council house shall betwixt the hours of seven and eight of the clock at night blow and play upon their instruments the space of half an hour to the rejoicing and comfort of the hearers thereof." Whether this was permissive or mandatory depends on the relative strength of its first and second parts, "shall have liberty" and "shall . . . blow." Although it refers only to the current year, 1553, the concerts may have recurred annually; on 13 May 1626 the court ordered that "there shall be no more sounding of the waits at the Market Cross upon Sabbath days in the evenings contrary to the law as well in regard of the law in that case made as of the contagion now being in the city." The waits evidently returned to Sunday playing, thereby allegedly drawing together many disorderly people, with the result that in May 1629 the court forbade "the waits of this city or any other" to play on Sunday "at the market cross or any other open place within the city." Perhaps playing a concert series annually never became as firmly established a duty for the waits in Norwich as it had in London.[11]

The growth in the number of waits kept in London was paralleled in the provinces as a whole. Some towns, including Sheffield and Liverpool, had only one, or one most of the time and two for a few years; many of the smaller, less wealthy, and less ambitious towns must have been satisfied with or unable to have more than one. The number in larger towns varied, apparently according to the availability of musicians and local interest in music.[12]

Nottingham had three waits in 1502-1503 and three from 1571 to 1587 except for a short time about 1580; presumably, therefore, three most of the time from 1503 to 1587. In 1587-1588 and 1589-1590, and probably the intervening year there were four, but by 1597-1598 three once more. By 1615 there were four again, by 1625-1626 seven, and seven in 1627-1628 (two had been replaced during the intervening year). In 1632-

---

[11] Stephen, *Waits of Norwich*, 9-10. On p. 9 Stephen states that the court "permitted" the waits to play. In 1576 "The whole company of the waits of this city . . . craved that they might have leave to play comedies and upon interludes [interlutes] and such other plays [places] and tragedies which shall seem to them meet . . . ," and the court granted the request "so far as they do not play in the time of divine service and sermons." *Records of the City of Norwich*, ed. Hudson and Tingey, II, 186.

[12] *Records of . . . Sheffield*, ed. Leader, 18-173; for brief periods Sheffield had two waits. *Liverpool Town Books*, ed. Twemlow, I, 7-456, II, 24-1060; 1558 to 1629, when the office of wait may have been done away with.

1633 there were only four, increased to five by 1634, when, as a result of a dispute among the waits, adjudged by the Nottingham common council in 1634, two waits were dismissed. The lists of town officers show seven again in 1637-1638 but only five in 1640-1641. In 1647, an unsettled year, the common council decided to have no more waits, but in 1653 reversed itself and hired six.[13]

The records for other towns, showing fewer fluctuations, also illustrate the tendency towards gradual increase. Canterbury had three waits at the beginning of Elizabeth's reign and five most of the time after 1577-1578; Leicester three in 1562, five in 1595 and 1603; Norwich three from at least the fifteenth century, four by 1437-1438, and five from 1553 on; Oxford two in 1577, three before 1588, five by 1588, and six in 1628; and York three in 1561, four in 1566, five from 1580 to 1596, and four thereafter. Three was perhaps the average number for all but the smallest towns; four was common for large towns; and five, rarely exceeded, and the most satisfactory number, was chosen by the wealthier and prouder towns.[14]

[13] 1502-1503: *Records of . . . Nottingham*, ed. Stevenson, III, 90. 1571-1587 (the sources for this period do not always specifically state the number of waits, which must therefore be inferred from the amounts of the livery payments): the same, IV, 137, 416-425, and Nottingham Chamberlains' Accounts, Book No. 1613, p. 3, and the succeeding books through No. 1626; Book No. 1621, p. 1 shows payment for 1581-1582 of one pound for liveries instead of the three pounds, more or less, which had been paid since 1576 and which were paid 1582-1583 and 1584-1587; accounts for the year 1583-1584 seem to be missing; and Book No. 1625 for 1585-1586 omits payment to the waits. 1587-1588 and 1589-1590: Book No. 1627, p. 39 and No. 1630, p. 17. 1597-1653: *Records*, ed. Stevenson, IV, 425, 335, V, 425, 426, 427, 165 (see also pp. 171-172), 425, 251, 281, 432.

[14] Canterbury: 1558-1559: Chamberlains' Accounts, Book 12, folio 84; 1577-1578: Book 14, folio 37; decision to have only four waits 1579: Canterbury Burmote Minutes 1578-1602, folio 14; five again by 1583: Minutes, folio 75; and in 1586: folio 101; and in 1587-1588: Chamberlains' Accounts, Book 15, folio 36.
Leicester: 1562: *Records of . . . Leicester*, ed. Bateson, III, 101; 1595: *Notices Illustrative . . . Leicester*, ed. Kelly, 228 (if the amount of cloth per livery in 1596, 1598, and 1601 was about the same as in 1595, the number of waits may have been six from 1596 to 1598, and perhaps seven 1598 to 1601; the increased amount of cloth may have been allowance for waits' boys or apprentices, on the other hand; compare items in Kelly, pp. 228, 229, 234); 1603: *Records*, ed. Bateson, III, 451.
Norwich: Stephen, *Waits of Norwich*, 6.
Oxford: 1577: *Selections from the Records of . . . Oxford*, ed. Turner, 394; 1588: *Oxford Council Acts, 1583-1626*, ed. Salter, 42; 1628: *Oxford Council Acts, 1626-1655*, ed. Salter and Hobson, 17.
York: 1561 and 1566: *York Civic Records*, ed. Raine, VI, 16, 121; 1580-1596: York House Book 27, folio 262, Book 31, folios 22 verso, 45, 206 (the record for five waits is not continuous for the years 1580 to 1596, but the references make it very likely; in 1597, however, the livery allowance was for four coats: Book 31,

Apprentices or "boys" participated in the waits' activities. At Leicester in 1583 the council agreed that the waits and their boys would have coats bought for them, and that two of the city's badges (cinquefoils) would "be made for the boys to wear with lace about their necks etc.," and at Canterbury in 1631 the city authorities had to settle a dispute among the waits over the number of boys they were to keep. For several years after about 1590 one of the York waits kept a boy (apparently in addition to one or more apprentices) for service with the group, more or less as one of the London waits, beginning in 1613, kept two boys pursuant to a special arrangement with the city. While the buying of livery and the making of badges for boys may have been uncommon, in most towns waits must have kept apprentices who performed with their masters as a matter of course.[15]

The threefold use made of the word "wait," ordinarily the designation for a municipal musician, occasionally for the shawm, and least often for a shawm player ("Sir Thomas Stanhope's waits"), is presumptive evidence that most waits played the shawm. Sir Peter Leycester, writing towards the middle of the seventeenth century, defined "the hautboys and shawms" as the instruments "such as the waits of our cities commonly use...," and town records mention shawms far oftener than any other instrument. A petitioner for the place of musician and head wait of Hereford in 1587, proud to say that he had "from his youth been brought up in music, and doth presently keep and maintain servants in the art of music to play on divers instruments," tacitly acknowledged that shawms were essential for Hereford waits by declaring that he would soon "attain to such knowledge in the instruments of shawms and loud noise as" would be to the "good liking and contentation" of the magistrates. Shawms seem to have been so long and widely

---

folio 318). A record of payment in 1612 of a reward to the waits of York, said to be seven, in Mss. of the duke of Devonshire, Cumberland Mss., Bolton 94, folio 97d, cannot be taken, in the absence of confirming evidence in the city archives, as proof that York had seven waits by 1612; perhaps apprentices were counted, or additional musicians joined the waits on this trip.

[15] *Records of ... Leicester*, ed. Bateson, III, 194, 206, 220. *Ancient Canterbury ... Bunce*, 18. York: see discussion in note to entry in York House Book 24, folio 267, in appendix C.

Ipswich, retaining four, five, or six waits 1582-1613, agreed in 1613 to pay five men and a boy for the next two years: Bacon, *Annalls of Ipswiche*, ed. Richardson, 453.

established as the proper instrument of the watch that they and waits had become almost inseparable.[16]

Another good marching instrument, the bagpipe, perhaps capable of the volume of sound of a whole noise of shawms, was the instrument of the lone wait of Liverpool and probably of some other towns that employed only one or two waits. The sackbut, also good on the march, was apparently the first instrument, after the shawm, that several towns bought for their waits.[17]

An extension of the variety of instruments waits played and the broadening of their duties seem to be twin aspects of a single phase in their history. The records are particularly reticent on the question of instrumentation, probably because towns must ordinarily have obliged waits to buy their own instruments; some waits must have played a wide variety of instruments long before municipal records began to tell about it. The Norwich waits played viol or violin or both, "a whole noise" of recorders, various sizes of shawms or hautboys, cornetts, and sackbuts, and a lyzardyne (probably a great cornett in *S* form) by about 1585, and the Chester waits hautboy, recorder, cornett, and "violens" by 1590. It is likely that most of the larger groups of waits played several kinds of instruments. The York House Books show that the waits had a double curtal (probably like a double bassoon) in 1602, and a sackbut in 1603 and 1623, that in 1561 one of the waits was officially warned to "leave his unthrifty gaming" and to "apply himself in the instruments and songs belonging to the said waits . . . ," and that in 1603 the waits

[16] Leycester: Mss. of C. Leicester-Warren, Esq., "Music," folio 30, "the Hoobies & Shalmes." HMC *21, Hereford Corp. Mss.*, 337.

Among the instances of shawms in municipal records: Norwich 1545-1546, Stephen, *Waits of Norwich*, 63-66; York 1561, "base shalme," and 1566, "a noise of four shalms," *York Civic Records*, ed. Raine, VI, 16, 121; Ipswich 1582 and 1583, "certain waits bought," and 1601, "playing with their waits," HMC *8, Ipswich Corp. Mss.*, 253, 255, 251, 250; Rochester 1640, Burtt, "On the Archives of Rochester," *Archaeologia Cantiana*, VI (1866), 111-112; Coventry 1615, "play with the waits about the city," Coventry Council Book 1556-1641, p. 394. Further selections will be found in the appendices below; see also Galpin, *Old English Instruments of Music*, 160 and following.

[17] *Liverpool Town Books*, ed. Twemlow, I, 79 (1558), II, 24 (1572), II, 681-682 (1594). Waits called "pipers" were probably bagpipers as a rule; the waits of Sheffield, for example: *Records of . . . Sheffield*, ed. Leader, 18 (1566), 26 (1572) etc. (the wait is still called piper in 1606: p. 89); and the waits of Richmond (probably Yorkshire) in 1630 and of Durham in 1634, called pipers in *Selections from the Household Books of Lord William Howard of Naworth Castle*, ed. Ornsby, 262, 316.

Sackbut: Salisbury 1540: HMC *55 Various* iv, *Salisbury Corp. Mss.*, 220; Norwich and York: see next note.

were required "to exercise and set up a consort amongst them . . . twice in the week at the least." If they had offered only shawms they would not have been invited into the earl of Cumberland's great chamber after supper in 1612, or been given five pounds as a reward for "attending all Christmas" in 1639, or been summoned to take part in the production of a masque at Skipton castle in 1636. The earl of Rutland must have rewarded more than wait-players at Belvoir castle in 1608 when he paid the waits of Grantham three pounds for playing at Christmas, and in 1612 the waits of Lincoln four pounds for playing when the king was there. If the waits of Lichfield had greeted Lieutenant Hammond only with shawms in 1634 he would hardly have praised them as he did, musicians, not fiddlers.[18]

The liberal compensation paid by the earls of Cumberland and Rutland testified their satisfaction with the quality of the music provided by the waits of York, Grantham, and Lincoln. Sir Francis Drake praised the Norwich waits in 1589 by asking the mayor to send them with him on his forthcoming Portuguese voyage; the waits wanted to go, the mayor's court accepted the invitation, and bought for them six cloaks, three new hautboys, and a treble recorder, provided a wagon to carry them and their instruments, and gave them ten pounds for their expenses. William Kemp gave provincial waits their most explicit praise in his description, published in 1600, of his nine days' dance from London to Norwich. As he entered Norwich through a great throng of people "on the cross, ready prepared, stood the city waits, which not a little refreshed my weariness . . . : such waits (under Benedicite be it spoken) few cities in our realm have the like, none better. Who, besides their excellency in wind instruments, their cunning on the viol, and

[18] Stephen, *Waits of Norwich*, 64-68. Chester: *Tudor Economic Documents*, ed. Tawney and Power, I, 129. York House Book 32, folios 200 verso, 254, Book 34, folio 262; the agreement to set up a consort in 1603 was the result of a complaint against one of the waits by two others: Book 32, folio 280 verso. Mss. of the duke of Devonshire, Cumberland Mss., Bolton 94, folio 97d; Bolton 177, folios 100 and 266; Bolton 175, folios 181-182. HMC 24, *Rutland Mss.*, iv, 462, 479.
A newly appointed Norwich wait in 1612 was to provide a "treable violyn" and in 1620 another wait was provided with a new sackbut: Mann Mss., Norwich Musical Events, VIII, folios 69, 78. The Coventry waits had a "bass pipe" in 1575 and two curtals (like bassoons) in 1593: Coventry Chamberlains' and Wardens' Accounts 1574-1636, pp. 8, 231. The Exeter waits had a double curtal in 1575: Langwill, "The Bassoon . . . ," *Proc. Mus. Assoc.*, 66th Session (1940), 1-2. The statement in *Records of . . . Leicester*, ed. Bateson, III, p. xxx, that the Leicester waits played bass and treble viol is not warranted by the reference given, which specifies only "base" and "treable" without naming the instrument (more likely shawm).

violin: their voices be admirable, every one of them able to serve in any cathedral church in all Christendom for quiristers."[19]

Tales of disputes between factions among city waits and instances of waits reproved or discharged for failing to do their duty satisfactorily are not uncommon, and reinforce the presumption, grounded on the nature of man, that not many waits, not even the waits of Norwich at all times, can have deserved such tribute. Perhaps in most towns most of the time, waits were but indifferent musicians. Their repertoires are now no better known than those of the London waits, but they must have extended from simple tunes and country airs, some of them melodies associated with particular towns and called by their names, to the finest music of the court, required for the festivities honoring Queen Elizabeth at Norwich in 1578 and for the masque at the earl of Cumberland's in 1636.[20]

Some indication of the quality of waits' musicianship, as well as of how they lived and of how much towns valued them, appears in the records that show the control maintained over them. Usually town councils appointed waits individually, but sometimes when several vacancies arose at one time they appointed one man and gave him responsibility for getting the others, as the mayor and aldermen of York did in 1567 when they thought that Robert Hewet, musician, was "a quiet and meet man to be the chief wait . . . taking to himself such his men or other three whom he think fit and able. . . ." Appointments, in effect ordinarily for life, were sometimes probationary. Peter Sandlyn's tenure of the place he received in the Norwich waits in July 1616 depended on a report four veteran waits were to make the following February as to whether or not he was "sufficient." While the most essential qualification seems generally to have been musicianship, the records of appointments are seldom as explicit as the one in the York House Book for 1623 that starts "And whereas Edward Easton is commended to be a very skilful musician. . . ."[21]

[19] *Records of . . . Norwich*, ed. Hudson and Tingey, II, 195. Stephen, *Waits of Norwich*, 13-14; three of the five waits died on the expedition. *Kemps Nine Daies*, C4 verso.

[20] Chappell, *Old English Popular Music*, ed. Wooldridge, II, 10-12, reprints from post-Restoration books the songs "London Waits," "Chester Waits," and "Colchester Waits."

[21] *York Civic Records*, ed. Raine, VI, 125. For other multiple appointments see: *Court Leet Records . . . Manchester*, ed. Earwaker, I, 126, II, 29; Bacon, *Annalls of Ipswiche*, ed. Richardson, 331, 350, 396 (the form used here may be a result of a wish to write less); HMC *18, Southampton Corp. Mss.*, 26. Sandlyn: Mann Mss., VIII, folio 72; another case, 1617, folio 73. See also *Notices*

When town councils discharged waits, which they seldom did, they usually were considerate enough to investigate fully first. They then, more often than not, soon rehired the former waits, perhaps sometimes because they could not find suitable replacements. The York council discharged all of its waits in 1566 and again in 1572, one wait in 1584 because of a fraudulent transaction having nothing to do with his duties, and two more in 1584 who could not deny their guilt when examined "touching their evil and disorderly behavior, to the discredit of this city. Viz. for that they have gone abroad, in the country, in very evil apparel, with their hose forth at their heels, also for that they are common drunkards and cannot so cunningly play on their instruments as they ought. . . ." Twelve years later three waits, who wanted another musician appointed wait, complained of one of the waits discharged in 1584: "he is become so disordered and distempered and such a person as will be oft drunk and is at diverse times troubled with the falling sickness and his hearing imperfect or almost deaf as that he is not sufficient to serve in his place, And that diverse times he hath so disordered himself in the exercise of his place in playing before the magistrates of this city and others as that he hath made the rest of them by his playing forth of tune and time to be ashamed of themselves and they to be thereby thought of the hearers to have no such skill as is requisite for their places to their great discredit. . . ." When other persons present agreed that the accused suffered the alleged "infirmities" and since he could not "sufficiently discharge himself touching the premises" the council "displaced" him, and the complaining waits, "in regard that he is a poor old man, . . . promised to give him yearly forth of their fee twenty-six shillings eight pence. . . ." All waits were discharged at Nottingham in 1578-1579, at Ipswich in 1597, at Leicester in 1602, at Manchester in 1620, and at Coventry in 1635, in one case because of neglect of duty, in two others because of disagreement among the waits themselves. Councils more commonly found less drastic ways of demonstrating interest in their waits.[22]

Illustrative . . . Leicester, ed. Kelly, 205 (1572).

York House Book 34, folio 275 verso.

[22] *York Civic Records*, ed. Raine, vi, 119; York House Book 25, folio 24; Book 28, folios 157, 159; Book 31, folio 206. Another wait was hired in 1575 who had been earlier discharged: Book 26, folio 23.

Records of . . . Nottingham, ed. Stevenson, iv, 421. Bacon, *Annalls of Ipswiche*, ed. Richardson, 388. *Notices Illustrative . . . Leicester*, ed. Kelly, 235. *Court Leet Records . . . Manchester*, ed Earwaker, iii, 32. Coventry Council Book 1557-1635, p. 634.

Their compensation, coming to them by several routes and in many forms, of which some were inappropriate or simply not used in London, included livery, municipal freedom, fixed wages, periodic collections from the townsfolk, rewards for performances at official functions and private gatherings in and out of town, monopoly, and protection on tour.

From early times virtually everywhere livery coats or cloaks seem to have been the basic perquisite, and badges or chains nearly as common. Nottingham's printed record of liveries, not the longest, extends from 1461 to after the middle of the seventeenth century, and of silver and enameled collars from 1495, when they were mended. In terms of money alone liveries were valuable as a rule. Coats for the four Nottingham waits cost £3.5.0 in 1589-1590, and six and three-quarter yards of cloth for the coats of the five Leicester waits £3.10.10 in 1595. The coat for the "piper or wait" of Sheffield cost only four shillings ten pence half penny (four shillings three pence for three yards of white cloth, seven pence for dyeing it, and twelve pence for making "the same coat") in 1566, but by 1605 it was costing one pound every year. While the records seem to indicate that waits always had livery, they are not conclusive as to how often they received it. Perhaps the rule adopted in 1571 by Leicester, to provide gowns for the waits in alternate years, was about average, but York, Canterbury, Coventry, Nottingham, and some others usually provided them every year, and others only every three years, and then by special appropriation.[23]

Orange, orange tawny, and tawny, the colors favored for liveries in Leicester from 1577 to 1623, were deserted for bastard scarlet in 1642

[23] *Records of . . . Nottingham*, ed. Stevenson, III, 416, 287; v, 282.

Cost: The same, IV, 230. *Notices Illustrative . . . Leicester*, ed. Kelly, 228. *Records of . . . Sheffield*, ed. Leader, 18-19, 88, 89, 90, and following. Record of payment of livery appears frequently, but seldom shows the number of waits provided for.

Frequency: *Leicester*, ed. Kelly, 204. Leicester was breaking its rule by 1573; see in the same, pp. 205, 207, 208.

Further examples of livery and recognizances furnished appear in the text and appendices; see also:

Livery: *Annals of Cambridge*, ed. Cooper, I, 231 (1483), II, 395 (1583), IV, 33 (1615). HMC *54, Beverley Mss.*, 184 (1578). *Oxford Council Acts, 1626-1665*, ed. Salter, 48 (1633; this minute reads as though it were a new decision for Oxford to buy cloaks for the waits), 417 (1633).

Recognizances: HMC *54, Beverley Mss.*, 161 (1423). *Annals of Cambridge*, ed. Cooper, I, 250 (1499, repairing the collars), 208 (1564). *Liverpool Town Books*, ed. Twemlow, 110-111 (1559). *Records of . . . Nottingham*, ed. Stevenson, IV, 177 (1577). Manchée, *The Westminster City Fathers*, 85 (1615).

and red in 1643. The Sheffield wait's coat in 1580, made "against Christmas," took a yard and a half of red flannel, two yards of white cotton "for to line the quarters of the said coat," and buttons, silk facing and lining "to the body of the said coat." Red was also the basic color of the coats authorized for the York waits in 1597. The cloaks made in 1627 for the waits of Coventry required eight yards of green baize (bayes), twelve yards of broadcloth of unspecified color, twenty yards of silk and silver lace, a quarter of an ounce of silk (thread?), and canvas for stiffening, all coming to £6.12.1. The black broadcloth coats worn by the five Southampton waits in 1607 must have displayed their silver escutcheons, bearing the town's arms, to brilliant advantage.[24]

The silver recognizances, usually provided for the waits on surety, and expensive to buy and to keep repaired, were sometimes badges hung on silver chains or ribbons, and sometimes chains or collars. The Salisbury waits had chains of silver, each made of forty-one "esses," and an "escutcheon of silver of the arms of this city," and the Beverley, Lincoln, Oxford, and York waits also both chains and badges. The Leicester waits periodically received broad ribbon to hold their badges, and Coventry, "to hang the crests about the wait players' necks," provided eight yards of broad ribbon in 1627, when the crests had just been dressed up, gilded, and enameled.[25]

According to common custom waits, as officials, should have been freemen of their town, ordinarily by right of birth as sons of freemen or by apprenticeship. The instances in which their admission, by purchase,

[24] *Records of . . . Leicester*, ed. Bateson, III, 170. *Notices Illustrative . . . Leicester*, ed. Kelly, 228, 229, 234, 246, 249, 253, 254, 255, 258, 266, 267. *Records of . . . Sheffield*, ed. Leader, 45. York House Book 31, folio 318. Coventry Chamberlains' and Wardens' Accounts 1574-1636, p. 776. *Assembly Books of Southampton*, ed. Horrocks, I, 43.

[25] HMC 55 *Various* iv, Salisbury Corp. Mss., 226 (1572). *Beverley Borough Records, 1575-1821*, ed. Dennett, 16 (1577; see also p. 23 for 1578, and p. 27 for 1582). The Lincoln waits in 1514 had collars of twenty-four to forty-eight links, two of the collars with "shields" and one with an "escocheon"; in 1541 badges were described as chains with a cross: HMC 37, *Lincoln Corp. Mss.*, 25, 38. The Oxford waits may always have had both badges and chains; in 1638 three of them were to furnish "Scutchens with silver Chaines": *Oxford Council Acts, 1626-1665*, ed. Salter, 79. *York Civic Records*, ed. Raine, VI, 119 (1566; silver collars), 121 (1566; "cognisans" and silver chains); York House Book 28, folio 137 verso (1584, chain), Book 29, folio 315 verso (1592, silver chain and "Scutchin"). In 1583 Leicester common hall agreed that two "skutchyns or sincke fyles" (cinquefoils) should be made for the waits' boys "to wear with lace about their necks . . .": *Records of . . . Leicester*, ed. Bateson, III, 194; *Notices Illustrative . . . Leicester*, ed. Kelly, 260 (1625; for earlier and later years see in the same, pp. 256-259, 262, 264). Coventry Chamberlains' and Wardens' Accounts 1574-1636, p. 775.

came with or after their appointment, were probably exceptional. John Baldwin received the freedom of Oxford in 1603 after paying purchase and other fees totaling twenty-seven shillings and agreeing to provide himself with a silver escutcheon worth twenty shillings, which seems to indicate that he received his appointment and freedom at the same time. The Leicester register for 1593-1594 shows the admission of George Ridgley, musician, already "one of the town waits," and Thomas Poyner, musician, "one other of the town waits." The small number of musicians admitted to freedom in Leicester, according to the register four, or possibly six, from 1558 to 1660, compared with the number of waits, five in 1595, for example, raises the question of whether freedom was required for the waits there at all. Perhaps some of the waits became freemen in other callings; or perhaps Leicester, which followed the exceptional practice of naming only the head wait in its appointing orders, did not require that the subordinate waits be freemen; in the case of George Ridgley "and his company," five altogether, appointed in 1603, the "company" may have been servants only. In 1628 Oxford appointed six waits, four of them not freemen; the council decided to excuse them from paying the purchase price of one pound provided that they paid the other fees (one received a further exemption because he had served as apprentice to a freeman) and furnished themselves with escutcheons if they did not have them already. Although the council feared that their successors might question the exemptions, three years later two waits were "admitted free for the officers' fees as is the custom." In 1638 the council again decided to admit waits on the 1628 terms, but agreed that "hereafter none but the apprentices of such musicians as shall be free of this city shall be admitted to be of the city waits. . . ." Oxford, like other towns at the same time, was trying to reserve more of its privileges for the families of its freemen.[26]

[26] *Oxford Council Acts, 1583-1626*, ed. Salter, 152. Baldwin's escutcheon was to belong to the city. A George "Bucknall" was appointed a wait in 1588 in Oxford; and a George "Bucknell," musician "of this city," was authorized freedom by purchase in 1596. Perhaps Bucknall and Bucknell were the same person, although it is odd that Oxford would have let a man have a city office for eight years before he became a freeman. A George "Buckner," musician, appears in the records for 1591 as bailiff of the hundred of Northgate, and a bailiff must have been a freeman. Sixteenth-century spelling being what it was, perhaps "Bucknall" and "Buckner" name one man, a freeman, and "Bucknell" another, not free until 1596 (the same, pp. 42, 61, 109).

Register of the Freemen of Leicester, ed. Hartopp, 92. Ridgley and Poyner were the first persons admitted as musicians in Elizabeth's reign; a third musician, a "stranger," was admitted in 1605-1606, and a fourth, the son of a husbandman,

By the first decades of the seventeenth century it seems to have been settled beyond question as far as York was concerned that appointments should go only to freemen. In 1605 Christopher Thompson, "late apprentice" of one of the waits, received an appointment effective as soon as he should become free. In 1623 the council appointed the skillful musician already mentioned and arranged for him to purchase his freedom. A year later, the new musician having departed, the council appointed another man on condition that he purchase his freedom by paying thirteen shillings four pence at his enfranchisement and twenty shillings yearly until a total of twenty nobles (£6.13.4) had been reached. An appointment order explicitly defined the custom in 1630: Thomas Girdler, "that hath been brought up as an apprentice with John Girdler, his brother, one of the city's waits, being first admitted to the freedom of this city, [shall] be admitted also to the place of third wait. . . ." Custom and the normal prejudice in favor of a home town man could be ignored when musicians were needed, but even so a stranger ought to become a freeman.[27]

---

in 1612-1613. The first son (occupation unspecified) of Ridgley was admitted in 1637, and the eldest son (occupation unspecified) of Poyner in 1638; both fathers were designated musicians, and their sons may have been musicians too. No other musicians were admitted under that title before the Restoration: *Register*, 102, 107, 124, 125. 1603: *Records of . . . Leicester*, ed. Bateson, III, 451.

Oxford Council Acts, 1626-1665, ed. Salter, 17-18, 35, 79. "Sampson's son, and William Hilliard and his eldest son" were to be admitted upon paying for the buckets and officers' fees (no purchase), and if they provided themselves with "Scutchens with silver Chaines" which were to be the city's property. The Sampson mentioned may have been the Sampson Stronge appointed a wait and made free with the others in 1628.

Henry Halewood, Liverpool wait, was admitted and sworn a free burgess of Liverpool in 1572, but when he was first appointed a wait, whether at this same time or before, does not appear: *Liverpool Town Books*, ed. Twemlow, I, 456.

[27] York House Book 32, folio 356, Book 24, folio 275 verso. Edward Easton was the skillful musician. The necessarily incomplete printed records for the earlier periods are inconclusive as to how long freedom had been an indispensable prerequisite to office. Nicholas Wright, Robert Husthwait, and Thomas Moore were waits in 1561, and Robert Hewet was made head wait in 1567 (*York Civic Records*, ed. Raine, VI, 16, 125); of these names only Nycoles Wright, mynstrell (c. 1547), and Robertus Husthwate, mynstrell (1558), appear among the names of freemen admitted as waits, minstrels, or musicians in *Register of the Freemen of the City of York*, ed. Collins, I, 266, 279; a Henricus Knight was admitted as "wayte" in 1541-1542, and a Johannes Bawderstone in 1564-1565 as "waite" (*Register*, I, 262, II, 7). Hewet and Moore seem not to be on the lists as musicians or waits.

Ipswich in this as in other respects may have been exceptional. The printed records do not indicate whether any of the musicians named (Martin, Betts, Oldham) or the members of their "companies" were burgesses or not, or whether

Waits

Many towns may have made no regular allowance, other than livery, to their waits, and let them live on rewards earned on special public occasions and in private employment. Some towns developed systems that gave substantial support if not living wages, several paying set amounts out of their treasuries, others having their waits collect wages from the magistrates and commons, still others using one, then the other system, or combining them.

Cambridge paid fixed wages of two pounds a year from its treasury, according to records of 1567 and 1622; perhaps the waits also collected assessments. In Barnstaple "Sherland, the player, one of the waits," received four pounds "for his wages," apparently as a matter of course, in 1610. The Lincoln common council decided in March 1599 to give the waits "one hundred shillings yearly towards the increase of their wages, and also four coats yearly at Christmas over and besides the coats they have now. . . ," but it is not certain that the hundred shillings increased a wage paid from the city treasury. Norwich, which paid its waits by assessment in the fifteenth century and early in the sixteenth century if not longer, was giving them one pound apiece a year by 1536, £2.6.8 apiece each year for livery and wages beginning in 1538, and £2.13.4 beginning in 1549. Because they had been "at greater charges than heretofore by providing sundry sorts of instruments" they asked for and received an increase again, in 1583, to wages of three pounds and livery of two pounds apiece each year, a rate still in effect in 1601-1602 and probably for many years after that.[28]

Until late in the period, the chamberlains of Nottingham paid out the little that the town council authorized for its waits. In 1568-1569

they were members of the Taylors' company, organized by the guild merchant in 1575-1576, which included musicians among many other occupations; see chapter five, below. In 1598 the order reappointing Betts and his company of three others specified that they "shall take none into their company dwelling out of town, without licence of the bailiffs and portmen. . . ." (Bacon, *Annalls of Ipswiche*, ed. Richardson, 396), which may imply that residence, without franchise or membership of any kind, sufficed.

[28] *Annals of Cambridge*, ed. Cooper, III, 176n, 146, 147n; the fee of two pounds may have been for all the waits rather than for each one. *Reprint of the Barnstaple Records*, ed. Chanter and Wainwright, II, 118. HMC 37, Lincoln Corp. Mss., 75. Stephen, *Waits of the City of Norwich*, 43-47; Stephen does not say that the collection of assessments for the waits was replaced by payments from the treasury but this seems to be implied.
The Beverley waits were paid a yearly fee of forty shillings in 1405 (HMC 54, Beverley Mss., 158) but I have not found record of later payments. See also *Some Municipal Records of . . . Carlisle*, ed. Ferguson and Nanson, 286.

the waits, apparently three at that time, received together twenty-five shillings and livery worth one pound, increased by 1571-1572 to one pound a man and livery. After 1575-1576 the chamberlains paid only for livery until 1617, when the council, "in regard of their poverty," granted the four waits forty shillings a year "amongst them," in addition to livery worth about a pound a man. Payments at this rate seem to have continued until at least 1636-1637, but in the meantime the number of waits grew to seven and each man's share became unduly small. In 1628 the council authorized the waits to collect "wages" yearly from "the inhabitants of the whole town" in accordance with a schedule of assessments starting at four shillings each from the mayor and aldermen and totaling about six pounds without counting the contributions of the commoners "of the better sort" at one shilling apiece and of "the lower rank" (whatever they cared to give). To help the waits in their collecting if they complained that "any be refractory," the mayor was to send an officer with them "to distrain the party so offending. . . ."[29]

Coventry seems to have paid its waits both out of municipal funds and by assessment. The chamberlains paid £1.6.8 a year for the four waits together from 1557 through 1613, and the wardens four pounds from 1574 through 1614; although these payments seem to have been intended at one time to provide livery, this was forgotten in 1610 when the wardens paid out three pounds for cloth for the waits. In addition to these regular payments, amounting together to £1.6.8 a man each year, the waits also collected quarterage, if authorizations for them in 1423, 1460, and 1610 indicate a continuous practice. In 1423 the leet appointed four minstrels who were "to have as others have had afore them. Also that they have of every hall place one penny, of every cottage ob. [half], every quarter, and after their bearing better to be rewarded. And also . . . they shall have two men of every ward every quarter to help them to gather their quarterage"; in 1460 it adjusted the provision for making the collection; and in 1610 set up a new quarterly schedule of four pence from everyone who had been mayor, three pence from

[29] Nottingham Chamberlains' Accounts, Book No. 1611, p. 3, No. 1612, p. 3, No. 1613, p. 3, No. 1614, p. 2, No. 1615, p. 3 (the manuscripts for various years, e.g. 1569-1571, are missing, and, most unfortunately, for all years 1592-1614). 1617: *Records of . . . Nottingham*, ed. Stevenson, IV, 350. Livery 1616-1617: Nottingham Chamberlains' Accounts, Book No. 1633(a), p. 9. Livery 1617-1618: the same, Book No. 1633(b), p. 13. For subsequent years see appendix, below. 1628: *Records of . . . Nottingham*, ed. Stevenson, V, 129-130. The waits of Nottingham were being paid by the chamberlains as early as 1462, and receiving livery also: *Records*, ed. Stevenson, III, 416.

anyone who had been sheriff, two pence from anyone who had been chamberlain or warden, and one penny from every "commoner." It is possible, then, that the waits had three sources of municipal pay from 1574 to 1610, chamberlains, wardens, and quarterage; and definite that they should have had all three from 1610 to 1613. In 1615 seven new waits received appointments with pay scheduled at one pound a man a year and quarterage, a reduction of six shillings eight pence a man from the old rate, and with "comely and sufficient cloaks" to be provided by the waits themselves. Something went wrong, however, for the accounts for 1616, 1617, and 1618 show only resumption by the chamberlains of their old payments of £1.6.8, and no payments at all from 1619 to 1626. Then in 1627 the council authorized annual pay for them of thirteen shillings four pence apiece and cloaks every three years; earlier in the year they had received cloaks costing altogether £6.12.1, and in 1629 cloaks again at £7.12.1 (they gained considerably by receiving livery in kind rather than a customary and inadequate allowance), and their wages were paid annually until 1632. The council then authorized wages at almost double the old rate but made no order about livery, nor about quarterage, which may have continued through all the changes. Finally in 1635 the council dismissed the waits and the wardens paid them £2.5.0 "in full discharge of their wages." During much of the period each wait had received from municipal funds more than a pound a year for wages or wages and livery, and had collected quarterage in addition.[30]

An order of 1583, providing that "Four persons meet for waits shall be retained in the town's service . . . and they shall have four pounds from the town, besides their common collection, and every of them a livery at the town's charge . . . ," sums up the analogous system used by Ipswich. Other orders make it clear that collections or "the benevo-

---

[30] Salaries: Coventry Chamberlains' Accounts 1498-1574, pp. 244 and following. (I did not follow these payments in the record back before 1557) and Chamberlains' and Wardens' Accounts, 1574-1636, pp. 1 and following. Payments were smaller in 1580 and 1582. See appendix, below.

Quarterage: *Coventry Leet Book*, ed. Harris, 59, 307. Sharp, *A Dissertation on the Pageants . . . at Coventry*, 210.

1615-1626: Coventry Chamberlains' and Wardens' Accounts 1574-1636, pp. 537-758; Coventry Council Book, 1556-1641, p. 394.

1627-1632: Coventry Council Book 1556-1641, pp. 554, 607, 634. Coventry Chamberlains' and Wardens' Accounts 1574-1636, pp. 766-851, 894-908. Payment of wages to the waits is not recorded for the years 1636-1640 in the Account Book 1636-1711, pp. 3-80. The rate set in 1632 was £4.10.0 a year, apparently for four waits.

lence of the town" had long standing, but not that a schedule of assessments had been set. The allowance from the treasury seems to have grown steadily, on the whole, from thirteen shillings four pence a year for each of three waits in 1538, to one pound for each of four in 1583, to £13.6.8 for "five musicians, and one boy," or about two and a half pounds a man, in 1613.[31]

Some towns, nominal patrons like many noblemen and gentlemen, gave their musicians the title of wait but neither pay out of the town chamber nor the right to collect scheduled amounts from the inhabitants. The Liverpool assembly, appointing a wait in 1571, agreed that he should "have the benevolence of the town," and in 1583, that a new man should receive "the rewards of the town's people." The Manchester jury found the system breaking down in 1577 and requested that "all those, who have withdrawn their good wills or such stipend of money, as they have been accustomed to give the waits, that they would the rather at our request extend their good wills to further their stipend and not to hinder it." The system lived on. In 1620 the jury, discharging the waits, told them not to "expect any pay or wages of any the burgesses or inhabitants . . . ," and in 1647, appointing waits again, authorized them "for their pains to ask and receive once every quarter the gifts and allowance of every inhabitant."[32]

York, which apparently did not pay wages regularly out of its chamber, had a well-developed system of collections. The schedule "for the minstrels of the said city" set up in 1484 called for fairly large annual payments, twenty pence from each alderman down to one penny from each of the lesser commoners except those too poor, and gave the constables and sergeants in each ward the responsibility for making the collections. Various entries in the House Books indicate that the system, if not necessarily the same schedule, continued: in 1593 the council answered the waits' request for "some better allowance" by ordering them to make up "a book of all their receipts" for it to study and, almost a year later, by appropriating £3.6.0 "forth of the common chamber . . . towards the amendment of [their] wages for the year

[31] Data for all years is not available in print, but see: Bacon, *Annalls of Ipswiche*, ed. Richardson, 212, 271, 278, 331, 336, 350, 363, 388, 396, 453; HMC 8, *Ipswich Mss.*, i, 251, 253, 255.

[32] *Liverpool Town Books*, ed. Twemlow, II, 269, 461. *Court Leet Records . . . Manchester*, ed. Earwaker, I, 186, III, 32, IV, 8; see also in the same II, 29, 163, 164 (quoted below). The Oxford waits customarily collected at Christmas, not necessarily to the exclusion of other times; see order of 1628 in *Oxford Council Acts, 1626-1665*, ed. Salter and Hobson, 17.

past and this year present"; in 1599 it directed a committee to meet "and assess the book of the waits' wages"; and later in the year it considered the problem of "the arrearages of the waits' bill . . . amounting to thirty-one shillings one penny" that the inhabitants of the ward outside the wall refused to pay because of the plague. The council's order at the time of the plague in 1632 that the waits should "go about at the accustomed time and receive the charity and benevolence of the aldermen, sheriffs, and four and twenty, and of all others which are disposed to do good unto them . . ." may indicate that the assessments had become voluntary contributions, but more likely reflects only a temporary change introduced because the plague was preventing the waits from playing and was making everyone short of money. A few clues point towards the amount each wait received. In 1581 the council admonished a wait, appointed nearly a year before, to mend his ways, and threatened to dismiss him with a payment of twelve shillings as compensation "for his pains heretofore taken." Three years later it discharged another wait and paid him one pound for the time, less than six months, that he had served. The £1.6.8 two waits promised in 1596 to give "yearly forth of their fee" to the "poor old man" who was being discharged for his drunkenness and general disability must have been a small part of their income. In 1602 a wait borrowed four pounds from the city in order to buy an instrument and agreed to repay it within two years, and in 1624 the council expected a new wait to be able to pay one pound a year for the next six years for his freedom. The basic wage of the York waits, probably collected throughout the period from the inhabitants of each ward, must have been well over two pounds a man by the 1580s, and, with other income, several times that by 1600.[33]

Leicester also used the collections system with a schedule of assessments, revised periodically. The rates adopted in 1583-1584, for the members of the council of forty-eight three times as high as in 1499, should have produced £9.12.0 annually from the councillors alone, or £3.4.0 for each wait. New rates, adopted in 1603 after the waits had been dismissed for their dissension, first set at half of the 1583 rates and then at two-thirds, should have brought from the councillors only

[33] *York Civic Records*, ed. Raine, I, 102; see also VI, 121. York House Book 27, folio 218, Book 31, folios 45, 46, 87, Book 32, folios 4 verso, 38, 43, Book 35, folio 128 verso.

1581: Book 28, folio 34. Book 28, folios 137 verso, 157. Book 31, folio 206. Book 32, folio 200 verso. Book 34, folio 301.

£1.5.7 for each of the five waits; perhaps the commons gave more than formerly.[34]

The least uncertain conclusion suggested by these figures is that wages, however paid, were so small that without other considerations to attract them few musicians would have gone into municipal service.

All towns, whether they paid wages out of their treasuries or not, seem to have rewarded their own waits when they played on special occasions. Nottingham, for example, besides a regular wage, gave its men two shillings for playing before the mayor and burgesses on Michaelmas and the following Saturday in 1557, four shillings for playing before the mayor to Saint Anne's well and on May Day in 1569, one shilling for playing at the bonfire in 1588, one shilling for playing on the day of rejoicing for the queen in 1588, dinner worth six pence a person for playing at the mayor's dinner in 1588-1589 (the dinner for the mayor and his guests cost one shilling a person), and one shilling for playing at the meeting of the "mayor and his brethren at John Veyryes" in 1590.[35]

Towns sometimes furnished instruments for their waits, a substantial contribution: the three "pipes" Norwich bought in 1569 cost £3.15.0, and the three hautboys and a tenor cornett in 1608 eight pounds.[36]

Sometimes waits were pensioned. John Bradley of King's Lynn, "late one of the town waits" and now, 1646, "aged and decrepid," was to receive a pension of forty shillings a year during pleasure. The Coventry council decided in 1585 that William Styffe, formerly a wait, should have from the wardens one pound a year for the rest of his life; "Old Styffe" was among those paid as waits in 1584 and 1585 and the wardens paid him his pension as late as 1590.[37]

[34] 1499: *Records of . . . Leicester*, ed. Bateson, II, 355. 1583-1584: the same, III, 192-193, 199. 1603: the same, III, 451 (for the dispute see III, 439-440, and *Notices Illustrative . . . Leicester*, ed. Kelly, 235). See also: *Records*, ed. Bateson, III, 192; *Notices*, ed. Kelly, 214; Nichols, *History . . . Leicester*, I, 418; *Records of . . . Leicester*, ed. Stocks, IV, 236.

[35] *Records of . . . Nottingham*, ed. Stevenson, IV, 117, 133, 217, 225; Nottingham Chamberlains' Accounts, Book No. 1629, p. 37; Book No. 1630, p. 29. For other examples see: *Notices Illustrative . . . Leicester*, ed. Kelly, 195, 203; *Annals of Cambridge*, ed. Cooper, III, 2, 29, 174; *Selections from the Records of . . . Oxford*, ed. Turner, 356; *Oxford Council Acts, 1583-1626*, ed. Salter, 367, 371; Canterbury Chamberlains' Accounts, Book 16, folio 35 verso, Book 17, folios 21 verso, 22-28; Coventry Chamberlains' and Wardens' Accounts 1574-1636, pp. 119, 260, 549, 575.

[36] Stephen, *Waits of the City of Norwich*, 66-68. See also: *York Civic Records*, ed. Raine, VI, 16, 121; York House Book 32, folio 254; Coventry Chamberlains' and Wardens' Accounts, 1574-1636, pp. 8, 231; Bacon, *Annalls of Ipswiche*, ed. Richardson, 331; HMC 8, i, *Ipswich Mss.*, 253, 255.

[37] Mann Mss., Norfolk Musicians, II, folio 33. Coventry Council Book 1557-1635,

At least two cities helped the waits solve their housing problem. Bristol allowed its waits £1.6.8 yearly towards the rent of the house they occupied, and Norwich granted the waits long leases of houses on what were apparently excellent terms. Waits lived in the Suffragan's Tenements, as certain city-owned dwellings were called, in the early 1580s, and after 1587 it became customary for them to live there. In 1588-1589 three of them leased Suffragan's Tenements for £1.13.4 a man, and further leases for long terms were made subsequently at about the same rates. By 1630, when they lost their leases because of failure to keep up the repairs, they all seem to have occupied city houses. That the waits were able to pay £1.13.4, or in one case £2.12.0 (corner house with "parcel of ground and stable") indicates, incidentally, that the Norwich waits had sizable incomes.[38]

Wages of one kind or another, rewards on special occasions from their own municipal employers, instruments furnished, pensions, housing, and reduced cost of freedom, all contributed in varying proportions to the income and welfare of provincial waits. Two reasons, perhaps the most important, why musicians wanted to become waits, remain for consideration: some waits had the sole right to perform music for pay in their town; and all waits enjoyed a protected status that many of them found particularly valuable because it enabled them to travel about the country for profit and pleasure.

A monopoly on the performing of music for pay within a town was probably recognized widely as an attribute of waits' freedom of the town: the town's qualified musicians were its musicians-freemen and at the same time its waits, and all other musicians could be excluded because of the principle that only freemen of a given town could trade or occupy a craft within that town. Specific legislation reinforced the principle in several towns.[39]

---

p. 187; Coventry Chamberlains' and Wardens' Accounts 1574-1636, pp. 86, 108, 195.

In 1486 York provided for an aged wait who had served for forty years. He was to have thirteen shillings yearly for life and use of a house (*York Civic Records*, ed. Raine, I, 170-171). In 1580 the widow of a wait was awarded the livery cloth her husband was to have received (York House Book 27, folio 262). The allowance three waits were to give annually to the aged wait being discharged in 1596 was, in effect, a pension.

[38] Murray, *English Dramatic Companies*, II, 211. Stephen, *Waits of . . . Norwich*, 60-62.

[39] On the principle see Gross, *Gild Merchant*, I, 118, II, 46; see also chapter five, below. In places like York where there were more musicians-freemen than waits, the latter could not be given a monopoly; in York they had a monopoly only on

The jury of Salford, adjacent to Manchester, in 1600 ordered that "no inhabitant of this town do permit or suffer any waits, musicians or minstrels to play in their houses at any wedding dinner saving the waits of Manchester and Salford sub pena of every householder so offending thirteen shillings four pence." Salford was much smaller than Manchester but apparently needed more music than its own waits could supply; Manchester did not reciprocate. Westminster, finding that since its appointment of six musicians in 1611 "diverse other foreign musicians of unknown and suspicious behavior and conversation of life . . . daily . . . resort unto the said city and liberties and there use to play" contrary to statutes and "the good government of the city . . . ," in 1615 ordered the constables to arrest all "foreign musicians that shall hereafter publicly play" at inns, alehouses, or elsewhere in the city. Oxford ruled in 1603 that "Order shall be set down by Mr. Mayor and the aldermen touching the inhibition of all musicians playing within this city and suburbs other than the waits . . . ; and if any musicians, other than the waits of this city, shall play in any other sort, to be imprisoned *toties quoties* by the mayor or any other alderman in his ward." A succession of orders defined the monopoly of the Lincoln waits. In 1590 the common council decreed, at the request of the waits, that musicians other than waits could play at a wedding only if they paid the waits a fee of two shillings. In 1607 it gave an almost complete monopoly by ruling that except at assize time no musicians of the city or elsewhere were to "use any music upon instruments either at any marriage or at or in any inn, alehouse or victualling house, or any other place within this city or the suburbs . . . without the leave and liking of the city's musicians. . . ." In 1617 another order added an exception permitting "the musicians of some nobleman" to play "for their own master only, at his house or lodging only," omitted the exception of assize time, and authorized fines for infringements of the monopoly, two shillings on any "housekeeper" receiving "foreign" musicians, and five shillings on the musicians themselves, the money to go to the waits who could if necessary sue for it as "the masters, fellows, and company of waits of the city of Lincoln."[40]

---

performing for huntsup: York City Mss., Book xxii, folio 143 verso (1578); House Book 31, folio 206 (1596); see also chapter five, below.

[40] *The Portmote or Court Leet Records of . . . Salford*, ed. Mandley, 1, 21. Manchée, *The Westminster City Fathers (The Burgess Court of Westminster) 1585-1901*, 84; the statutes cited seem to refer generally to the acts against vagabondage. *Oxford Council Acts, 1583-1626*, ed. Salter, 151. HMC 37, *Lincoln Corp. Mss.*, 73, 81, 91.

If monopoly made inhabitants of a town completely dependent on their waits for professionally performed music, they had a right to expect them to remain in town at their service. Some towns had, therefore, as a corollary to the monopoly principle, orders limiting the absences of their waits or forbidding them to travel at all. Nottingham seems not to have enacted specific legislation either granting monopoly or limiting the waits' travel, but memoranda on a dispute settled in 1634 and 1635 show that the waits were supposed to enjoy a monopoly, and that its connection with their presence in town was recognized. Two of the waits, Homfrey Coggs and his son William, were discharged after failure of attempts to reconcile their dispute with the rest of the waits. The settlement agreed on in 1634 was that annually three of the waits were to pay Homfrey three pounds and his son one pound, on condition that they "not play with their instruments in this town when the other waits are in the town, unless they be invited to play at weddings or churchings. . . ." Two principles, that musicians who were free of the town had a right to perform there, and that the waits ordinarily had a monopoly, were recognized; the compromise between them, reached now that the town had musicians-freemen besides the waits, preserved the waits' monopoly as long as they were in town and let the other freemen play when they were not. At least two towns, Leicester and Manchester, had specific legislation covering both the monopoly principle and its corollary.[41]

Defining the whole position of its waits in 1582, Leicester ordered them to play every night and morning "and not to go forth the town to play except to fairs or weddings then by license of Mr. Mayor," and in return gave them quarterly allowances and a monopoly: "no estraungers, viz. waits, minstrels, or other musicians whatsoever, be suffered to play within this town, neither at weddings, or fair times, or any other times whatsoever." Early the next year, as the council set up a specific schedule of assessments, it redefined the monopoly, which now excluded even residents of Leicester except at the time of general assizes, when anyone could "play but only to strangers," and provided again "always that the said town waits shall keep the town and do their duty. . . ." A new act in the following year repeated the schedule of assessments and ordered that the waits "not go forth of the town to play, without license, neither any strangers to be suffered to play within the town." The absence of reference to competition from musicians dwelling in the town may indicate that any who had been there the

[41] *Records of . . . Nottingham*, ed. Stevenson, v, 165, 171-172.

year before had since moved on. About twenty years later Leicester faced the problem that troubled Nottingham in the 1630s. After the waits had been discharged for quarreling, and some of them rehired in 1603, George Ridgley, one of the rehired waits, complained that although he and his company had been appointed "the waits and musicioners for this corporation and therein to have the benefit, gain, and privilege above all others of that science," Thomas Poyner and his company (evidently former waits) "daily intrude themselves to play before strangers at common inns [and] at weddings and oftentimes have been accepted and your suppliants rejected by some of the company to his disgrace and great hindrance." Ridgley then asked for himself and his company the "profit and . . . preeminence above all others, especially at all lawful assemblies, meetings, and merriments . . . within this borough. . . ." Both Ridgley and Poyner had been freemen since 1593 or 1594. The published record does not show what compromise between the monopolistic rights of waits and the general rights of freemen the council discovered, but it seems to have enabled both men to remain in Leicester; Ridgley's eldest son gained his freedom in 1637 and Poyner's in 1638.[42]

The Manchester orders, issued during approximately the same period, finally arrived at the logical climax, invocation of the laws against vagabondage. The first relevant order, in 1567, appointed two men to hold office for so long as they should fulfill their duties and "not absent themselves without license . . . ," but said nothing about a monopoly, which the waits may have held by custom or earlier grant. In 1588 the jury pointed out that while the waits "cannot be maintained sufficiently without reasonable allowance of every inhabitant in Manchester, . . . strange pipers, or other minstrels come and sometime play before weddings to the church, sometime at the wedding dinner, by reason whereof, they draw to themselves some gains, which ought to redound to the waits of this town," and for remedy ordered "that no piper or minstrel shall be allowed to play at any wedding dinner, or before any wedding within the town to the prejudice of the waits. . . ." The jury strengthened its order in 1602 by directing that the waits should "have the commodity and benevolence of the whole company" present at a wedding, "sub pena to everyone offending . . ." two shillings, and by forbidding any inhabitant to "suffer any other

---

[42] *Records of Leicester*, ed. Bateson, III, 192-193, 199, 439, 450, 451. *Records of . . . Leicester*, ed. Stocks IV, 53 (undated; perhaps c. 1605). *Register of the Freemen of Leicester*, ed. Hartopp, 92, 124, 125.

minstrel to play at his house at wedding dinners but only the waits" on pain of a fine of three shillings four pence; at the same time it also admonished the waits not to miss their evening and morning playing without permission. The next year the jury discovered that the waits had "been secluded by foreign and other musicians at wedding dinners" and had therefore lost the contributions that "the inhabitants of this town their loving friends would willingly and liberally have imparted and bestowed upon them." The waits must "be received to play music at all and every wedding dinners in this town . . . and the foreign musicians and all others . . . rejected . . . ," and any innkeeper or alehousekeeper admitting any musicians except the waits must pay a fine of three shillings four pence. In 1606, again finding that its orders "for the secluding of other minstrels then the waits to play within this town" (weddings not specified) had "taken small effect," the jury instructed the waits to prosecute every offender against the old orders and the constables to see that the statute "for the punishment of rogues, vagabonds, and sturdy beggars may be duly executed."[43]

Grants of monopoly, or even of the exclusive right to play for certain of the more profitable kinds of engagements such as weddings, served to provide, by apparently easy and equitable means, at least part of waits' pay, and, at the same time, by discouraging the visits of outsiders, and by encouraging the local musicians to stay at home, to support the campaign for the suppression of vagabondage. Nevertheless, as long as vagabondage and the wandering life in general flourished, and as long as waits, even those with monopolistic rights, and other musicians wanted to go on the road as their fathers had done, enforcing monopolies was bound to be a most difficult problem.

Many towns, perhaps most, let their waits travel. It was another inexpensive way of providing for them, as the Nottingham council acknowledged in 1617 when it granted its waits forty shillings yearly because of their poverty "and for that their gratuities abroad in their travels are not so beneficial as heretofore they have been." A regard for equity and the desire for variety gave towns that let their own waits travel good reason for allowing visiting waits to play for them; doing so was not necessarily incompatible with grants of monopoly, for visit-

[43] *Court Leet Records . . . Manchester*, ed. Earwaker, I, 115, II, 29, 163, 164, 196, 223. The statute mentioned acted to continue and amend the statute of 1597.
The Beverley waits may have had a monopoly in 1578 ("Waits of the town for a fine taken of foreign minstrels twelve pence": *Beverley Borough Records, 1575-1821*, ed. Dennett, 18). The Norwich waits had a monopoly in 1672: Stephen, *Waits of . . . Norwich*, 29.

ing waits could play for the magistrates and perhaps publicly a time or two elsewhere without depriving the town's own waits of weddings and other private engagements.[44]

Towns that gave musicians chiefly livery and the right to use their names were not merely like nominal private patrons; they were better, for while the protective power of barons and others of greater degree waned during Elizabeth's reign, that of towns remained undiminished. Waits, wearing town livery and insignia attesting their official status, were safe anywhere as long as they behaved honestly and respectably; they knew that anyone could identify them as law-abiding musicians and freemen, and distinguish them at a glance from vagabond minstrels and fiddlers, and that they could count on welcome and reward wherever they went. Both towns and waits tried to protect their livery from debasement: the magistrates of Coventry spoke for their peers in 1615 when they ordered their waits to provide themselves with "comely and sufficient cloaks for the credit of the place," and the York waits for theirs in 1584 when they complained that two others of the group had "gone abroad, in the country, in very evil apparel, with their hose forth at their heels." The case of the waits of Nottingham, "stead" at Stomford in 1573 or 1574 and rescued by one of the Nottingham chamberlains at a cost of over eight shillings, is exceptional if not unique, so safe were waits on their travels.[45]

Waits wandered about a great deal, usually fairly short distances but occasionally from one end of the kingdom to the other, and at all times of the year. The records of the chamberlains of Nottingham for the years 1558-1592 and 1614-1640 (the records for some of these years are missing), show rewards paid to the waits of thirty-five towns for one hundred and forty-six visits to Nottingham; many more groups must have passed through, unrewarded and unrecorded by the chamberlains. Waits from nearby towns came to Nottingham oftenest, of course: Newark's twenty-five times between 1571 and 1592, Grantham's fourteen times between 1558 and 1590, Derby's thirteen times between 1557 and 1584, Boston's eleven times between 1576 and 1592, and Leicester's nine times between 1569 and 1588. (It may have taken the waits of Derby and Leicester as long to get to Nottingham as it took those of Boston.) Similarly Coventry rewarded most often waits of nearby towns: Nottingham's eleven times between 1631 and 1640

[44] *Records of . . . Nottingham*, ed. Stevenson, IV, 350.
[45] *Records of . . . Nottingham*, ed. Stevenson, IV, 150 (1573-1574). The record does not show that Nottingham punished its waits in any way.

(Coventry's waits were rewarded in Nottingham only three times between 1569 and 1590), and Derby's eight times between 1630 and 1639; after these, waits of relatively distant places came more frequently than those of some closer towns: Newark's five times between 1621 and 1638, and Ripon's (Yorkshire) five times between 1631 and 1637. Nottingham's waits were evidently among those accustomed to taking longer trips. In 1635, when ruling on the case of Homfrey Coggs and his son, the Nottingham common council forbade them to "go abroad, or into the country, to the prejudice of the said waits, to play with their instruments; and when the other waits have a purpose to travel to London or elsewhere, as usually they have done, that then Homfrey Coggs, nor his son, shall not travel that way, to forestall them, until a fortnight after they be gone, at the least." The waits of York seem to have taken fairly long tours: the chamberlains of Nottingham rewarded them in 1569, 1578, 1579, and 1582, and the fact that they were rewarded twice in 1579, on 7 June and 13 September, suggests that this year, contrary to their probable custom, they may have gone and returned by way of Nottingham, and traveled south of Nottingham between June and September. Perhaps the waits of Chester were on a similar long tour in 1613, when the city assembly, after hearing the petition of one George Callie that he and his "fellow musicians" be appointed waits "instead of the waits now absent," deferred its answer until it could find out what had become of the old waits. The waits of Westminster were rewarded in both Coventry and Nottingham in 1586, and the waits of Bristol twice in 1587 in Nottingham. Records of such long tours are comparatively uncommon, however.[46]

Most of the longer trips seem to have been made in the warmer months, probably because duty and weather often kept them at home in the winter: the waits of Westminster were rewarded in Nottingham in June 1586, of York three times in May and once each in June, July and September 1569-1590, and of Ripon in Coventry in May 1631. The waits of Bristol were rewarded at Nottingham in August 1587, but they had also been rewarded there in January. The waits of Lincoln, evidently making much shorter tours, seem always to have gone out in the spring or summer: to Nottingham between April and August 1577-1588 and to Coventry in June and August 1623-1636. Pontefract ("Pomfret") may also have let its waits travel only in spring and summer; they were rewarded in Nottingham in May 1569 and 1585 and

---

[46] Nottingham Chamberlains' Accounts and Coventry Chamberlains' and Wardens' Accounts. HMC 7, *Chester Corp. Mss.*, 364.

in June or July 1590, and at Coventry in May 1623. Nearly all other waits who visited Nottingham and Coventry came both winter and summer. When they came in the winter they probably were usually making only one-day or overnight visits that would not interfere seriously with the performance of their duties; if their duties were primarily musical, waits of other towns were as likely as not to be taking their place, in fact if not officially, for the time being. The waits of Newark went the twenty miles (more or less) to perform in Nottingham at the beginning of January at least seven or eight times between 1575 and 1590; they were also at Nottingham twice in May, once in July, once in August, once in September, six times in October, and once in November between 1571 and 1588. On the other hand, Coventry, many times farther than Nottingham (and then much more difficult to reach) from Newark, rewarded them only in the spring and summer, in June 1623 and on 2 and 29 August 1636; the month was not recorded for two earlier visits. They also visited, and received rewards at, Winkburn, a residence of the earls of Rutland in Nottinghamshire and therefore relatively close, on 30 December 1590 and 1 May 1591. That the waits of Boston had to make a relatively long trip to get to Nottingham perhaps explains why, that of the ten trips 1576-1592 for which the month is given in the records, only three came at the first of the year and the others between April and October. All four of the recorded visits to Nottingham of the waits of Rotheram were made early in January, 1585-1588; the journey must have required at least one night's absence from Rotheram. Grantham, then about as far as Rotheram from Nottingham, let its waits go to Nottingham at least six times during the winter holidays 1576-1588 and at least six other times between May and October 1569-1590. Some of the times that waits passed through a town they may have been journeying in response to the summons noblemen and gentlemen occasionally sent them; town officials could hardly forbid their waits to absent themselves when a neighboring magnate sent for them. On the whole waits seem to have traveled chiefly during the warmer months and to have made almost all of their long tours then, but they also often visited nearby towns in December and January.[47]

Their travels must have paid them well. At Nottingham about 1558 they usually received a shilling, but it might be as much as a shilling four pence or as little as four pence. By the 1580s waits' rewards in

[47] Nottingham and Coventry accounts. Winkburn: HMC 24, *Rutland Mss.*, iv, 399, 400. For instances of summons from noblemen see chapter nine, below.

Nottingham were smaller, averaging about six pence at the most, apparently about a penny a man; a great many rewards, to waits and others, were being paid in these years. Comparable payments were made elsewhere. The waits of Bristol received a shilling at Southampton in 1582, the waits of Cambridge a shilling and of Westminster six pence at Coventry in 1586, of Leicester a shilling at Coventry in 1587, of Bath a shilling at Southampton in 1587. Rewards were higher, probably for more service, at the establishments of the earl of Rutland: the waits of Newark received three shillings six pence in 1590 and five shillings (five waits) in 1591 at Winkburn. In 1600 the Spencers of Althorp gave the Northampton waits five shillings. Waits visiting the household of the earl of Cumberland at Bolton or Londsborough about 1612 were usually well rewarded: in 1611 three waits from Rotheram received two shillings six pence, and in 1612, seven waits of York thirteen shillings four pence, three from Ripon two shillings, four from Richmond three shillings four pence, four from Pontefract three shillings four pence, four from Lynn three shillings four pence, and three from Leeds also three shillings four pence, three from Lincoln two shillings four pence, four from Carlisle five shillings, and three from Bewley two shillings six pence. Rewards tended to be smaller at the Howard establishment at Naworth castle near Carlisle about 1620, like those paid in Coventry in 1623, usually a shilling to each group. In the 1630s rewards at Coventry were higher, two shillings six pence as a rule, occasionally as little as a shilling or as much as three and six. The rewards, sometimes several pounds, paid by noblemen for services extending over several days, belong in another category. The surviving accounts, although showing scores or hundreds of rewards to waits, must record only a fraction of the number actually paid.[48]

The wages paid quarterly or annually to waits increased in some relation to inflation, but much of their income, coming from voluntary offerings, did not. Rewards were not a percentage of a bill. In this respect waits, even when fortunate enough to have adjustable basic incomes, suffered along with nominal retainers and independent musicians. Of the signs appearing throughout the chapter that waits made

[48] Nottingham and Coventry accounts. Bristol waits: Murray, *English Dramatic Companies*, ii, 399, 462, 479. Bath waits: Murray, ii, 398. At Winkburn and Belvoir: HMC 24, *Rutland Mss.*, iv, 399, 400. At Althorp: BM Ad. Ms. 25,080, folio 12 verso. At Bolton or Londsborough: see appendix, Entries pertaining to music, from household accounts, below. At Naworth: *Selections from the Household Books of Lord William Howard of Naworth Castle*, ed. Ornsby, 89, 131.

out fairly well on the whole, perhaps the clearest is the continuous demand for waits' places.

Nearly every town had waits, valued and nourished them, and often increased the size of the group. Their duties, becoming more predominantly musical and still requiring the shawm as an essential instrument, called for an increasing variety of instruments and sometimes for trained voices. The protected status they enjoyed both in and out of town, probably even more than their small stipends, made their places valuable. Neither wealthy nor in rags, waits led respectable and reasonably secure lives, probably comfortable according to lower middle class or artisan standards but more interesting than most: waits shared in every festivity, public and private, knew everyone in the town and its countryside, worked late, and took to the road now and then. Necessarily circumspect in an age suspicious of wandering fiddlers, and therefore not as glamorous in memory as the old minstrels, waits contributed nonetheless mightily to the pleasures of their communities.

CHAPTER V. INDEPENDENT MINSTRELS OR MUSICIANS

THE independent minstrels and musicians of the provinces formed a homogeneous group only by definition: all lacked permanent municipal or private patrons and all resorted to music for at least part of their livelihood. Some were skilled and respected freemen of their town, others vagabonds using music as a cloak for lives of petty crime and idleness. No sharp line divided the men of these extremes: between them were the mediocrities, including men able enough musically who were either incapable of managing their lives or who simply preferred the wandering life with its hazards; those who were so poor musically that they could not, no matter how hard they tried, earn even subsistence at music alone; and those, not really professional musicians at all, who eked out what they earned at their basic occupation (tailoring, for example), by playing rude music at fairs and festivals. All these and others were likely to clash with officers of the law sooner or later and to be considered then members of the class of rogues and vagabonds rather than of the class of professional musicians. It was recognition of these extremes that led in the sixteenth century to the distinction between minstrel and musician.

The number of competent and respectable independent musicians in the provinces was probably small by the end of Elizabeth's reign. Dominated by the conditions that led to the enactment of the vagrancy statutes, they necessarily established themselves in one town or another and became dependent on the inhabitants of a comparatively restricted area. Few towns could support many musicians: in contrast to London with its population of perhaps one hundred and twenty thousand in about 1580 were Norwich, in population the second city of the kingdom, with perhaps seventeen thousand inhabitants, York, politically second, with perhaps ten thousand, and Leicester, with perhaps four thousand; Bristol, with an estimated six thousand about 1550, was probably then the third or fourth largest. In most towns waits probably had no difficulty in meeting the ordinary day-to-day demands for music and had an effective monopoly whether or not one had been specifically granted to them. Competent independent musicians must have lived chiefly in towns large enough to support more musicians than were needed as waits, or in towns that had no waits at all. Facing all the problems known to the musicians of London, they needed badly the organization that their numbers seldom allowed them to have.

In the provinces only the musicians of York seem to have maintained a company. The musicians of Canterbury tried and failed, those of Hull united with the men of several other occupations, and those of Beverley attempted to control the musicians of a wide area. What was most common, apparently, was no organization at all, except for the overall union of all freemen in a town or the informal but recognized union of the waits of the town, who were not independent musicians and not always all of the musicians-freemen in the town.

In 1561 the independent musicians of York received what seems to have been their first formal grant of authority, an "ordinary," as craft ordinances are called in the York House Books. Minstrels had been freemen of York long before: Willelmus Plombre, Robertus Lemyngton, and Robertus Comylton, minstrels, had all "paid in full" for their freedom in 1486-1487. Why they had not united formally long before, if they had not, is hard to understand. It may be that when York was in its ascendancy minstrels in the train of the great, rather than independent minstrels resident in the city, supplied most of its music, and that later, when the great visited less often and rarely brought minstrels with them, and when wandering minstrels were losing favor, the city could then support more independent musicians, a number large enough to make formal organization possible. In 1578 the council gave them a new ordinance in which six paragraphs reinforced the twelve paragraphs taken over from the thirteen in the old ordinance, and amended it in 1579, 1602, and 1603.[1]

The ordinances of the York and London companies, both modeled on those of other crafts, are similar. The officers of the York company, a master and two searchers, were to be elected at an annual meeting, and anyone elected but refusing to serve was to pay a fine of twenty shillings, half to the city, half "to the behoof of the said art," as were all fines. All brothers were to pay two pence dues quarterly, attend the quarter day and other assemblies, and keep secret everything said there. No one "enfranchised in the said art or brother of the same" was to "presume to rebuke, revile, or give any slanderous or villainous words"

[1] York Corp. Mss. 1561: Book B/Y (20A), folios 222-223 verso; see also *York Civic Records*, ed. Raine, VI, 30-31. 1578: Book 22, folios 142 verso-143 verso. 1579: York House Book 27, folio 196 verso. 1602: York House Book 32, folio 223. 1603: York House Book 32, folio 294 verso. *Register of the Freemen of the City of York*, ed. Collins, 211; these names are the first designated minstrels in the printed register.

to the officers or any other "brother or freeman of the said fellowship or art" on pain of a fine of six shillings eight pence. Both ordinances end by requiring the fellowship at its own expense yearly "when the play shall be played [to] bring forth . . . the pageant of Corpus Christi . . . sometime brought forth by the late masons of the said city."[2]

The regulations governing apprenticeship differed in a few details from those of the London company. No freeman was to "take any servant by covenant for a year or otherwise unless he be apprentice for the term of seven years at the least. . . ." In London the ordinance of 1500 had prescribed seven years exactly. An exception in favor of the waits allowed them to hire a man to help them. The penalty for violating this rule, twenty shillings, was heavier than most. In 1561 the penultimate paragraph of the ordinance provided, on pain of a fine of twenty shillings, that no freeman of the craft should have more than one apprentice at a time except that brothers who had been masters or searchers of the craft could have two at a time; this paragraph does not appear in the record copy of the ordinance of 1578. Within one month of the binding of each apprentice the brother was to present him to the master and searchers and pay twenty pence to the common box, or pay a fine of ten shillings. A paragraph added in 1578 and unmatched by any London rule looked to the qualifications of masters taking apprentices: "Item that no brother . . . shall take any apprentice except he be able to teach him in that art both such cunning and conversation as he may be well thought on to serve a nobleman or man of worship without the whole consent of the brethren. . . ." Even without the 1561 paragraph limiting the number of apprentices a master could keep at one time, the 1578 ordinance gave the company adequate authority over the taking of apprentices. In 1594 the council issued an order, directed to all occupations, limiting the choice of boys to be apprenticed by requiring that every "newly set up" master take a freeman's son as his first apprentice, and that one of the apprentices of every master having two or more be a freeman's son; the head searchers of every occupation were to bring in their ordinances for the addition of this amendment, evidently designed to protect the fortunes of old York families, but eight years later the council had to issue a special order in an attempt to get it into the musicians' ordinance.

[2] The use of the word "searcher" illustrates the close connection between the musicians' ordinances and others; searchers were guild or company officials who searched goods, such as cloth or shoes, to see that craftsmen and shopkeepers were maintaining standards.

Both the 1561 and 1578 ordinances regulated the employment of apprentices: they were not to be "set forth . . . to labor in any company as a minstrel within the said city or liberties thereof before [they were] examined and admitted by the said master or searchers. . . ." The 1578 ordinance required also that no person, presumably including an apprentice at the end of his term, was to "be made a free brother . . . except he be examined by the master and whole fellowship aforesaid and be well thought on by them to be a fit man for that purpose . . . ," a rule required by logic but not adopted by the London company. Both ordinances forbade any brother to teach anyone except his own apprentice "in any point or feat of minstrelsy" without the permission of the master of the brotherhood, but he could nevertheless teach the son of another musician who was a freeman in the brotherhood and "any freeman or gentleman of this city and their children disposed to learn anything for his pleasure." The equivalent London rule restricted teaching much more severely.[3]

The ordinance of 1578 added three measures calculated to preserve order. One, for the welfare of the city as a whole, forbade masters or apprentices "to play on the night before any man's apprentices or servants after ninth of the clock at night. . . ." The others, by moderating competition between the masters, should have helped keep them from quarreling. "No brother . . . shall seek for any weddings or proffer himself or cause himself to be hired to the same, to the hindrance of other his brethren . . . except the parties so to be married or their friends do send for him or them . . . ," and no brother was to "offer to play in any place within this city or suburbs where any of his brethren is playing whereby they shall be the worse thought of unless he be willed or sent for by the best man of that company. . . ."[4]

Competition from outsiders concerned them even more. The first rule in both the 1561 and 1578 ordinances forbade any "manner of foreigner of what condition he be [to] occupy any minstrelsy, singing or playing upon any instrument within any parish within this city or franchise thereof upon any church holidays or dedication days hallowed or kept within the same parish, or any brotherhood's or freeman's dinner or dinners. . . ." A later paragraph reinforced this by forbidding any brother to "go with any stranger to any wedding or any

---

[3] Apprenticing freemen's sons, 1594: York House Book 31, folio 86.

[4] Intramural competition was also limited by a provision, added in 1578, reserving huntsup playing to the city waits "unless the goodman of the house" sent for other musicians of the company. This was probably designed rather to reward the waits than to preserve order.

other feast only to labor with him within the said city or liberties . . . without license of the master of the said art. . . ." A little over a year after thus reserving the more important occasions, the council ordered the exclusion of all but "such as be allowed by statute," that is, the servants of barons and others of greater degree, from playing in York at any time, and gave the primary burden of enforcement to the searchers of the company, called here "the searchers of the waits," who were to forfeit six shillings eight pence if they allowed "any strange musicians or minstrel to go abroad . . . playing at men's doors or in their houses . . ." and to inform the magistrates "at all times when any such minstrels and musicians, as shall be allowed by statute, shall repair to this city. . . ."

In 1603 the council barred strangers altogether, as it could only after passage of the act of 1597, by agreeing "that no waits of any city or town whatsoever nor no musicians of any place whatsoever not being freemen of this city and free of the company of the musicians of this city shall be from henceforth permitted or suffered to play at any time hereafter within this city upon any instruments whatsoever without license of the lord mayor . . . and of the searchers of the said company. . . ." Here the York company received not only a grant excluding strangers, but also what the London company sought and failed to get, a grant excluding from the practice of music in York freemen who were not also free of the company. If the members of the York company could have enforced the order they should have been satisfied, for no ordinance could give them more. Apparently they could not. In 1608 the council noted that various "waits or musicians dwelling in the country do resort unto this city in the assize week times playing of their instruments, which is contrary to the statute . . ." and ordered that they be brought before the mayor or any alderman and warned to be gone, and then, if they failed to go, that they "be apprehended and used according to the statute." The House Books seem to contain no further reference to this problem for the next quarter century; perhaps it was thought that no new order would be more effective, or perhaps the problem became less urgent as countrywide enforcement of the vagrancy statutes began to succeed.

The company was probably unsuccessful. Although it existed through most of Elizabeth's reign, it seems to have left only signs of weakness. Listed among the least important companies in 1579, those whose searchers "have no voices at the election of the mayor, aldermen and sheriffs," by the end of the century it was so insignificant that the fact that its searchers had not brought in its ordinance for insertion of "the article for taking of freemen's sons' apprentices," as they and the searchers of all companies were required to do in 1594, was not noticed and ordered corrected until 1602. It may even have become inactive altogether within the next few years: in the order of 1608 against outsiders playing during assizes the council did not mention the company or its searchers as it had done in the related orders of 1579 and 1603.[5]

The story of the Canterbury fellowship is similar but shorter, starting and ending in the latter part of the reign of Henry VIII. During an administration of John Alcock, mayor four times between 1525 and 1545, the city court ordained that all waits and minstrels inhabiting Canterbury should be a "fellowship of the craft and mystery of minstrels" so to "continue from henceforth forever," and in 1546, without alluding to the fellowship or its ordinance, put all the waits and minstrels freemen of the city into the fellowship of barbers and surgeons. The fellowship of minstrels may have lasted only a year. The ordinance, more detailed on certain matters than the London ordinances, contains passages that may indicate why the fellowship failed. It did not give a monopoly to the waits and minstrels. In the first place the waits had priority over the other members, who were not to "prevent," or forestall, them in any alderman's or common councillor's house on dedication days or with noblemen staying at inns. The other restrictions favored the whole fellowship. No "foreigner minstrels" should take employment at "weddings, dedications, may games or garlands" from a freeman on pain of a fine of six shillings eight pence, nor should any freeman join himself "to any foreigner minstrel to the intent to occupy their instruments within the said city or liberties . . . except he be his apprentice. . . ." A later paragraph weakens these prohibitions by ordaining "that if it shall fortune any person . . . to hire the waits for any wedding, may game or other suchlike thing by the space of one, two or three days," each wait should be paid for each day twelve pence, and if the waits cannot or will not play for these rates "then it shall be lawful . . . to take any other minstrel meet and able. . . ." Still another paragraph further weakens the monopolies by providing that nothing in the ordinance "shall be at any time hereafter anything prejudicial or hurtful to any of the king's minstrels, the queen's, my lord prince's or any honorable or worshipful man's minstrels of this realm." Most of the best minstrels of England must have belonged to one or another

---

[5] No voice at election, 1579: York House Book 27, folios 160-164 verso. The other orders are mentioned in the preceding paragraphs.

of these categories, with the result that Canterbury's own minstrels must have continued to share with strangers the employment offered by both citizens and travelers. The ordinance and therefore the fellowship cannot have helped them appreciably. After the failure of their fellowship and consignment to the barbers and surgeons, the waits and minstrels freemen of Canterbury, like those of many towns, probably tended to think of themselves as an informal group, primarily of waits, and to look directly to the mayor and aldermen for help and guidance.[6]

Hull had long had religious, merchants', weavers', and many other guilds and fellowships, when in 1599 the goldsmiths, smiths, pewterers, plumbers and glaziers, painters, cutlers, stationers and bookbinders, basketmakers, and musicians, some of whom had had separate fellowships of their own earlier, formed a company "to the intent that the said arts . . . may better flourish within the town of Kingston upon Hull. . . ." Their "composition," as they called their basic agreement, had no extraordinary features, being concerned mostly with organizational and formal matters and leaving details on apprenticeship and the like for the "ordinances" they were authorized to make. Three of its provisions show how they hoped to monopolize business. They were to take as apprentices only persons "borne or remaining within this town" unless they had permission of the mayor and a majority of the aldermen to take others. Only musicians free in the town and company were to "keep any dancing school [or to] play at all without the consent of the mayor . . . and of the warden" of the company, and no inhabitant was to "let any place or room to any musician or others wherein any dancing school shall be kept [or to] learn to dance or play within this town with any musician not free of the said company. . . ." Thirty-seven freemen are named in the composition, eleven smiths, five goldsmiths, four in each of three other occupations, two in each of three others, and three musicians. If they were mutually accommodating they should have gotten along as well as a more homogeneous company.[7]

Another attempt at organization, more a medieval relic than a forerunner of the Elizabethan age, appears in the order of the fraternity

[6] Canterbury Corp. Mss., Bundle A54, Mss. 18 and 20, and Burmote Minutes 1542-1578, folio 25 verso (26 January 1546).

[7] Lambert, *Two Thousand Years of Gild Life*, 264-268, prints the composition in full. The provision barring outside musicians ends with the general saving clause, "unless they be licensed by the laws and statutes of this realm."

On amalgamated trades and crafts in general see Kramer, *English Craft Gilds*, Study 1, and Lipson, *Economic History of England*, 1 (7th edition), 423-425.

of Beverley, granted in 1555 by the "governors" of Beverley in accordance, the preamble says, with custom going back to the time of King Athelstone whereby "all or the most part of the minstrels playing of any musical instruments, and thereby occupying their honest living, inhabiting, dwelling or serving any man or woman of honor, and worship of any city or town ... between the rivers of Trent and Tweed, have accustomed yearly to resort unto this town and borough of Beverley; and then and there to choose yearly one alderman of the minstrels" and other officers. Besides this order almost no other record of this fraternity seems to survive. The famous minstrels' pillar in St. Mary's church Beverley of about 1525, with its statuettes of four minstrels in stone on the capital and the inscription "Thys pyllor made the meynstrels," may be a memorial of the fraternity's more prosperous days. Of two entries in borough accounts posterior to 1555 that may refer to it, the first 1556-1557, almost certainly does, but the second, 1578, "Waits of the town for a fine taken of foreign minstrels twelve pence," more likely pertains only to an informal association of the waits, or waits and musicians, of the borough alone. It would be surprising if the fraternity had flourished long, for in the latter half of the sixteenth century an organization deriving its authority from one town and attempting to rule all minstrels between the Trent and the Tweed rivers, a region including York, Durham, Newcastle, and Hull, could hardly have succeeded. The order was a belated attempt to recreate a defunct organization: "the governors of the said town ... do grant unto the said brotherhood of minstrels the renewing of all godly and goodly orders concerning the said science, of late partly omitted, to be revived in as large and ample a manner as they have been hitherto at any time used. ...." The basic idea of the order, perhaps a product of an age when wandering minstrels retained their popularity, makes it earlier in spirit than even the Canterbury ordinance and relates it to the fifteenth century patent authorizing the royal minstrels to govern all the minstrels of England save those of Cheshire.[8]

[8] The composition is printed in Lambert, *Two Thousand Years of Guild Life*, 134-137, and Lambert took it from Oliver, *History and Antiquities of the Town and Minster of Beverley* (1829), 557-559. It is also printed in Poulson, *Beverlac, or the Antiquities and History of the town of Beverley* (1829), 302-306. Both Oliver and Poulson used BM Lansdowne Ms. 896, folios 153-156 verso, a copy, made apparently about 1724 by Bishop Warburton from a source not cited. The readings by Oliver and Poulson differ in details of wording.

Pillar: Hope, "Notes on the Minstrels' Pillar," *East Riding Antiquarian Society Transactions*, 1895, pp. 67-68. 1556-1557: IIMC 54, *Beverley Corp. Mss.*, 179. 1578:

The provision intended to revive the active membership of the fraternity, "minstrels to men of worship, waits, cunning men, being honestly esteemed, and within the liberties of the brotherhood of Beverley shall come in and be brothers . . . at the next Rogation days," authorized a fine of one pound on minstrels who neither came nor explained their absence, but its effect at most was probably to deter waits and other musicians from visiting Beverley. Determination to promote high standards found unusual expression. No alderman was to "take in any new brethren unless he be minstrel to some man of honor and worship, or wait of some town corporate, or other ancient town, or else of some honesty and cunning, as shall be thought laudable and pleasant to the hearers. . . ." According to the letter of the provision, an incompetent minstrel could gain admission if he held a job somewhere. And the officers were to expel a brother of the fraternity "not being able as aforesaid, or has been so able, and now declineth from the same for lack of honest usage . . . as they will make answer to the king's officers when they speak of vagabonds and valiant beggars." Brothers should have only one apprentice at a time "and he to be presented to the alderman in one year and one day to be enrolled and made full brother. . . ." If this means that apprentices had to serve only one year in order to become freemen, it is highly unusual, to say the least; perhaps the writers meant to require enrollment of the contract within a year and a day in accordance with the common practice. The first of the two regulations on teaching is unusual too, for it provides that no minstrel shall "teach his own son or any other for a particular sum of money" but only persons presented as apprentices; and the second anticipates the York ordinance of 1578 by requiring that no minstrel "take any apprentice to teach or any other . . . except the same minstrel be able and approved" by the officers. Another provision, reserving to musicians who were burgesses of Beverley all weddings and aldermen's feasts held there excepting on fair days, points to what the order probably became, the authority for a municipal company, and if the fraternity survived this is probably what it soon became.

Two other attempts at regional control, but of quite different character, have likewise left scant evidence of their effect. "Le roy des minstraulx" of the honor of Tutbury (Staffordshire, Derbyshire, Nottinghamshire, Leicestershire, and Warwickshire) held annual court on the feast of the Assumption and had the right to arrest all minstrels

Beverley Borough Records, ed. Dennett, 18. Fifteenth century patent: see chapter one, above.

within this honor not doing service at this court. The jurisdiction, apparently dating from 1380 and confirmed in 1443, was not recognized in the patents to the royal minstrels and musicians or in the vagrancy acts but was apparently still operative in 1636 when a royal proclamation postponed Tutbury fair, the minstrels' court, and related activities, until 23 August because the king was to be in Staffordshire on the fifteenth. In Cheshire minstrels were under the supervision, at least in legal theory, of the Duttons of Dutton by virtue of rights recognized in the patents to the royal minstrels and musicians and in the vagrancy laws, and allegedly granted in the reign of Richard I. According to the story as told in the seventeenth century by Sir Peter Leycester, the earl of Chester, sorely besieged by the Welsh, was relieved by his constable, Roger Lacy, who gathered together all the "fiddlers, players, cobblers, debauched persons, both men and women" at the Chester fair and took them to the rescue. Lacy's reward, perpetual authority in Cheshire over all these people, he passed on to his steward, Dutton of Dutton; Dutton's heirs maintained at least a show of their authority until 1756, when they held their last court. Courts convened annually on the feast of St. John the Baptist (midsummer, 24 June) in St. John's church in Chester and, according to Leycester, "none ought to use their minstrelsy but by order and license of that court, under the hand and seal of the Lord Dutton or his steward. . . ." Leycester described the court held in 1642: The lord of Dutton rode with his gentlemen friends, banner, drum and trumpet, to a place above the Eastgate in Chester, and there paused for the reading of a proclamation ordering all musicians and minstrels "either resident or resorting within or to the county" to come and play in procession for the lord, at that time Robert Viscount Kilmorey. The lord then rode, with all the musicians playing before him, to St. John's. As soon as he and his friends had seated themselves in the chancel "a set of loud music upon their knees [played] a solemn lesson or two" and the musicians, standing, blessed the king and the heir of Dutton. Then, in a different place, a jury was impaneled, and inquiry made as to whether any persons present knew of any treason, whether any persons were known to have practiced minstrelsy without license from this court, whether any prophaned the Sabbath by playing music except by special license of the court, whether any got drunk, and so on. After a dinner for the lord and his friends, the presentation of a lance and banner to him by the musicians, and payment by each of them of their annual fee of two shillings two pence for a license, the court adjourned for the year. The Duttons had on the whole a kind of negative control. Their rights were recognized by statute, but apparently extended only to licensing. Presumably any musician traveling or performing in Cheshire who did not have a license from the Dutton court, or some other legal justification such as a baron's protection, could be seized and prosecuted under the vagrancy acts, which only provide that nothing in them should act to the prejudice of any Dutton "liberty, privilege, preeminence, authority, jurisdiction or inheritance," none of which are defined. The jurisdiction seems not to have acted positively to regulate apprenticeship and to perform the other functions of a fellowship or company.[9]

The picture of how independent musicians looked out for themselves, obscure and fragmentary for York, Hull, and Beverley, is dim indeed for the other provincial towns. Those that had granted their waits a monopoly had no independent musicians; in each the waits, uniting to defend and exploit their monopoly, presumably managed all their common interests as well as any company could have—the waits of Lincoln even had the right to sue as a company. If the half dozen or so towns known to have granted monopolies to their waits fairly represent many more, it would seem that independent professional musicians cannot have existed in much of urban England. There were, however, some independent musicians. The towns known to have granted monopolies to waits did not do so until the decades immediately before and after 1600, and no doubt in some cases before then independent musicians lived and worked in these towns in competition with the waits and in competition with visiting musicians, but the fact that the ordinances granting the monopolies usually refer particularly to strangers seems to indicate that in most cases these waits already formed a closed group of musicians-resident. Specific grants of monopoly were probably made in reaction either to an excessive number of musicians-resident in a town, or, more commonly,

---

[9] Tutbury: Chambers, *Mediaeval Stage*, II, 260. Hardy, *Syllabus*, II, 892 from *Foedera*, ed. Rymer, IX, ii, 34. Hawkins, *History of Music* (3d edition, 1875), 192-194, gives further information.

Dutton: Ormerod, *The History of the County Palatine and City of Chester . . . incorporated with a republication of King's Vale Royal, and Leycester's Cheshire Antiquities* (2d edition, revised and enlarged by Thomas Helsby, London, 1882; first edition 1819), I, 36 (account of the origins of the jurisdiction, from Leycester's *Antiquities*, first published 1673), I, 654-655 (the description of the court of 1642, an addition to Leycester's published work, from an autograph manuscript by Leycester). Compare Chambers, *Mediaeval Stage*, II, 259. For example of the reservation in favor of the Duttons in the vagrancy statutes, see 14 Elizabeth, chapter 5, paragraph 42.

to increasing pressure from the royal government and local dignitaries for help in repressing unessential travel. No specific grant was necessary, presumably, in most towns because the problem of an excessive number of musicians who were residents did not arise, and because national legislation and local custom combined, as the position of waits became more settled towards the end of the sixteenth century, to give adequate grounds for exclusion of strangers. Perhaps most independent town musicians lived in towns not employing waits, places not easily identified because in the absence of both waits and companies of musicians the records tend to lack positive information; Reading, whose printed records speak of musicians resident in the town but not of waits of its own, may have been one. Whatever town they lived in, if they had no company their status was in general that of any resident of a small town who pursued a minor occupation.[10]

Independent town musicians could be simply inhabitants of their town, not freemen or burgesses or brothers of the corporation or guild merchant, or freemen or brothers of any craft guild, however local affairs were organized. The musicians of Rye may have had this status in 1617 when the mayor and jurats of the town made a certificate "of the good behavior of Thomas Maxwell, a musician, an inhabitant of Rye, formerly an inhabitant of Battle, who desires to go to Middleborough in the Low Countries to visit his brother, John Maxwell, a merchant there, and to take with him John, son of the said John Maxwell, Oliver Sanders, his servant, Michael Borne, an apprentice, and Ambrose Drury, one of his company, with their musical instruments and to return again to Rye." Thomas Maxwell is designated an inhabitant, not a freeman or burgess; a musician, not a wait, which Rye may not have had; and his standing must have been regular and good, for the town officials were not only helping him to leave but also to return. If no one had a particular interest to defend, if there was no

---

[10] *Diary of the Corporation of Reading* (*1431-1654*), ed. Guilding (in four volumes). Barton-upon-Humber may have been another. Although waits from Barton-upon-Humber were rewarded at Nottingham in 1572 (*Records of . . . Nottingham*, ed. Stevenson, IV, 137), the earl of Cumberland's accounts for 1611-1613, which mention waits much more often than musicians, always refer to the musicians, not waits, of Barton (Mss. of the duke of Devonshire, Cumberland Mss., Bolton 94, folios 86, 96b, 96c verso, 97j; these accounts do not specify "-upon-Humber," but that this is the Barton meant seems to be indicated by its proximity to Londesborough).

English local government follows a multitude of patterns, as a glance at Gross, *Gild Merchant*, makes clear; Lipson's caution, "every town has its own history and . . . no one generalization can cover the whole field," must be remembered (*Economic History*, I, 373).

company of musicians or group of musicians freemen in a town, the general rule that no one could work or do business in a town except its freemen and members of its companies could be ignored with respect to musicians who lived in the town. In Oxford inhabitants who did not want to set up in trade or hold office usually did not incur the expense and obligations of taking freedom in the guild merchant. Any man who was an inhabitant only was perhaps less secure than a burgess or freeman, and a musician would have to be particularly circumspect.[11]

Independent town musicians might also be freemen or burgesses of the town or of the guild merchant (sometimes these were the same) without membership in any craft guild. This was the case, apparently, in Oxford, where there were some craft guilds but none for many minor occupations such as music, and where, at the same time, the waits were freemen in spite of a rule, often unenforced, passed in 1551 that no one should be admitted by purchase unless he were recommended by the craft he practiced. In Reading the crafts were grouped into five companies, and although the lists of the occupations included in each, made in the latter half of the sixteenth century, do not name minstrels or musicians, by the time of James I musicians were freemen of the town. If they were members of one of the five guilds then their status may have been similar to that of the musicians of Ipswich, where the guild merchant had in 1575-1576 divided the occupations or trades among four companies, one of which, called the Taylors' company, included "mynstrells" besides tailors, cutlers, smiths, barbers, chandlers, plumbers, millers, tinkers, and ten others. Such a company was quite different in origin and character from the miscellaneous company of Hull, apparently formed, like any of the regular craft guilds of Hull, initially by voluntary association of craftsmen who asked for and received an ordinance; in Ipswich the four groupings were evidently a result of the attempts of the guild merchant to improve and simplify control over all the occupations followed in the town. Ipswich had waits, of course. That members of so many crafts belonged to one company called the Taylors' suggests, incidentally, a possible reason for the absence or rareness of the names of persons admitted to freedom or burgess-ship as minstrels or musicians in some municipal registers: in Ipswich musicians may have been listed as tailors. Devizes and Dorchester likewise

[11] HMC *31, Rye Mss.*, 151. *Oxford Council Acts, 1583-1626*, ed. Salter, p. vi. See *Records of . . . Leicester*, ed. Bateson, III, p. xviii; Leicester was not typical, however, and had waits who were freemen and had a monopoly.

had their free craftsmen divided into several companies, each of many occupations, but music was not named among them. Perhaps neither town could support professional musicians, and depended on amateurs, on the semiprofessional efforts of men primarily following other occupations, and on professionals called in from nearby, larger towns. An idea of how such musicians, free of a town but without a regular company of their own, or merely residents of a town, were governed professionally and how they promoted their interests, can be formed only by considering the custom and law that applied to merchants and craftsmen generally.[12]

Length of term for apprenticeship, tending during the first half of the sixteenth century to become more uniform throughout the country, was set definitively at seven years or more by the statute of apprentices in 1562. While the court of King's Bench held in the case of Tolley, an upholsterer, that the statute did not govern occupations that it did not name, musicians and municipal authorities before and after 1615, the date of the ruling, acted as though they thought it did govern musicians. That the musicians of several provincial towns took apprentices has already been shown incidentally in the preceding pages, and in Reading, where musicians had apprentices in 1624 and 1628, the municipal authorities in 1634 applied the statute of apprentices to the apprentice of an Oxford musician. There can be little doubt that apprenticeship was the only normal way in which boys who were expected to become professional musicians were trained, and that because of old custom, contemporary practice in the other mysteries, and the statute of apprentices, seven years was the minimum term. Neither the statute nor uniformity of custom set the number of apprentices that musicians might take. What did were practical considerations: for the individual musician, how many apprentices he could profitably keep, for the several musicians of a town, how many would be most profitable to them collectively. Restrictive agreements like that reached in Reading in 1623, described in the next paragraph, may have been common.[13]

[12] Oxford: *Oxford Council Acts, 1583-1626*, ed. Salter, p. vii; Gross, *Gild Merchant*, II, 193. Reading: Gross, I, 69, 118, II, 208-209; Man, *The History and Antiquities . . . of Reading*, 347-353; *Diary of . . . Reading*, ed. Guilding, II, 104, 179, 210. Ipswich: Gross, I, 332, II, 129-130; Wodderspoon, *Memorials of . . . Ipswich*, 168-179. Devizes: Gross, II, 55-56 (1614). Dorchester: Gross, II, 57 (1629).

By 1715, and probably long before, Andover had made similar arrangements: Gross, II, 349. Carlisle had divided its occupations into seven guilds but the whole municipal structure was considerably different from that of the other towns here considered: Gross, II, 359.

[13] In Tolley's case the court held that "if the artisans which . . . were assistants

Independent Minstrels

Local custom, prejudice against strangers, and the vagrancy statutes apparently combined sometimes to give even unorganized town musicians monopolistic rights. In 1622 freemen of the "faculty" of music in Reading, including one James Shiler, complained to the mayor and burgesses against certain "foreigners" who were working in the "quality of musicians . . . to the great damage" of the freemen, and against one James Belgrove (apparently a freeman) who was employing or working with ("entertaineth") these foreigners. One of them "was forbidden and willed to return" to his own town, and Belgrove and the complaining freemen, who apparently had an income-sharing arrangement and cloaks like waits, reached an agreement whereby Belgrove was "to take his place" and keep "company with them for his share." The agreement did not work out; Shiler and two other musicians complained five months later that Belgrove was keeping two boys and working in town, to which he replied that his share would not keep him and his children. Evidently the mayor and burgesses had granted Shiler and his associates a monopoly or had forbidden Belgrove to work in Reading: the rights of musicians-freemen had not been definitely settled yet, apparently. By a new agreement Belgrove, "keeping company with them" and getting rid of one boy, was to receive an equal share with the rest of them for himself and one boy. The group now consisted of James Shiler, Philip Shiler, John Jarrard, Belgrove, each with his boy, William Costyn, and Richard Burren. "Every of them shall have equal share of all gains, and hence and abroad. And the four masters first named shall yearly pay to William Costyn over and above his share twenty-six shillings eight pence," for what reason the agreement does not indicate. In December 1624 the mayor and burgesses

---

unto the committees for the expressing of all manner of trades, had thought that the trade of an *Upholster* had been such a trade that required art and skill for the exercising of it, they would not have failed to make mention of it": *Tudor Economic Documents*, ed. Tawney and Power, 1, 381-382. Minstrels and musicians are not mentioned in the act. Certainly the art or mystery of music requires "skill or experience" even if upholstering does not ("And the intent of this statute was not to extend unto any other trades, but as required art and skill for the managing of them": Tolley's case, in the same, 1, 382). Lipson, *Economic History*, III (2d edition), 281-282, discusses the case, and Chambers, *William Shakespeare*, II, 83, with respect to actors.

Reading apprentices: *Diary of . . . Reading*, ed. Guilding, II, 213, 405. Oxford apprentice lurking in Reading: the same, III, 228; the provision of the statute applied was evidently paragraph 39.

There seems to be virtually no specific evidence showing how musicians trained their apprentices.

"Agreed that there shall be no other company of musicians but Mr. Shiler and his, provided that old Mathew Jackson and his son shall be permitted in town." It is unlikely that this ruling was a consequence of further misbehavior by Belgrove, for a little over a month later Shiler promised to give the overseers of the poor ten shillings a quarter to help support Belgrove's widow and children. Reading musicians had been able, with the help of the municipal government, to drive out a stranger, to restrict the number of apprentices to be kept by musicians within the town to one apiece, and to secure a monopoly for themselves within the town; and perhaps not too happily had promised to help the widow and children of an associate. Their success may not have been typical but what they sought was sought in many places and widely regarded as reasonable and desirable. Even in towns where there were no musicians-freemen, those permanently resident should have fared better than strangers. The custom barring all but freemen and guildsmen could be enforced against visiting musicians, perhaps violators of the vagrancy statutes, and ignored with respect to the local musicians, men with local interests that tended to predispose them to respectable behavior.[14]

These independent urban musicians, apparently conforming to standard professional practices and probably less numerous than waits, on the whole can hardly have been paid much or deserved much. Lacking the basic income received by many waits, they may usually have subsisted on a level with the poorer waits. The man of Rye, off to visit his brother in Middleborough, was perhaps better off than most, and Robert Paycock, "musitioner" in York, perhaps worse: Paycock, "a very poor man," was "licensed to keep an ale house or tipling house" in 1611, and four years later received thirteen shillings four pence from the stock of the parishes to bind a son apprentice to a tailor. Belgrove's widow and children had to depend on the overseer of the poor in Reading. Their musicianship, too, was probably mediocre. If they were expert, and dependable, they must usually, by finding permanent employment, have ceased to be independent musicians; a few of them, including the musicians of Barton, sent for by the Cliffords and well paid, must have been quite competent; and not many can have been both down at the heels and incompetent, for the chances are that before long

---

[14] *Diary of . . . Reading*, ed. Guilding, II, 104, 179, 210, 216. Other details were in the original manuscript and appear fragmentarily in the printed transcription; the abstract given here seems to be all that can be taken with much certainty out of the transcription. The widow complained in 1627 that Shiler was not making the payments and he then agreed to keep his promise: the same, II, 375.

they would have been condemned as lawless minstrels and forced into menial labor. Their employers and occasions of employment, their instruments and repertoires, probably rustic more often than courtly, must have varied in the same ways and as widely as those of waits.[15]

Most of the other provincial musicians were perhaps semiprofessional, men who engaged in more than one occupation, villagers who played on Sundays and holidays for their fellow rustics, and latter-day minstrels or counterfeit musicians who performed wherever and whenever fancy called them. All took money that professional musicians felt was rightly theirs, and many of them injured the credit of the profession.

The men of small towns who tried to live wholly by music or who divided their time between it and another occupation are known now chiefly because of their difficulties and poverty. The name of Richard Towler of Yxworth, musician, appears in the records of the sessions of the peace for the borough of Thetford in Norfolk for 1589 because of a bond posted for the maintenance of his children, and of "Thomas Coombes of Trucketts hill in Nunney, a musician," in the records of the sessions of Bridgewater, Somerset, for 1616, because debt had compelled him to forsake the county and to leave behind his apprentice, taken shortly before for seven years and now again dependent on his father, an inmate of the Wells almshouse. A petition, recorded in the Essex sessions rolls in the year of the first Elizabethan vagrancy statute, shows how the very statute that should have helped honest musicians sometimes made life more difficult for them. John Holinshed, gentleman, William Martin, and eight others began their petition to the justices of the peace with a general address, "To all true Christian people to whom this present writing shall come to be seen, read or heard [hard]," and then stated their case: "George Writt, tailor and musician, inhabiting in Maplested Magna in the county of Essex, being a poor man, having a wife and five children and two prentices, laboring for his living with these two sciences as an honest man may ought to do, and whereas the foresaid George Writt was wont to travel the country with his instruments to brideales and to other places, being thereunto required [sent for], and using himself in good order according to honesty and truth, whereas it is now set forth by the laws of this realm . . .

[15] Rye: see above, including note 11. York: York House Book 33, folio 252, Book 34, folio 64 verso; another son was to be given thirteen shillings four pence for clothing in 1619 when being bound apprentice to a musician: the same, Book 34, folio 165. Barton: sent for from Londesborough by the Cliffords 1611-1613; see note 10, above.

that none shall travel without license granted out by the honorable and worshipful of this realm, the queen's majesty's justices, wherefore we would desire your favor to grant unto this poor man license, that he may travel the country and maintain his poor living according to the laws of this realm. Wherefore we do certify you to the honorable and worshipful, that this man is well known unto us to be of honest conversation and living. . . ." Writt, one of the marginal, semiprofessional, rural musicians, found it difficult to support himself and a fair-sized family even with two occupations. To supplement the little that he could earn in Maplested Magna itself he had to track down employment in other communities, a practice threatened by the new statute. The published record does not give the justices' decision. The plight of such musicians grew worse after the statute of 1597 removed the licensing provision. Nicholas Yeomans, "a poor man who is a musician dwelling with his wife and children in Hutton," had to ask for relief at the sessions in Wells early in 1616 because "he is now likely to be dealt with according to the statute of rogues and vagabonds . . ." for having "lately traveled to the house of one Marten, and other places not above two or three miles from Hutton, to such persons as have sent for him, and did in short time return home orderly again. . . ." The justices, "conceiving the said Yeomans not to be within the compass of the said statute," ordered that he "be no farther troubled for the said matter by the constables, tithingman, or other officers." He might have fared differently had the justices been like Glandville, justice of the common pleas 1598-1600, of whom it is told that "upon a time, when fiddlers pressed to play before him, made them sing also, and then asked them if they could not cry too; they said his worship was a merry man; but he made them sad fellows, for he caused them to be used like rogues as they were." The confining effect of the statute appears also in the privy council's instructions to the constables of Grafton-Underwood, Northamptonshire, in 1618, on maintaining order at the coming "feast" of their town: "And if any fiddlers come to the town, not being sent for by some of the inhabitants and agreed with before they come what they shall have for their music, that you shall give them notice they are within the compass of the statute against rogues; and if they will not depart, that you punish them accordingly. . . ." Unable to earn a living from music in their own little town, and unable to travel out of the neighborhood without danger of running foul of the law, many rural musicians must have turned to other pursuits, as Writt did to tailoring, for at least part of their livelihood.[16]

The village musician, even less professional than these, has been omnipresent since before the days of Daphnis and Chloe. Laborer or craftsman during working hours and piper or fiddler at other times, he too kept bread out of the mouths of better qualified professional musicians. The fifteenth-century commissions to the royal musicians speak of "many unskilled rustics and artificers . . . pretending that they are our own minstrels, by [the use of] their livery and by color of the said art or occupation, deceitfully collect and receive great exactions of moneys from our lieges. . . . And although they are by no means skilled or expert in that art or occupation, and practice divers arts and labors on working days and thence amply obtain their living, nevertheless on festal days they run about from place to place and entirely win that gain whereby our minstrels and others . . . not practicing or in any other way enjoying any other labors . . . ought to live. . . ." Some ignorant impostors may have tried to pass as the king's minstrels but most musical rustics probably played only in their own and neighboring villages where they could not have been mistaken for even ordinary professional musicians. If the latter could not get the farthings paid to the rustic in his own village, they could try to keep him there: the Beverley order of 1555 directed that "no shepherd or husbandman, or husbandman's man, or man of other occupation playing upon pipe or other instrument, shall sue any wedding, or other thing that appertaineth to the said science, except it be within the parish wherein he dwelleth. . . ."[17]

Far greater enemies of honest professional musicians, whether of London or of Hutton, were the miscreants who continued to disgrace the name of minstrel.

Some of them, with good intentions but restless natures, were like John Felde, servant to Robert Crispe of Norwich, who confessed in 1561 that he "did absent himself from his master his service and went running about the country with a gittern," and like Wheler, Jackson,

[16] Towler: HMC 55 *Various* vii, *Thetford, Norfolk Mss.*, 145. Coombes: *Quarter Session Records for the County of Somerset*, ed. Harbin, I, 193. Writt: HMC *13, Custos Rotulorum and Justices of the Peace . . . Essex . . . Mss.*, 474. Yeomans: *Quarter Session Records . . . Somerset*, ed. Harbin, I, 166; Yeomans had fled from the parish to avoid punishment as a vagabond. Glandville: John Manningham, *Diary*, ed. John Bruce, 117; in brackets after this story appears *Ch. Dauers*, apparently Manningham's source. Grafton: HMC *45, Buccleuch Mss.*, iii, 207.

[17] Commission: quoted from the patent dated 1429 in *Records of . . . Norwich*, ed. Hudson and Tingey, II, 328; see note 2 in chapter one, above. Beverley: Lambert, *Two Thousand Years*, 136.

and Jones, "idle boys professing themselves musicians living basely and of themselves without masters in this town," Reading, in 1623. What the future could have brought to these boys is indicated in the presentment, for "marvelous ill life and conversation," made at the Wiltshire quarter sessions in 1605 of Robert Craundon of North Bradley; Craundon "useth no trade to live by, but is sometimes a weaver, sometimes a surgeon, sometimes a minstrel, sometimes a dyer, and now a bullard, running from place to place with a bull or two, and sets men on the Sabbath day a quarrelling and fighting . . ."; his religion unknown, when he was presented for incontinent living he came to the vicar "and called him knave. . . ." Bishop John Earle's portrait of "a poor fiddler," although probably drawn more from literature than life, and therefore more characteristic of the sixteenth century than of the reign of Charles, when it was written, personifies the less vicious of the species: he "Is a man and a fiddle out of case: and he in worse case then his fiddle. One that rubs two sticks together (as the Indians strike fire) and rubs a poor living out of it: Partly from this, and partly from your charity, which is more in the hearing, then giving him, For he sells nothing dearer then to be gone: He is just so many strings above a beggar, though he have but two: and yet he begs too, only not in the down-right *For God's sake, but with a shrugging God bless you*, and his face is more pin'd then the blind man's. . . . A good feast shall draw him five miles by the nose, and you shall track him again by the scent [sent]. His other pilgrimages are fairs, and good houses, where his devotion is great to the Christmas: and no man loves good times better. He is in league with the tapsters for the worshipful of the inn, whom he torments next morning with his art, and ha's their names more perfect then their men. A new song is better to him then a new jacket: especially if bawdy, which he calls merry, and hates naturally the Puritan, as an enemy to this mirth. A country wedding, and Whitson-ale, are the two main places he domineers in, where he goes for a musician, and over-looks the bagpipe. The rest of him is drunk, and in the stocks."[18]

Allusions in contemporary literature, often collected since, have immortalized the petty criminals, or associates of criminals, who worried the privy council, parliament, and local magistrates. Chettle, writing

[18] Felde: *Records of . . . Norwich*, ed. Hudson and Tingey, ii, 179; for another case see in the same, ii, 188. Wheler: *Diary of . . . Reading*, ed. Guilding, ii, 122. Craundon: HMC 55 *Various* i, *Wiltshire Mss.*, 77; not in quotation marks in HMC. Earle, *Micro-cosmographie*, signatures E10-E11; quoted from the sixth, 1633, edition.

about 1592, told of how ballad singers and hawkers, unsatisfied with their own efforts at stirring up unchaste thoughts, and trying to escape the notice of authority, employed innocent boys; one Barnes, using "the blushless faces of certain babies," his sons, would leave them singing ballads, "the one in a sweaking treble, the other in an ale-blown bass," while he, walking among the bystanders and feigning admiration, sent "straggling customers to admire the roaring of . . . the lascivious under songs of Watkins ale, the Carmans whistle, Choping knives, and Frier Foxtail. . . ." That musicians are "toys to prick up wenches withal" was another charge often stated more or less plainly. Gosson (*Schoole of Abuse*, 1579 and 1587) alleged that prostitutes, welcome in inns because they increased business, tried to explain their throng of visitors by putting an "instrument of music in sight to dazzle the eyes of every officer" and by claiming that "all that are lodged in the house by night, or frequent it by day, come thither as pupils to be well schooled." According to Sir Peter Leycester's account, the Dutton jurisdiction over the minstrels of Cheshire began as an authority over all the "lechers and whores" of the county: "the custom seems to have been altered to the fiddlers, as necessary attendant on revellers in bawdy-houses and taverns." In other ways, too, the underworld and music were said to be associated: ballad-singers served as efficiently as tumblers and steeplejacks to distract attention while pickpockets relieved the gawkers. The arrival of a dusty, and thirsty, musician, however honest, would please the simple and alarm the prudent.[19]

Chettle, Gosson, and the rest deepened the shadows, but legal records show that they did not write wholly from imagination. The vagrancy laws witness the opinion of the ruling classes, as do measures taken "for the advancement of true religion," such as the statute of 34 and 35 Henry VIII, chapter 1, which lists ballads, plays, rhymes, and songs among the weapons used by schismatics to pervert the people. During Mary's reign Norwich officials traced one case of infection to its apparent source when they examined two boys on their singing against the faith and led their master to admit that he had received a book of songs from a minstrel of Wymondham; and a generation later, in

---

[19] Chettle, *Kind-Harts Dreame*, from Aydelotte, *Elizabethan Rogues and Vagabonds*, 48-49; I have modernized the spelling. "Toys to prick up . . .": Beaumont (?), Fletcher and Massinger, *Thierry and Theodoret* (first acted about 1608), act 1, scene i, from Cowling, *Music on the Shakespearian Stage*, 103. Gosson, *Schoole of Abuse* (1579), folios 18 verso-19. Leycester: in Ormerod, *Chester*, I, 644. For the part that music played in helping pickpockets, see Greene, *Thirde and Last Part of Conny-catching* (1592).

1576-1577, the thirty-third article for inquiry in Darlington ward, Durham diocese, dealt with "all minstrels and jesters [singing] popish superstitious songs or bawdy ballads full of filthy ribaldry or any seditious songs or rhymes in commendation or defense of popery or of any rebels or fugitives." Hersey, sedition, and minstrelsy could unite a dangerous crew. Just as the potboiling authors alleged, women, music, and male visitors together aroused the suspicions of officers; the Middlesex sessions in 1616 took two men's recognizance for a spinster of Bethnal Green suspected of disorder because she had "had in an evening musicians at her house and certain men . . . unknown . . . ," and indicted eight persons, including the wife of a musician, for keeping houses of prostitution; the same charge is implied in the record of the sessions at Thirske, North Riding, Yorkshire in 1606. Musicians were suspected, indicted, and convicted of many kinds of felonies, more often of stealing than anything else. A report made in 1618 of "disordered persons" in Cumberland includes "James Routledge, piper, and Archie his son, both thieves and of bad behavior." In Norwich a musician from Romford in Essex, found wandering and suspected of "miching" (pilfering), was locked up in 1615, presumably pending indictment and trial. Conspiracy with thieves seems to have been suspected in Reading in 1625 when a musician's apprentice was examined about silver plate left at the musician's house by a stranger a few weeks earlier.[20]

Anyone prone to distrust musicians would have found his worst suspicions virtually confirmed by the Middlesex sessions records of about 1615. Two minstrels of Clerkenwell, Nicholas Doninge and Robert Goodman, appeared in sessions in 1613 as surety for behavior of a cooper and of Thomas Sheppard of Charterhouse Lane, St. Sepulchre's, musician, who had been found guilty of breaking into a house at night and stealing money and clothing; let off with branding instead of hanging because he could read, Sheppard (or Shephard) appeared twice again in court the next year, both times as sureties, once with several other persons for a yeoman (literate) found guilty of stealing ten pounds worth of cloth, and later with the minstrel Nicholas Doninge (Douninge) and other persons for a married couple

[20] Gold: Mann Mss., *Norwich Musical Events*, VIII, folio 45. Darlington: *Tudor Parish Documents of the Diocese of York*, ed. Purvis, 15. *County of Middlesex, Calendar to the Sessions Records. New series*, ed. Hardy, III, 294. Thirske: [North Riding] *Quarter Sessions Records*, ed. Atkinson, I, 34. Cumberland: *Selections from the Household Books of Lord William Howard of Naworth Castle*, ed. Ornsby, 440. *Diary of . . . Reading*, ed. Guilding, 213.

found with stolen goods in their house; and it was Sheppard's wife Katherine who was indicted in 1616 for keeping a brothel. Besides this underworld company, at least ten more minstrels or musicians appeared at Middlesex sessions during these years, some as sureties, some as common vagrants, and one for assaulting and beating a pregnant woman. Musicians probably got into no more trouble than other men—ordinarily hundreds of pages of sessions records must be turned to uncover the case of one suspected musician—but everywhere the lawless or unfortunate confirmed year after year the common impression that musicians are an untrustworthy lot.[21]

Living on the fringes of the profession, the tailor-musicians, the Sunday-pipers, the roguing minstrels, made life harder for all musicians and especially for the independent, usually unorganized, musicians of the middling and larger towns; with them they provided a large part of the music heard in rural England.

[21] *Middlesex . . . Sessions Records*, ed. Hardy, 1, 4, 5, 18, 35, 65, 78, 79, 198, 277, 306, 413, 11, 155-156.

CONCLUSION

By the reign of James the musical profession in the provinces seems to have reached a relatively stable condition in which most professional musicians were waits, a few of the best served in private households, and a few others remained independent. During the reign of Elizabeth, the time of the culminating phases of the transition to this stability, the vagrancy statutes and all that accompanied them bade minstrels look for refuge. They found it, not in private households, which tended to hire fewer rather than more men, but in towns: from being a profession of men characteristically itinerant, whether independent or privately retained, it became one of townsmen, municipally employed and protected. Town magistrates, because less and less able to count on visitors for their entertainment, and eventually less willing to welcome and reward them, had reason to want to retain the better musicians now ready to settle down, and the utilitarian tradition attached to the office of wait obviated the necessity of justifying the expenditure of town money for what otherwise might have been a completely new institution, assailable as an unproductive luxury. Municipal employment provided provincial musicians the security that they could find in almost no other way.

The change probably increased the quantity and quality of purely musical entertainment heard by the country as a whole. Waits, specializing more in music than their guardian and minstrel forebears, playing an increasing variety of instruments and presumably more of the music best known in London and at the court, and still permitted to travel, could bring to each other and to audiences throughout their counties new fashions, new standards, and new pleasure. At the end of Elizabeth's reign and until the civil wars, before waits fell into disrepute, the provinces may have enjoyed more secular music, and particularly more concerted instrumental music, than ever before, and perhaps more than they were to have again until the coming of modern concert tours and the radio.

PART THREE
THE CHURCH

CHAPTER VI. "THAT GOD MIGHT BE PRAISED WITH A CHEERFUL NOISE"

REAT MUSIC was written for the church of England in Elizabethan and Stuart times, but the church itself played a relatively minor part in the musical life of the country at large. Religious music was not a treasure participated in and enjoyed by people generally in their parish churches throughout the country; it seems to have been cultivated mainly by professional musicians in cathedrals and in a few other endowed churches. However much psalms were sung in parish churches and elsewhere, the fine religious choral music of the age was virtually the monopoly of some two dozen cathedrals, royal peculiars such as Westminster, the principal colleges at Oxford and Cambridge, and schools such as Eton.[1]

Whether originally secular foundations and therefore comparatively unchanged by the reformation, or monastic like Canterbury, or newly established like Peterborough, all of the cathedral choirs included priests, called variously minor canons or vicars choral; laymen, called vicars choral (also), singing-men, or lay clerks; a master of choristers; and choristers or singing-boys. Their size varied considerably from place to place and time to time. Winchester, about average, was to have six minor canons, ten lay clerks, and eight choristers, according to Henry VIII's foundation, and according to that of Charles I, six minor canons, ten lay clerks, organist-master of choristers, and six choristers. Canterbury's new foundation in 1542 called for twelve minor canons, twelve lay clerks, a master of the choristers, and ten choristers; in 1560 five minor canons (one had died recently), eighteen lay clerks,

[1] Throughout this chapter the word "cathedral" stands for all churches having choirs like those of cathedrals.

Sources found particularly useful for this chapter include: *Reports* of HMC, and especially the papers relating to Archbishop Laud's visitations in HMC 3, *House of Lords Mss.*, 124-159; *Visitation Articles and Injunctions*, ed. Frere; *Elizabethan Episcopal Administration*, ed. Kennedy; cathedral statutes, including *The Statutes of the Cathedral Church of Durham*, ed. Thompson (includes bibliography of cathedral statutes, p. xix, and good introduction on cathedral statutes and organization in general); and parish records.

Among the useful modern secondary works, besides the standard histories of the church of England, are: Jebb, *The Choral Service of the United Church of England and Ireland*; Robertson, *Sarum Close*; Atkins, *The Early Occupants of the office of organist and master of the choristers of the cathedral . . . Worcester*; Fellowes, *English Cathedral Music*; Christie, *Some Account of Parish Clerks*.

a master of the choristers, and eight choristers actually held places, and in 1634 six minor canons, eighteen lay clerks, a master of the choristers, and the "full" number of choristers. London, of the old foundation, had thirteen minor canons, six vicars choral, and ten choristers serving in 1561, and in 1636 eleven minor canons (one place temporarily unfilled), six vicars choral, an almoner (master of the choristers), and ten choristers.[2]

Expropriation of endowments and inflation seem to explain a general diminution in the size of cathedral choirs between the time of Henry VIII and the civil war; when income from endowments could not keep pace with the cost of living the obvious and usual solution was to leave places unfilled as they became vacant and to divide the money saved among the remaining men and boys. Exeter reduced the number of secondaries from twelve to nine in order to increase the pay of the "best deserving" and of the organist, according to the answer to Archbishop Laud's visitation articles in 1634. At Canterbury, where there should have been twelve minor canons, it was reported in 1560 that the full number was kept up only by bringing in men from the city at a low salary, and in 1634 that although the foundation was meant to provide twelve minor canons, "time out of mind" six substitutes had been appointed. St. George's chapel, Windsor, had to make rearrangements in 1547 and 1550 "because the choir cannot now be so well furnished with priests that are cunning singing men, for the rareness of them, as . . . in time past. . . ." Thomas Lawes, father of the famous composers Henry and William Lawes, became a lay vicar of Salisbury cathedral in 1602, resigned in 1604 because the pay was inadequate, and resumed his place only after salaries were raised by reducing the number of lay singers from eight to six. The reduction of the number of choristers at Salisbury in 1550 from fourteen to eight seems to reflect directly the recently reduced income. The answer, made in 1634 to one of Archbishop Laud's visitation articles, tells the

[2] Winchester, 32 Henry VIII: Tanner and Nasmith, *Notitia Monastica*, sig. Xx2 verso; 1638: *The Statutes Governing the Cathedral Church of Winchester*, ed. Goodman and Hutton, 43-44, 54. Canterbury, 1542: *Visitation Articles*, ed. Frere, II, 247n; 1560: the same, I, 153; 1634, HMC 3, *House of Lords Mss.*, 124-126. London, 1561: *Visitation Articles*, ed. Frere, I, 191 (the manuscript is unclear about the number of minor canons); 1636: HMC 3, *House of Lords Mss.*, 154-157. See also *Statutes of . . . Durham*, ed. Thompson, p. xlix (Durham and other cathedrals); Bristol: Tanner and Nasmith, *Notitia Monastica*, sig. Ee verso, and HMC 3, *House of Lords Mss.*, 141; Bannister, *The Cathedral Church of Hereford*, 164 (compare Tanner and Nasmith, sig. Aaa verso); Stanier, *Magdalen School*, especially pp. 25 and 61.

story at Bristol: ". . . there are but four petty canons who have the stipend of the other two vacant places by the direction of the late bishop . . . only until provision can be made to fill up the number. And these said four petty canons . . . undertaking to discharge the office of gospeller, by the direction aforesaid, the stipend of that place is conferred upon the singing-men and organist for their encouragement until things may be better settled. The place of the episteller hath been for many years executed by one of the vicars choral, who receiveth the stipend for the same. . . ."[3]

Obviously the fixed stipends can rarely have given much satisfaction. In 1539 Henry VIII seems to have been proud of his design for the reestablishment of Canterbury cathedral. In it he allotted ten pounds a year for each of eight petty canons, and £6.13.4 a year for each of twelve lay clerks. If this was thought to be more than adequate in 1539, such salaries, or ones not much larger, could only be regarded as pitifully small by the time of the Stuarts. Towards the middle of the century the singing-men in orders at Windsor received £13.6.8 a year and the laymen ten pounds, those at York ten pounds and eight pounds, and the laymen at Norwich £6.13.4. In 1604 the laymen at Salisbury were receiving £8.13.4, raised then to twelve pounds, enough to bring Lawes back. The dean and chapter of Bristol reported in 1634 that until fairly recently the wages of the minor canons had been ten pounds a year and of the lay clerks £6.13.4, but that they were now twelve pounds and ten pounds.[4]

Some men, usually priests, received additional compensation from various sources. In the secular cathedrals of the old foundation the priest vicars choral, or minor canons, sometimes had collegiate organization and properties of their own which gave them some income, apparently small as a rule. The minor canons of St. Paul's had both

[3] Exeter: HMC 3, *House of Lords Mss.*, 137. Canterbury: *Visitation Articles*, ed. Frere, I, 153; HMC 3, 125. Windsor: see the fifth of the second set of royal injunctions of 1547 and the twenty-third of the injunctions of 1550, in *Visitation Articles*, ed. Frere, II, 161-162, 223. Salisbury: Robertson, *Sarum Close*, 169, 127. Bristol: HMC 3, 141 (notice the disagreement on the need for the diversion, in "v. Additional explanations").

[4] Henry VIII: *The Remains of Thomas Cranmer*, ed. Jenkyns, I, 291. Windsor: *Visitation Articles*, ed. Frere, II, 161-162. York: the same, II, 316. Norwich: Norwich Public Library, Mann Mss., Norwich Cathedral Musical Events, III, folio 30; rates for later years are given in subsequent folios. Salisbury: Robertson, *Sarum Close*, 169. Bristol: HMC 3, *House of Lords Mss.*, 141. For Rochester see the same, p. 146.

stipends from the dean and chapter, and rents due to their corporation, as did also the vicars choral of Wells and of Salisbury.[5]

Quite commonly housing and a common table were perquisites, at least in theory. The vicars choral of York had a residence called the Bedern given to them in the thirteenth century, in which they continued to reside until the eighteenth century; and the minor canons and vicars choral of St. Paul's had houses, but by 1634 because of long leases made years before, some of the minor canons and all of the vicars choral lived away from the cathedral. The dean and prebendaries of Rochester, replying with some indignation to the charge, made after the archiepiscopal visitation of 1634, that they paid their choirmen inadequately, stated that they not only paid good wages and provided the minor canons with houses, but took care of the repairs and from time to time distributed gifts of money amongst the choirmen. At Exeter, where since 1612 the choir had been supposed to include four priest vicars, ten lay vicars, and twelve secondaries (later reduced to nine, in practice), two of the lay vicars reported in 1634 that the priest vicars "used to keep commons at their hall weekly, but now they have not done it these many years," that they ought to repair the lay vicars' houses but did not, leaving it up to the lay vicars themselves, and that all of the lay vicars should be living in houses in the vicars' college, but instead "set out their houses to others." One of the canons of Salisbury declared in 1634 that "the choral vicars have a hall, where they have in my time taken their commons together, which now they have left altogether." In 1635 the archbishop of Canterbury ordered the dean and chapter of Gloucester to do "all right" to their minor canons and singing-men "concerning their houses," and a year earlier the archiepiscopal visitation of Bristol brought forth the charge that "The house of commons (anciently for the use of the quire) is alienated from them, and let out by lease to a stranger, . . ." with the result that "Our quiremen wanting houses convenient for their service in our church, and ofttimes neglecting their duty by reason of their remote dwelling in the city." Housing should have been an important part of the compensation, but it seems often to have been lost completely or to have survived only in money payments become tokens because of inflation.[6]

[5] HMC 3, *House of Lords Mss.*, 154, 140, 130-131, and for Exeter, pp. 137-138. For the general picture see *Visitation Articles*, ed. Frere, I, 130-132, and *Statutes of . . . Durham*, introduction.

[6] York: *Visitation Articles*, ed. Frere, II, 316. St. Paul's: HMC 3, *House of Lords Mss.*, 154-155. Rochester: the same, 146. Exeter: the same, 137. Salisbury: the same, 131. Gloucester: the same, 157. Bristol: the same, 144.

Common tables, which would also have softened the effects of rising prices, disappeared in many places too, no doubt partly because priests, as well as lay-singers, now wanted to eat privately with their families. The royal injunctions for Worcester, 1559, point out that the cathedral statutes require all the minor canons and temporal ministers of the church, including the children, to eat together, and suggest that the practice could be resumed if, when certain leases expired, the land were kept to the cathedral's use and the provisions raised on them kept for the table. Winchester's new statutes of 1638 order that "they who assemble together and praise God together in the choir," that is, all the unmarried minor canons, lay clerks, other inferior ministers, and the choristers, should "take their meat at the same time and board in a common hall" if the dean and chapter can arrange it conveniently, and if not the wages of the cooks and other, then unnecessary, persons should be divided amongst the choirmen. The statutes also order the furnishing of livery, four yards of cloth at five shillings the yard yearly to each minor canon, down to two and a half yards at three shillings four pence a yard for each chorister and the undercook. On the whole the common benefits, such as collegiate income, housing, and common table, seem to have contributed little by 1600, sometimes because of careless administration, and often because managers were insufficiently aware of the nature of inflation.[7]

Outside employment supplemented the income of many choirmen. The Winchester statutes of 1638 expressly allowed each minor canon and some other officers to have "one ecclesiastical benefice . . ." if it were not over twenty-four miles from the city and if each canon saw to it that his benefice had divine service provided at his expense. The archiepiscopal visitors in 1634 learned that one of Rochester's minor canons had a vicarage: the practice had probably long been as common as minor canons could make it. According to the report of Bristol in 1634, some of the singing-men were "clerks of parishes or organists in the city," and some of the singing-men of Norwich may have held places as city waits, all harmonious pairings of occupations. Mace's comments on the church in the reign of Charles II could have been written about the church at the end of the sixteenth century: singing-men get in some choirs only eight, ten, or twelve pounds a year, "but none amounting to one quarter so much as may sufficiently, or com-

[7] Worcester: *Visitation Articles*, ed. Frere, III, 44-45. Winchester: *Statutes . . . of Winchester*, ed. Goodman and Hutton, 59-64. See *Statutes of Durham*, ed. Thompson, pp. li and lxvi.

fortably maintain such officers. . . . Yet I do verily believe, that such stipends or wages might plentifully suffice them, in those former cheap times. . . ." After amplifying these remarks Mace continues by asking how singing-men with such incomes could be "otherwise then well-nigh starv'd, were it not for that notable piece of connivance, or con-trivance of the worthy prelates and masters of our churches, who suffer them to work and labor (otherwise) for their necessary livelihoods, some in one calling, and some in another, viz. in the barbers' trade, the shoemakers' trade, the tailors' trade, the smiths' trade, and divers other (some) more inferior trades or professions (God knows)."[8]

Organists and masters of the choristers suffered no less. The reason in the case of the organists is immediately apparent: even though men were sometimes appointed and called organists, cathedral foundations and statutes usually did not provide special places with special pay for them, and in consequence organists seem usually to have been in fact ordinary minor canons or singing-men. Many organists also held simultaneously the office of master of the choristers, and perhaps usually then received the pay of two places. Why the masters suffered is not as quickly apparent; more than one man schemed to get a post as master of the choristers and then found the seemingly large allowances for the maintenance of the boys too small to begin with and even less adequate as time went on.[9]

[8] Winchester: *Statutes . . . of Winchester*, ed. Goodman and Hutton, 48. Rochester: HMC 3, *House of Lords Mss.*, 144. Bristol: the same, 141. Norwich: An Anthony Wyllson was one of the Norwich waits who died on Drake's Portuguese voyage in 1589, an Anthony Wilson received a singing-man's place in the cathedral in 1573, and an Antony Wylson received eight pounds as a singing-man in 1581; a Peter Sandyn received eight pounds as a singing-man in 1608, and a Peter Sandley and a Thomas Quashe eight pounds apiece as singing-men in 1625, while a Thomas Quashe, admitted to freedom as a musician in 1613, was a wait, and a Peter Sandlyn, admitted to freedom as a musician in 1622, was a wait also: Stephen, *Waits of Norwich*, 20, and Mann Mss., Norwich Cathedral Musical Events, III, folios 48, 56. Mace, *Musick's Monument*, 23-25. The anonymous churchman, quoted in chapter three above, wrote in BM Royal Ms. 18Bxix, folio 7 verso, that places were given to "tailors and shoemakers and tradesmen, which can sing only so much as hath been taught them since they were men . . ."; the manuscript is an inscribed, rather than ordinarily written, copy of what amounts to a petition, undated but probably of the earlier part of the seventeenth century.

[9] Chapter twenty-seven of the Durham statutes of 1555, in *Statutes of . . . Durham*, ed. Thompson, 142-143, is like chapter twenty-five of most of Henry VIII's cathedral statutes: "We appoint and ordain that in the Church aforesaid there be ten choristers, boys of tender age and with voices tuneable and fit for singing, to serve, minister and sing in choir. For their instruction, as well in gentle behavior as in skill of singing, we will that, beside the ten clerks before enumerated, one

The scheme of 1539 for Canterbury apparently provided no special place for an organist, but did allow ten pounds a year for a master of the children, and £3.6.8 a year for each of ten choristers (£33.6.8), presumably for finding their meals, laundry, and the rest. At Salisbury the "keeper and player of the organs and schoolmaster of the choristers" in 1538 received £6.11.8, and food and drink daily if he went in turn to the tables of the resident canons; a choristers' house and the income from choristers' properties were supposed to provide everything they needed. By 1569 the posts of organist and master had been separated, and the master, in return for teaching music to not more than ten boys and finding them in "good, wholesome, meet, and convenient meat, drink, lodging, washing, polling, and all such and the like, apparel and other necessaries," and keeping the choristers' house in repair, was to receive £52.5.8 a year, use of the house, two cows, and pasturage for them. In 1580 or earlier the number of boys the master had to teach and keep was reduced from ten to eight, and the money compensation reduced also, but not in proportion, to £45.11.0. In 1587 the master received in addition the place of organist, promised to him in 1580; and in 1593 a new master apparently received the income of three places, master of the choristers, organist, and lay vicar. (It is likely that masters of the choristers commonly held places either as minor canons or singing-men, besides their places as masters.) Apparently because three places were too much for one man to serve well, the place of organist was separated again from the mastership in 1598; when the new organist received his formal appointment in 1600 it was as both vicar choral and organist. The master appointed in 1593 had been granted only forty pounds a year to maintain the eight boys, and if this rate remained in effect it helps explain why the master appointed in 1600, apparently an inefficient man in many respects, failed to take care of the boys properly, with the result that by about 1602 they were all living at home with their parents instead of in the choristers' house; what started by default remained the practice for the next two hundred

---

shall be elected, a man of honest report, of upright life, skilled in singing and in playing the organs, who shall zealously give his time to teaching the boys, playing the organs and chanting the divine offices. And that he may give his labor the more diligently to the discipline and instruction of the boys, we permit him to be absent from choir upon ordinary week-days, so that he be bound to serve in choir and at the organs every Sunday and feast-day and on double feasts as above. And on the days whereon he is permitted to be absent we will that some other person with knowledge of organ-playing be appointed from among the minor canons or clerks by the precentor so to play. . . ."

and fifty years. In 1629 the dean and chapter decided that there should be six choristers thereafter, and that the two seniors should have four pounds a year apiece and the others three pounds apiece; the chapter was in effect paying the parents to keep the choristers and accepting the termination of the ancient community life of the choristers.[10]

At Worcester from about 1541 to the middle of the seventeenth century the master of the choristers was also organist, and received £11.6.8 a year; the master was to be skilled in playing the organ and in singing, to train the boys in proper behavior and singing, and to play the organ and to sing in divine service. Norwich had places for both organist and master, sometimes held by one man. Between 1569 and about 1608 the master received yearly for himself and the keeping of eight boys £26.13.4, or £3.6.8 for each boy, and the organist ten pounds a year; singing-men at this time received from eight to twelve pounds apiece a year at Norwich. The master of the choristers in 1569 received £36.13.4, and the same amount (£10 and £26.13.4) in 1581, probably because he was also organist; the posts were held by different men in 1599. By 1608 the organist's salary had risen to twenty pounds, and the master of the choristers, still paid at the old rate for keeping the boys, was also a minor canon, as some of his predecessors may have been. The rates of payment seem to have remained unchanged thereafter until at least 1640. At Bristol, a cathedral of the new foundation, in 1634 the organist had the duties of master of the choristers, apparently as a matter of course. Formerly his salary had been ten pounds a year, and the allowance for each of six boys £3.6.8; by reducing the number of boys to four the rates had been increased to £13.6.8 and four pounds; and later two probationary choristers, slated for the next regular vacancies, had been made room for at two pounds a year apiece. The visitation records imply that the organist, an aged man no longer capable of discharging his duties, was not responsible for the maintenance of the boys, who may have lived at home. At Winchester the new statutes in 1638 provided only £5.2.0 for the master of the choristers and one pound apiece for each of the choristers, besides "the commons and liveries," but the whole scale of payments there was low, probably because of these allowances. Why provincial musicians departed for the royal chapel at Windsor if they could is obvious: Nathaniel Giles, master of the choristers and organist of Worcester 1581-

[10] Henry VIII: *Remains of Thomas Cranmer*, ed. Jenkyns, 1, 291. Salisbury: Robertson, *Sarum Close*, 122, 140, 147, 166 (compare with pp. 171, 178), 171 (1600), 166 (1593), 172-173, 180 (see also HMC 3, *House of Lords Mss.*, 131).

1585 at £11.6.8, took a post as one of the organists and master of the choristers of Windsor in 1585, with compensation set at £81.6.8 a year, a house, and other perquisites calculated to enable him to maintain ten choristers. The master of the choristers at Windsor had, besides suitable allowances and prestige to begin with, a vantage point that made it easy to see further profitable opportunities as well as excellent facilities for making an enduring reputation as a musician.[11]

Along with their elders the choristers seem to have been losing their common lodging and table towards the end of Elizabeth's reign. Their masters could not keep them on the old allowances, and the easy course, to give parents a small sum of money yearly for the services of their children whom they continued to maintain, seems to have been followed more and more commonly. No doubt some masters still managed to make good profits out of their pay and allowances, but they must have been the exceptions by the time of Charles I.

From more than one point of view it is unfortunate that the pay and allowances of cathedral organists and masters of choristers could not have been better maintained. Several of them, including Orlando Gibbons (organist), Nathaniel Giles (organist and master), and Nathaniel Patrick (organist and master), not only selected the music for the services, but wrote much of it and thereby gave England some of its greatest music. The quality of the performance of the whole choir depended on them, immediately, because the choir as a whole could be no better than its boys, and, in the long run, both because choirmen ordinarily had received their training as choristers and because the future composers of ecclesiastical music usually received their first technical training and standards as choristers. A distinguished modern organist has written that "almost without exception, [England's] best composers have been brought up under the fostering care of the Church, and indeed the large majority of them actually began their musical career as choristers." If the posts were too badly paid, training, and therefore finally, all ecclesiastical music, suffered. Full support for the masters of choristers would not have been quite enough; some parents must have hesitated about letting their boys become choristers if it was becoming true, as the anonymous churchman, quoted in chapter three,

[11] Worcester: Atkins, *Organist and Master of the Choristers of . . . Worcester*, 20-41. Norwich: Mann Mss., Norwich Cathedral Musical Events, III, folios 36, 40, 43, 44 (to the master for new singing books, Morley's Service), 48, 49, 52, and following. Bristol: HMC 3, *House of Lords Mss.*, 141-144. Winchester: *Statutes*, ed. Goodman and Hutton, 64. Giles: Fellowes, *Organists and Masters of the Choristers of St. George's Chapel in Windsor Castle*, 35-38; Atkins, *Worcester*, 26-27.

wrote, that for a man "to bring up his son in a cathedral church is to make him a beggar by profession. . . ."[12]

When the masters did their work well, their choristers received broad and thorough training, both in the ordinary studies of schoolboys and in music. At Windsor in 1550 the "Grandsire of the choristers" was to teach them their ordinary studies, writing, reading, behavior, and religion, from six in the morning until eight, and from noon until two, while the rest of the day belonged to music. Nathaniel Giles, appointed master of the choristers at Windsor in 1585, agreed to teach "the knowledge of music, that is to say, in singing, pricksong, descant, and such as be apt to the instruments"—probably a fair statement of the chief teaching responsibilities of masters of the choristers in most cathedrals too. By studying pricksong they learned to perform from written or printed music, and by studying descant to improvise vocally, or, according to a seventeenth-century meaning of the term, the rules of composition; a successful student of descant, in either sense of the word, had taken a big step towards becoming a composer. The bishop visiting Worcester cathedral in 1569 asked whether the master of the choristers "was apt and willing to bring them up and instruct them in singing and playing on the organs according to the statutes," the organist appointed at Durham in 1628 promised to train the boys "to play upon the virginals or organs," at Ely in 1567 teaching the viol was a duty of the master of the choristers, and the Winchester statutes of 1638 required the master to train the choristers "in playing cunningly upon instruments of music," but did not specify what they should be. Perhaps choristers were likely to have the widest opportunities in cathedrals where a variety of instruments were used regularly or frequently in the service.[13]

[12] Nicholson, *Quires and Places where they Sing*, 2. Royal Ms. 18Bxix, folio 19 verso. On the precentor, who at least nominally had charge of the service, see *Statutes of . . . Durham*, ed. Thompson, p. xlviii.

[13] Windsor, 1550: *Visitation Articles*, ed. Frere, II, 227; 1585: Fellowes, *Organists . . . Windsor Castle*, 36 (the commas are not in Fellowes). For Salisbury, 1538, see Robertson, *Sarum Close*, 122; Worcester, 1522: Atkins, *Organist . . . Worcester*, 19; Winchester, 1562: Visitation Articles, ed. Frere, III, 138; St. Paul's: Bumpus, *The Organists and Composers of St. Paul's Cathedral*, 17; and for a romantic picture of a day in the life of a chorister see Brennecke Jr., "A day at Christ Church, 1573," in *Music and Letters*, XIX (1938), 22-35 (later a chapter in Brennecke's book, *John Milton the Elder and his Music*).

"Descant," in Scholes, *Oxford Companion to Music*, is a brief and clear introduction to the subject.

Worcester, 1569: *Visitation Articles*, ed. Frere, III, 230. Durham, 1628: Nicolson, *Quires*, 46. Ely, 1567: Arkwright, "Note on the Instrumental Accompaniment of

"That God Might Be Praised"

In principle the church was to provide for the continued education of choristers after their voices had changed; it was not an innovation in 1547 when a royal injunction ordered all cathedral chapters to "find choristers as have served in the church five years or more, or hath their voices changed, at some grammar school and give them yearly £3.6.8 out of the revenues of the common lands for the space of five years." That practice came close to principle is doubtful. Archbishop Parker felt obliged to admonish the Canterbury chapter in 1570 "that in placing of scholars hereafter in the grammar-school, the choristers in the said church . . . be preferred," and the royal injunctions for Salisbury in 1559, noting that former choristers attending the grammar school had to ring bells and "to do such other service as had a yearly stipend" in order to earn their charges, directed the chapter to give them "the full stipend of the altarist, and meat and drink. . . ." Probably the chief determinants of whether or not former choristers went to one of the universities after grammar school were their own ability and initiative and the interest and initiative of their families and friends. Some did go, and royal policy in the Chapel Royal provided that all qualified former choristers should be sent. A visitation article for Exeter, 1634, may represent a complementary, or alternative, general rule, "whether the secondaries be elected out of the number of the choristers whose voices be changed, according to the statutes, customs, and practice of the church," and certainly choristers frequently did receive subordinate posts and singing-men's places.[14]

Choristers should always have received a good education, in music at least, but sometimes they can hardly have learned much of anything. At Salisbury the master, outrageous in general conduct, made so little progress in his teaching that the choristers "under him utterly mock at work"; he had to be removed in 1568, after five years or more in office, by direct order of the bishop. Conditions were different but

Church Music in the Sixteenth and Seventeenth Centuries," in John Milton, *Six Anthems*, ed. Arkwright, 14. Winchester, 1638: *Statutes*, ed. Goodman and Hutton, 54.

[14] 1547: *Visitation Articles*, ed. Frere, ii, 139; see also in the same, ii, 93, 223, iii, 40. Canterbury, 1570: the same, iii, 235. Salisbury, 1559: the same, iii, 32-33; see also Robertson, *Sarum Close*, 130, 140. On the Chapel Royal, see chapter seven, below. Exeter: hmc *3, House of Lords Mss.*, 139. Durham's statutes provide that poor boys, not past their fifteenth year, should be preferred to the cathedral grammar school, but "we suffer the choristers of the said church to be admitted as scholars, even if they have passed their fifteenth year; and we will that these, if they be suitable and shall have done good service in choir by their great proficiency in music, shall be preferred to the rest." *Statutes*, ed. Thompson, 142-145.

no better about 1602. The master had promised when taking over the unsatisfactory choir four years earlier that he would train it properly in two years, but the boys were still unable "(by reason of their want of knowledge and practice in the church songs and music) to sing surely and perfectly but (did) often miss and fail and (were) out in their singing"; he had often absented himself without leave, had not appeared to "overview" them in the cathedral for six months, said that his duties did not include teaching them but only boarding them, and then failed to give them good food, lodging, and clothing (it was during this master's regime that the Salisbury choristers stopped living in their house). Bishop Bancroft visited St. Paul's in 1598 and found that the boys spent "their time in talk and hunting after spur-money, even in service-time; the hallooing [hallowinge] and hooting above in the steeple were intolerable at divers times." Of St. Mary's college, Winchester, in 1635, the visitor reported that "Divers of the choristers are not fit to come into the college school, and other are detained many times in the particular employments of the fellows. . . ."[15]

Music became the vocation, in or out of the church, of many choristers. Others, profiting from their general educational opportunities, entered the ministry; in supervising the teaching of the choristers at St. Paul's the almoner was to keep in mind for them a career in the ministry. Several became distinguished indeed: Thomas Cooper, son of a poor tailor, chorister at Magdalen, author of several important works including a famous English and Latin dictionary, became bishop of Lincoln in 1571 and of Winchester in 1584; when he was master of the Magdalen school one of his pupils, and perhaps a chorister, was William Camden; Thomas Bickley, chorister at Magdalen along with Cooper, became warden of Merton and then bishop of Chichester; and Richard Hooker was probably a chorister at Corpus Christi college about 1567. Still others found careers in lay occupations: John Milton the elder became a scrivenor and gained a reputation as a fine amateur musician; and some of the boys of St. Paul's cathedral and the Chapel Royal followed up the training they received in the theatre and became actors. Parishioners could have profited greatly, in and out of church, from ministers who had learned music well as choristers; music must have enriched the lives of most former choristers, whatever careers

[15] Salisbury: Robertson, *Sarum Close*, 137-139, 171-173. St. Paul's: Bumpus, *Organists . . . of St. Paul's Cathedral*, 28. Winchester college: HMC *3, House of Lords Mss.*, 150; other instances of the improper employment of choristers appear in these visitation papers.

they found, and must often have enhanced the pleasures, and musical standards, of the communities they dwelt in.[16]

The careers of most ecclesiastical musicians were quiet and obscure. Often born in the close and sons of choirmen and other churchmen, usually receiving their general elementary education and a large part of their musical training as choristers, they seldom saw much of the world during their boyhood unless the master of the choristers of the Chapel Royal, Westminster abbey, St. Paul's, or Windsor chapel, armed with a royal commission, descended on the cathedral and took them away to sing where the monarch might hear them now and then. If this perhaps unnerving, certainly exciting, and rare, intervention did not change their careers at the outset, and if they were not dismissed as "incorrigible boys," like Thomas and Richard Longe, choristers of Gloucester in 1635, they sometimes stayed on, after their voices began to change, to continue their education, and took subordinate posts in the cathedral, or, exceptionally, received singing-men's places at once. Later, those who could took orders and became vicars choral, and perhaps added care of a parish to their duties. While it is probably true that most choirmen died at last in the service of the cathedral where they had started long before as choristers, and where their sons and grandsons might then be serving, some, particularly masters of choristers, moved once or twice as they found better opportunities or came to dislike their old surroundings or associates. For the ambitious the goal seems to have been a place in one of the choirs near the court, in St. Paul's, in Westminster, in Windsor, and, above all, in the Chapel Royal. It is doubtful that many of them accumulated much property. Perhaps better off than most, the master of the choristers at Worcester who died in 1581 could bequeath his clavichord, song books, some money, and other property inventoried at over twenty-eight pounds; and one of his successors, the composer Nathaniel Patrick, who died in 1595, could leave to his wife lands as well as "an old virginal and an old recorder," books, and other valuables. "One Richard Jackson," singing-man of Bristol in 1634 who held also the epistoler's place, was "reputed to be able to dispend two hundred pounds per annum . . . ," an extraordinary income for a man in his position; perhaps he married

---

[16] St. Paul's: Bumpus, *Organists . . . of St. Paul's*, 17. Cooper: Stanier, *Magdalen School*, 82-89; *Lincoln Episcopal Records*, ed. Foster, p xvi. Bickley: Stanier, 72-73. Hooker: Stanier, 83. Milton: Brennecke Jr., *John Milton the Elder*. St. Paul's and Chapel Royal boys: see Wright, *Historia Histrionica*, 15 and following; Chambers, *Elizabethan Stage*; Arkwright, "Elizabethan Choirboy Plays and their Music," in *Proc. Mus. Assoc.*, 40th session (1914), 117-138; and part four, below.

well, as Edward Gibbons, composer and "priest vicar" (although a layman) of Exeter from 1609 to sometime in the 1640s (?), was said to have twice done. The life, which most of them must have liked, offered, if not wealth, security for life to all but those unfortunate enough to live until the civil war.[17]

Of their work, of what the worshipers heard, little need be said here. During this period the Anglican liturgy, and the distinctively English musical forms, such as the anthem and cathedral service, were assuming their character, but the history of these developments is outside the scope of this study. By the end of Elizabeth's reign the general design had been so well laid out, and the work of the composers had been so brilliant, that, were it possible to recreate a cathedral service of the year 1600, few in a modern congregation would find it remarkably different from what they know. They might find unfamiliar music: while some of the music of Tallis, Byrd, Gibbons, and many others, is often heard now in English cathedrals, sixteenth- and seventeenth-century worshipers heard much more of the work of their contemporaries, for all the music the choirs had at their disposal had been written within living memory—they did not have the treasury of four centuries to draw upon as twentieth-century choirs do—and they had almost always to perform from manuscript music, much of which has been lost or is for some reason generally unknown today. The first great collection of Anglican services and anthems, edited by John Barnard, minor canon of St. Paul's, was published only in 1641.[18]

[17] Pressing boys: see chapter seven, below; Chambers, *Elizabethan Stage*, II, 17; Murray, *English Dramatic Companies*, I, 338. A warrant to Sebastian Westcot, master of the children of St. Paul's, 30 June 1560, was copied into the York City House Book under the date 11 May 1571; apparently he or his agents were then trying to get choristers in York: York Corp. Mss., House Book 24, folio 241 (from transcript furnished by the Reverend Angelo Raine, Hon. Archivist to the City of York). Gloucester: HMC 3, *House of Lords Mss.*, 157. Continuity of family service is particularly evident in the Mann Mss., Norwich Cathedral Musical Events, III. For examples of movements of masters of choristers see Robertson, *Sarum Close*. For illustrations of the courtward movement of musicians see the lives of the composers in *Grove*, and Robertson, 166-171. Worcester, 1581: Atkins, *Organist . . . Worcester*, 24-26; 1595, the same, 32-34. Jackson: HMC 3, *House of Lords Mss.*, 137. "Gibbons," in *Grove*. The expectations of members of cathedral choirs received recognition in 1632 when an endowment was made for the support of one widow of a vicar or singing-man of the cathedral: HMC 37, *Lincoln Corp. Mss.*, 18.

[18] Surveys include: Procter and Frere, *A New History of the Book of Common Prayer*; Jebb, *Choral Service*; Fellowes, *English Cathedral Music*; Phillips, *The Singing Church*; Nicholson, *Quires and Places where they Sing*.

Barnard, *The First Booke of Selected Church Musick, consisting of services and*

"That God Might Be Praised"

In one conspicuous element cathedral music then differed sometimes from what the modern congregation knows, in the use of instruments. The organ, employed in the service of the church for centuries, was assuming its modern role by Elizabeth's time, in spite of strenuous efforts by numbers of sixteenth-century reformers, including some of the Elizabethan bishops, to expel it. The failure of their efforts, at least as far as cathedrals were concerned, is testified by the English organists, including Orlando Gibbons and John Bull, who earned European reputations, and by the record of organ building under the Stuarts, when great new organs were installed at Worcester (1613-1614), Durham (1621), Salisbury (1635), Gloucester (1639-1640), and elsewhere. Besides the organ, which did not have the virtual monopoly it holds in the twentieth century, cathedral choirs employed several other instruments, and not only on extraordinary occasions. Cornetts and sackbuts were often used, the cornetts being thought to blend particularly well with voices and apparently found especially useful for strengthening a weak treble section. The regular employment of two cornett and two sackbut players seems not to have been an innovation at Canterbury in 1532, and in 1634 the visitation brought out that the dean and chapter substituted "two corniters and two sackbutters" instead of the deacon and subdeacon called for by the foundation. Worcester cathedral used cornetts in 1619, Salisbury cornetts and sackbuts in 1625, and Durham both in 1633, and Lincoln "Organs with other instruments, suited to most excellent voices" in 1634. Both times that Queen Elizabeth visited Worcester cathedral in 1575 cornetts and sackbuts were used; the Sunday service included "a great and solemn noise of singing of service in the quire both by note and also playing with cornetts and sackbuts. . . ." In 1604 as the king, queen, and Prince Henry passed through London their welcomers included the "quiristers" of St. Paul's cathedral, "upon whose lower battlements [they sang] an anthem . . . , to the music of loud instruments . . . ," and in 1620 when

---

anthems, such as are now used in the cathedrall, and collegiat churches of this kingdome. Never before printed. Whereby such bookes as were heretofore with much difficulty and charges, transcribed for the use of the quire, are now to the saving of much labour and expence, publisht for the generall good of all such as shall desire them either for publick or private exercise. Collected out of divers approved authors, by John Barnard one of the minor cannons of the cathedrall church of Saint Paul, London.

Reading of the catalogues of the manuscript music remaining in cathedrals reveals unfamiliar names; see for example, Dickson, A Catalogue of Ancient Choral Services and Anthems Preserved among the Manuscript Scores and Part-books in the Cathedral Church of Ely.

James visited St. Paul's the gentlemen of the Chapel Royal and the cathedral choir "with solemn singing brought the king into the quire [and] they began to celebrate Divine Service, which was solemnly performed with organs, cornetts, and sackbuts." (More information concerning the employment of instrumentalists in the Chapel Royal appears in part five, below.) Cathedrals also used recorders and viols, but the evidence is less extensive. Byrd and Orlando Gibbons, pioneers in the composition of the verse anthem, had viols accompany the solo passages, and other composers, writing for the Chapel Royal in particular, also employed strings as well as the organ. Lieutenant Hammond reported that at Exeter cathedral in 1635 "a delicate, rich, and lofty organ . . . with their viols, and other sweet instruments, tunable voices, and the rare organist, together [made] a melodious, and heavenly harmony, able to ravish the hearer's ears." Norwich cathedral, having a connection, already noted, with musicians-freemen, paid the city waits for their services at Christmas 1575, and in 1638 and later; Chester paid its city waits in 1591 and in the 1660s; and York gave the waits thirty-three shillings four pence in 1623 "for playing in the quire five services this year." This collaboration between city and cathedral musicians furnishes unusually concrete instances of how different classes of musicians could influence each other.[19]

[19] See "Organ," in *Grove*, and Miller, "Sixteenth-Century English Faburden Compositions for Keyboard," *Musical Quarterly*, xxvi (1940), 50 (with bibliographical references).

For objections to the organ see Scholes, *Puritans and Music*; and for the attempts of Tudor bishops to silence them, see *Visitation Articles*, ed. Frere, ii, 200, 235n, 258, 320, iii, 331.

Organs built: Worcester: Atkins, *Organist . . . Worcester*, 46; Durham: *Journal of Sir William Brereton 1635*, ed. Hodgson, 13; Salisbury: HMC 55 *Various* i, *Salisbury Dean and Chapter Mss.*, 353; Gloucester: Atkins, 53.

Other instruments: Canterbury, 1532: Galpin, "The Sackbut, its Evolution and History," *Proc. Mus. Assoc.*, 33d session (1907), 15-16, and Galpin, *Old English Instruments of Music*, 191; 1634: HMC *3, House of Lords Mss.*, 125. Worcester: Atkins, 47. Salisbury: HMC *55, Various* i, *Salisbury Dean and Chapter*, 352. Durham: Nicholson, *Quires*, 44-45. Lincoln: Hammond, *Relation 1634*, ed. Legg, 6-7. At Gloucester cathedral, in the visitation of February 1663 it was reported that according to ancient custom there ought to be two sackbuts and two cornetts for the singing-service and anthems: HMC *55, Various* vii, *Gloucester Diocese Mss.*, 64. Elizabeth, 1575: Nichols, *Progresses . . . of Queen Elizabeth*, i, 538-539. Royal family, 1604: Nichols, *Progresses . . . of King James*, i, 367. James, 1620: the same, iv, 601 (quoted, in part, in introduction to Milton, *Six Anthems*, ed. Arkwright, 18-19; this provides a good outline of the subject). Recorder: see Arkwright's introduction to Milton, *Six Anthems*, 13-21. Viol: see "Anthem," *Grove*; Ouseley, "Considerations on the History of Ecclesiastical Music of Western Europe," *Proc. Mus. Assoc.*, 2d session (1876), 38;

Some of the evidence already presented, on compensation, on the dwindling size of choirs, on masters of choristers, makes it clear that the quality of performance often sagged badly. Mace, after describing the decline of which he had been "an experimental witness . . . for more then these fifty years," points out the consequences: ". . . first in reference to the clerks' pitiful-poor-wages, and likewise to the general dead-heartedness . . . in these our times, towards the encouragement of such things; how can it be imagined, that such clerks should be fit and able performers in that duty, which necessarily depends upon education, breeding, and skill in that quality of music, which is both a costly, careful, and a laborious attainment, not at all acquirable (in its excellency) by any inferior-low-capacitated men. . . ." Mace's observations apply as well to the earlier period; only the "dead-heartedness," the absence of consistent and general effort to encourage and improve cathedral music, changed for the better for a while during the reign of Charles I. More than cynicism gave rise to visitation articles inquiring whether choristers and singing-men were chosen for "friendship, rewards, or money," rather than for their "aptness, voices, and towardness in singing" and to injunctions such as that sent to the dean and chapter of Worcester in 1635, "that none be admitted into any place of your quire before he be first approved of for his voice and skill in singing, by such of your church as are able to judge thereof, and that the places there, as they fall void, be supplied with men of such voices as your statutes require." In 1634 Archbishop Laud wrote to the dean and chapter of Norwich cathedral to point out the poverty of their choir and to require that suburban livings be given to the petty canons; "But I hear withal there is a purpose amongst some of you, without any regard to the honor and good of the church, to bestow those livings, when they fall, upon their private friends, without any respect had to the choir; which, if it be, will utterly overthrow the choir service, and you will not be able to retain either voices or skill amongst you." St. David's in 1577 had only one chorister, and Salisbury, which had so much trouble with its masters of choristers around 1600, had no choristers at all in 1629 because of a dispute over the office of master. While employment outside the cathedral, by dividing the attention and energy of the choirmen, might have no worse results than to lower the effectiveness of the choir, the absence from Bristol cathedral in

---

Meyer, "The 'In Nomine' and the Birth of Polyphonic Instrumental Style in England," *Music and Letters*, XVII (1936), 29-30; and chapter eight, below. Exeter: Hammond, *Relation 1635*, ed. Legg, 74. Norwich: Stephen, *Waits of Norwich*, 59.

1634 of those singing-men who had extra employment as parish clerks or organists, and of the minor canons with benefices, usually resulted in the giving up of singing altogether at ten o'clock prayers on Sunday mornings. The Chapel Royal, to which cathedral choirs were indebted in major but intangible ways, contributed also to their difficulties because men appointed to it usually kept their old places along with the new, in spite of the fact that they seldom could, or bothered to, serve in their old places themselves or provide substitutes. This problem appeared throughout the period. Queen Elizabeth hurt cathedral services, more than by simple negligence, in 1600, when she wrote to the dean, chapter, and college of vicars of Exeter to the effect that they had ejected one of their vicars from his place worth ten pounds a year and a house because he had taken a place in her chapel, that it was unreasonable that anyone called to her service should lose any benefit thereby, that they could the better afford to let him keep his place because they had long left vicars' places vacant, and ordering them therefore to restore him. St. Paul's complained of such absences in 1636, and Rochester in 1634 lacked "three of the ablest men of the quire" because of their attendance at the Chapel Royal. It is not surprising that Lieutenant Hammond wrote that at Carlisle (in a region distasteful to him in general) "The organs, and voices did well agree, the one being like a shrill bagpipe, the other like the Scottish tone," and that at Chichester, Bristol, and Peterborough the voices were "but indifferent." The visitorial injunction to Peterborough in 1635 that "those of your choir who are defective in skill or voice be removed . . ." seems to confirm the lieutenant's finding. Thomas Morley, whose competence to judge in the matter is unimpugnable, wrote towards the end of Elizabeth's reign that as "to the expressing of the ditty, the matter is now come to that state that though a song be never so well made and never so aptly applied to the words, yet shall you hardly find singers to express it as it ought to be, for most of our church men (so they can cry louder in the quire then their fellows) care for no more. . . . But this for the most part, you shall find amongst them, that let them continue never so long in the church, yea though it were twenty years, they will never study to sing better then they did the first day of their preferment to that place, so that it should seem that having obtained the living which they sought for, they have little or no care at all either of their own credit, or well discharging of that duty whereby they have their maintenance."[20]

[20] Mace, *Musick's Monument,* 25. Visitation articles: *Elizabethan Episcopal Ad-*

"For the most part," as Morley qualified his stricture. The tendency to denounce faults and to pass over the acceptable in silence, as well as the widespread antagonism of men who objected to elaborate religious music in principle, may partly explain the preponderance of censure over praise for cathedral choirs; the function of ecclesiastical visitations is to discover and to correct abuses and shortcomings, not to award honors. Now and then, here and there, where the dean and chapter liked music and believed strongly that it had great importance in the service, or where a fine and competent musician exercised authority, choirs no doubt reached creditable standards "whereby to draw the hearer in chains of gold by the ears to the consideration of holy things," as Morley put it. Lieutenant Hammond gave moderate praise to the choirs of several cathedrals, and declared that at Winchester the organist was "one of the rarest . . . that this land affords . . . ," and that the choristers were skillful and their voices good. The music at Salisbury should have been deplorable, yet George Herbert, whose "chiefest recreation was music," according to Izaak Walton, usually went there twice every week when he was rector at Bemerton (1630-1633) not only for prayers but for the cathedral music and for singing and playing with his friends afterwards. What speaks most strongly in praise of cathedral choirs, what indicates most clearly that some of them fulfilled their trust, is the great music written for them. Not all of it was composed in and for the Chapel Royal and the great churches in and near London, and the Chapel Royal itself depended partly on the provincial cathedrals for its men and boys. Although not because of foresight and design, the cathedrals formed a kind of a system, not as efficient as it might have been, which trained musicians for service throughout the country and for the crowning organizations in and near the court. Composers of religious music could find the security, the musical resources, and the stimulus they needed in many cathedrals and collegiate churches throughout England.[21]

---

ministration, ed. Kennedy, II, 31, III, 253, 279; HMC 12, *Wells Cathedral Mss.*, 256; *Visitation Articles*, ed. Frere, II, 261. Worcester: HMC 3, *House of Lords Mss.*, 158. Laud: Trevor-Roper, *Laud*, 172; see also p. 209. St. David's: Atkins, *Organist . . . Worcester*, 39-40. Salisbury: Robertson, *Sarum Close*, 175-185. Bristol: HMC 3, *House of Lords Mss.*, 141. Exeter: CSPD *1598-1601*, 438. St. Paul's: HMC 3, 154. Rochester: the same, 144-146. See also HMC 12, *Wells Cathedral Mss.*, 245; and HMC 3, 137 (small service of Edward Gibbons at Exeter). Hammond, *Relation 1634*, ed. Legg, 37, 94; *Relation 1635*, ed. Legg, 34, 87. Injunction to Peterborough: HMC 3, 158. Morley, *Plaine and Easie Introduction*, 179.

[21] Morley: from the omitted portion of the passage quoted in the preceding paragraph. Winchester: Hammond, *Relation 1635*, ed. Legg, 46. Walton, *Lives*

Parish churches apparently had very little music. Composers seem to have written almost nothing for them, nothing comparable to what they wrote for the cathedrals but suited to parish resources, which were slender. Records of the century preceding the reign of Edward VI show that it was not extraordinary then for a parish church to have an organ: St. Margaret's, Southwark, bought a new organ in 1447 and hired an organist; St. Andrew Hubbard bought one about 1460; Rye had organs early in the reign of Henry VIII, as did Allhallows, Barking, London, in 1519, St. Giles's, Reading, also in 1519, Stoke-Courcy, Somerset, from at least 1520 to 1544, St. Margaret's, Norwich, which was given a new organ in 1537, and St. Leonard's, Bridgnorth, Shropshire, where in 1542 the bellman's duties included digging graves and blowing "the organs Sundays and holidays. . . ."[22] Organs do not appear with equal frequency in records of Elizabeth's reign, probably because most of the old ones were destroyed and new ones were not built. The tradition that many organs disappeared during Edward's reign, and that "over a hundred organs were taken down at one place or another" soon after Elizabeth's reign began, seems to be well founded. The accounts of the wardens of St. Mary's, Dover, from 1537 to 1541 show yearly payments to children "for helping to mass," "to help the priests sing," and in 1550-1551 the selling of the church's plate, copes and other vestments, and fifty-three pounds of organ-pipe metal; the money was not used to buy a new organ. Charges for repair of organs occur in the wardens' accounts of All Saints, Tilney, Norfolk, from 1451, but stop in 1551. Shortly after Elizabeth's accession "it was agreed by the worshipful of [St. Lawrence parish, Reading] that the organs in St. John's chancel, for that they should not be forfeited into the hands of the organ takers, should be taken down and sold. . . ."[23] In the seventeenth century new

---

(World's Classics), 303. For what a powerful political ecclesiastic, John Williams (lord keeper, bishop of Lincoln), with a taste for music could do see the dedication in Michael East, *The Sixt Set of Bookes, wherein are anthemes* (1624), Hacket, *Scrinia Reserata*, 46, and Chambers, *Shakespeare*, II, 349.

[22] St. Margaret's, Southwark, and St. Andrew Hubbard: Corner, on a contract for an organ for Allhallows, Barking, 1519, in *Proc. Evening Meetings of the London and Middlesex and Surrey Archaeological Societies*, 1862, p. 89. Rye: Macdermott, *Sussex Church Music in the Past*, 57. Allhallows: Corner, *Proc. Evening Meetings*, 1862, pp. 86-89 (indenture for organ to cost fifty pounds). Reading: Man, *The History . . . of Reading*, 331. Stoke-Courcy: HMC 5, *Acland-Hood Mss.*, 349. St. Margaret's, Norwich: Mann Mss., Norwich Musicians, XI, folio 57. St. Leonard's: HMC *13, Bridgnorth Mss.*, 425.

[23] Tradition: Knappen, *Tudor Puritanism*, 433; Scholes, *Puritans and Music*, 230-231. St. Mary's Dover: BM Egerton Ms. 1912, particularly folios 6, 7 verso, 10, 16-16 verso, 19 verso, 34 verso, 41 (sale), 43, 49-49 verso, 88 verso. All Saints,

interest in organs seems to have arisen, perhaps largely as a result of the influence of the Anglican or conformist elements in the church and particularly of the authority of Archbishop Laud. In the 1630s Wigan in Lancashire, Romsey in Hampshire, Waddesdon in Buckinghamshire, Grantham, Bath, Cheddar in Somersetshire, and Prescot in Lancashire, all the churches in Salisbury, and most of them in Bristol, had organs; it was in Bristol, a most prosperous city, that the cathedral singing-men also served as parish organists and clerks. Yet most parish churches seem still to have lacked organs: notes taken during a visitation of one hundred and fifteen churches in Buckinghamshire in 1637 show that only a few, including Beaconsfield and Bishop's Woburn, had them, and that several others, including Edgeborough and Ivinghoe, had remnants of them ("An organ case is there and organs in the memory of man," at Edgeborough). Even the "stately fair church" of Coventry, "which may compare with many cathedrals," had none in 1634. Why there were so few is partly explained by the complaint made to Laud in 1637 that "in Lancashire . . . all the orders of the church go down the wind, for they call the surplices the rags of Rome; they do it at Preston and at Manchester, and will suffer no organs, nor sign no children with the cross when they are christened. . . ."[24]

Without suitable scores, and without organs and therefore organists and choirmasters, few parish churches can have had choirs. In the sixteenth century "learned parish clergy were the exception rather than the rule," an authority on Elizabethan episcopal administration has written, and if the parson could not teach his parishioners to sing in

---

Tilney: Mann Mss., Norfolk Musical Events, 1, folios 240-242. St. Lawrence: Man, *History . . . of Reading*, 315. An exhaustive search in parish records, a work of years, could alter the picture.

[24] Wiggan: Hammond, *Relation 1634*, ed. Legg, 46-47; Hammond states that the bishop of Chester was parson of the church and paid for the organ. Romsey: Hammond, *Relation 1635*, ed. Legg, 60; "given by an old and rich snudge." Waddesdon: *Journal of Sir Simonds D'Ewes from the Beginning of the Long Parliament*, ed. Notestein, 306, 385-386, 446-447. Grantham: the same, 38. Bath: Hammond, *Relation 1634*, 108. Cheddar: HMC 2, *Cheddar Parish Mss.*, 330. Prescot: HMC 35, *Kenyon Mss.*, 57. Salisbury: Hammond, *Relation 1635*, 64-65. Bristol: HMC 3, *House of Lords Mss.*, 141; of Bristol Hammond wrote, in *Relation 1634*, 92, that "In her we found (besides . . . the cathedral . . . eighteen churches . . . in the major part of them, are neat, rich, and melodious organs, that are constantly play'd on." Buckinghamshire: names of places having organs taken from CSPD *1637*, 398, and of places having remnants from the manuscripts calendared, PRO Ms. SP 16/366, folios 171 verso, 172. Coventry: Hammond, *Relation 1634*, 68. Laud: CSPD *1637*, 26; compare the remarks of Trevor-Roper, *Laud*, 174, about the difficulties of the bishop of Chester in the 1630s.

choir from written parts they were unlikely to learn. Occasionally some parishioner, a gifted amateur or professional musician, encouraged by his parson and by favorable sentiment in the parish, or the parish clerk, as in the case of the Bristol singing-men, perhaps found it possible to train a choir. When Archbishop Parker went to Sandwich early in Elizabeth's reign he "found the service sung in good distinct harmony and quiet devotion: the singing-men being the mayor and jurats, with the head men of the town, placed in the quire, fair and decent." St. Margaret's, Westminster, hardly a typical church, bought four books of psalms, in metre, and four other songbooks for its choir in 1562, and in 1600 paid "The charge for the organs, in all" £17.2.7. An endowment, somehow rescued during the confiscations, could give a parish a choir. At Newark-on-Trent a song school remained, in which the master, a priest, was to teach six capable children singing and playing the organ, and on Sundays and festival days they and their master were to help with the service at the Newark church. Lieutenant Hammond noticed Newark particularly in 1634 for its fine church with its "sweet organs, some 'queristers,' and singing boys."[25]

Although it is doubtful that more than a few parish churches had organs and choirs, many congregations probably raised their voices together in metrical psalms. Unaided by instruments, hobbled by the illiterate who sometimes made "lining out" (reading each line before it was sung) essential, congregations must usually have found their psalm singing almost wholly a spiritual exercise, and very little musical; many protestants seem to have regarded this as one of the merits of psalm singing. It did not require formal training, but it may have been, for the literate, a gateway to musical knowledge, for from 1562 to the nineteenth century Sternhold and Hopkins's psalter opened with

[25] Kennedy, *Elizabethan Episcopal Administration*, I, p. xcvii. Parker: Frere, *The English Church in the Reigns of Elizabeth and James I*, 110-111. St. Margaret's, Westminster: Nichols, *Illustrations of the Manners and Expences of Antient Times in England . . . from the Accompts of Churchwardens*, 16, 17, 26; Christ Church, London, another exception, decided about 1580 that "the poor singing-men [should] be continued in the quire 'in respect they have been trained in the science of music all their life' ": CSPD *1547-1580*, 703. Newark: Brown, *A History of Newark-on-Trent*, II, 188, 206-207 (grammar master also); the school inventory of 1595, indicating a broad music education, includes: six surplices for "quirristers" and one for the master, "five long church books," four anthem books, "two sets of service books of four parts," five "violine" books, five "violins" with a chest, and six "mathringal" books (from manuscript Newark-on-Trent Corporation minutes, folio 80 verso; I was able to see these by the kindness of Guy Parsloe, Esq., who had temporary custody of the manuscript and noticed the inventory). Hammond, *Relation 1634*, ed. Legg, 10.

a discourse on the theory of reading music. Parish clerks undoubtedly helped here too sometimes. According to custom, perhaps a growth of this age, parish clerks were to name the psalm tune, set the pitch, and lead the singing, and in London, where they had a company, many of them seem to have known more than the rudiments. According to the company's charter of 1612 prospective clerks were to be examined in the singing of psalms with the usual tunes, and according to its charter of 1640, the most skillful were, in continuation of ancient custom, to sing psalms and anthems every Michaelmas in the Guildhall chapel. For the country as a whole well-trained parish clerks were probably as much the exception in the sixteenth century as learned parish clergy.[26]

Psalm singing was at least as well known outside the parish church as in. Calvinists found particular virtue in it as part of private devotions, and the great crowds that gathered for singing at Paul's Cross after service time in Elizabeth's reign suggest its attraction to the general public. It became an institution even in Worcester cathedral, if in no others. There in the 1630s on Sunday afternoons a lecturer gave a sermon and then the organist, choir, and congregation joined in the psalms; it was said that no greater congregation could be seen anywhere except at St. Paul's. Religious feeling, patriotic or partisan emotions, and the intoxicating effects of familiar music, were frequently compounded during the crises of Tudor and Stuart times, but perhaps never more powerfully than at York in 1644. Then royalists, enduring an eleven weeks' siege, thronged into the great minster in such numbers that it was "cramming or squeezing full" and there participated in "the very best harmonical-music" that Mace ever heard. "Now here you must take notice," Mace wrote, "that they then had a custom in

---

[26] Lining out: John Cotton, the New England divine, told how lining out should be done: "The last scruple remaining in the manner of singing, *Concerneth the order of singing after the Reading of the Psalm. . . .* We for our parts easily grant, that where all have books and can read, or else can say the *Psalm* by heart, it were needless there to read each line of the *Psalm* before hand in order to singing . . . it will be a necessary help, that the words of the *Psalm* be openly read before hand, line after line, or two lines together, that so they who want either books or skill to read, may know what is to be sung, and join with the rest in the duty of singing. . . ." (*Singing of Psalmes a Gospel-Ordinance,* London, 1647, 62.) Sternhold: Scholes, *Oxford Companion to Music,* "Hymns and Hymn Tunes, 5," and others have noticed this. Parish clerks: Christie: *Some Account of Parish Clerks,* 122, 128-129; see chapter two, above, at note 18. On congregational psalm singing see also: Knappen, *Tudor Puritanism,* 182; Kennedy, *Elizabethan Episcopal Administration,* III, 214-215; *Visitation Articles,* ed. Frere, III, 121, including note and references; and *Hymns Ancient and Modern, Historical Edition,* ed. Frere, pp. xlii-xliii.

that church (which I hear not of in any other cathedral, which was) that always before the sermon, the whole congregation sang a psalm, together with the quire and the organ; and you must also know, that there was then a most excellent-large-plump-lusty-full-speaking-organ, which cost (as I am credibly informed) a thousand pounds. . . . This organ, I say (when the psalm was set before the sermon) being let out, into all its fulness of stops, together with the quire, began the psalm. . . . But when that vast-conchording-unity of the whole congregational-chorus, came . . . thundering in, even so, as it made the very ground shake under us; (Oh the unutterable ravishing soul's delight!). . . ."[27]

Although able to sustain England's heritage in ecclesiastical music by continuing to maintain cathedral choirs, the church stayed far below its heavenly model, so far below that, if it had not been for the court's patronage of the Chapel Royal, Westminster, and Windsor, England might never have known the works of its great Elizabethan and Stuart composers.

[27] Private devotions are mentioned in chapter nine, below. Paul's Cross: Knappen, *Tudor Puritanism*, 182. Worcester: Atkins, *Organist . . . Worcester*, 48. Mace, *Musick's Monument*, 18-19; the whole passage, worth reading, appears conveniently in Scholes, *Puritans and Music*, 272-274. Mace put perhaps one-third of the words in this passage, as in his whole book, in italic type.

PART FOUR

THE COURT

INTRODUCTION

THE church of England had many musical establishments but none which rivaled that of the court. A few noblemen of the age stand in the shadowy background of musical history because grateful or hopeful composers dedicated works to them, but none—and some had wealth enough—maintained a great instrumental or choral group for their own pleasure and prestige and for the encouragement of composers; the city of London did much more for musicians than any one of them. By sustaining the Chapel Royal and the King's Musick, Elizabeth, James, and Charles, and only they in their time, earned the title of great patron of English music.

CHAPTER VII. THE CHAPEL ROYAL

B OTH because of its work and of its constitution the Chapel Royal must be considered a part of the court rather than of the church. It pertained to the person of the sovereign and traveled with him to the various royal palaces, on progresses, and even to the Field of the Cloth of Gold with Henry VIII and to Scotland with James I and Charles I; it had no charter or endowment, and was fully and directly subject to royal commands and a direct charge on royal revenues. In all this it differed from a royal foundation such as St. George's chapel at Windsor castle. Wholly a product of royal patronage, the Chapel Royal was an institution and not a building.[1]

By Queen Elizabeth's time the Chapel Royal had centuries of service behind it. Household regulations of about 1135 mention it in some detail, records of 1401 show that its membership by then included boys, and a description of the court written about 1478 (*Liber Niger*) outlines what proved to be the permanent essentials of its organization. It had listed distinguished musicians on its rolls, too, including Henry Abyngton (died 1497), singer and organist, Robert Fairfax (died 1521), composer, and William Cornyshe (died 1523), composer and dramatist, besides Thomas Tallis (died 1585), who continued to serve in the Chapel Royal and to compose during much of Elizabeth's reign.[2]

Chaplains and singing-men, all called gentlemen of the chapel, and

---

[1] See Chambers, *Elizabethan Stage*, II, 25; Hillebrand, "The early history of the Chapel Royal," *Modern Philology*, XVIII (1921), 239; "Chapel Royal," *Grove*.

The chief sources for the history of the Chapel Royal are: *The Old Cheque-Book, or Book of Remembrance, of the Chapel Royal from 1561 to 1744*, ed. Rimbault; the manuscript printed on pp. 251-268 in the Hillebrand article named above; *The King's Musick A transcript of records relating to music and musicians (1460-1700)*, ed. Lafontaine; and manuscripts in the PRO including state papers domestic and lord chamberlain's accounts. Brief accounts include: Fellowes, "Chapel Royal," *Grove*; Hayes, *King's Music*; Manly, "The children of the Chapel Royal and their masters," *Cambridge History of English Literature*, VI, 279-292 and bibliography, 467 468 (earlier history); Flood, "Queen Mary's Chapel Royal," *English Historical Review*, XXXIII (1918), 83-89; Hillebrand (as above), pp. 233-251 (earlier history); Chambers, *Elizabethan Stage*, II, 23-61 (bibliography); Roper, "Music in the English Chapels Royal c. 1135-present day," *Proc. Mus. Assoc.*, 54th session (1928), 19-34; Wallace, *Children of the Chapel at Blackfriars* (contains some useful material).

CB and KM are used in part four as abbreviations for *Cheque-Book*, ed. Rimbault, and *King's Musick*, ed. Lafontaine, respectively.

[2] For the earlier history in general see references in the preceding note, and for the specific details given see Chambers, *Elizabethan Stage*, II, 24, and *Grove*.

choristers or singing-boys, were the basic components of the organization. Under Elizabeth the lord chamberlain, who maintained a general supervision over the chapel and was its "chief governor under her sacred majesty," had to exercise direct, if not day to day, control. James, returning to an earlier practice, appointed deans, the first, James Montague, later a bishop, being sworn in on Christmas day 1603, and the second, Bishop Launcelot Andrewes, on 1 January 1619; Charles followed the revived precedent by appointing Bishop William Laud in 1626 after the death of Andrewes. In general the deans passed on appointments, ruled on difficult disciplinary cases, and issued standing orders, sometimes drawn up in assemblies over which they occasionally presided.[3]

One of the gentlemen, designated subdean, exercised the actual daily supervision. The title brought no extra pay, but it seems to have been coveted, perhaps partly for the dignity and partly for the more tangible returns authority usually attracts. Ordinarily the subdean subscribed his name first to the rules and agreements adopted by the gentlemen, authorized absences, prescribed penalties for minor offenses, and chose the service and anthems to be sung.[4]

By the middle of the sixteenth century the regular number of gentlemen, besides the subdean but including chaplains, singing-men, the master of the children, and the clerk of the check (secretary) was thirty-two. "A note of the names of the subdean, gentlemen and others of the chapel, at the time of the coronation of King James the First,"

[3] On the position of the lord chamberlains and deans see in general CB (*Cheque-Book*, ed. Rimbault). The office of dean, described in *Liber Niger Domus Regis* (*A Collection of Ordinances and Regulations*, pp. 49-50), is mentioned in the Elizabethan records of the Cheque-Book only once, apparently; in 1593 the subdean ordered that a gentleman guilty of a certain offense should remain suspended until "he can get relief at the hand of the dean, and, for the present, of the . . . lord chamberlain, our chief governor under her sacred majesty" (CB, 66-67). It also appears incidentally in an item for 1580 in the manuscript printed by Hillebrand, *Modern Philology*, XVIII (1921), 253. A minute made in 1608 refers to the time when "six lord chamberlains had the government of the chapel (in the vacancy of a dean). . . ." (CB, 141); Queen Elizabeth had altogether six lord chamberlains.

Deans under James and Charles: CB, 39, 126, 80-81 (Bishop Matthew Wren).

Orders of 1603 and 1604, CB, 39-40, illustrate the character of the control and its shift from lord chamberlain to dean.

Duties illustrated: CB, 71-81, 101-104, 143.

[4] CB, 62-80; from 1630 to 1640 the standing orders were signed by the dean. Absences: rule first entered in 1593, CB, 66-67. Choice of services and anthems: rule first entered 1604, CB, 70-71.

entered in the informal register of the chapel, the Cheque-Book, represents fairly the normal establishment: it lists first the subdean, then seven "mynisters" in order of seniority, the master of the children, the clerk of the check, "Jo. Bull, doctor in music" (listed apart because of his degree, presumably), twenty-two "gentlemen" also in order of seniority, and four officers of the vestry. Many lists vary widely from this one, but usually for some obvious reason, when larger often because they include the names of honorary gentlemen ("extraordinary") and when smaller usually because they include the names of only those gentlemen who happened to attend a particular vestry or chapter meeting or to agree to some proposal.[5]

Not all thirty-two gentlemen attended every service, however. An order of 1619 refers to those "grown aged or taken with sickness, so that there is no expectation of their service. . . ." Robert Stone, ninety-three years old when he died in 1613, Thomas Sampson, just starting his fifty-second year as a gentleman of the chapel when he drowned in 1615, and William Byrd, about eighty and in his fifty-fourth year as a gentleman of the chapel at the time of his death in 1623, must have been among these. In a few instances places were left vacant for a considerable time and the pay diverted to other uses; one place remained unfilled from February 1622 until April 1623, "the wages in the meantime . . . disposed of by the dean for pricking of songs and for a new set of books for the Chapel, and other disposings and allowances. . . ." For ordinary occasions the gentlemen took turns according to a roster made up annually so that each month there should be "a competent number of gentlemen. . . ." On Sundays, principal times at Christmas, Easter, and Whitsuntide, "upon holy days at both services," and certain

[5] The authorized number is indicated by warrants for livery for the chapel, e.g. PRO Ms. LC 5/37, p. 47 (1595) and p. 276 (1601).

"Note," coronation 1603: CB, 127-128.

For other lists see Stopes, "Mary's Chapel Royal and her Coronation Play," *Atheneum*, No. 4063 (9 September 1905), p. 347; CB, 60-62 (1604); CB, 156 (1625; compare *King's Musick*, ed. Lafontaine, 58).

Lists of gentlemen attending meeting: CB, 62-63, 64-65, 67-68 (and errata, p. 241), 140-141, 122-123, 104.

For an example of a misleading list see CB, 70, a record signed by forty men, nineteen of whom became gentlemen in ordinary at dates subsequent to the date of the record.

Something seems to be wrong with the draft of a warrant to increase the annual allowance of the gentlemen (1604) as calendared in CSPD *1580-1625*, 450. It specifies thirty-eight gentlemen.

The number of gentlemen who were ministers varied.

other great times, all the gentlemen on the list were to attend at the same time, "as well out of their appointed month as in it. . . ." Some gentlemen, and particularly those who had places elsewhere too, often found it inconvenient to attend, and unless they made arrangements, satisfactory to the dean or subdean, for a substitute, ran the danger of checks on their wages and even of forfeiture of their places.[6]

In addition the membership included an inconstant number of gentlemen who received no wages. Most of them were gentlemen extraordinary, appointed because the sovereign, dean, or a majority of the gentlemen in ordinary wished to honor them, and sometimes because they had helped the chapel in some way, as in the notable cases of "Mr. William Phelps of the town of Tewkesbury . . . , being trained up in the noble science of music, . . . for that he did show a most rare kindness to Mr. Doctor Bull in his great distress, being robbed in those parts . . ." (1592), and of William West "the rather for that he did attend by the space of eight days at the great solemnity of the league of Spain to his great charge" (1604). Usually when taking their oath of office gentlemen extraordinary also swore not to try by any means whatever to get a place in ordinary, but occasionally their appointments carried with them reversions, and many gentlemen extraordinary did in fact later receive regular places. At least six times between 1601 and 1618 men were sworn in ordinary without pay, four of these times with reversions specified and once with the man taking oath not to seek a regular place "until he shall be called and approved fit for the same by the dean, subdean, and major part of the gentlemen then attending." Except for this man, not recorded in the Cheque-Book as taking a regular place but listed among the gentlemen in the lord chamberlain's accounts for the funeral of James I in 1625, all received regular places very quickly. Several of the gentlemen extraordinary and gentlemen in ordinary without pay accepted their appointments with specific understanding that they would serve either regularly or whenever needed.

[6] CB, 123, and list of appointments, pp. 1-10. Sampson's successor as clerk had acted as clerk for the preceding eight years or more (p. 8). Byrd was succeeded by one John Croker (p. 10). Long vacancy: CB, 10 (see also pp. 11 and 57-58).

Order of service: CB, 71-73; other rules are given concerning absences, including provision for fines for absence and lateness. The order is signed by the dean, William Bath and Wells, that is, William Laud, bishop of Bath and Wells 1626-1628, and dean of the chapel from 1626, and must therefore have been written between 1626 and 1628. The provisions for substitutes in the orders of 1592 and 1593 (CB, 66-67) seem to imply that the principle of alternation in service had been long established. See also CB, 79 (1637).

The chances are that all the gentlemen with reversions and all who strongly wanted regular places served gladly when asked. Gentlemen extraordinary, as well as ordinary, received mourning livery ("blacks") for both Queen Elizabeth's and King James's funeral ceremonies and presumably sang at them. Perhaps they always participated on great occasions of state.[7]

The gentleman next in dignity to the subdean was the master of the children. He had, above all, to see that they were ready to sing their parts in the chapel, a task which should have been easier when the dean and subdean heeded the rule of 1604 that they should choose the music "not without the advice of the master of the children, for such songs as are to be performed by the children in the chapel." Several of the masters also employed the boys as actors, thereby winning considerable notice in the history of Elizabethan drama. In order to get suitable boys, the masters, from at least 1420, used royal warrants empowering them to seize boys anywhere in England, excepting (sometimes, perhaps always) Windsor chapel, Westminster abbey, and St. Paul's. Responsibility for the boarding, lodging, clothing, and general well-being of the boys also fell on the masters, who found it a considerable burden, requiring as it did the keeping of an usher and another man servant to attend them and a woman servant to keep them clean. On the whole the masters seem to have discharged their duties well.[8]

The prescribed number of boys was twelve; the actual number may have been much larger when they were acting regularly, but not neces-

[7] Most of the appointments extraordinary recorded in CB are given on pp. 31-48. Phelps, CB, 31-32; West, CB, 40. Appointments in ordinary without pay: CB, 37, 45-48; lord chamberlain's accounts in KM (*King's Musick*, ed. Lafontaine), 58 (LC 2/6). Irregular appointees to serve: CB, 37, 38, 41; see also rule of 1663: CB, 83. Funerals, 1603: KM, 44 (LC 2/4[4]); 1625: CB, 156 and KM, 58 (LC 2/6). Chambers, *Elizabethan Stage*, I, 52, states that "all royal servants, whatever their office, and whether 'ordinary' or 'extraordinary,' received a customary allowance of red cloth at the coronation and of black cloth at a royal funeral. . . ." If there were any gentlemen extraordinary in 1558-1559, and if the accounts in PRO Mss. LC 2/4(2), pp. 61-62 and LC 2/4(3), p. 97 are complete, they do not seem to have had livery for the funeral of Queen Mary and the coronation of Queen Elizabeth.

[8] Choice of music: CB, 71. Pressing boys: Hillebrand, *Modern Philology*, XVIII (1921), 80; Roper, *Proc. Mus. Assoc.*, 54th session (1928), 21-22; *Privy Purse . . . Henry the Eighth*, ed. Nicolas, 140; Chambers, *Elizabethan Stage*, II, 33-34; CSPD 1595-97, 450; CSPD 1603-10, 151; PRO Ms. AO 1/390/53 (warrant 1616 for expenses of N. Gyles going for boys for forty days); see also chapter six above (at note 17). On caring for the boys see petition of William Hunnis, 1583, below. The exemptions of St. George's chapel, Windsor, and the others occur in various of the warrants to the masters, and Elizabeth gave a standing exemption to St. George's in 1560: see Chambers, *Elizabethan Stage*, II, 62 note 3.

sarily to the musical advantage of the chapel, for the masters may not have trained the extra boys as choristers.[9]

Long as they had served in the chapel, organists had no fully established post like that of master of the boys. In the fifteenth century all the gentlemen may have been expected to take turn at the organ, for the *Liber Niger* includes among their general qualifications "sufficient in organs playing," but by the middle of the sixteenth century organ playing had definitely become a specialty. Thomas Tallis and William Byrd described themselves, on the title page of the *Cantiones* they published in 1575, as "generosis et organistis," and Tallis had served in the chapel from about 1540 and Byrd from 1570. William Blitheman, another composer, served as organist from 1585 until his death in 1591, and taught John Bull, soon famous on the continent as in England for his playing. It was not until 1592, however, that the keeper of the Cheque-Book described one of the gentlemen as an organist, and this in recording the appointment extraordinary of Phelps, the musician of Tewkesbury who had helped Bull ("organist of her said majesty's chapel") when he had been robbed. The first appointment of an organist, so specified in the Cheque-Book, came nine years later, in 1601, when Arter Cocke took an oath as "gentleman in ordinary and organist (without pay)"; he was to serve "until an organist place shall become void . . . and to supply the wants of organists which may be through sickness or other urgent causes. . . ." Thereafter the record usually gave organists the title, and at least twice they received the same, larger, quantities of cloth for livery that gentlemen who were ministers received: in 1603 for Queen Elizabeth's funeral, Bull, along with the sub-dean and ministers, received nine yards for himself and two for his servant while the other gentlemen received seven yards and two yards apiece; and in 1625, for King James's funeral, Orlando Gibbons, "senior organist," similarly received nine yards and two for his servant. Any man who succeeded Gibbons, described at the time of his death as having at the virginals and organ "the best hand in England," was almost sure to have troubles, and Thomas Warwick, gentleman-born, did, suffering in 1630 "a check of his whole pay for the month of March because he presumed to play verses on the organ at service time, being formerly inhibited by the dean [Laud] from doing the same, by reason

---

[9] On the authorized number see Chambers, *Elizabethan Stage*, ii, 25 and references there given. Hunnis, 1583, mentions twelve (see petition below), and twelve is the number for 1603, 1612, 1618 and 1625 according to KM, 44, 49, 53, 58. On the requirements for plays see Chambers, especially chapter xii (vol. ii) at p. 48.

of his insufficiency for that solemn service." Thomas Tomkins, organist of Worcester cathedral, and John Tomkins, organist of St. Paul's, were both organists in the Chapel Royal and apparently worthy successors of Tallis, Byrd, Bull, and Gibbons.[10]

The clerk of the check carried on his work as secretary in addition to his regular duties as gentleman; the clerkship, evidently valued, like the office of subdean, for its dignity and privileges, was filled by vote of the gentlemen. The recorder of songs, mentioned once in the Cheque-Book, was likewise a gentleman, in this case evidently happy to supplement his income by copying parts. The offices of gospeller and episteller, sometimes used to support boys after their voices had changed, were frequently given as preliminary appointments to musicians waiting for gentlemen's places; the record for the 1620s shows clearly a regular practice of appointing a man first episteller, then gospeller, and then gentleman, as the deaths of gentlemen made promotions possible. An organ blower must have been employed as soon as the chapel used organs, but the office entered the Cheque-Book only in 1625. The bellringer and the vestrymen—a sergeant, two yeomen, and a groom—seem to have had no musical duties.[11]

During Elizabeth's reign the gentlemen received seven and half pence a day wages and a shilling a day board wages (paid since 1544 instead of dinner and supper in kind), a total of £29.13.1½ a year, perhaps increased late in the reign to an even thirty pounds. In 1596, acting at last to counter the effects of long felt inflation, the gentlemen banded together to bear the costs of a suit, to be conducted through "one Mr. Hills, of London, gentleman," to the queen for "some gift or grant . . . for the yearly increase of [their] livings." Over eight years later, in

[10] *Liber Niger* in *Ordinances and Regulations*, 50. Blitheman: *Grove*, I, 392. Phelps: CB, 31. A Cheque-Book entry July 1592 names one of the witnesses, a gentleman of the chapel, organist: CB, 33. Cocke: CB, 37-38. Bull's livery: PRO Ms. 2/4(4); Gibbons's livery: CB, 156. Gibbons "the best hand": John Chamberlain to Sir Dudley Carleton, as quoted by Fellowes, "Gibbons," *Grove*. Warwick: CB, 78; see also p. 207. Tomkins: CB, 10, 11.

[11] Clerk: CB, 57, 58, and particularly 75-76. Recorder of songs, 1625: CB, 156. Gospeller and episteller: CB, 3, 4, 7, 10, 11, 12, 33, 34, 44, 56. Organ blower: CB, 156 (1717: p. 148). Bellringer: CB, 139 (1606), 144, 156. Vestry: CB, 76-78, 130-145. Chambers, *Elizabethan Stage*, II, 24, and Rimbault, CB, p. iii, seem to suggest that the gospeller and episteller were yeomen (as *Liber Niger*, in *Ordinances and Regulations*, 50, indicates), but comparison of the record of appointments of gospeller and episteller with those of the vestry shows that in the reigns of Elizabeth, James, and Charles they were distinct, the former on the liturgical side, the latter on the menial side.

A common servant is mentioned in 1626: CB, 144.

1604, the gentlemen, "after a long and chargeable suit," won an increase of ten pounds a year "to every man, so increasing their stipends from thirty to forty pounds. . . ." The memorial of the great event, inscribed in the Cheque-Book for the delighted gentlemen, ends: "Now it was thought meet that seeing the entertainment of the chapel was not augmented of many years by any of his majesty's progenitors . . . that therefore his kingly bounty . . . should be recorded, to be had ever in remembrance, that thereby not only we (men and children now living), but all those also which shall succeed us in the chapel should daily see cause (in our most devout prayers) humbly to beseech the Divine Majesty to bless his highness, our gracious Queen Anne, Prince Henry, and all and every of that royal progeny, with blessings both spiritual and temporal, and that from age to age and everlastingly, and let us all pray Amen, Amen." And in the margin: "Cursed be the party that taketh this leaf out of this book. Amen." "The names of the gentlemen living at the time of this augmentation granted," and of the vestrymen, follow. If they thought of the wages of singing-men in cathedrals they had the more reason for rejoicing in their fortune.[12]

Various other perquisites of less importance came to them from time to time. Nine or seven yards, according to rank, of black cloth for royal funerals or of red cloth for coronations, went to each gentleman, each of whom also received a cloth allowance for a servant; the singing-men of Westminster usually received only four yards apiece on these occasions. Two surplices of "fine holland cloth" ("gathered in the collar for the subdean") were supplied for each gentleman every three years, normally. Weddings now and then brought in two pounds, two pounds and a buck, or five pounds. A regular schedule of compensations for "removes," from one palace to another or on royal progresses, although probably calculated only to cover the extra expense, may have added a little to their income. The extraordinary removes to Scotland required special allowances. In 1617 the dean received for the chapel four hundred pounds and a well-furnished ship, and in 1633 three

---

[12] Seven and a half pence: *Liber Niger*, in *Household Ordinances*, 50. Board wages: *Household Ordinances*, 169, 212. The record in the Cheque-Book of the increase ("from thirty to forty pounds"), and the patent appointing Giles master of the children in 1597 (Wallace, *Children of the Chapel*, 59-60 note 3) mentioning thirty pounds as a gentleman's fee, both seem to indicate that the wages and board wages may have been combined into a thirty-pound fee. See, however, Hillebrand, "Early History . . . ," *Modern Philology*, XVIII (1921), 266.

Suit 1596: CB, 59-60. Increase granted: CB, 60-62; and draft of warrant: CSPD *1580-1625*, 450.

hundred and fifty-three pounds and the *Dreadnought*; the nineteen gentlemen who went on the latter trip received twelve pounds apiece. Exemption from payment of subsidies added substantially, in effect, to their incomes during the Stuart reigns, and an annual feast on deer, provided with a gratuity by the sovereign, to the amenity of the life.[13]

Some of the gentlemen profited from being near the monarch and the great men who guided the flow of royal bounty. "The king's grace advanceth these priests and clerks by prebends, churches of his patrimony, or by his letters recommendatory, . . . or pensions," the *Liber Niger* declares. Perhaps the most famous instances of the royal patronage were grants to Tallis and Byrd, and later Morley, of monopolies on the printing of music. Bull received from Queen Elizabeth a lease worth twenty marks a year, and on her recommendation received the first appointment as music professor in Gresham college. William Hunnis, gentleman of the chapel from about 1550, master of the children from 1566 until his death in 1597, and conspicuous in the history of the stage, enjoyed several marks of Elizabeth's appreciation, including the keepership of the orchards and gardens at Greenwich from 1562, and grants of crown lands at Great Ilford and elsewhere in 1585. Orlando Gibbons in about 1611 asked for a lease in reversion worth forty marks a year, said to have been promised by the queen, and re-

---

[13] Funeral and coronation liveries: PRO Mss. LC 2/4(1), p. 17 (funeral of Edward VI); LC 2/4(2), pp. 61-62 (funeral of Mary); LC 2/4(3), p. 97 (coronation of Elizabeth; amounts of scarlet only five and four yards); LC 2/4(4) (funeral of Elizabeth); LC 2/4(6) (funeral of Prince Henry; four yards); LC 2/5 (funeral of Queen Anne 1618); LC 2/6 (funeral of James; also CB, 156); Chambers, *Elizabethan Stage*, I, 52.

Surplices: PRO Mss. LC 5/37, pp. 47-48 (1595); LC 5/37, pp. 134-135 (1598; note at end: "That these wants are very needful to be supplied and for the which no warrant hath passed in four years . . ."); LC 5/37, p. 276 (1601; note as in 1598); LC 5/115, a similar warrant for 1675, folded, is labeled on outside "The Triennial warrant for the Chapel . . ."; KM, 63 (1626), 65 (1628).

Weddings: CB, 160-161.

Removes: Hillebrand, *Modern Philology*, XVIII (1921), 264-265; and to Scotland: CSPD *1633-34*, 38, 47, and Hillebrand, pp. 267-268.

Subsidies: CSPD *1623-25*, 286; *1625-26*, 550; *1628-29*, 196; CB, 91, 92.

Although the gentlemen seem to have received livery regularly in earlier reigns I do not remember seeing evidence that they did under Elizabeth and later. *Liber Niger*, in *Household Ordinances*, 50, says that they should have winter and summer livery. See CB, p. ix. Collier, *Annals* (2d edition, 1879), I, 174, from an Elizabethan fee list, gives £15.0.8 as the value of an annual livery (caution on fee lists: Chambers, *Elizabethan Stage*, I, 29). See also Chambers, II, 26-27, including note I on p. 27.

Annual feast: *Privy Purse . . . Henry the Eighth*, ed. Nicolas, 64, 242; PRO Ms. AO 1/381/7, 10; CB, 122-126; CSPD *1611-18*, 53.

ceived royal grants in 1611 and 1615. A warrant in 1623 to preserve the king's game in certain of his lands must have contributed to William Heather's prosperity, which was evidently considerable, for in 1627 he founded the music lecture or professorship at Oxford with an endowment of £17.6.8 a year. Church livings, including posts as cathedral singing-men, also supplemented the wages of many of the gentlemen. Sometimes they simply retained places they held before entering the chapel. Thomas Tomkins, organist of Worcester, and John Tomkins, organist of St. Paul's, have been mentioned already, and the preceding chapter told of Queen Elizabeth's reprimand to the dean and chapter at Exeter for depriving a vicar of his place after his appointment to the chapel. Nathaniel Giles, organist and master of the choristers at St. George's, Windsor, kept his post there after his appointment to the chapel. Orlando Gibbons, in addition to his other special grants, enjoyed two posts, virginalist and ordinary musician, in the King's Musick, and, for the last two years of his life, the position of organist in Westminster abbey. John Savelle received a parsonage in Norwich in 1579 and kept his chapel position. Sometimes the order in which gentlemen received their many places is not evident, as in the case of Thomas Day, gentleman of the chapel, master of the choristers in Westminster, and musician in the King's Musick (reigns of James and Charles). The subdean, Robert Green, died in 1592 at "his benefice in Norfolk," and his successor, "Preacher since the first year of her majesty's most happy reign," was vicar of Stepney and gospeller in the chapel at the time of his election. While pluralities enriched the gentlemen they also made it difficult to secure adequate attendance at times; the Cheque-Book records several attempts to stop unauthorized absences, and in 1663 the dean, reissuing ancient rules, ordered that no one should be admitted a gentleman of the chapel "but shall first quit all interest in other quires." The rule may have been ancient, but it had not applied to the more distinguished musicians and other gentlemen of influence.[14]

[14] *Liber Niger*, in *Household Ordinances*, 50. Printing monopoly: Kidson, *British Music Publishers*, xi-xii, and *Grove* (Tallis, Byrd, Morley). Bull: *Grove*. Hunnis: Chambers, *Elizabethan Stage*, III, 349. Gibbons: request for lease, CSPD *1611-18*, 107; grants, "Gibbons," *Grove*. Heather: warrant, CSPD *1623-25*, 1; "Heyther," *Grove*. Exeter: CSPD *1598-1601*, 438. Giles: *Grove*. Gibbons's posts: "Gibbons," *Grove*. Savelle: HMC *9, Marquess of Salisbury Mss.*, ii, 248; CB, 3. Day: KM, 58-59. Green and his successor: CB, 33. Absences: see CB, especially section v, pp. 62ff. Rule in 1663: CB, 81; see also pp. 99-100. For another grant to Tallis and Byrd, 1577, see HMC *9, Marquess of Salisbury Mss.*, ii, 155-156.

The regular allowances of the masters of the children, gigantic in the eyes of provincial musicians, seemed pitifully meagre to the men who received them. Hunnis, petitioning in 1583 for increased allowances, presented a sorry picture: "May it please your honors, William Hunnis, master of the children of her highness chapel, most humble beseecheth to consider of these few lines. First, her majesty alloweth for the diet of twelve children of her said chapel daily six pence a piece by the day, and forty pounds by the year for their apparel and all other furniture. Again there is no fee allowed neither for the master of the said children nor for his usher, and yet nevertheless is he constrained, over and besides the usher still to keep both a man servant to attend upon them and likewise a woman servant to wash and keep them clean. Also there is no allowance for the lodging of the said children, such time as they attend upon the court, but the master to his great charge is driven to hire chambers both for himself, his usher, children, and servants. Also there is no allowance for riding journeys when occasion serveth the master to travel or send into sundry parts within this realm, to take up and bring such children as be thought meet to be trained for the service of her majesty. Also there is no allowance nor other consideration for those children whose voices be changed, who only do depend upon the charge of the said master until such time as he may prefer the same with clothing and other furniture, unto his no small charge." Then Hunnis pointed out how times had changed: "And although it may be objected that her majesty's allowance is no whit less then her majesty's father of famous memory therefore allowed: yet considering the prices of things present to the time past and what annuities the master then had out of sundry abbeys within this realm, besides sundry gifts from the king, and divers particular fees besides, for the better maintenance of the said children and office: and besides also there hath been withdrawn from the said children since her majesty's coming to the crown twelve pence by the day which was allowed for their breakfasts as may appear by the treasurer of the chamber his account for the time being, with other allowances incident to the office as appeareth by the ancient accounts in the said office which I here omit. The burden hereof hath from time to time so hindered the masters of the children viz. Master Bower, Master Edwardes, myself and Master Farrant: that notwithstanding some good helps otherwise some of them died in so poor case, and so deeply indebted that they have not left scarcely wherewith to bury them. In tender consideration whereof, might it please your honors that the said allowance of six pence a day apiece for the children's diet might be reserved in her majesty's coffers during the time of their attendance. And in lieu thereof they to be allowed meat and drink within this honorable household for that I am not able upon so small allowance any longer to bear so heavy a burden. Or otherwise to be considered as shall seem best unto your honorable wisdoms." As Chambers observes, Hunnis failed to mention any profits from the boys' acting. Although his particular remedies seem not to have been accepted, his own distress was probably relieved by the grant of crown lands in 1585. The great suit of the gentlemen for an augmentation brought some relief to Hunnis's successor, Nathaniel Giles, the board wages for each boy being increased from six pence to ten pence a day. The fixed allowances of the master were, therefore, his pay as a gentleman of the chapel, about thirty, then forty pounds a year; an allowance of forty pounds a year for teaching and keeping the boys; and six pence a day, then ten pence a day, for the feeding of each of the twelve boys. In addition the masters during the reigns of James and Charles seem to have received compensation for the cost of their "riding journeys" for new boys (in 1616 ten shillings a day for forty days); at least once some clothing besides the funeral and coronation liveries; to have had a gentleman of the chapel as deputy master for several years at least (warrant for his expenses of twenty-five pounds 1626-1630); and, as always, to have been rewarded for special services rendered by the boys. Perhaps too little at times, the allowances apparently were never, in the sixteenth century and the first half of the seventeenth, so inadequate that they caused deterioration of the high standards of the chapel and a break in the brilliant line of masters.[15]

The boys, unpaid in cash, received for their services an education in music and in general elementary subjects, and, when their voices had changed, sometimes places in the chapel or some collegiate church, or, if not that, at least the promise of university training. The *Liber Niger* states that "when they be grown to the age of eighteen years, and then

[15] Petition: Chambers: *Elizabethan Stage*, ii, 37-38 (from PRO Ms. SP 12/163, no. 88; Chambers gives an endorsement). Giles's journey 1616: PRO Ms. AO 1/390/53; the warrant gives the total as eighteen pounds. Shirts 1605: KM, 46. Deputy: KM, 77. Rewards for special services including plays: see particularly Hillebrand, *Modern Philology*, xviii (1921), 264-265; Chambers, *Elizabethan Stage*, ii, 23-61; Manly, *Cambridge History of English Literature*, vi, 279-292; Arkwright, "Elizabethan Choirboy Plays and their Music," *Proc. Mus. Assoc.*, 40th session (1914), 117-138; "Early Elizabethan Stage Music," *Musical Antiquary*, i (1910), 30-40.

their voices be changed, nor cannot be preferred in this chapel, nor within this court, the number being full; then if they will assent, the king assigneth every such child to a college of Oxford or Cambridge, of the king's foundation, there to be in finding and study sufficiently, till the king otherwise list to advance him . . . ," presumably in the church. Henry VIII paid the university expenses of chapel boys or otherwise took care of them, but before or during Elizabeth's reign the practice was suspended, according to Hunnis's petition. James restored the old custom in 1604 by authorizing the master to send any boy who had served at least three years in the chapel and was then no longer able to serve because of his changed voice, to any college or school of royal foundation in Oxford, Cambridge, or elsewhere, where he was to have the place of a "scholar of the foundation." Charles also followed precedent in 1629 when he granted a chapel boy's request for a recommendation to a singing-man's place in Salisbury cathedral. Some of the boys, given clothing as they departed, seem merely to have "gone off." As a rule a boy who became a chorister in the Chapel Royal could expect to get an education, and had fair assurance of some kind of an honorable career, probably in the church.[16]

The primary duty of the Chapel Royal was to provide daily religious services for the court in any of the palaces of the London area it occupied for the time, and sometimes when it was on progress. Rest periods, set by precedent but variable at the will of the sovereign, gave the gentlemen opportunity for some change, and even to serve in their provincial posts if they cared to. At the beginning of Charles's reign the dean, Bishop Laud, acknowledged that the "ancient times of liberty and playing weeks" included the quarter from St. Peter's day (29 June) to Michaelmas, the week before Christmas, the week after Twelfthtide (6 January), the week after Candlemas (2 February), the week after Easter, the week after St. George's day (23 April) and all "removing weeks," during which times the gentlemen waited only on Sundays and holidays. No doubt they earned a rest by their work during the great festivals immediately before these weeks, or after in the case of the Christmas "playing week." A few years later Charles issued

---

[16] CB shows several instances of the preferment of chapel boys: see pp. 4 and 8 for examples. *Liber Niger*, in *Household Ordinances*, 51. Henry VIII: Hillebrand, *Modern Philology*, xviii (1921), 246; *Privy Purse . . . Henry the Eighth*, ed. Nicolas, 13, 46, 82, 125, 165, 260. James: Hillebrand, p. 250, from writ of impressment granted to Giles. Charles: CSPD *1628-29*, 564. Clothing: KM, 46 (1605), 89 (1634).

a new order: "When we are absent: as our express pleasure is that our chapel be all the year thorough, kept both morning and evening with solemn music like a collegiate church: unless it be at such times in the summer, or other times when we are pleased to spare it. . . ." Charles, or Laud, may have meant to see that services ran more continuously for the court, but it is likely that the gentlemen convinced the king that he should excuse them about as often as in former times. Besides its daily function the Chapel Royal rendered important service on many great state occasions, when to its own full strength often were added instrumentalists from the King's Musick, and sometimes the choir of Westminster abbey.[17]

An echo from these great days still sounds from the pages of the Cheque-Book. The subdean ("one very near") devoutly recorded "the princely coming of her majesty to the holy communion at Easter" in 1593; "Dr. Bull was at the organ playing the offertory." In 1611 music helped solemnize the taking of the royal oath to the French ambassador "for the maintenance and continuation of the league" between "the Christian King" and "the king's majesty of Great Britain." As James and the ambassador entered the chapel and went to their seats "the organs played" and then the choir sang an anthem; "after the taking of the oath, the king and ambassador kissed each other, and then went again [to their seats] till another anthem was sung. That ended, they went out . . . the organs playing till they were gone. . . ." The chapel in Whitehall palace "was in royal sort adorned" in 1613 for the wedding of Prince Frederick and Princess Elizabeth: "This royal assembly being . . . settled in their places, then began the gentlemen of the chapel to sing a full anthem . . . the sermon being ended, which continued not much above half an hour, the quire began another anthem which was the psalm, Blessed art thou that fearest God, &c. While the anthem was in singing, the archbishop of Canterbury and the dean of the chapel . . . put on their rich copes and came to the communion table, where standing till the anthem was ended, they two ascended the throne, where these two great princes were married. . . ." After the benediction, "God the Father, God the Son, &c. the quire sang the same benediction in an anthem made new for that purpose by Doctor Bull [then] versicles and prayers were sung by the archbishop and answered by the quire. The prayers being ended, began another anthem;

[17] Rest periods: cb, 73; for date of memorandum see note 6 above. Charles's order: pro Ms. LC 5/180, pp. 19-20, a book of household regulations ascribed in catalogue to 1630.

that done, Mr. Garter, principal king at arms, published the style of the prince and princess. . . ." All then departed, the king and queen leaving the newly married couple to dine in state in the new banqueting house with the princes, ambassadors "and the whole troupe of lords and ladies."[18]

For the gentlemen of the chapel the "Funerals of King James" were arduous but not without profit: "His dead corps were brought from Theobalds to Denmark house . . . where all his officers attended and waited during the time that his corps lay there, except the chapel, who waited upon King Charles at Whitehall. . . . Two days before the day of the funerals the corps were brought into the said chapel in great solemnity with an anthem, . . . and the gentlemen of the chapel from that time waited there, and performed solemn service with the organs brought thither for that purpose; they also waited with the corps by night and day: by night, first decani side, and next cantoris side, and twice in the night, viz. at nine of the clock and at midnight, they had prayers with a first and second chapters, and ended with an anthem. . . ." The black hangings, chairs, screens, cloths and other furnishings of both the chapel set up in Denmark house and at Whitehall "were fees to the gentlemen of the chapel, and divided amongst them. . . ."[19]

The greatest opportunity of all came with a coronation. That of "our sovereign lord King Charles" took place on Candlemas day, 1626: "Upon which day all the chapel met at the college hall in Westminster, where they had a breakfast at the charge of the college, from thence they went by a back way into the church, and so into the vestry, where together with the quire of Westminster they put on surplices and copes and went into Westminster hall, and there waited until the king came thither . . . by water . . . into the great hall, where was a large scaffold covered all with cloth, and upon it a throne and chair of estate. . . . The chapel followed the Knights of the Bath, . . . next the quire of Westminster, then the chapel, who went singing through the palace yard and round about the church, through the great sanctuary till they came to the west door of the church: when all the chapel were within the church they began the first anthem." After singing this, "I was glad when they said unto me we will go into the house of the Lord . . . ," and after the archbishop had "done at the corners of the scaffold, and the people's acclamation ended," the choirs sang another anthem, "Strengthened be thy hand, and exalted be thy right hand. . . ." A third

[18] CB, 150, 152-153, 163-166. [19] CB, 154-155.

anthem followed the sermon and the king's oath taking, then a prayer, then the reading of the litany by two bishops with the answers sung by the choirs, and then, while the archbishop anointed the king, a fourth anthem, "Sadock the priest and Nathan the prophet anointed Solomon king and joyfully approaching they cried, God Save the King . . . Allelujah." At further stages in the ceremony the choirs sang the fifth anthem, the Te Deum, the sixth anthem, the Nicene Creed, and the seventh anthem, at the beginning of the offertory; "the organs play till the offertory be ended." After the communion the choirs sang their eighth and last anthem, "O hearken then unto the voice of my calling," and after the final prayers "the king returned back again into Westminster hall in the same manner as he went, the chapel going in their former order, and singing all the way till they came to Westminster hall door, and there they stayed, making a lane for the king and all the lords to pass betwixt them, and continued singing till the king was within the hall. . . ." The gentlemen and children now could take off their copes and surplices and return to Whitehall for what they must have welcomed, "some allowance of diet for their suppers."[20]

[20] CB, 157-160. Extensive bibliography on coronations will be found in Schramm, *A History of the English Coronation.*

CHAPTER VIII. THE KING'S MUSICK

LTHOUGH minstrels had served the predecessors of Henry VIII for centuries—Berdic, *joculator regis*, listed as a property-holder in Domesday book, was probably one of them —the King's Musick as a large establishment of many instrumentalists and a few singers continuously attendant on the sovereign, arose only in the sixteenth century. By then the king's minstrels with their guild, marshal, and authority to govern all the minstrels of the realm, and regular wages and livery, were losing their importance: most of them were wanderers who served the sovereigns at certain intervals rather than household musicians in daily attendance. Still holding their places and fees in the reign of Henry VIII, some of them fitting into the King's Musick, a few of them surviving into Elizabeth's reign, they sank into obscurity; by the end of the century they were little more than a memory, their authority over the minstrels of the realm apparently forgotten until used by the new musicians against the London company, their places, fees, and glory usurped by the King's Musick.[1]

Henry VIII, passionately fond of music as of other pursuits, and willing to spend money freely, gave the King's Musick a great start. The lord chamberlain's accounts of liveries supplied to the household for the funeral of Henry VII in 1509 list two minstrels who had been Prince Henry's, three minstrels of the chamber, four sackbuts and shawms, eight minstrels called in another account "still shalms," of whom one was marshal, and three "tabretts" who had once been minstrels to Queen Elizabeth, wife of Henry VII, besides trumpeters, who are not taken into account in this study. By 1540 Henry VIII had attracted to his court, from various parts of England and the continent,

---

[1] On the minstrels of the medieval kings see Chambers, *Mediaeval Stage*, chapter three, especially pp. 48-50; for Berdic see p. 43. Hayes, *King's Music*, 30-49, has notices of payments from 1252. On the guild, marshal, and authority over minstrels generally, see chapter one, above.

The chief sources for the history of the King's Musick are PRO manuscripts, particularly lord chamberlain's accounts, audit office declared accounts, and state papers domestic. Much material drawn from these is printed in *King's Musick*, ed. Lafontaine (KM); "Lists of the King's Musicians from the Audit Office Declared Accounts," *Musical Antiquary*, I-III (1909-1912); "Lists of the King's Musicians," *Musical Antiquary*, IV (1913); *Annalen der englischen Hofmusik* . . . (1509-1649), ed. Nagel; and CSPD.

MA is used in this chapter as an abbreviation specifically for the "Lists . . ." published in the *Musical Antiquary*, I-IV.

and particularly from Italy, about thirty-seven minstrels and musicians, and by 1547 perhaps fifty-eight. According to a list based on an account of liveries supplied to the household for Henry's funeral (forty-two persons) and supplemented from other sources (sixteen persons), there were then eight viols including Hans Hosenet, Fraunces de Venice, Marke Anthony Galyardo and Ambrose (Lupo) de Milano; seven sackbuts including Robert May, Mark Anthony Petalo and Anthony Mary (Galyardo or Galiardello); seven flutes including Guillam de Trosse, Thomas Pagington and Piero Guye (senior); two lutes, Peter van Wilder and Philip van Welder; four singers, all English apparently; nine singing-men and children under Philips (Philips was in the chapel but the others seem not to have been); a virginalist, John Heywood; three harps including William More; two instrument-makers; a songpricker (copyist); a bagpipe; a Welsh minstrel; six musicians including four or five Bassanos; eight minstrels including Hugh Woodhouse, marshal; and a rebec, John de Severnacke. A full study of how Henry gathered so many musicians and how he employed them would be an interesting history in itself.[2]

Elizabeth, less affluent and less willing to spend than her father, kept a smaller musical establishment. The exact size of the establishments of any of the sovereigns in the sixteenth and seventeenth centuries is almost impossible to determine; although lists of musicians have been extracted and published from many sources, none of them are complete, as comparison of the lists and checking with other published and unpublished official records show. The French ambassador wrote that in 1598 Elizabeth told him that she entertained at least sixty musicians, but the figure is misleading: he reported incorrectly, or she knowingly or unknowingly exaggerated, or, contrary to customary usage, called the singers of the Chapel Royal musicians and counted them to make her total. Because she may have had forty-one musicians in 1558, and thirty-eight in 1603, the mean of these figures may represent the average size of her secular musical establishment. But the figures for these years may well be representative rather of larger establishments maintained by Mary and James, or merely of establishments specially augmented for funeral and coronation ceremonies. Elizabeth had about thirty-three musicians in 1570, about twenty-four in 1580, and about

[2] Liveries 1509: KM, 2-3. Lists for 1540 and 1547: see appendix, The King's Musick, below. The "tabretts" are identified as Elizabeth's from *Privy Purse Expenses of Elizabeth of York*, ed. Nicolas, 100.

twenty-nine in 1590, and therefore probably on the average thirty musicians.[3]

James seems usually to have kept about forty musicians, his wife, Queen Anne, about fifteen, and the prince of Wales about fifteen. Counting only once musicians serving both the king and prince, and excluding the chapel and trumpeters, the total number of professional musicians at James's court seems to have been between sixty-five and seventy.[4]

Charles again augmented the King's Musick, perhaps mainly by incorporating into it the musicians who had served him before his accession. It may have included about seventy-eight men in 1625, but the names of nine of them seem to appear only in the 1625 lists. By 1635 the number had been reduced to about sixty-five, and by 1640 to about sixty-two, not counting musicians serving without pay. Sixty-five is probably about the average number of men Charles kept in the Musick. During at least part of the reign Queen Henrietta Maria also had a musical establishment, apparently of about fifteen men and two or three singing-boys.[5]

The King's Musick, then, had on the average thirty men under Elizabeth, forty under James, and sixty-five under Charles. In addition to these, under James the princes kept perhaps fifteen men, and under James and Charles, the queens another fifteen men.

Most of the musicians received £46.10.10 a year, that is, sixteen pence a day wages, four pence a day board wages, and £16.2.6 a year for livery. During Charles's reign about fourteen received forty pounds a year and livery money, a total of £56.2.6.[6]

[3] Maisse, *A Journal of all that was accomplished by Monsieur de Maisse*, ed. Harrison and Jones, 95. On the size of the Musick according to accounts see appendix, below.

[4] I have found satisfactory annual accounts for only about twenty-five of the forty in James's establishment (MA, II, 239, for example). Records of appointment, pay, etc., give the other fifteen names. See appendix, below.

[5] See appendix, below.

[6] Originally they received livery, and the value varied (Nicholas Lanier, appointed 1561 with livery at £13.6.8: MA, I, 59; see also MA, II, 176) but in 1564 thirteen musicians were paid £16.2.6 "for their apparel accustomed to be paid out of the great wardrobe, in lieu of their liveries" (MA, I, 59-60) and thereafter nearly all of the musicians seem to have been paid for livery at this rate. It is not entirely clear, however; some warrants dormant to the master of the great wardrobe specify in detail the cloth and trimmings, made up into gowns, jackets and doublets to be furnished annually before Christmas to named musicians; for example: PRO Ms. LC 5/51, pp. 15-16, 27 (1625); LC 5/50, pp. 8, 9, 143 (1604, 1619). On the other hand, a warrant of 1622 to the treasurer of the chamber added

Some had much higher pay. From 1626 Nicholas Lanier, composer, painter and favorite of Charles I, received as master of the music two hundred pounds a year, originally granted to him by Charles before his accession, in addition to livery as master, and pay at forty pounds and livery as a lutanist. His total income was thus £272.5.0 a year. Stephen Nau, who had been in royal service as violinist since 1627, and additionally as composer from 1628, was receiving at least two hundred pounds a year and livery by 1635. An earlier Nicholas Lanier, who served from 1561 till about 1615 as flutist, received thirty-eight pounds a year and £13.6.8 livery, evidently because he was a superior foreign musician whom the queen particularly wanted at the court. Certainly this was why Elizabeth granted the famous Italian composer, Alfonso Ferrabosco, a pension of one hundred pounds a year in 1569. The annual rates of pay of Queen Anne's four Frenchmen were in 1612 one hundred and fifty-five, one hundred and thirty, one hundred and fifteen and one hundred pounds apiece, and in 1620 they received, as they probably had before the queen's death, large additional payments for rent; Queen Henrietta Maria's musicians apparently received even more.[7]

Several times wages were doubled or more, in effect, by granting two or more places to one favorite. Alfonso Ferrabosco, son of the Italian composer pensioned by Queen Elizabeth, "enjoyed four places, viz., a musicians's place in general, a composer's place, a viol's place, and an instructor's place to the prince in the art of music," according to a note made after his death in 1627. His places were then granted to two of his sons. Orlando Gibbons, the composer, held two posts under James, with fee of eighty-six pounds together, in addition to his position as organist of the chapel. He was succeeded by Thomas Warwick, also of the chapel, in both places.[8]

A few unhappy musicians struggled along on less than the normal

---

to a previous fee (forty marks a year to Thomas Lupo) £16.2.6 a year "of like money" "for his apparel, or livery," to be paid quarterly (LC 5/115).

Chief sources for rates of pay are MA, KM, and notices of appointments in CSPD.

[7] For references see appendix, where further examples of large payments will be found.

For Lanier's career see *Grove*, III, 88-89, which, however, confuses him with an earlier Nicholas Lanier who served as flutist 1561-1615 (MA, I, 59-61, 119-124, 182-187, 249-253; II, 51-55, 114-118, 174-178, 235-239; KM, 19-43, 45-52), and whose son Andrew was appointed to succeed him in 1618 (KM, 52).

On Ferrabosco see *Grove*, II, 216-217.

[8] Ferrabosco: KM, 63; see also CSPD *1628-29*, 44. Gibbons: MA, III, 58, 110-114. There are several other cases, e.g. Robert Johnson, composer, two places.

pay of £46.10.10. Robert May, a sackbut about 1547-1577, received six pence a day (£9.2.6 a year) and livery, and several other musicians received eight pence, twelve pence, fourteen pence, or sixteen pence a day and livery. Before the end of Elizabeth's reign all of these rates, evidently survivals of rates set much earlier, had disappeared. Three musicians appointed about 1579, and some of their successors, received only twenty pounds a year and livery. Instead of having two places, several musicians held under Charles half a place, usually with reversion to full place. William Lanier took a place jointly with his father, Jerome, in 1626; two other men shared an appointment in 1629; and two others, John Hixon and Francis Smith, took the place of Edward Bassano in 1638 with reversion to full places when vacancies should arise. The evidence in previous chapters, showing that musicians could live on far less than the forty-six pounds normal in the King's Musick, is reinforced by the existence of these lower rates, in some cases paid for many years.[9]

All of the musicians, as servants in ordinary in daily attendance on Queen Elizabeth, had several valuable rights and privileges. According to a letter from the lord chamberlain to the lord mayor of London in 1573, they were not to be chosen churchwarden, constable, scavenger, watchman, or to other office, nor charged with subsidies and other taxes. In practice they sometimes were assessed for subsidies, as in 1559 and 1590, and sometimes exempted by royal warrant, as in 1624, 1625, and 1628. In 1640 a newly appointed musician received a certificate listing his privileges: he should not be arrested, chosen into any office, warned to attend any assizes, impanelled on juries, charged with any contributions, taxes, or payments "but in court only as other of his majesty's servants," and he should be "free from watching and warding in regard of his nightly and late attendance at court." In spite of these privileges local authorities were apt to make charges and to give duties to the musicians, who, the privy council wrote in 1638, did not refuse to pay reasonable duties, but did object to being "commonly overcharged in respect of other richer parishioners."[10]

[9] May: KM, 7, 9, 14-16, 18, 19, 21-28; MA, I, 57-61, 119-124, 182-185; *Annalen*, ed. Nagel, 22. For the other low daily rates, and the three musicians at twenty pounds, see appendix. The Laniers: CSPD *1625-26*, 559; Dorney and Parker, 1629: MA, III, 172 (apparently temporary); Hixon and Smith: KM, 102, 103. Petro Guy jr. may have received only sixteen pence a day according to PRO Mss. SP 16/301(9) and SP 16/474(2) (1635, 1640).

[10] Letter 1573: *Analytical Index to the . . . Remembrancia . . . London*, ed. Overall, 428. 1559: PRO Ms. SP 12/8(10). 1590: *Returns of Aliens . . . London*,

Most or all of them probably benefited a little from Christmas gifts and perhaps special rewards at other times. Sir Henry Sydney's "rewards" of twenty shillings to the flutes, thirty shillings to the violins and twenty shillings to the sackbuts on 1 January 1579 and Secretary Windebank's of ten shillings to the wind instruments, ten shillings to the violins, and five shillings to the chapel boys' "box," on 1 January 1637, seem to reflect long-standing tradition. The sovereigns apparently rewarded the musicians each new year's day, but these gifts may not have been profitable because of an obligation to reciprocate: a record for 1600 shows that fifteen musicians each received five ounces of gilt plate from the queen and presented in turn perfumed gloves.[11]

Musicians could be courtiers as well as servants, and some of them sued successfully for special favors, licenses, and monopolies. William Treasorer, instrument maker to Mary and Elizabeth, received licenses to export vast quantities of ashes and old worn shoes, and several of the Bassanos, licenses from 1593 to 1614 to export thousands of dickers of calf-skins. The office, for twenty years, of weigher of hay and straw brought into London, with a fee of six pence for each load of hay and three pence for straw, went to Alfonso Lanier in 1604. The valuable license, renewed from time to time, gave rise to dissension in the Lanier family and protracted trouble for the privy council. Innocent Lanier, involved in the hay business, had also a patent for taking ballast out of the Thames, and, according to his partner's complaint to the duke of Buckingham in 1625, caused no end of trouble by cutting the ropes of the ballast engines. The partner, of course, had put up the money for the project. Other patents indicate similarly the high favor musicians enjoyed at the court and how difficult it was to compensate them satisfactorily.[12]

---

ed. Kirk, ii, 427. 1624: CSPD *1623-25*, 300. 1625: CSPD *1625-26*, 566. 1628: CSPD *1628-29*, 220. 1640: KM, 104. 1638: CSPD *1638-39*, 33.

[11] Sydney: HMC *77, de l'Isle Mss.*, i, 266. Windebank: CSPD *1636-37*, 335-336. 1600: Nichols, *Progresses of Queen Elizabeth*, iii, 457-458, 465; all of the musicians were foreigners, and are listed under "Gentlemen." According to the same, iii, 24-25, fewer musicians made gifts in 1589 of "sweet water," lute strings, "sweet gloves," and so on, and received in turn five ounces of gilt plate. Only two musicians are represented in the lists of 1578 and 1579 (the same, ii, 78-79, 89, 263, 272). The lists are probably incomplete. Rewards 1530 to 1541: MA, iv, 181, 183; *Annalen*, ed. Nagel, 20-21. Warrant to deliver a gift "such as the musicians have" to a new musician, 1638: KM, 99 (see also pp. 107 and 111).

[12] William Treasorer," MA, iii (1912), 104-105. Calf-skins: CSPD *1598-1601*, 90, CSPD *1603-10*, 165. Hay: CSPD *1603-10*, 146; *1634-35*, 516-517, 564; *1635-36*, 301-302, 316-317; *1636-37*, 36; *1637*, 71, 115, 116; *1637-38*, 472. Ballast: CSPD *1623-25*, 466. Patent for soil of Thames, Alfonso Ferrabosco III: CSPD *1636-37*, 384-385. Patent for transport of lamphries, Jerome Lanier: CSPD *1639-40*, 409.

At times they needed supplementary sources of income because their salaries were in arrears. In 1616-1617 many had received only part or none of their wages, in 1635 most of them had a quarter- or half-year's wages overdue and in 1640 a whole year's. Usually they seem to have been paid fairly punctually, and on the whole to have been very well off, more prosperous than even the gentlemen of the Chapel Royal.[13]

By the end of the reign of Henry VIII the resources of the King's Musick included, besides voices, all of the instruments important in the music of western Europe in the sixteenth and seventeenth centuries, viols, sackbuts, flutes, lutes, virginals, harps, bagpipes, rebecs, and probably recorders. It is possible that some of Henry's Italian musicians played the violin, and quite probable that Queen Elizabeth's did. Under Elizabeth the instrumentation underwent little change except perhaps for the dropping out of some of the older instruments. Apparently the last record of a rebec player in the Musick is for 1558, although some of the other string players may have played the rebec for dancing, and the last musician listed as bagpiper in the Musick died in 1570.[14] A roster for this year gives a good idea of the composition of the Musick during most of Elizabeth's reign:

viols			
or	Thomas Browne		Ambrose [Lupo] de
violins:	George de Comye		Myllayne
(8)	Innocente de Comye		Joseph Lupo
	Mark Anthonye		Petro Lupo
	[Galliardello]		Fraunces de Venyce

[13] MA, III, 56-57. PRO Mss. SP 16/301(9), folio 25-25 verso and SP 16/474(2), folios 6-7 (probably 1640).

[14] Henry VIII's players: KM, 6-8; MA, IV, 55-56. Henry had at least sixty recorders (Galpin, *Old English Instruments*, 292-300); it is likely that some of his musicians listed for other instruments, or some called simply "musicians," played recorder; the first time royal musicians are listed as recorder players seems to be 1603 (KM, 45), but the four Bassanos thus listed appear on a subsidy list of 1590, instruments unspecified (*Returns of Aliens*, ed. Kirk, II, 427).

Galpin, *Old English Instruments*, 93-95, holds that the violin was in use at the English court in Henry VIII's reign; Hayes, *Musical Instruments*, II, 189-198, suggests 1561 or 1572 and says nothing about Galpin's arguments. Straeten, *History of the Violin*, I, 8, conjectures that the violin replaced the rebec for dances at court about 1588. Pulver, *Dictionary of Old English Music*, 232-233, argues for the last years of Charles I. See also note 19, below.

Rebec: John Severnake, appointed as rebec in 1518, also named as rebec many times 1528-1552 and perhaps 1553 (*Annalen*, ed. Nagel, 14; MA, IV, 180; *Annalen*, ed. Nagel, 16; MA, IV, 55, 58; *Annalen*, ed. Nagel, 24), appears as flute in 1547, 1557 and finally in 1558 (KM, 6, 8-10, 12).

Bagpipe: see next note.

flutes: (6)	Gillam Duvet James Funyarde Petro Guye [sr.]	Nicholas Lanneer Thomas Pagington Ranaldo Paradizo
sackbuts: (7)	Mark Anthony Bassany Anthonye Maria [Galliardello] Raphe Grene	Robert Howlett John Lanneer Robert Maye Edwarde Petala
lutes: (4)	Augustine Bassanye Anthonie Countie	Alfonso Ferrabosco [I] Roberte Woodwarde
virginals:	Anthonie Countie (also listed as lutanist)	
bagpipe:	Richarde Woodwarde (died 1570)	
"musicians": (6)	Anthonye Bassanye Baptista Bassanye Jasper Bassanye	John Bassanye Lodovico Bassanye Anthonie Maria [Galliardello?]

Since many of the musicians undoubtedly played more than one kind of instrument, the list, to be complete, should include recorders, shawms, hautboys, and cornetts.[15]

The instrumental resources changed little if at all under James. It is certain that the musicians now included men who played recorder, hautboy (hoboies), and cornetts. A harper, Gormock McDermott, came about 1603, perhaps the first harper in the Musick since the death in 1565 of blind old William More, long in service to the court. The harp must have become popular, for McDermott's successor in 1618, Philip Squire, received an appointment to teach a child on the Irish harp and other instruments.[16]

[15] From MA, I, 123 supplemented as follows: Mark Anthony Bassany, sackbut: KM, 23. Lutes: for Ferrabosco see *Grove*, II, 216-217; the others are listed as "musicians" in MA, I, 123; Bassano is identified as lutanist from 1599 (MA, II, 118) and recorder in 1603 (KM, 45); Countie as lutanist from 1555 (KM, 9, 10, 17-30) and virginalist in 1552 and probably 1553 (MA, IV, 58; *Annalen*, ed. Nagel, 24); Woodwarde as lutanist in 1594 (*Annalen*, ed. Nagel, 33). Bagpipe: Richard Woodward was listed as bagpiper in 1547 and 1552 (MA, IV, 55, 58; KM, 6, 8) and as "musician" thereafter, and died in 1570 (KM, 9, 10; MA, I, 58-61, 119-123). The "musicians" are so listed in MA, I, 123; Anthonie Maria was probably the person listed above as sackbut (Anthony Maria Galliardello named as sackbut player 1570 in *Annalen*, ed. Nagel, 29).

Paradizo, flute, died in 1570 and was succeeded by Gomar van Oustrewike (MA, I, 123).

[16] Recorders and "hobies": KM, 45. Anthony Bassano, Andrea, Clement and Jerome Lanier played cornett although more frequently listed for other wind instruments; see KM, 61, 75, 77, 83, and appendix, below. More's death: MA, I, 60; McDermott: *Annalen*, ed. Nagel, 35, 37; Squire: CSPD *1611-18*, 599; *Issues of the Exchequer*, ed. Devon, 234; PRO Ms. SP 16/474(2), folios 6-7.

Under Charles no new instruments were added. There was, however, new emphasis on lutes and voices when the musicians that had
served Charles as prince of Wales were taken into the Musick after
his accession. By 1635 the Musick had perhaps nineteen viols and
violins, nine hautboys and sackbuts, seven flutes, three to five recorders, eight cornetts (who also played other instruments), eighteen or
more "lutes and voices," two virginals, and a harp. Many of the men
played more than one instrument, of course. The following list, while
probably not entirely accurate or complete in itself, should give a
reasonably sound idea of the strength and resources of the King's
Musick in 1640:

Master of the Musick: Nicholas Lanier (also lute)

viols	Ambrose Beeland	Thomas Lupo	Symon Nau
and	Richard Comer	Davis Mell	Robert Parker
violins:	Richard Dorney	Leonard Mell	Nicholas Piccart
(14)	John Hopper	Estienne Nau,	Thomas Warren
	Theophilus Lupo	*composer for the violins*	John Woodington

wind
instruments:
(20)

flute: John Ferrabosco, William Gregory,
  Thomas Mell and Peter Guy.

flute and cornett: Andrea Lanier, Henry Ferrabosco,
  Francis Smith, John Hixon and Alfonso
  Ferrabosco.

flute, cornett and recorder: Anthony Bassano and
  John Adson.

cornett, recorder and sackbut: Clement Lanier.

cornett, recorder and sackbut or hautboy: Robert Baker jr.

cornett and sackbut or hautboy: Jerome Lanier.

sackbut or hautboy: Christopher Bell and John Mason.

sackbut: Henry Bassano, John Strong, Richard Blagrave
  and John Snowsman.

lutes and
voices:
(24)

lutes: John Coggeshall, John Lanier II, John Kelly, Nich-
  olas Duvall, William Lawes, Henry Lawes, Lewis
  Evans, Timothy Collins, Dietrich Steifkin (?),
  Robert Dowland and Thomas Ford.

(*theorbo*?): Anthony Robertes.

virginals: Giles Tomkins.

harp: Philip Squire.

viol: John Friend, Daniel Farrant; John Taylor (viol?).

. . . . : Thomas Day, John Drew, Edward Wormall,
  John Wilson, Robert Tomkins, Angelo Notary and
  Charles Coleman(?).

harp: John le Flelle (another listed above).
organ keeper and tuner: Edward Norgate
virginals: Thomas Warwick (another listed above). [and pupils.]
Queen's musicians: master, fourteen men and two boys.[17]

Apparently no Cheque-Book survives to suggest the outlines of the government or organization of the King's Musick. Even the title, "master of the musick," seems to appear in the records for the first time only in the second year of the reign of Charles I, when Nicholas Lanier, already a lutanist in the Musick, became master. Otherwise the records seem to leave unanswered the question of the management of the musicians. It is likely, however, that various kinds of duty tended to cause the formation of more or less permanent groups, and that management of each group fell to its senior musician if not to a designated favorite or virtuoso. Sometimes favorites and virtuosos seem to have created and guided their own groups.[18]

Information about the duties of the Musick is a little more plentiful but far from concentrated. One of its principal functions must have been the giving of concerts of many kinds. Princess Mary's privy purse accounts disclose that sackbuts regaled her at "Mr. Page's" in 1537, a type of concert enjoyed at the court for perhaps the next century and more, and not entirely unknown in the twentieth century. A quieter concert attracted the notice of the French ambassador in 1597: Queen Elizabeth "was having the spinet played to her in her chamber," his journal records. Concert-giving must have been the principal function of the group known from at least 1614 as "the consort," and later also as "the lutes and voices," or "the lutes, viols and voices." In Charles's reign it included about twenty-five musicians, among them the master of the Musick, lutanist-singers, singers, a harper, violists, and a virginalist. The band of violins, probably next in importance to "the lutes and voices," comprised in 1631 three treble, two contratenor, two tenor, three low tenor, and four "basso" violins,

---

[17] Charles's musicians as prince and king: most of the musicians listed in CSPD *1625-26*, 372 (see also p. 145) are given in the list "For the lutes and voices" of 1628 in KM, 66; some in the 1628 list played viol or other instruments.

1635: see appendix (chiefly from PRO Ms. SP 16/301(9), folio 25-25 verso and MA, III, 176.

1640: PRO Ms. SP 16/474(2), folios 6-7; MA, III, 230-231; KM, passim, for Hixon, Coleman, John Ferrabosco, Flelle, France, and Woodington. Their instruments are identified chiefly from these and earlier records in the same series.

[18] KM, 61; CSPD *1625-26*, 372; see also Pulver, *Biographical Dictionary*. See below for groups named for their leaders.

a total of fourteen, and had from 1621 its own composer (who was evidently also its master) appointed by James that it might "be the better furnished with variety and choice for our delight and pleasure in that kind. . . ." Evidence of another consort, perhaps temporary, appears in a warrant of 1635 authorizing payment of "Mons. Nicholas DuVal, for a lute provided by him, to play in the consort of Mons. le Flelle. . . ." John le Flelle, a harper, may have organized a group similar to Lanier's "lutes and voices." At least the simpler groupings, particularly those of one family of instruments, must have originated long before the Stuarts reached England; the modern practice of using large numbers of all types of instruments together in one orchestra had not yet developed: the King's Musick was not one band, not a symphony orchestra.[19]

Another type of music, not exactly a concert, came at dinner time. In 1598 a traveler reported that while Elizabeth's guard brought her dinner, "twelve trumpets and two kettle-drums made the hall ring for half-an-hour together." The report does not say that she had any music during the dinner, and by stating that she dined alone with very few attendants may indicate that ordinarily she did not. Rosters made in 1630 and 1633, showing that the musicians customarily played at dinner, probably in continuation of long-established practice, name the players on wind instruments required to attend at the king's table. For week days in 1630 the list includes two companies, to serve in alternate weeks, of four musicians each, one company of cornetts, recorders, and hautboys, the other of cornetts, flutes, and hautboys. Sundays and holidays also had alternating groups, similarly composed, but with sackbut players added, and with six in one group and seven in the other. The companies were larger in 1633, having six musicians

[19] *Privy Purse . . . Princess Mary*, ed. Madden, 30. Maisse, *A Journal*, ed. Harrison and Jones, 55.

"The Consort": warrant, 4 December 1614, to Andrea Bassano for making two sets of jacks and new stringing of his majesty's virginals for the consort, in PRO Ms. AO 1/390/52; KM, 58 (1625, list headed "The Chamber of our late . . . King James"), 66, 83, 92, 95, 111; see also 1640 list above.

The violins: KM, 53 (1621), 64, 76 (1631, an order directed to the composer of the violins, Estienne or Stephen Nau, successor to Thomas Lupo). The PRO Ms. (LC 5/115) abstracted in KM, 53, clearly says "violins"; in the sixteenth century and perhaps still in 1621 writers sometimes meant "viols" when they wrote "violins," of course. Note Sachs, *History of Musical Instruments*, 358: "A violin orchestra . . . had first been formed to accompany the *ballets de cour* [of France] in the middle of the sixteenth century. . . ." The English masque was reaching its height towards 1615.

Le Flelle: KM, 91, 70.

in each on ordinary days, and being combined and adding three more musicians, a total of fifteen, on special days. Andrea Lanier may have been immediately responsible for them, as warrants for payments to him in 1630 and 1633 suggest; the first warrant authorizes payment for three tenor and three treble cornetts, and the second warrant, which names, besides Andrea Lanier, five of the men also named on the dinner lists, payment for one tenor and five treble cornetts and a set of books for them. The master of the Musick, although not a member of these groups, was ultimately responsible for them; appended to the 1633 list is an order that any of the musicians unable to be present must provide substitutes, and that in case of neglect of the order, the master should "complain or be liable to the like punishment himself as they by their negligence may incur." These groups were also to perform on "play nights." They probably played before and between the acts when the children of the Chapel Royal or other players acted at court, and may well have been the inspiration for similar entertainment in the so-called private theatres in London at the end of the sixteenth century and early in the seventeenth. On at least one occasion music seems to have been .composed for a new play, *The Royal Slave*, "lately acted at Hampton court"; the costs of the production, for which payment was authorized in 1637, included "the charge of dancers and composers of music . . . viz., . . . to Estienne Nau [composer for the king's violins] and Sebastian la Pierre for themselves and twelve dancers, fifty-four pounds." *The Royal Slave* seems to be the play by Cartwright, produced by Archbishop Laud with scenery by Inigo Jones and music by Henry Lawes (of the Chapel Royal), for the entertainment of Charles at Christ Church, Oxford, in 1636; Charles must have enjoyed the play thoroughly if he had it presented again at Hampton court with new sets, music, and dances.[20]

Queen Elizabeth took a keen interest in dancing. In 1589 a courtier wrote that Elizabeth "is so well as I assure you six or seven galliards in a morning, besides music and singing, is her ordinary exercise." The French ambassador recorded that she told him that "in her youth she danced very well, and composed measures and music, and had played them herself and danced them." He noted also that then, Jan-

[20] 1598: Hentzner's *Travels*, in *England as Seen by Foreigners*, ed. Rye, 106-107.
1630: KM, 72; this list mentions only, and incidentally, "play nights," but the groups were almost the same as those of 1633, in KM, 87-88, which were to wait in the chapel and at the king's table. Warrants for cornetts: KM, 75, 83.
Play at Hampton court: CSPD *1636-37*, 563; the Oxford *Royal Slave*: Trevor-Roper, *Laud*, 293.

uary 1598, "She takes such pleasure in it that when her maids dance she follows the cadence with her head, hand and foot. She rebukes them if they do not dance to her liking, and without doubt she is a mistress of the art, having learnt in the Italian manner to dance high." Two years later it was reported that during the Christmas festivities she came out into "the presence" almost every night "to see the ladies dance the old and new country dances, with the taber and pipe." The last two witnesses intimate that she had about given up dancing for herself, but apparently not altogether: a secret agent in London reported to the Spanish in 1599 that "on the day of Epiphany the queen held a great feast, in which the head of the Church of England and Ireland was to be seen in her old age dancing three or four galliards." For galliards taber and pipe, quite fitting for country dances, would hardly have done; a consort of the queen's musicians must have set the measure for her. James and Anne, Charles and Henrietta Maria, were not less fond of dancing.[21]

Some of the musicians instructed the princes and princesses in music. This was not an ordinary duty which might fall to any musician from time to time; some musicians had appointments only as instructors, apparently, while others had appointments as instructors in addition to their regular places as musicians. Prince Henry seems to have had three teachers of music, and Prince Charles another, early in the seventeenth century.[22]

In some instances musicians kept and trained boys for the royal service. From 1618 one musician was paid to teach a boy on the "Irish harp" and other instruments, from at least 1625 another musician was paid to teach two boys flute and cornett, and still another musician to teach singing to two boys. A warrant, much better reading than most, issued at Westminster in 1626, almost brings these boys to life: "We will and command you that at the feast day of St. John Baptist next coming you deliver or cause to be delivered to our well beloved servant Andrea Lanier, one of our musicians, these parcels hereafter following for the summer liveries of two boys which we appointed to his custodie and keeping, for the training up, and to be made fit for

[21] 1589: Nichols, *Progresses . . . Elizabeth*, III, 32, from Lodge, *Illustrations of British History* (1st ed., 1791), II, 411. 1598: Maisse, *A Journal*, ed. Harrison and Jones, 95. 1600: HMC 77, *de l'Isle Mss.*, ii, 427. 1599: *Calendar of Letters and State Papers . . . Simancas*, IV, 650 (not in quotation marks); my attention was drawn to this by Pattison, *Music and Poetry in the English Renaissance*, 16.

[22] See *Issues of the Exchequer*, ed. Devon, 35, 142; KM, 49, 50; Hardy, *Syllabus*, II, 834; HMC 3, *de la Warr Mss.*, 310.

our service, in the knowledge of the flutes and cornetts (that is to say) to each of them severally nine yards of broad cloth for a cloak jerkin and breeches at thirteen shillings four pence the yard; to each of them, two yards and a half of bayes [baize] to line their said cloaks at four shillings the yard; ten dozen of silk lace at three shillings four pence the dozen for each of them; to each a quarter of a yard of velvet for a cape at six shillings. Five yards of fustian for doublets for them at four shillings the yard; twelve dozen of silk buttons for them at six pence the dozen; two pair of worsted stockings at ten shillings the pair to each of them; one pair of silk garters to each of them price six shillings; one hat with a band price ten shillings to each; and for shirts, bands, and cuffs for one half year, six pounds for them both. And for the making of the said cloak, jerkin, doublet, and breeches, and all small furnitures, forty shillings. And further our pleasure and command is that you deliver or cause to be delivered to the said Andrea Lanier for the said two boys at the feast of St. Andrew the Apostle next coming, after the date hereof the like parcels for their winter liveries, and so forth every half year yearly. . . ." Several of these boys became royal musicians.[23]

Some of the musicians assisted in divine service in the Chapel Royal. At the baptizing of Princess Mary in 1605 the chorus of one of the anthems "was filled with the help of musical instruments," and after the banquet which followed the ceremonies, "the chapel and the musicians joined together, making excellent harmony with full anthems. . . ." Later in the year at Queen Anne's churching anthems were sung "with organ, cornetts, sackbut, and other excellent instruments of music." Similarly, after the death of Prince Henry in 1612, when his body was brought into the king's chapel, the gentlemen and children sang "several anthems to the organs and other wind-instruments." When the musicians started to play regularly in the chapel is unknown, but it was probably long before 1633, the year of the order that mentions "waiting in the chapel" as one of the duties of the groups of wind instrumentalists assigned to perform at the king's table. A warrant for surplices indicates that "waiting" meant participation in the services. Several prominent composers, members of the

[23] Harp: *Issues of the Exchequer*, ed. Devon, 234 (pupil admitted to service: KM, 86; MA, III, 174).

Flute and cornett: KM, 61, 67, 74, 75, 77, 78, 81 (called singing-boys: 82), 86, 88, 93, 98, 101 (pupils admitted to service: 102), 104 (called singing-boys: 106).

Singing: KM, 61, 64, 73, 74, 76-78, 81, 84, 86, 98, 101, 106.

Warrant: PRO Ms. LC 5/51, p. 37.

chapel, wrote music which called for the services of the instrumentalists. William Byrd composed an anthem, published in 1611, in which
viols accompany the solo passages, and Orlando Gibbons wrote verse
anthems with organ or string accompaniments for the solos. In an
anthem book of the chapel, 1635, number 119 was "An anthem with
verses for cornetts and sagbuts" by William Lawes. Ordinarily a verse
anthem has solo voice passages with accompaniment, usually on the
organ; perhaps in this case Lawes wrote an instrumental interlude
for cornetts and sackbuts, instead of a vocal solo, and thus anticipated the anthems with string interludes which became the style after
the Restoration.[24]

The musicians heightened the majesty of many other great cere-
monials. During the state banquet at Whitehall palace following the
investiture of Henry as prince of Wales in 1610 "the hall resounded
with all kinds of exquisite music." The recipients of rewards when
Charles was made prince of Wales in 1616 included twenty-nine musicians in four companies (twelve pounds), as well as sixteen trumpeters (sixteen pounds) and four drummers (five pounds). Musicians
and gentlemen of the Chapel Royal journeyed to Canterbury in 1625
to help King Charles welcome Queen Henrietta Maria to England.
Annually, from 1627 at least, members of the band of violins played at
Windsor during the week-long meeting of the Knights of the Garter;
from 1627 to 1633 twelve went each year, in 1637, thirteen, and in 1638,
fifteen, each violinist receiving a reward of five shillings.[25]

Tilts and masques, the most brilliant of the royal entertainments,
gave the Musick perhaps its greatest opportunities to display its virtuosity. Summary descriptions of one tilt and one masque, standing here
as representatives of them all, will give a hint of the rich variety of
music enjoyed by the court.[26]

[24] Baptism 1605: CB, 167-169. Churching: Nichols, *Progresses . . . King James*, I,
514. Funeral 1612: Birch, *Life of Henry Prince of Wales*, 361. Order 1633: KM,
87-88 (the abstract quoted here is not in quotation marks in KM). Surplices 1634:
KM, 90. Anthems by Byrd and Gibbons: see Fellowes, "Anthems," *Grove*. Lawes:
"The Chapel Royal Anthem Book of 1635," MA, II (1911), 108-113.
[25] 1610: Birch, *Life of Henry*, 195. 1616: *Issues of the Exchequer*, ed. Devon,
193-194. 1625: CSPD *1625-26*, 22 (Secretary Conway to lord treasurer. For two
hundred and sixty pounds for the musicians who are to go into Kent for the reception of the queen); CB, 11. Garter: KM, 89, 99, 103-104.
[26] On tilts and masques see for example: Reyher, *Les Masques Anglais*; Steele,
Plays and Masques at Court; Sullivan, *Court Masques of James I*; Welsford, *The
Court Masque*; Dent, *Foundations of English Opera*; Chambers, *Elizabethan
Stage*; Evans, *Ben Jonson and Elizabethan Music*; and other works listed in
Nicoll, *Stuart Masques*, 22, note 2.

In about 1570 Sir Henry Lee established an annual tilt at court in honor of Queen Elizabeth's accession, with himself as her champion. By 1590 Lee, forty-seven years old, thought that it was time for him to give up tilting, and at a great ceremony, turned his place over to George Clifford, earl of Cumberland. After doing their service at arms, Lee and Cumberland prepared to present themselves to the queen, who was watching from a gallery window overlooking the tilt yard in Westminster. As they approached her, a pavilion appeared and music sounded, "so sweet and secret, as every one thereat greatly marvelled," to which verses were "sung by M. *Hales* her majesty's servant, a gentleman in that art excellent, and for his voice both commendable and admirable." After the arming of Cumberland and other ceremonies, the spectacle ended. Robert Hales, a lutanist, served in the Musick from 1583 to 1615.[27]

The Stuart masques, fantastically elaborate spectacles, required the cooperation of England's greatest talents in poetry, music, scenic design, and dancing, as well as prodigal spending of borrowed money. Among the items on a warrant for one masque are twenty pounds "To Master Johnson, for making the dances," five pounds "To Thomas Lupo, for setting them to the violins," forty pounds to "Master Giles, for three dances," thirty-two pounds for the "company of violins," ten pounds to "Thomas Lupo, the elder, Alexander Chisan, and Rowland Rubidge, violins" (these, like the others named, members of the royal establishment), thirty-two pounds to "ten singers, and five players on the lute, provided by Alphonso [Ferrabosco?]," three pounds for two cornetts, forty pounds for "twenty lutes, provided by Master Johnson for the prince's dance," and twenty-one pounds for "sixteen other instruments, for the satyrs and fairies"; and on a warrant for another masque, £66.13.4 to Doctor "Capian" or Campion, fifty pounds to Inigo Jones, about two hundred pounds to several other designated musicians including John Coperario, Robert Johnson, and Thomas Lupo, forty-two pounds to forty-two musicians not named, eleven pounds to "two that played to the antic mask," and ten pounds to "ten of the king's violins." Thomas Campion, lutanist, singer, composer, poet, and doctor of physic, wrote a particularly full account of one of his masques, *The Description of a Maske, presented before the kinges majestie at Whitehall, on Twelfth Night last, in honour of Lord*

[27] Chambers, *Sir Henry Lee*, 38, 135-140, quoting Segar, *Honor, Military and Civil*, iii, ch. 54. Hales: MA, I, 251; III, 54, 55; Chambers, *Lee*, 142, says Hales "is traceable as a royal lutanist from 1568 to 1603," but gives no references.

Hayes, and his bride, daughter and heire to the honourable the Lord Dennye, their marriage having been the same day at court solemnized (1607). In the hall, toward the upper part where the king sat, were scaffolds and seats, and a dancing place. On one side sat a consort of ten musicians, who played large and medium sized lutes, a bandora, a double sackbut, two "treble violins" and a harpsichord; and on the other side a consort of nine violins and three lutes. Back farther (the consorts marked the points of a triangle) were "six chapel voices" and six cornetts; this consort was "in a place raised higher in respect of the piercing sound" of the cornetts. In another portion of the setting many trees shadowed "those that played on the hautboys [Hoboyes] at the king's entrance into the hall." After giving these preliminaries Campion went on to describe the alternation of the various consorts, the songs, dialogues, and dances. One "*Chorus* was in the manner of an echo, seconded by the cornetts, then by the consort of ten [lutes, bandora, sackbut, violins and harpsichord], then by the consort of twelve [nine violins and three lutes], and by a double *chorus* of voices standing on either side, the one against the other bearing five voices apiece, and sometime every chorus was heard severally, sometime mixt, but in the end altogether: which kind of harmony so distinguished by the place, and by the several nature of instruments, and changeable conveyance of the song, and performed by so many excellent masters, as were actors in that music; (their number in all amounting to forty-two voices and instruments) could not but yield great satisfaction to the hearers." Somewhat later, during a procession, "the six cornetts, and six chapel voices sung a solemn motet of six parts," after which "the violins began the third new dance. . . ." Two bass and two treble voices then sang "a dialogue," which was followed by "lighter dances." Prompted by "Night's" reminder that the bride must be growing impatient, the violins took up the last dance, the company sang a final chorus "with several echoes of music, and voices," and the dancers unmasked.[28]

Tilts and masques, occasion for music yielding such "great satisfaction to the hearers," must have seemed to the court justification enough for the maintenance of the King's Musick.

[28] Warrant 1611: *Issues of the Exchequer*, ed. Devon, 136-137. Warrant 1613: *Issues*, 164-165. Campion, *Description* (1607).

CONCLUSION

THE records give several signs that even the Chapel Royal and the King's Musick had to contend with the careless, the lazy, the dissolute, and the inept: in the case of the Chapel Royal, repeated attempts to require examination before appointment, a rule requiring a year's probationary service before permanent appointment, and schedules of fines for lateness and absences; and in the case of the King's Musick, the admonition concerning absences of musicians required to play for the king's dinner. But for once it would seem to be wrong to interpret such evidence as signs of low standards and lax discipline: excellence sought perfection. Their excellence and preeminence appear when the roll of the greater English composers is exhibited: Tallis, Byrd, Morley, Bull, Dowland, Gibbons, and Lawes, are among the many who became famous at the English court. In part the preeminence of the Chapel Royal and the King's Musick can be attributed to their great size, to the virtuosity of many of their members, to the completeness of their instrumental resources, and to the keen interest taken in them by the sovereigns.[1]

The royal musicians were a very select group. The immediate provenance of about seventy of the gentlemen appointed to the chapel between 1563 and 1640 is readily ascertainable. About half came from places in and near London: at least three, probably many more, graduated directly from choristers' places in the Chapel Royal; eight came from St. George's chapel, Windsor; eleven from Westminster abbey; and twelve from St. Paul's. Originally some of these had come from provincial posts. The other half came directly to the chapel from all over England:

Cambridge	2	Exeter	5	Norwich	1
Canterbury	3	Gloucester	1	Salisbury	2
Chester	1	Hereford	3	Wells	2
Chichester	1	Lichfield	6	Winchester	2
Durham	1	(5, 1567-1580)		Worcester	1
		Lincoln	3		

The records are less helpful in the case of the King's Musick, and except in the cases of a few musicians from the band of waits of London, and sons or pupils of members of the King's Musick, indicate

---

[1] CB gives many indications of continuing efforts to raise and maintain standards; see especially pp. 8-10, 70, 80.

the origins only of the foreign musicians. During Elizabeth's reign between half and two-thirds of the men in the King's Musick were immigrants. In 1590, for example, nineteen of the twenty-nine musicians were aliens, mostly members of the Bassano, Lupo, Lanier, Comy, and Galliardello families. Under James and Charles a larger proportion were English born, but the sons and grandsons of immigrants—Bassanos, Ferraboscos, and Laniers—continued predominant.[2]

The court attracted musicians from all over England because, in the first place, of the excellent pay, far better than that of English cathedral musicians and of waits, even of the city of London. Henry VIII and Elizabeth offered special pay to certain foreigners, who came and probably pulled others in their wake, and Anne and Henrietta Maria brought musicians with them. Some of the foreigners fled from the continent because of difficulties over religion, and a few came originally as servants of noblemen.[3]

Good pay counted for much, but with it the musicians needed, and had, what was at least as important, a feeling of security. Their immunity from the vagrancy laws, their freedom from local restrictions and duties, the permanence of their positions, along with their superior pay, enabled them to be at their ease, to devote themselves to the improvement of their talent, whether playing cornett or writing madrigals. Bach estimated the importance of this feeling in about 1730: "let anyone visit Dresden and observe how the royal musicians there are paid. They have no anxiety regarding their livelihood, and consequently are relieved of *chagrin*; each man is able to cultivate his own instrument and to make himself a competent and agreeable performer on it."[4]

The court establishment excelled also because of the incentive its musicians had. The resources available to the royal composers included not only excellent singers and fine instrumentalists on all instruments, but the best instruments that could be had: foreign and English instrument makers worked at court, and the best Antwerp virginals, Cremona violins, and other instruments were imported. The many occasions at court, more numerous than in any other establishment in

[2] Chapel: compare names in CB and biographical reference works. King's Musick 1590: aliens identified in *Returns of Aliens*, ed. Kirk, II, 427.

[3] See, for example: *Privy Purse . . . Henry the Eighth*, ed. Nicolas, 157, 165, 170, 173, 174; *Returns of Aliens*, ed. Kirk, II, 126 (Gomer) and 127 (Markantonie Galliardell, Esquire); Arkwright, "Notes on the Ferrabosco Family," MA, III (1912), 220-228, IV (1913), 42-44; and "Damon," *Grove*.

[4] Terry, *Bach: A Biography*, 203.

England, requiring composition and performance, stimulated composers and performers alike. The number and diversity of the performers and composers promoted excellence: by association, competition, and cooperation, they created for themselves a stimulating environment. They worked under the eyes, or for the ears, of accomplished amateur musicians; Henry VIII, Mary, Elizabeth, Prince Henry, Charles, all played more than one instrument, and several of them composed. Some of the courtiers too were amateur musicians, and probably even more of them could offer helpful criticism. The more or less steady influx of foreign musicians, the occasional continental travels of a few of the English musicians, the importation of foreign scores, introduced new ideas. The royal musicians necessarily made full use of their abilities.[5]

They were foremost, too, in setting the styles and standards for the other musicians of England. The developments in instrumentation and in composition, introduced partly by the foreigners attracted to the court, and partly by Englishmen, including Walter Porter, a pupil of Monteverdi, and Giovanni Coperario (John Cooper), who traveled and studied abroad, were emulated in the provinces. Organists of provincial cathedrals, obtaining copies of the music written for the Chapel Royal, could develop their own compositions in the patterns conceived there; the court, rather than the provincial cathedrals, gave England most of the great ecclesiastical music it inherits from Tudor and Stuart times. Even the manner of performance was copied, especially when the sovereign was expected. In 1613 when James visited Salisbury cathedral the chapter sent for lay clerks and choristers from Winchester, Wells, Windsor, and London in order to make the cathedral services conform to the standard the king knew at court.[6]

In short, the Chapel Royal and the King's Musick together held a position in England corresponding to that of a great academy. Here the best English singers, players, and composers worked in security

---

[5] Instruments: see, for example, "William Treasorer," MA, III (1912), 103-106; records relating to Andrea Bassano in *Returns of Aliens*, ed. Kirk, II, 427; *Annalen*, ed. Nagel, 32, 33; MA, II, 175-178, 238-240, III, 54-58, 110-115; James, *Early Keyboard Instruments*, especially from p. 99; KM, 71, 83, 89, 92, 93, 98, 99 (Cremona violin).

On the sovereigns as composers see Hayes, *King's Music*, 20-25, 52-64.

[6] "Walter Porter," *Grove*. "John Cooper," *Grove*. "Coperario," Pulver, *Biographical Dictionary*.

Provincial organists: see, for example, Dickson, *A Catalogue of Ancient Choral Services and Anthems . . . of Ely*.

Salisbury: Robertson, *Sarum Close*, 160-161.

with the best foreign musicians whom the monarchs could attract. They had every material resource and great men in other arts to collaborate with them. They trained boys for their own service and set standards and indicated new ways for the musicians of the whole country. Their work was encouraged and pushed to high levels by the informed criticism of sovereign and courtier and the challenge of new men from the provinces and abroad.

The importance of the royal establishment should not be exaggerated. It depended on the rest of England, and on the continent, for many men and ideas. Music was a very important form of entertainment at court, but not the only form. It appears in perspective in Sir John Throckmorton's description of the excitement at court during the visit of the king of Denmark in 1614: "The exercises for the time have been hunting, running at the ring, excellent music, great cheer, and sound drinking, and on the last of July at night, for a parting blow, the king of Denmark did exhibit certain curious and excellent fireworks. . . ." The court had work to do, too.[7]

There was some political and diplomatic significance to the maintenance of the Chapel and the King's Musick, but probably very little. They were conspicuous signs of wealth and therefore of power, and so may have contributed something, indirectly, toward the strengthening of England's position in European affairs. They did, of course, help in the entertainment of foreign envoys and visiting princes. In the internal political situation their significance may have been a little greater. Although their cost, possibly three thousand pounds a year during Elizabeth's reign and seven thousand a year under James and Charles, was relatively small, the lavishness of the musical establishment perhaps symbolized the improvidence of sovereigns unable to live of their own. Prudent merchants may have felt about the Chapel and Musick as it was reported the "commonalty" felt about a masque in 1609: they "do somewhat murmur at such vain expenses and think that that money worth bestowed other ways might have been conferred upon better use. . . ."[8]

Without the Chapel Royal and the King's Musick, Elizabeth, James, and Charles could not have satisfied as fully their taste for music and for the display of dignity and power; with their help they enjoyed courts in harmony with renaissance ideals.

---

[7] HMC 75, *Downshire Mss.*, iv, 484.
[8] 1609: W. ffarington, quoted in Chambers, *Elizabethan Stage*, I, 211, from Chetham Society, *Publications*, xxxix, 151.

PART FIVE

AMATEURS OF MUSIC

CHAPTER IX. "IT ONLY SERVETH
FOR RECREATION"

E VERY domestic hearth was the scene of musical performance of a very high standard." "The art of singing [was] cultivated with equal zeal and discernment, in every grade of social rank." Such generalizations, familiar to nearly everyone who has read studies of Elizabethan music and society, conjure up a picture so charming and so beloved that it will not disappear soon, yet so patently unreal that the wonder is that only recently have scholars begun to correct it. Something approaching reality appears when account is taken of the dependence of musical accomplishment on aptitude, interest, and the availability of time, money, and teachers.[1]

The illiteracy indicated by the need for lining out psalms shows clearly that a large part of the population of England could hardly have acquired the accomplishments required by the madrigals of Wilbye or the ayres of Dowland. Agricultural and other laborers and artisans, while no doubt as capable of learning music as any other members of society, in past ages have seldom had time to devote to serious study of music, and seldom money to pay music teachers or to buy expensive instruments or books. It is doubtful that in Elizabethan times many of them even wanted to learn how to sing madrigals or to play the finer music for virginals, lute, and viol. Many of them must never have heard madrigals, and those who had may often have found the more elaborate polyphonic flights as far beyond their comprehension as most people today find the later works of Schoenberg; those who saw and heard an expert performer on the virginals probably admired more his technical skill than the music, found it entertaining in the same way that they found a rope-walker entertaining, and as likely an accomplishment for themselves as preaching in York minster. Lacking time and money and usually opportunity to acquire a taste for the more highly developed music of their day, the mass of the people of England in the reigns of Elizabeth and the

[1] Since nearly every class of documents and nearly every kind of literature of the period provide materials for the subject of this chapter, brief and useful classification of the sources is almost impossible, as the following footnotes should make clear.

For an example of the more realistic approach used by some scholars recently, see Westrup, "Domestic music under the Stuarts," *Proc. Mus. Assoc.*, 68th session (1942), 19-54.

first Stuarts could not have performed and perhaps not even have appreciated this music.

That they did sing and, to a lesser extent, play music, is certain. Every people seems always to have folk music, which tends to flourish most where people are most dependent on themselves for entertainment, which survives and grows by use or personal contact rather than by formal record and instruction, and which costs little or nothing but affection and happily spent·time.

Most of the music performed by the poorer people must have been vocal, but some was instrumental; the more primitive instruments, such as pipes, bagpipes, drums (tabers), prototypes of the violin, and others, which could be made cheaply and easily at home or by local craftsmen, could be learned without formal instruction and played by ear for solitary amusement in the pastoral tradition, for entertainment in the cottage, and at village festivities. Some of the more skilful of the performers tended to become semi-professional musicians of the kind mentioned in chapter five on the independent musicians, who were called on to play for neighboring communities, and who were tempted sometimes by the pennies their music brought to forsake their fields or village in pursuit of the apparently carefree life of the minstrel. Town boys had perhaps more opportunity than countrymen to learn some of the more fashionable instruments. Most apprentices in non-musical occupations, however, could hardly have had the money to buy good instruments or to pay teachers, and professional musicians preferred not to teach persons who might become their competitors. Masters, moreover, usually tried to keep their apprentices from idle or mischievous ways, among which the learning and practice of music was sometimes counted. In 1554 it was complained that whereas formerly "in the education and bringing up of apprentices" in Newcastle, reverence, obedience, and temperance were taught to apprentices, now "lewd liberty, instead of the former virtuous life, hath of late taken place in apprentices, and chiefly of those as are serving in this worshipful fellowship of merchants, . . . that regardeth little the good lessons of us their masters (for never among apprentices, and chiefly of this said fellowship, hath been more abused and inconvenient behavior than is of them at this day frequented, for what dicing, carding, and mumming, what tippling, dancing, and brazing [brasenge] of harlots; what guarded coats, jagged hose, lined with silk, and cut shoes; what use of gitterns by night; what wearing of beards, what daggers is by them worn cross overthwart their backs, that these their doings are more comely and decent for raging ruffians than seemly for honest apprentices). . . ." Some of the same troubles still bothered the Newcastle Merchants Adventurers half a century later, for in 1603 one of their rules forbade their brothers to permit their apprentices to "dance, dice, card, mum, or use any music either by night or day in the streets." Merchant adventurers were apt to be wealthier than the average master, and their apprentices to come from well-off families which perhaps gave them more money than was good for them: while not exceptional in their predisposition to disorderly conduct, these apprentices can hardly have been typical if they had money for dicing, tippling, silk-lined hose, and gittern-playing. Nor is it likely that many of the poorer townsmen patronized the kind of barbershops, if they patronized any at all, where musical instruments were likely to be hanging for every man to play (and so to give poets a vivid figure of speech to belabor). Even a gentleman would hesitate to play in a barbershop: good manners would not permit him to boast of his accomplishment by playing for the common public. Those barbers who had instruments may have had them chiefly to help themselves pass the time while waiting for custom, and perhaps allowed their less bashful patrons to play them, or to pick out a tune with one finger. For most of the poor, opportunity to perform music was probably confined to folk song, hymns and psalms; fewer played primitive instruments; and perhaps a very few, some of the newer instruments.[2]

Their opportunities to hear music extended beyond what each family could provide for itself, of course. Sooner or later most people must have visited some town where they could hear waits and perhaps a choir and organ. More frequently, particularly before the laws against vagabondage became effective, they could hear wandering minstrels who, more often than not, must have performed folk music. Some of the music least familiar to them must have been heard at the gates, in the courtyards, and even inside the houses of the local magnates, performed by wanderers and sometimes by a domestic ensemble of one or two professional musicians and members of the family and household staff: all the people of the countryside were likely to gather when an important local family celebrated some regular holiday or extraordinary event. These festivities too probably became rarer as the fashion of hospitality waned.

[2] *Extracts from the Records of the Merchant Adventurers of Newcastle-upon-Tyne*, ed. Dendy, I, 20-21, 22.

At the traditional communal festivals such as May games and church ales, folk music flourished in its native soil. Extracts from the accounts of the churchwardens of Melton Mowbray, Leicestershire, hint at their character:

"1563. This is the reckoning and account of me Robt Odam Junior, being chosen and nominated the Lord of Melton at Whitson day A° 1563 to gather the devotion of the town and country which is to be bestowed for the repairing and mending the highways.

Charge [includes]:—
Imprimis received of Hawe [Holy] Thursday at the choosing of the
    Lord and Lady   18s.10d.
Item at the gathering of the malt and wheat [for the Whitsun ales] 18s.

. . . .

    Discharge [includes]:—
Item to the piper of hawe Thursday   12d.
Item for spice for the cakes   21d.
Item for nails to the lord's hall   2d."

Philip Stubbes, violently against such goings-on, described them with some animosity but otherwise probably with reasonable accuracy, in the discourse on "The Lord of Misrule" in his *Anatomie of Abuses*, 1583: "The name, indeed, is odious. . . . First, all the wild-heads of the parish, conventing together, choose them a grand-captain . . . and him they crown with great solemnity. . . . This king anointed chooseth forth twenty, forty, threescore or a hundred lusty guts [who] bedeck themselves with scarfs, ribbons and laces . . . they tie about either leg twenty or forty bells. . . . Thus all things set in order, then they have they their hobby-horses, dragons and other antiques, together with their bawdy pipers and thundering drummers to strike up the devil's dance withal. Then, march these heathen company towards the church and church-yard, their pipers piping, their drummers thundering, their stumps dancing, their bells jingling, their handkerchiefs swinging about their heads like madmen, their hobby-horses and other monsters skirmishing amongst the route: and in this sort they go to the church (I say) and into the church (though the minister be at prayer or preaching), dancing and swinging their handkerchiefs, over their heads in the church, like devils incarnate, with such a confused noise, that no man can hear his own voice. . . . Then, after this, about the church they go again and again, and so forth into the churchyard, where they have commonly their summerhalls, their bowers, arbors, and banquetting houses set up, wherein they feast, banquet and dance all that day and (peradventure) all the night too. . . ." A more temperate witness, Archbishop Grindal, bears out part of Stubbes's testimony in his forty-fourth injunction for the province of York, 1571: "*Item*, that the minister and churchwardens shall not suffer any Lords of Misrule or summer lords or ladies, or any disguised persons or others in Christmas or at May games, or any minstrels, morrice-dancers, or others, at rush bearings, or at any other times, to come unreverently into any church, or chapel, or churchyard, and there dance or play any unseemly parts, with scoffs, jests, wanton gestures, or ribald talk, namely in the time of divine service or of any sermon."[3]

Repeated orders and presentments show that in spite of the efforts of many civil and ecclesiastical authorities such games continued, although perhaps less widely and frequently. The very fact that the games and many other common forms of amusement became involved in high problems of state, which need not be considered here, may have encouraged rather than discouraged their survival. An order made at quarter sessions in Devonshire in July 1595 suggests reasons both why magistrates attempted to impose restraints and why active opposition appeared; the justices declared that all "Church or parish ales, revels, May-games, plays, and such other unlawful assemblies of the people of sundry parishes unto one parish on the *Sabbath day* and other times, is a special cause that many disorders, contempts of law, and other enormities, are there perpetrated and committed, to the great profanation of the Lord's 'Saboth,' the dishonor of Almighty God, increase of bastardy and of dissolute life, and of very many other mischiefs and inconveniences, to the great hurt of the commonwealth." The justices therefore ordered that these assemblies be abolished on the Sabbath, that no drink be "used, kept, or uttered" on Sundays at any time nor on any holiday or festival day during divine

---

[3] Melton Mobray: *Notices Illustrative . . . Leicester*, ed. Kelly, 65-67.

Stubbes, *Anatomie of Abuses*, ed. J.P.C., 141-143.

Grindal: *Visitation Articles*, ed. Frere, iii, 291. For similar items see *Elizabethan Episcopal Administration*, ed. Kennedy, ii, 125 (archdeaconry of Middlesex, 1582) and iii, 166 (Coventry and Lichfield, 1584).

Webb, *English Local Government*, vii, 11-12, gives a good description of parish ales, and further references. A description of summer lords ("vulgariter vocatum Somergame") c. 1469 is printed in a footnote in *Tudor Parish Documents of the Diocese of York*, ed. Purvis, 160-161. Machyn's *Diary* gives vivid sketches of May games c. 1555; because the games he saw were in and near London and the court, they were more elaborate than most games can have been, and had more music, including waits and viols. Extracts from St. Mary's parish, Reading, wardens' books c. 1555, given in Man, *Reading*, 308, are illuminating also.

service, nor at night time at all, and that there should be no "Minstrelsy of any sort, dancing, or such wanton dalliances" allowed at the May and other games. In January 1599 the justices ordered the complete suppression of parish and church ales, and revels.[4]

Division of opinion is again illustrated by a case in Somerset sessions in 1607, when articles were presented against two church wardens of Yeovil for participating in disorders at their church ale; it was alleged that it was a usual thing on the Sabbath to have minstrelsy and dancing and "carrying men upon a cavell stafe," and that the accused wardens were themselves willingly "so carried to the church." At the Somerset sessions held at Wells in January 1608 the justices ordered the suppression throughout the county from then on of "all bull baitings, bear baitings, church ales, clerk ales, woodwards-ales, briales and all kinds of such like ales whatsoever"; the order was repeated in 1624. Worcestershire records for 1616 and 1617 likewise show strong feelings. A petition to the justices declares that the youths of Longdon in summer dance every Sunday, and that in one case during the previous year, "the dancing again taking place in Longdon, the petitioner being then constable there, endeavored peaceably to take the minstrel there playing and to punish him on the statute against rogues" but the crowd so terrified the constable that he fled. A letter written from Coventry in November 1618 reports that during evening prayer at Allbriton or Allerton, Staffordshire, a company with drums and guns entered the churchyard, shot off the guns, and cried, "Come out, ye Puritans, come out" and so on; and that at Lea Marston, near there, parishioners, "coming into the church in their fools' coats, . . . sat awhile ridiculously, and ere the second lesson was read, impatient of delay, they rose up and went into the churchyard, where, and at an alehouse [close] by, they tabred and danced the whole sermon time. . . ."[5]

Such incidents probably bear about the same relationship to the ordinary amusements of the country people as caricatures to the cari-

[4] Hamilton, *Quarter Sessions from Queen Elizabeth to Queen Anne . . . Devon,* 28-29.

[5] *Quarter Session Records for the County of Somerset,* ed. Harbin, I, 5-6, 7, 344. HMC 55, *Various* i, *County of Worcester Mss.,* 295. HMC 45, *Buccleuch Mss.,* iii, 213-214.

See also *Hertford County Records . . . 1581 to 1698,* ed. Hardy, I, 13 and *Liverpool Town Books,* ed. Twemlow, II, 753.

The story of the music connected with community festivities is closely bound up with the history of puritanism. See the bibiographies by Read and Davies for studies on puritanism, sabbatarianism, the Book of Sports, and so on.

catured. Where feelings were less strong, traditions, with some modification, must have quietly prevailed. The success of the vagrancy laws probably decreased the quantity of music heard by countryfolk, but it is doubtful that action against church ales, May games and similar festivals, and against piping and dancing on Sundays, decreased it much, for when one festivity was discouraged another, such as Guy Fawkes day, sprang up. Then too, communal religious music may in some places have taken the place of the old folk music for people who regarded it as pagan or popish. "You may now sometimes see at St. Paul's Cross, after the service, six thousand persons, old and young, of both sexes, all singing together and praising God," Bishop John Jewell wrote to Peter Martyr in 1560, thus describing an extreme instance; and Lady Hoby's diary in 1600 describes another extreme: "I went to supper, then to the lecture: after, I sung a psalm with some of the servants and, lastly, read a chapter, prayed, and so went to bed." Neither kind of gathering can have been familiar to more than a small part of the people of England.[6]

Search for evidence that many in the lower classes performed or heard and appreciated much sophisticated music is discouraged at the outset by consideration of the inhibiting effects of lack of time and money. In the upper classes time and money can hardly have been as dominant. While not everyone in the elastic middle class, nor even all members of the aristocracy, had both to spend on music, by and large members of these classes were not restrained by illiteracy, inability to pay teachers and buy instruments, or lack of time for practice: for them the more important factors were aptitude and inclination. Aptitude, as an innate quality, is not created or destroyed by social conditions and need here only be remembered as a factor. Inclination to exercise an aptitude, to learn, to practice, to hear, to patronize music, varying in strength from one person to the next according to the force of usually imponderable variables in personality and personal circumstance, is greatly affected by the prevailing attitude of society: inclination will be strongest, most widespread, in a society which holds music in highest esteem. It is important, therefore, to get some idea of how music was regarded in England about 1600.

In spite of the feeling of many people against elaborate music in the church, no important group seems to have regarded music as bad

[6] Bumpus, *The Organists and Composers of St. Paul's Cathedral*, 26; see Knappen, *Tudor Puritanism*, 181-182. Lady Margaret Hoby, *Diary (1599-1605)*, ed. Meads, 138-139.

in itself. Percy Scholes, ardent partisan of the English puritans, searched long and diligently for evidence justifying to any degree the hackneyed allegations against them, and found none (*The Puritans and Music*). Extracts from two essays, both written in the reign of Elizabeth, represent fairly the serious opinions of stricter divines. John Northbrooke, a puritanical clergyman, in *Spiritus est vicarius Christi in terra. A treatise wherein dicing, dauncing, vaine plaies or enterludes with other idle pastimes, &c. commonly used on the Sabboth day, are reprooved*, published in London in 1579, covers the whole problem "dialoguewise" in a lengthy discussion between Youth and Age: "*Youth*. 'What say you to music and playing upon instruments, is not that a good exercise?' *Age*. 'Music is very good, if it be lawfully used, and not unlawfully abused. . . .' *Youth*. '. . . some men dispraise it too much, and think it unlawful, others commend it as much, and think nothing so lawful: and a third sort there are, which make it a thing indifferent.' *Age*. '. . . but the third sort is to be commended. . . .' " (signature L3). Dudley Fenner, "preacher of the word of God in Middleburgh," whose *A Short and Profitable Treatise of Lawfull and Unlawfull Recreations* was published there about 1587 (perhaps two editions, 1587 and 1592) taught about the same conclusions, but with emphasis upon the idea that recreation is approved insofar as it will refresh the mind and body and so make one better able to praise God. He defines a Christian recreation as "an exercise of something indifferent," something neither enjoined nor forbidden, and instances use of the bow, of music (Nehemiah 7:67), hunting, riddles. "Exercises must be only for the refreshing . . . of the body or mind. . . . So in the prophet Esa [Isaiah] 5:12 a woe is threatened to them, in whose banquets is the Harp, Viol, Pipe, &c. . . . So we are commanded, To redeem the time. Ephasians 5:16 which we do not, when our exercises do not make us more fit to all godly duties. . . ." Games of chance he found bad, better replaced by "many other recreations, as pleasant and of greater praise, as chess, music &c." (signatures A5-A8). Northbrooke, Fenner and the rest, then, do not condemn music out of hand; it is for them, in fact, better than many other means men find to amuse themselves. Perhaps it is not altogether idle, however, to wonder whether divines, and their followers, who found it necessary thus to weigh seriously the innocency of music, might not have had less inclination to practice music and patronize musicians, than those who were ordinarily content to assume without question that music in itself is "a thing indifferent." Men most intensely concerned with religion, and particularly the more puritanical Englishmen, who were preoccupied with doctrinal and ritualistic problems, and especially obsessed with a repugnance towards elaborate vocal music in the church and towards any instrumental music whatsoever in the church, might well find less need for madrigals and mixed consorts than their less precise neighbors, even though they would not condemn music altogether. This conjecture cannot easily be supported: expression of lack of inclination by not singing, not playing or not patronizing musicians, is not apt to leave much of a record. That it is not wholly insupportable is indicated in a letter written in 1596 by Posthumous Hoby, a member of the well-known puritan family, inviting to his wedding his cousin, Anthony Bacon, and informing him that there would be no music because his mother did not want it, nor dancing because far from his "humour," and that he would "have all let alone, and seek only to please the beholders with a sermon and a dinner, and myself with beholding my mistress. . . ." Margaret Hoby's diary, too, reveals that while she knew how to play the orpharion, she almost never, if ever, sang anything but psalms (c. 1599). Some contemporaries, perhaps mistakenly, attributed antagonism towards music to puritans. An innkeeper in Rye allegedly told a musician in 1610 that "We have a puritan to our mayor and therefore you may play as long as you will at his door, but he will give you nothing." Some members of the middle and upper classes, perhaps a very few, who could afford to indulge in the best secular music, apparently refrained because of lack of inclination, which in turn may have stemmed from their religious beliefs, or perhaps from inner currents predisposing them both to their religious beliefs and to lack of inclination for music.[7]

The renaissance ideal of the gentleman and lady undoubtedly affected the inclination of all persons who were, or who wished to be considered, gentlemen and ladies. The ideal, product of centuries of assimilation of classical to Christian ideals and to the ever changing needs of medieval civilization, received many definitions in the sixteenth and seventeenth centuries, of which a few, including those of Elyot, Castiglione, Ascham and Peacham, may here be taken as representative.[8]

Sir Thomas Elyot, in *The Boke Named the Governour*, first pub-

[7] Lady Margaret Hoby, *Diary (1599-1605)*, ed. Meads, 32. HMC 31, *Rye Mss.*, 144.

[8] For fuller accounts of the idea of the gentleman see Kelso, *The Doctrine of the English Gentleman in the Sixteenth Century*, and also works referred to in Wright, *Middle-Class Culture in Elizabethan England*, 121-130.

lished in 1531, endorsed music, but unenthusiastically, as an element in the training of a gentleman. The seventh chapter, entitled "In what wise music may be to a noble man necessary: and what modesty ought to be therein," begins: "The discretion of a tutor consisteth in temperance: that is to say, that he suffer not the child to be fatigued with continual study or learning, wherewith the delicate and tender wit may be dulled or oppressed: but that there may be therewith interlaced and mixed some pleasant learning and exercise, as playing on instruments of music, which moderately used and without diminution of honor, that is to say, without wanton countenance and dissolute gesture, is not to be contemned." After giving many biblical and classical examples, he warns the reader that he "would not be thought to allure noble men to have so much delectation therein, that, in playing and singing only, they should put their whole study and felicity: as did the emperor Nero. . . . It were therefore better that no music were taught to a noble man, than, by the exact knowledge thereof, he should have therein inordinant delight, and by that be elected to wantonnesss, abandoning gravity, and the necessary cure and office, in the public weal, to him committed." He then cites Philip's rebuke to Alexander for being able to sing so well, and explains that Philip meant "that the open profession of that craft was but of a base estimation. And that it sufficed a noble man, having therein knowledge, either to use it secretly, for the refreshing of his wit, when he hath time of solace: or else, only hearing the contention of noble musicians, to give judgment in the excellence of their cunnings. These be the causes whereunto having regard, music is not only tolerable but also commendable." Elyot concludes by showing how the tutor can "adapt the pleasant science of music to a necessary and laudable purpose": "And if the child be of a perfect inclination and towardness to virtue, and very aptly disposed to this science, and ripely doth understand the reason and concordance of tunes, the tutor's office shall be to persuade him to have principally in remembrance his estate, which maketh him exempt from the liberty of using this science in every time and place: that is to say, that it only serveth for recreation after tedious or laborious affairs, and to show him that a gentleman, playing or singing in a common audience, appaireth [impaireth] his estimation: the people forgetting reverence, when they behold him in the similitude of a common servant or minstrel. Yet, notwithstanding, he shall commend the perfect understanding of music, declaring how necessary it is for the better attaining the knowledge of a public weal: which . . . is made of an order of estates and degrees, and by reason thereof, containeth in it a perfect harmony. . . ." The work as a whole evidently harmonized with the ideals of educated Englishmen in the sixteenth century, for seven more editions were published by 1580.[9]

Perhaps the most celebrated of the books of the gentleman, Castiglione's *The Courtier,* was first printed in Italian at Venice in 1528, three years before *The Governour,* but did not appear in English until 1561; in the intervening thirty-odd years Englishmen could have become acquainted with it in Italian, Spanish, and French editions, and after the English edition of 1561 they could also obtain it in German and Latin. In contrast to the rather grudging Elyot, Castiglione is enthusiastic for music, trusting on the whole the good judgment of the properly educated gentleman to keep him from abusing an essential accomplishment.

The turn of music in the description of the courtier comes just after a member of the duchess of Urbino's company (whose discourse on the nature of the good courtier Castiglione pretends to be reporting) protests to Count Lewis of Canossa, the principal speaker, that "there is never a vessel in the world possible to be found so big that shall be able to receive all the things that you will have in this courtier." The count resumes: "My Lords (quoth he) you must think I am not pleased with the courtier if he be not also a musician, and beside his understanding and cunning upon the book, have skill in like manner on sundry instruments. For if we weigh it well, there is no ease of the labors and medicines of feeble minds to be found more honest and more praiseworthy in time of leisure than it. And principally in courts, where (beside the refreshing of vexations that music bringeth unto each man) many things are taken in hand to please women withal, whose tender and soft breasts are soon pierced with melody and filled with sweetness. . . ." When it is objected that music is more fit for women than men the count reminds the company of the praise the ancients accorded to it and cites, among others, Plato and Aristotle, who held that it "ought necessarily to be learned from a man's childhood, not only for the superficial melody that is heard, but to be sufficient to bring into us a new habit that is good, and a custom inclining to virtue, which maketh the mind more apt to the conceiving of felicity. . . ." The necessity of drawing and painting as accomplishments of the courtier

[9] Elyot, ed. Croft, I, 38-43.

is next taken up. At the following meeting of the company the manner in which the various accomplishments should be exercised is discussed, and it is found (here Castiglione and Elyot agree) that the courtier should not exhibit his skill in public or contest with peasants and other inferior people. "I will have our courtier," Sir Frederick Fregoso (principal speaker for the session) says, "therefore to do this and all the rest beside handling his weapon, as a matter that is not his profession: and not seem to seek or look for any praise for it, nor be acknowen that he bestoweth much study or time about it, although he do it excellently well." He should not be willing to sing or play for a company on the slightest excuse, and, "for all he be skilful and doth well understand it, yet will I have him to dissemble the study and pains that a man must needs take in all things that are well done." Sir Frederick then tells of the kinds of music suitable to the courtier, and discusses "the time and season" for it. Whenever a man is in "familiar and loving company, having nothing else a do," and particularly in the presence of women, music is appropriately used; but performing for the multitude, and particularly the unnoble, must be avoided. The appropriateness of the time and place must be left, on the whole, to the discretion of the courtier.

The perfect lady, too, must know music, as the next evening's discourse makes clear. She must have many of the accomplishments of the courtier, but must do them "with heedfulness and the soft mildness that . . . is comely for her. And therefore in dancing I would not see her use too swift and violent tricks, nor yet in singing or playing upon instruments these hard and often divisions that declare more cunning than sweetness." Even the instruments must befit womanly mildness. Lord Julian sums up by willing "that this woman have a sight in letters, in music, in drawing or painting, and skilful in dancing, and in devising sports and pastimes," of very great price in everything, of staidness, nobleness in courage, wisdom, temperance, "and the other virtues." Castiglione has no misgivings as to whether the perfect courtier and lady should study music.[10]

Roger Ascham, younger contemporary of Elyot and Castiglione, secretary of an embassy to Germany, a teacher to Queen Elizabeth as princess, and latin secretary to Mary and Elizabeth, although cultivating music himself, held opinions of it more like Elyot's than Castiglione's. In *Toxophilus, The Schole of Shootinge*, dedicated to Henry VIII but

[10] Castiglione, ed. Raleigh, 88-91, 115-120, 220-221.

addressed "To all gentlemen and yeomen of England" (not simply to gentlemen), Toxophilus and Philologus discuss informally at Cambridge the worth of shooting and how to shoot the long bow. First they find that shooting is an honest recreation fit for princes and great men, and then, while considering whether it is appropriate for scholars, debate the relative merits of shooting and music. The argument, drawn chiefly from the customary classical sources, seems to be well epitomized in the preliminary table of contents: "Shooting fitter for students than any music or instruments." Philologus, more enthusiastic for music than Toxophilus, maintains that while shooting may be appropriate sometimes for some scholars "yet the fittest always is to be preferred. Therefore if you will needs grant scholars pastime and recreation of their minds, let them use (as many of them doth) music, and playing on instruments, things most seemly for all scholars. . . ." Toxophilus rejoins that both shooting and music are fitting, but that some kinds of music are bad, leading to sinfulness, effeminacy and dulling of wits: ". . . the minstrelsy of lutes, pipes, harps, and all other that standeth by such nice, fine, minikin fingering (such as the most part of scholars whom I know use, if they use any) is far more fit for the womanishness of it to dwell in the court among ladies, than for any great thing in it, which should help good and sad study. . . ." Philologus replies that he would gladly have this kind of music decay among scholars, but wishes "that the laudable custom of England to teach children their pricksong, were not so decayed throughout all the realm as it is." (The table of contents describes this section "Youth ought to learn to sing.") A utilitarian note enters when Philologus declares that two kinds of men holding the highest offices under the king "shall greatly lack the use of singing," that is, preachers and lawyers, for if they do not learn singing they shall not "be able to rule their breasts." All voices "may be helped and brought to a good point, by learning to sing. Whether this be true or not, they that stand most in need, can tell best, whereof some I have known, which, because they learned not to sing, when they were boys, were fain to take pain in it, when they were men." The times are decaying: "for of them that come daily to the university, where one hath learned to sing, six hath not." Except for singing the effect of the argument for music is unenthusiastic. Two more editions of *Toxophilus* appeared in Elizabeth's reign.

Twenty years after the first edition, between 1563 and his death in 1568, Ascham wrote *The Scholemaster or plaine and perfite way of*

teachyng children, to understand, write and speake, in Latin tong, but
specially purposed for the private brynging up of youth in jentlemen
and noble mens houses . . . (published 1570), and he refers specifically
to what he had written in his "book of shooting" to support his contention that some moderate wits are often marred by "over much study
and use of some sciences, namely, music, arithmetic, and geometry."
Farther on, Ascham, in urging that young gentlemen "use and delight
in all courtly exercises, and gentlemanlike pastimes," includes music,
without apparent hesitation, in the list of these: "Therefore, to ride
comely: to run fair at the tilt or ring: to play at all weapons: to shoot
fair in bow, or surely in gun: to vault lustily: to run: to leap: to wrestle:
to swim: to dance comely: to sing, and play of instruments cunningly:
to hawk: to hunt: to play at tennis, and all pastimes generally, which
be joined with labor, used in open place, and on the day light, containing either some fit exercise for war, or some pleasant pastime for peace,
be not only comely and decent, but also very necessary, for a courtly
gentleman to use." Perhaps he had been influenced by Castiglione, for
a few paragraphs after giving this catalogue he cites Castiglione as an
authority for the joining of "learning with comely exercises," and
marvels that *The Courtier* "is no more read in the court, than it is, seeing that it is so well translated into English. . . ." *The Scholemaster*,
perpetuator of Ascham's name, was also well received by Elizabethan
readers, at least two more editions appearing before the end of the
century.[11]

Richard Mulcaster (c. 1530-1611) differs from all of the authors already considered in that he was a distinguished schoolmaster himself,
and presumably could put some of his ideas into effect. An "esquire
borne" (as he described himself), university-educated, familiar at the
court, where his pupils presented plays, the first master of the Merchant-
Taylors School (1561-1586), then master of St. Paul's (1596-1608),
teacher of boys who became famous, among them Edmund Spenser
and Lancelot Andrewes, and holder of church livings, Mulcaster was
well qualified to express for his day the highest ideals in education as
well as his own ideas on how to achieve them. Both in his *Positions*
(1581) and his *Elementarie* (1582) he writes for the advancement of
the whole man, in the best renaissance tradition. Music he includes in
the studies of the young rather as a matter of course than apologetically

[11] Ascham, *Toxophilus*, ed. Arber, 22, 38-43. *The Scholemaster*, ed. Arber,
34, 64, 66.

or hesitatingly, although he does give reasons why music should be studied. Four things are to be taught in the elementary school: reading, writing, drawing, and "*Music* by the instrument, besides the skill which must still increase, in form of exercise to get the use of our small joints, before they be knit, to have them the nimbler, and to put musicians in mind, that they be no brawlers, least by some swash of a sword, they chance to lease a joint, an irrecoverable jewel unadvisedly cast away. *Music* by the voice, besides her cunning also, by the way of *physic*, to spread the voice instruments within the body, while they be yet but young. As both the kinds of *music* for much profit, and more pleasure, which is not void of profit in her continuing kind." Music is included for girls too, who should also learn reading and writing. The virginals and lute are named as especially suitable instruments for the elementary pupils "because of the full music which is uttered by them. . . . I will also set down so many chosen lessons for either of them as shall bring the young learner to play reasonable well on them both, though not at the first sight, whether by the ear, or by the book alway provided that pricksong go before playing. . . ." Mulcaster and his employers, the Merchant-Taylors, did not always agree on either his wages or his performance of his duties: his ideals were probably somewhat ahead of what his employers would have him do. But he was able to teach music to at least some of his pupils, for Sir James Whitelocke, who proceeded to Oxford from the school in 1588, wrote: "I was brought up at school under Mr. Mulcaster . . . where I continued until I was well instructed in the Hebrew, Greek, and Latin tongues. His care was also to increase my skill in music in which I was brought up by daily exercise in it, as in singing and playing upon instruments. . . ." Mulcaster was the last great Tudor writer on education, and he did not finish his self-appointed task, for although he lived twenty nine years after the publication of the first part of his *Elementarie*, the second part never appeared.[12]

Two other well-known and, in their day, popular, books which reflect more dimly the renaissance ideal, appeared before the civil wars: Henry Peacham's *Compleat Gentleman*, published in many editions with the first in 1622, and Richard Brathwaite's *English Gentleman* (1630; *English Gentlewoman*, 1631). Both want their gentlemen to have polite accomplishments, but Peacham seems more superficial about it all than the older writers, making it a great part of the duty of

[12] Mulcaster, *Positions*, ed. Quick, 39. *Elementarie*, ed. Campagnac, 66. Quick mentions Mulcaster's difficulties with the Merchant-Taylors in a biographical appendix, pp. 301-302, and quotes Whitelocke, *Liber Famelicus*, on p. 304.

a gentleman to be able to blazon his own coat of arms, as Raleigh points out, and Brathwaite expresses more interest than some of the older authors in religious and moral ideas.[13]

Peacham's book, designed, according to the title, to "fashion" the complete gentleman "absolute in the most necessary and commendable qualities concerning mind or body that may be required in a noble gentleman," starts with general considerations such as the definition of nobility—an innate quality—and the duty of teachers, which varies according to the abilities, tastes and other characteristics of pupils. It then takes up various subjects of study, including history, geometry, poetry, music (chapter eleven, pp. 96-104), drawing and painting, armory and blazonry, exercise, and general conduct, and concludes with a chapter on travel. Peacham, often cited to prove that all gentlemen had to be accomplished in music, recognizes explicitly if reluctantly that some men lack aptitude or taste or both for music. His chapter "Of Music" starts: "Music, a sister to poetry, next craveth your acquaintance (if your *genius* be so disposed). I know there are many . . . of such disproportioned spirits, that they avoid her company. . . . I dare not pass so rash a censure as . . . the Italian . . . proverb . . . *Whom God loves not, that man loves not music*: but I am verily persuaded, they are by nature very ill disposed, and of such a brutish stupidity, that scarce anything else that is good and savoreth of virtue, is to be found in them." (p. 96). Peacham next defends the use of music, "an immediate gift of heaven," in the church, against the arguments of "our sectaries," and then proceeds to the direct benefits music brings to the body and mind: singing "openeth the breast and pipes," is "an enemy to melancholy," cures some diseases, and is a "help for a bad pronunciation, and distinct speaking. . . ." After quoting liberally the usual classical authorities in favor of music Peacham calls a halt; the praise of music must be measured, for gentlemen must restrain their indulgence in music: "I might run into an infinite sea of the praise and use of so excellent an art, but I only shew it you with the finger, because I desire not that any noble or gentleman should (save his private recreation at leisurable hours) prove a master in the same, or neglect his more ·weighty employments: though I avouch it a skill worthy the knowledge and exercise of the greatest prince." (pp. 98-99). Like *The Courtier, The Compleat Gentleman* cautions against display by gentlemen of real mastery in music; Peacham's warning might easily

[13] See Raleigh, introduction to Castiglione, *The Courtier*, p. lxxxv.

be mistaken for advice not to learn to play and sing well, although his meaning probably corresponds closely to Castiglione's. After discussing this point, the fitness of the practice of music in moderation for the greatest of men, Peacham tells how much skill he would have a gentleman attain: "I desire no more in you then to sing your part sure, and at the first sight, withall, to play the same upon your viol, or the exercise of the lute, privately to yourself." (p. 100). This sentence is often quoted, commonly in association with the famous dialogue from the beginning of Morley's *Plaine and Easic Introduction*, and taken somehow to prove that to have any title to proper breeding a man must be able to sing well at sight, play well on the viol at sight, and be a master on the lute. Even out of context the sentence does not say this. It asks that a gentleman be able to sing his part sure at first sight (an accomplishment fully attainable only by persons of unusual aptitude or by persons of moderate aptitude after diligent and extended practice), and (perhaps *or*) play a part on the viol (an accomplishment more easily attainable by the moderately gifted). Or the gentleman may learn to play the lute for his own solitary recreation; a lutanist playing for himself alone has no social obligation, as a part-singer does, to acquire much skill. Perhaps Peacham lists the three accomplishments in order of desirability, with the singing of a part sure the best; he does not require all three; and he is expressing simply a desire, an ideal, and not describing a fact: "I desire no more. . . ." The sentence should be considered in relation to the preceeding passages. Peacham acknowledges the fact that some gentlemen lack aptitude or taste for music: they are not the less gentlemen, he grudgingly admits, because they do not pursue music. And Peacham urges restraint in the practice of music: too much time must not be spent at it, and professional skill must not be displayed; thorough competence in singing, moderate or little aptitude, and rigorously limited exercise in singing are scarcely compatible. Peacham was writing with a flourish. A discussion of composers and compositions, and praise of "the theoretique of musicke" and of music itself close the chapter. The ideals expressed in this chapter (taken by itself) differ little from those expressed in *The Courtier*. Peacham's great fondness, perhaps immoderate, for music, shown by the chapter itself, makes it somewhat suspect as a mirror of the effective standards of his day.

Brathwaite has much less to say about music, and is inclined to be somewhat condescending towards it. When he first discusses music he cites the usual authorities and opinions; after writing of rhetoric, grammar, mathematics, and physics, he comes "lastly" to music and tells the story, from Du Bartas, of how a tortoise shell first gave rise to music, the story of Pythagoras and the drunken banqueters sobered by an appropriate change of music, the precepts of Aristotle, and "diviner effects of music, confirmed by holy writ" (Saul, David, St. Augustine's *Confessions*). Somewhat farther on Brathwaite takes up recreations, and praises amongst others hawking, hunting, fishing, swimming, running, and fencing and then, "to descend to more soft and effeminate *recreations*: we shall find, of what great esteem *music* was, even with some, who were in years as ripe, as they were for wisdom rare." Many of the ancients are again introduced, including Socrates, Minerva, Alcibiades, Plato, Aristotle, and Lycurgus. Every now and then he uses music to adorn his style, as when writing on acquaintance: the discourse of friends "like some choice *music* delights our *hearing*; their sight like some rare object contents our seeing. . . ." A pious flight, in the chapter on perfection, comes near the end, and profane music is, at least by implication, put in its place. If you have closed your heart to sensual ideas, to lust for women, "done with your *midnight revels*, and court pleasures, you shall be filled with the *pleasures* of the *Lord's house* . . . ; or left frequenting masks, tilt-triumphs and enterludes, the glorious spectacles of vanity, you shall be admitted to those angelical triumphs, singing *heavenly hymns* to the God of glory. . . ." Brathwaite lacks the enthusiasm for music that Castiglione and several of the other earlier writers had. Music can be all right, but no harm can come of neglecting it.[14]

James Cleland's Ηρω-παιδεια or *The Institution of a Young Nobleman* (Oxford, 1607) is more explicit. Chapter twenty-five of the fifth book, "Of those house-games from the which a nobleman should abstain," condemns dicing as fit only for "deboshed" soldiers, warns against stage plays excepting performances at the king's court or approved plays presented at home, and then considers music in two paragraphs: "*Delight not also to be in your own person a player upon instruments, especially upon such as commonly men get their living with*: because you may employ your time better then so: and for the most part we see that those who are most given to play upon them, are fantastic and full of humors, accounting more sometimes of the tuning

[14] Brathwaite, *The English Gentleman* (1630), 132-134, 167, 242, 416-417 (see also pp. 87, 98, 101).

of their lute, then of the entertaining and pleasant company of their friends. *Enervant animos citharae, cantusque, lyraque.* [In margin: "Ovid. l. de. 'rem," i.e. *Remedia Amoris*, 753] I may add that oftentimes the holding of the lute hath hurt the breast, and made many crooked bodies, as also that playing upon instruments doth disgrace more a noble man then it can grace and honor him in good company, as many think. For he should rather take his pastime of others, then make pastime unto them." (pp. 229-230). The chapter concludes with a paragraph condemning the chase. Cleland's utilitarian point of view, and his development to the logical extreme of the snobbish principle, found in *The Courtier* and many other works, that gentlemen must not perform in such a way that music will seem to be their profession, comes as a shock after the enthusiasm, or at worst, indifference, towards music of the other authors.

Cleland, although a Scot, may have represented a school of opinion widespread in England, a new attitude which was making Peacham's views, first published in 1622, old-fashioned. Apparently of an old and distinguished Scottish family, and graduate of the University of Edinburgh in 1597, Cleland became acquainted with the highest circles of English society as tutor to Sir John Harington, friend and companion of Prince Henry in his court or academy at Nonesuch. Here Cleland wrote *The Institution*, and perhaps met the duke of Lennox, to whose service he went in 1607. In 1614 he was appointed rector of the church at Old Romney, presumably through the duke's influence, and in 1618 to the rich rectory of Chartham also. That the second appointment was made by the king, probably at the request of Lennox, indicates that Cleland cannot have been conspicuously puritanical, if puritanical at all. He died in 1627. As Molyneux, editor of a facsimile edition of *The Institution* points out, Cleland was heavily indebted for his educational philosophy to the classics and to Castiglione, Patrizi, and Vives. But while Cleland follows Castiglione in stressing lack of affectation as the essence of manners, his objective is utilitarian: "For to be learned and experimented in those things which are pleasant, and to be ignorant of those which are necessary and profitable, that learning is little worth." (p. 95). Thus Castiglione, Elyot, and the rest are guides for Cleland until they advocate training in painting and music: for Cleland even pastimes, to be good, must increase the young nobleman's efficiency in peace and war. His attitudes seem puritanical, but in spite of his biblical references his standard for judgment of conduct is less ethics or fitness than profit or loss: only virtue can ennoble, but of the virtuous only those are noblemen or gentlemen "whose virtue is profitable to the king and country; whom his majesty esteems worthy to bear a coat of arms, and to enjoy diverse privileges for services done to him and his kingdom." (pp. 5-6). That Cleland's book was re-issued twice with new title-pages, in 1611 as *The Scottish Academie . . .* and in 1612 as *The Instruction of a Young Noble-man*, and apparently had no second edition, indicates that it may have failed to gain wide circulation. Cleland's prudent attitude towards the arts may have been widely held, nevertheless; veneration of the principle of the universal man and practice on an earthier level perhaps flourished together. Society, as well as Cleland, may have been anticipating Lord Chesterfield's advice, "Eat game, but do not be your own butcher and kill it." "If you love music, hear it; go to operas, concerts, and pay fiddlers to play to you; but I insist upon your neither piping nor fiddling yourself."[15]

The weight of authority supported musical attainment as an attribute desirable in gentlemen and ladies. Degree of enthusiasm varied, of course, and so did the justifications for music, which was a relaxation from more important affairs, an accomplishment desirable and appropriate in itself, a help to the vocal chords and lungs and to good public speaking, good exercise for the fingers, and a reminder not to be a brawler. Several authorities caution against display of skill in public, particularly before the lower classes, and against showing anywhere that much effort has gone into the acquiring of musical skill. This warning against display of professional virtuosity could lead to the idea that no more than mediocre skill should be attained by a gentleman, an idea which Peacham, for all his enthusiasm for music, almost expresses and may imply.

Perhaps most Englishmen of the upper classes accepted these precepts as their theoretical standards. At least a few did not. Some took the view that musical skill is commendable but by no means essential. Clarendon (1609-1674) expressed this when describing William Cavendish, duke of Newcastle (1592-1676): "He was a very fine gentleman, active and full of courage, and most accomplished in those qualities of horsemanship, dancing, and fencing, which accompany a good breed-

[15] Cleland, *The Institution of a Young Noble Man, I: Introduction and Text.* Introduction by Molyneux: see especially pp. xxxiv-xxxvi and xlvii-xlviii. The biographical details are drawn from this introduction, and quotations from this facsimile.

Chesterfield, as quoted by Raleigh in the introduction to his edition of *The Courtier*, p. lxxxvi. Raleigh points to the contrast between eighteenth century practice and Castiglione's ideals.

ing; in which his delight was." So much was indispensable. "Besides that, he was amorous in poetry and music, to which he indulged the greater part of his time." Others had a more inclusive but perhaps really lower ideal, that of Sir Gervase Holles (1547-1627), of whom his grandson wrote: "He was as well furnished with learning as in his own opinion fitted a gentleman; for I have heard him say that he would have a gentleman to have some knowledge in all the arts but that it did not become him to be excellent in any of them. . . ." Margaret, duchess of Newcastle, born about 1625, youngest daughter of well-to-do Sir Thomas Lucas, in describing her own education and that of her brothers and sisters, said that while they had tutors in "all sorts of virtues, as singing, dancing, playing on music, reading, writing, working, and the like, yet we were not kept strictly thereto, they were rather for formality then benefit. . . . As for my brothers . . . [they amused] themselves with fencing, wrestling, shooting, and such like exercises, for I observed they did seldom hawk or hunt, and very seldom or never dance, or play on music, saying it was too effeminate for masculine spirits. . . ." The ninth earl of Northumberland, writing about 1595, rejected music altogether as a gentlemanly accomplishment: "Dancing amongst the rest may be admitted to grace the carriage; tennis for variety to procure nimbleness and health; but music, singing, cards, dice, chess, and the rest of this nature are but lost labor, being qualities neither profitable to themselves, nor anything else. For pastimes and recreations they are of most men tolerated, but he that cannot pass his time without them, in my conceit shall incur the suspicion of an idle member, and he that yields to them for recreation's sake, must withal be delighted in them, or else are they none; for laborsome it is that is not to the mind pleasing, and in them to be pleased I nominate a fault." Some forty years later Viscount Conway wrote in a letter from Newmarket, ". . . when we do not hunt we hawk, . . . the rest of the time is spent in tennis, chess, and dice, and in a word we eat and drink and rise up to play; and this is to live like a gentleman, for what is a gentleman but his pleasure." This is hardly an attitude of which the earl of Northumberland could have approved; nor can it have been typical of the Elizabethan nobility or gentry, but it no doubt expresses fairly the gross standard of a minority in Elizabethan as well as Stuart England. Not all gentlemen even wanted to play and sing well; Cleland's attitude towards music reflected at least part of what he saw.[16]

[16] Clarendon, quoted in Firth, *The House of Lords during the Civil War*, 124. Holles, *Memorials of the Holles Family 1493-1656*, ed. Wood, 125-126. Margaret,

Acceptance of the ideal, in principle, did not make attainment of it practicable. Lack of aptitude, as Peacham pointed out, excused some gentlemen, who were gentlemen nonetheless. The gap between parents' intentions and their performance was bound to cause many sons and daughters to grow up with little or no musical training. Parents who had managed well enough themselves without proficiency in music were as likely as not to be ineffective when trying to force their reluctant children to practice their music lessons faithfully, week in and week out; they were especially likely to fail when the actual superintendence of the children was in other hands. Children learn to read and write, even Latin and Greek, usually because their masters, at home or school, leave them no way out. The learning of music because of the pleasure and the social grace it will bring usually depends very largely on the willingness and desire of the child, and children seldom choose present sacrifice for future gain.

Even apt and willing children of parents anxious to have them acquire all courtly graces could fail to learn music for lack of teachers. More than one handbook to the easy learning of music advertised itself as the answer to the needs of those who could not get teachers—"they cannot all dwell in or near the city of London where expert tutors are to be had," as it was expressed in *A new booke of tabliture, containing sundrie easie and familiar instructions, shewing how . . . to play on sundry instruments* . . . (1596). Schools seldom remedied the deficiency, for very few of them taught music notwithstanding the opinions of Mulcaster, Sir Humphrey Gilbert, and others that they should. Besides the cathedral and collegiate-church schools, and the Newark song school, only about half a dozen seem to have taught music (or have been supposed to): the Merchant-Taylors school under Mulcaster, Christ's Hospital, London (for orphans), Dulwich college, Rivington grammar school, the school at Burford, Oxfordshire, and perhaps Repton school, Derbyshire. Gentlemen were unlikely to send their sons to several of these, and even in most of them music was apparently not a regular and usual part of the curriculum for all the boys. It was almost a rule that boys and girls had to learn music at home, or not at all; the exceptions include the cases of Sir James Whitelocke, already mentioned, and Gervase Holles (1607-1675), who when about six went to the free

duchess of Newcastle, *Memoirs*, printed with her *Life of the Duke of Newcastle,* Everyman's Library edition, pp. 190-191. Henry Percy, ninth earl of Northumberland, *Advice to his Son,* ed. Harrison, 64. Conway: HMC 29, *Portland Mss.,* ix, 52.

grammar school of Grimsby where his first teacher taught him music in addition to the regular subjects. Ordinarily there cannot have been time for such special instruction, for most masters could seldom have had the leisure, inclination, and ability together; and the full school day must have pretty well exhausted the patience and energy, for study at any rate, of most students.[17]

That many gentlemen or would-be-gentlemen knew little or no music is almost proved by Morley's often quoted dialogue in which a young man tells how he was shamed in polite company because he could not bear his part at sight in a madrigal.[18] Instead of indicating, as many writers have supposed, that it was hardly possible for a gentleman to live in polite society without consummate musical skill, the passage seems to be an appeal, of a kind known in today's advertising, to the socially ambitious. Morley and other writers could hardly have hoped that their manuals would sell if musical Utopia had already been reached. Great emphasis has sometimes been placed on the large num-

[17] *A new booke of tabliture*, sig. A3 verso. The editor seems to have been the publisher, William Barley.

Schools: in general see Watson, *The English Grammar Schools to 1660*, 216-217; the chapter "The teaching of music," is a useful summary in spite of some inaccuracy. The first four schools named above are described or mentioned in Watson, pp. 212-215. At Dulwich in 1634 the organist was "said not to be able to instruct the poor scholars in prick song, nor on the viol and other instruments. His incompetency was alleged to be connived at because he was the master's son, or because church music was contemned. . . ." (CSPD *1633-34*, 419-420). Psalm-singing, perhaps not musical education, was ordered at the Burford free school: HMC *55, Various* i, *Burford Corp. Mss.*, 54-55. Regarding Repton school Sir John Harpur wrote to Henry, fifth earl of Huntington, in 1622: "Upon the great desire of Mr. Whitehead to have a boy to teach others to sing, I placed one with him at Michaelmas was twelve months. . . ." (HMC *77, Hastings Mss.*, ii, 60).

The duke of Buckingham was said by his biographer, Wotton, to have been "taught the principles of music, and other slight literature" at his school (quoted in Mathew, *The Jacobean Age*, 109).

The Gresham college, London, music lectures seem to have had no importance. John Bull, professor 1596-1607 (the first), was the only one with any considerable knowledge of music until the late eighteenth century (see "Gresham Musical Professorship," in *Grove*).

Holles, *Memorials of the Holles Family 1493-1656*, ed. Wood, 227-228.

The school day: see Watson, and Brown, *Elizabethan Schooldays*.

[18] Original publication: Morley, *A Plaine and Easie Introduction* (1st edition, London, 1597), 1. Quoted in Chappell, *Old English Popular Music*, ed. Wooldridge, 1, 60; Byrne, *Elizabethan Life* (2d edition), 222-223; Fellowes, *English Madrigal*, 19; *Shakespeare's England*, ed. Onions, 11, 22; and elsewhere. For superior comment on this passage see Fellowes's introduction to the Shakespeare Association facsimile edition of Morley's *Plaine and Easie*, pp. x-xi; and Davey, *History of English Music* (2d edition), 156.

ber of technical allusions to music in the plays of Shakespeare and others and in poetry in general; they prove, of course, only that music has an adaptable vocabulary and that many Elizabethans may have understood it. Even Sir Philip Sidney, model of his age, could not amuse himself with music privately: "You will not believe what a want I find of it in my melancholy times," he wrote to his brother, when advising him not to neglect music among his studies. In 1589 it was stated, perhaps with some exaggeration, that "it is hard to find in these days of noblemen or gentlemen any good *mathematician,* or excellent *musician,* or notable *philosopher,* or else a cunning poet. . . ."[19]

Even if musical skill was less obligatory than scholars have sometimes believed, it is possible that predominant opinion favored music as a gentle accomplishment. Certainly many boys and girls started music lessons at home. Often the children were quite young. Peregrine Bertie was six or seven when his lute was mended in 1562, and William Cavendish about eight when learning viol and singing in 1599. Musical instruction seems always to have included singing, while the most common instruments seem to have been virginals, lutes (and similar instruments), and viols. Although it may be true that usually girls rather than boys practiced at the virginals, and boys rather than girls the viols, this was not necessarily a rule. About 1555 both Francis (then about nine) and his sister Margaret Willoughby were taking lessons on the virginals, and in 1602 Philip Gawdy wrote to his sister that he was sending her "two songs for the viol." Since nearly all instruments then made—excepting perhaps trumpets, shawms, and bagpipes—appear in household inventories it is unlikely that the fashionable instruments fully monopolized the attention of amateurs.[20]

That teachers of music were frequently, perhaps usually, not house-

[19] On allusions in Shakespeare see Naylor, *Shakespeare and Music* and Elson, *Shakespeare in Music* (quotations and interpretations).

Sidney quoted by Lee in Edward, Lord Herbert of Cherbury, *Autobiography,* ed. Lee (2d edition), 23 note 2, from *Sidney Papers,* I, 283-285. See Pattison, "Sir Philip Sidney and Music," *Music and Letters,* xv (1934), 76, and Pattison, *Music and Poetry of the English Renaissance,* 62.

The scarcity was lamented by George Puttenham, *The Arte of English Poesie,* ed. Willcock and Walker, 21.

[20] Bertie: HMC *66, Ancaster Mss.,* 466. Cavendish: Mss. of the duke of Devonshire, Cavendish Ms. 23, folios 3 verso-49 verso. Willoughby: HMC *69, Middleton Mss.,* 407ff. Gawdy: HMC *6, Frere Mss.,* 525.

For a charming paragraph on the activities and recreations of the ladies of the court (the youngest "apply their lutes, citharns, pricksong, and all kind of music . . . only for recreation sake") see Harrison, *An historicall description of the iland of Britaine,* I, 330.

hold servants is indicated by family accounts showing that they were paid separately and according to the number of pupils in the family. Sometimes a teacher may have boarded with the family in which he was teaching, particularly when the residence was remote from a large town, and sometimes he may have been primarily a musician in residence and only secondarily a teacher. Nearly anyone, guild rules notwithstanding, might be a teacher. Sir Thomas Chaloner's daughter had a "fleming musician" to teach her Italian songs in 1552; a young widow in 1579 planned to support herself by giving virginal lessons in Gloucester; Lady Anne Clifford "learned to sing and play on the bass viol of *Jack Jenkins*, my aunt's boy"; and some composers dedicated their published works to the fathers of their former pupils. Nearly every professional musician of any respectability is likely to have done some teaching, of course. Some teachers received relatively high pay. About 1550 various music teachers of the Willoughby children received usually five shillings a month for each pupil; for a while at least the virginals teacher also taught "arethmetick" to young Francis; in 1594 and 1595 "Judith's" lute teacher in London received fifteen shillings a quarter; and about 1600 William Cavendish's teacher received ten shillings a quarter and a gift of five shillings at New Year.[21]

Girls perhaps tended to keep at their music lessons longer than boys, who were more likely to go off to school not long after they had made a start and who had, even if they stayed home, more subjects and skills competing for their time and interest. There can be little doubt, moreover, that many gentlemen and ladies neglected when grown whatever musical proficiency they had obtained as children. This happened so often that it could be presented in literature as an easily recognizable, and common human failing, and seemed important enough as a deter-

---

[21] Evidence that some families living in rural areas kept a teacher in residence includes the dedications of several songbooks which seem to imply that the composers had lived with the patrons; e.g. dedication in Henry Youll, *Canzonets to Three Voyces* (1608); see chapter three, above. An amusing but certainly unreliable discussion of the hours at which pupils' various masters come to give lessons is given on signature F3 verso of Peter Erondell, *The French Garden for English Ladyes and Gentlewomen to Walke in* (1605).

Chaloner: BM Mss., Lansdowne 824, folio 38. Margaret Partridge planned to teach sewing, "the book," and virginals: CSPD *1566-79*, 562. *The Diary of Lady Anne Clifford*, ed. Sackville-West, 16.

In general see household account entries relating to music, especially Cavendish, Pelham, and Willoughby accounts. "Judith" and her teacher appear in Bodleian Ms. 31,542 (Malone Ms. 44), folios 19, 39 and 63 verso; she was probably a daughter of "a lady of position of Milk Street" in London.

rent to prospective purchasers of *The Schoole of Musicke: wherein is taught, the perfect method of true fingering of the lute* . . . (1603), that Thomas Robinson, the author, brought it into the preliminary discussion. A knight, who is thinking of having his children take lute lessons, tells Timotheus, a teacher, that he fears for various reasons that all his expense may be wasted: ". . . but I fear none so much as . . . that they [his children] will be careless and forgetful, of so excellent a quality as is playing upon the lute; and my fear is the greater, for that it was mine own fault, that in my youth could have played so well as any in those days, and now it is as clean forgotten, and which is more, I have no willing mind in the world, either to practice (to recover that I lost,) or to learn anew: for the play that is now, and the lessons (that are now a days) are so curiously set, that we of the old mine, are smoked [smoakt] up like to sea-coal, and this age hath the golden ore, and sparkling diamonds of divine musicians, that for mine own part, I am content, to give place both to youth, and the time, only content to be an auditor, and lover of the best. . . ." Timotheus agrees "that many, both men and women, that in their youth could have played . . . passing well, in their age, or when they once have been married, have forgotten all," but, as becomes a teacher, has a ready answer that satisfies the knight. Going off to the universities or the inns of court did not necessarily put an end to boys' study of music, in spite of the fact that neither the universities or inns offered practical instruction in singing or playing. Whatever music boys learned there was by private arrangement, as in the case of the diarist Evelyn, who "began to look upon the rudiments of music" in his third year at Oxford, and of Lord Herbert of Cherbury who wrote of how he learned to sing his part "at first sight" and to play on the lute in order that he "might not need the company of young men, in whom [he] observed . . . much ill example and debauchery." For young gentlemen the study of law at the inns of court was not so serious a business as to preclude the practice of music. Philip Gawdy about 1581 found that because of eye trouble he "durst not much look of a book but only tend playing of the lute."[22]

[22] Robinson, signatures B1, 2. The title continues, after *lute: pandora, orpharion and viol de gamba; with most infallible generall rules, both easie and delightfull. Also, a method, how you may be your owne instructer for prick-song, by the help of your lute, without any other teacher: with lessons of all sorts, for your further and better instruction.*

Universities: see "Degrees in Music," in *Grove*; Williams, *A Historical Account of Musical Degrees at Oxford and Cambridge*; and Mee, *The Oldest Music Room in Europe. A record of eighteenth century enterprise at Oxford*, especially pp.

Few amateur musicians can have been more than mediocre performers; Holles's rule was probably seldom broken. Michael Est, while intending no doubt to flatter his patron, Sir Thomas Gerard, inadvertently expressed the truth when in the dedication of his *Second Set of Madrigals* (1606) he spoke of Sir Thomas's "perfection in music . . . rare in a gentleman of your rank." Several composers evidently had had unhappy experience of the more ordinary gentlemen-musicians. Orlando Gibbons obviously refers to them in the dedication, to Sir Christopher Hatton, of his *First Set of Madrigals and Mottets*, 1612: "Experience tells us that songs of this nature are usually esteemed as they are well or ill performed, which excellent grace I am sure your unequalled love unto music will not suffer them to want. . . ." It is not pleasant to have your compositions condemned when the fault is the performers'. Several composers tried to find a large market by emphasizing the easiness of their works. The long title of *Musicke of Sundrie Kindes* (1607), by Thomas Forde, a musician of Henry, prince of Wales, concludes with the inviting phrase, "very easie to be performde." The nature of the compositions, the scoring of them, and the dedications indicate that Forde and his publisher expected their buyers to be of the gentry. The "sundrie kindes" of music were "set forth in two books. The first whereof are ayres for four voices to the lute, orpharion, or bass-viol, with a dialogue for two voices, and two bass-viols in parts tuned the lute way. The second are pavans, galliards, almains, toys,

---

vii-xvi. Although degrees in music have been granted from at least the later Middle Ages, they have not until recent times indicated completion of a course of study at the universities; professional musicians sometimes received degrees after proof of many years of practical work and after submitting a "degree exercise." Theoretical music, as a part of the quadrivium, seems to have been neglected in the sixteenth and seventeenth centuries. The music lectures at commencement time apparently were a relic of the quadrivium and used only as an occasion for speech on a subject of the orator's choice (see CSPD *1603-10*, 447, for example). A professorship of music was endowed in 1626; the situation does not seem to have been changed materially thereby. For accounts of student expenses at the universities (some including indications of musical activity) see the following: Maitland, "Archbishop Whitgift's College Pupils," *The British Magazine and Monthly Register of Religious and Ecclesiastical Information*, xxxii (1847), 650-656, xxxiii (1848), 17-31, 185-195 and 444-463; HMC *19, Townshend Mss.*, 13-17 (Cambridge c. 1610); Bennet, "Notes from a Norfolk Squire's Notebook," *Communications, Cambridge Antiquarian Society*, v (1884), 201-224 (Cambridge c. 1614, p. 215); HMC *23, Cowper Mss.*, 191, 284 (Cambridge c. 1625).

Evelyn, *Diary*, ed. Dobson, i, 18. Edward, Lord Herbert of Cherbury, *Autobiography*, ed. Lee (2d edition), 23. Lord Herbert studied music both at Oxford and "at home" "with very little or almost no teaching." *Letters of Philip Gawdy of West Harling, Norfolk, 1579-1616*, ed. Jeayes, 5-6.

jigs, thumps and such like, for two bass-viols, the liraway, so made as the greatest number may serve to play alone. . . ." (title-page; spelling modernized). "Not full twelve years," and "What then is love" are among the eleven songs in the first book, while the second includes "The wild goose chase" (designated "Sir John Philpot's delight"), "The Bagpipes" ("Sir Charles Howard's Delight"), "A Pill to Purge Melancholy" ("M. Martin's Thump"), and "Why not here." In the dedication of the first book (to Sir Richard Weston whose "delight," a pavan, appears in the second book), Forde declares that he need not apologize for "these musics, since none are so much in request . . . then of these kinds . . . some of them have been graced of your special favor and liking. . . ." The second book is dedicated to Sir Richard Tichborne, whose "toy," "And if you touch me I'll cry," is the eleventh "lesson" in this book. Thomas Ravenscroft also called attention to the easiness of two volumes of his songs, both published in 1609. *Pammelia. Musicks Miscellanie. or mixed varietie of pleasant roundelayes, and delightful catches, of 3. 4. 5. 6. 7. 8. 9. 10. parts in one . . . ,* containing one hundred songs, mostly drinking songs (cuckoldry and so on) but with some of a serious flavor, is, according to the prefatory address "consonant to all ordinary musical capacity, being such indeed, as all such whose love of music exceeds their skill, cannot but commend . . ." (signature A2). *Deuteromelia, or the second part of musicks melodie, or melodius musicke of pleasant roundelaies; K. H. mirth, or freemans songs. And such delightfull catches. Qui canere potest canat. Catch, that catch can,* is described as a collection "of things of the same *condition*" as *Pammelia,* and of which likewise "*most* men . . . are capable, that are not altogether immusical . . ." (signature A3; italics in 1609 edition). The testimony of these composers, and of others, is corroborated by the reports of the performances of the masques at court: the aristocracy danced and professional musicians played and sang. Perhaps it was felt that to dance in a more or less public spectacle was more becoming than performing music; but the determining reason for the practice must have been that the musicianship of the aristocracy was inadequate to the demands of the scores composed for the masques.

No doubt there were many devoted practitioners of music in the upper classes in late Tudor and early Stuart England, and some of them must have been highly skilled; that not all of them were is hardly surprising. The public that had studied music and had retained an active interest in it was large enough to give printers hope of profit from the publication of music in editions of a few hundred copies each and large enough to give English composers an important corps of discriminating critics and patrons.[23]

Authentic information on how and when ladies and gentlemen entertained themselves by performing music is quite rare, rare first of all because not many people thought it worth while to record even their important activities, and, next, because comparatively few people could and did perform music for their own entertainment. Instances of solitary performances have already been mentioned—playing on the lute or gittern and presumably singing too, and playing on the virginals—and study of the appendices of this book will indicate the relatively great popularity of these solo instruments; the possession of instruments and music is at most a suggestion of intention, sometimes only of service to fashion, and never by itself a sure sign of intensive musical activity.

A few instances of groups of friends joining to amuse themselves with music have also been noticed. Of these, the best known were those George Herbert attended in Salisbury. What were in some respects the most famous musical parties of Elizabethan England gathered in the 1580s at the house of Nicholas Yonge, a lay clerk of St. Paul's cathedral. Yonge, who compiled *Musica Transalpina*, the first printed (1588) collection of Italian madrigals with English words, mentions the parties in the dedication: ". . . since I first began to keep house in this city, it hath been no small comfort unto me, that a great number of gentlemen and merchants of good account (as well of this realm as of foreign nations) have taken in good part such entertainment of pleasure, as my poor ability was able to afford them, both by the exercise of music daily used in my house, and by furnishing them with books of that kind yearly sent me out of Italy and other places, which being for the most part Italian songs, are for sweetness of air, very well liked of all, but most in account with them that understand that language. As for the rest, they do either not sing them at all, or at the least with little delight. And albeit there be some English songs

---

[23] For size of editions (ordinarily about one thousand copies) see Gregg and Boswell, *Records of the Court of the Stationers' Company, 1576 to 1602*, p. lvi. Dowling, "The Printing of John Dowland's *Second Booke of Songs or Ayres,*" *The Library*, 4th series, XII (1932), 365-380, gives an enlightening account of the publishing of a successful book (about one thousand copies altogether in four editions) and of the profits of dedications. (Dr. J. W. Kerman, formerly of the Westminster Choir School, Princeton, and now of the University of California, Berkeley, called my attention to this article).

lately set forth by a great master of music [Byrd], which for skill and sweetness may content the most curious: yet because they are not many in number, men delighted with variety have wished more of the same sort. . . ." The fame these meetings gained came chiefly later, and stems, it seems, from the support this dedication gives to the notion that nearly everyone in Elizabethan England was an accomplished musician. Yonge's editorial initiative, if not universally acclaimed, won appreciation sufficient to encourage him to prepare *Musica Transalpina. The second booke of madrigalles, to 5 and 6 voices*, which was published nine years after the first set, in 1597. The meeting of similar groups is implied by other dedications, such as that of Morley's *Canzonets. or little short songs to foure voyces: celected out of the best and approved Italian authors*, 1597, to "Master Henrie Tapster citizen and grocer of the city of London," whom Morley thanks for past courtesies and asks to accept the songs for "the honest recreation" of himself and others.

Casual passages mentioning non-professional musical groups seem usually to refer to the most informal and lighthearted of effort, ready renderings of pills to purge melancholy, rather than to delicate readings of subtle polyphony. John Greene, nineteen years old and reading law at Lincoln's Inn, hardly suggests straining after, or achievement of, perfection in madrigal or motet in his diary references to student pastimes: "On the 31 [of October 1635], being all Saints Eve, we had fire in the hall, no gaming, no revels. We had music and mirth and solace and the measures. It was fasting night. On the first of this month [November], being Sunday and also all Saints day the judges dined here. Solace was song and measures danced, and also after supper. I danced the measure after dinner. . . . [10 November 1635] I at lottery and dance. Corrante in music. . . . [4 December 1635] . . . being Saturday after supper we had no mirth and solace, but Mr. Chamber and four couples danst the measure. After they were done four benchers came into the hall and we had songs as usual; nothing else, no gaming. . . ." Such informal entertainment was in the Lincoln's Inn tradition, mentioned in a letter of 1613: "The first of this month the lord chancellor [Thomas Egerton, Lord Ellesmere] was at Lincoln's Inn (as he said) to take his leave, and sang and danced about the fire after their laudable custom." Besides their knowledge of the law the gentlemen-students took back to their counties (if they had not brought it with them) a taste for such music; it was what the Lieutenant Hammond of Norwich encountered at an outing near Harwich in 1635: ". . . I discovered there were a civil, merry, genteel company of both

sexes, who that morning were come upon that stream, from Wood-
bridge, to take their recreation on the sea for their health, and afterwards for their pleasure to laugh and be merry at land, with that good
wine and other provision that they had brought along with them: . . .
I had a free participation of their good cheer, which was wine, oysters,
music, mirth, &c. . . ."[24]

Mace, a clerk of Trinity college, Cambridge, whose enthusiastic
reporting was quoted in chapter six, devotes many pages in *Musick's
Monument* to musical customs he knew in his youth, and one of these
passages may depict, not unfaithfully, some of the more sophisticated
musical parties of the last decades before the civil war: "We had for
our grave music, fancies of three, four, five, and six parts to the organ;
interpos'd (now and then) with some pavins, allmaines, solemn, and
sweet delightful ayres. . . . The authors of such like compositions, have
been divers famous English men, and Italians; some of which, for
their very great eminency, and worth, in that particular faculty, I will
here name, viz. Mr. Alfonso Ferabosco, Mr. John Ward, Mr. Lupo,
Mr. White, Mr. Richard Deering, Mr. William Lawes, Mr. John
Jenkins, Mr. Christopher Simpson, Mr. Coperanio, and one Monte-
verde, a famous Italian author; besides divers . . . others. . . . [In margin: "What instruments were us'd, and how in the best old music."]
And these things were performed, upon so many equal, and truly siz'd
viols; and so exactly strung, tun'd, and play'd upon, as no one part
was any impediment to the other; but still (as the composition required) by intervals, each part amplified, and heightened the other;
the organ evenly, softly, and sweetly according [acchording] to all.
Whereas now the fashion has cry'd these things down. . . . We had
(beyond all this) a custom at our meetings, that commonly, after such
instrumental music was over, we did conclude all, with some vocal
music, (to the organ, or (for want of that) to the theorboe). The best
which we did ever esteem, were those things which were most solemn,
and divine, some of which I will (for their eminency) name, viz. Mr.
Deering's Gloria Patri, and other of his Latin songs; . . . besides many
other of the like nature, Latin and English. . . . But when we would
be most airy, jocund, lively, and spruce; then we had choice, and
singular consorts, either for two, three, or four parts, but not to the
organ (as many (now a days) improperly, and unadvisedly perform

[24] Greene: Symonds, "The Diary of John Greene," *English Historical Review*,
XLIII (1928), 389. Lincoln's Inn, 1613: *The Letters of John Chamberlain*, ed.
McClure, I, 489. Hammond, *Relation 1635*, ed. Legg, 3.

such like consorts with) but to the harpsicon; yet more properly, and much better to the pedal, (an instrument of a late invention. . . . Then again, we had all those choice consorts, to equally-siz'd instruments, (rare chests of viols) and as equally perform'd: For we would never allow any performer to over-top, or out-cry another by loud play; but our great care was, to have all the parts equally heard; by which means (though sometimes we had but indifferent, or mean hands to perform with); yet this caution made the music lovely, and very contentive."[25]

Since Mace lived both by and for music, groups in which he participated can hardly be taken as typical. The passage does however call to mind some of the musical resources available to ladies and gentlemen, and makes clear the great importance of instruments; they were used not only for what we now call chamber music, but with singing. About a hundred music books, some in more than one edition, were printed in England during the reigns of Elizabeth, James, and Charles, most of them for voice, and a great deal of music was imported (Morley and others complained of the partiality of Englishmen for Italian music). References to the copying of music occur fairly frequently in the sources, an indication that manuscript was probably more common than printed music; and in the manuscripts instrumental music is more common than vocal.[26]

---

[25] Mace, pp. 233-236. Mace disparages, in contrast, the new fashion of "High-priz'd noise, viz. ten, or twenty violins . . . ," with its strong contrasts.

[26] For Morley's complaint see *A Plaine and Easie Introduction*, 179. Carleton, *Madrigals* (1601) states in "A preface to the skilful musician" that he has "labored somewhat to imitate the *Italian*, they being in these days (with the most) in high request" but also that he cannot forget that he is an Englishman (signature Aij verso).

The catalogue of the library of John Baron Lumley (1534?-1609) furnishes an example of what might be found in a library gathered mostly in the earlier part of this period. Nearly all of the more than forty-five sets of music books were of Netherland or Italian origin, c. 1550-1570 (from Huntington Library photostatic copy of the original catalogue, Trinity College, Cambridge Ms. 0.4.38). See also appendices, especially Cavendish accounts in Entries Relating to Music, from Household Accounts.

For the troubles which William Trumbull encountered in getting virginal lesson books written up for himself about 1609 see HMC 75, *Downshire Mss.*, iii, 163-164, 171-172, 182-183, 197-198, 219-220, 253, 490-491. See also in the same, pp. 438-439 (Trumbull is requested to secure "chansons pour la violle") and p. 394.

For an example of the kind of music to be found in manuscript part-books, see the description of Bodleian Ms. Mus. folios 1-6, in Madan, *A Summary Catalogue of Western Manuscripts in the Bodleian Library at Oxford*, IV, 31.

On instrumental music in manuscript see the catalogue in Meyer, *Die Mehrstimmige Spielmusik des 17. Jahrhunderts*, 133-148 (English only). See also Meyer's *English Chamber Music*; on p. 125 he states that "It is true that more

Of the recurring musical parties mentioned in the preceding paragraphs, the two most probably devoted largely to the careful performance of the more advanced and often more difficult music had in each case as a participant a professional musician—Yonge and Mace were both lay clerks. It seems likely that this was the general rule: certainly the guidance and participation of a professional musician would make easier the performance of difficult music by a family or group of friends. For gentlemen truly devoted to music this must have been one of the principal reasons for retaining a professional musician in residence and for obtaining musical servants.

Even in those households, probably a majority, where the master and his family had no serious pretenses to musical accomplishment and rarely raised their voices in song unless for a psalm or catch, music might often be heard. In the earlier decades of the period vagabond minstrels and nominally-retained musicians—and throughout the period waits—were fairly frequent visitors, stopping to play or sing at the gates or in the hall. Some of them were almost certain to attend the greater, or more generous, gentry at the great holiday times and other important occasions. While uninvited attendance was more common, special summons appear now and then in the records of some of the noble families and others particularly devoted to music.

Christmas more regularly demanded the services of musicians in the great houses than any other festival. Sir Henry Sidney, when lord president of the council for Wales, paid a large sum for musicians in Christmas 1570. The earl of Rutland had the waits of Grantham at Belvoir castle for Christmas 1607, Franklyn and his men (and a bear and bull) in for Christmas 1609, musicians again ("all the twelve days") in 1611, and Franklyn again in 1614. The earl of Cumberland had "Stephen Gryges the musician of Barton . . . and four more for playing and attending" Christmas 1611 and 1612 (and probably in the succeeding years), the waits of York at Christmas 1633, Roger the piper in 1637 and 1638, and "the music of York . . . all Christmas" in 1639. In most cases several musicians served, they seem to have come by invitation rather than on speculation, and to have stayed for the whole holiday period; in every case they were very well paid. A passage in Robert Armin's *A Nest of Ninnies*, 1608, describes no particular house or Christmas, but may nevertheless indicate fairly accurately the

---

vocal music than instrumental was printed, but far more instrumental music than vocal survives in manuscript, and the sum total of instrumental music composed surpasses that of secular vocal music."

spirit and some of the older traditions of the holiday: "At a Christmas time, when great logs furnish the hall fire—when brawn is in season, and, indeed, all reveling is regarded, this gallant knight kept open house for all comers, where beef, beer, and bread was no niggard. Amongst all the pleasures provided, a noise of minstrels and a Lincolnshire bagpipe was prepared—the minstrels for the great chamber, the bagpipe for the hall—the minstrels to serve up the knights meat, and the bagpipe for the common dancing."[27]

Weddings took an eminent place among the great special occasions calling for music. Thomas Wilcox's pious *Exposition uppon the Booke of the Canticles, otherwise called Schelomons Song*, 1585, in commenting on Song of Solomon, iii, 5, refers to "the custom used then, and yet even at this day in some places used amongst us, namely that songs are sung before the bride chamber, and certain noises of instruments brought, to wake the bride and bridegroom from sleep. . . ." How extensive the musical requirements of a great wedding were is indicated by two entries in the accounts of the earls of Cumberland for July 1634, when Lady Elizabeth Clifford married (at Skipton castle, Yorkshire) Richard Boyle, heir to the earl of Cork: "This day to certain French musicians and a singer, which were at my Lady Dungarvan's marriage for their reward by his lordship's command, six pounds," and "The same day to the music of Stamford for their reward and service done here at my Lady Dungarvan's marriage nine weeks the sum of fifteen pounds."[28]

Music was often employed to help honor distinguished guests; the earl of Leicester's entertainment of Queen Elizabeth at Kenilworth in 1575 is only the most famous of these great fetes. The waits of Lincoln received four pounds for playing at Belvoir castle during the visit of King James in 1612, and George Mason and John Earsden wrote music to help honor James when he was the guest of the earl of Cumberland in 1617 (mentioned in chapter three). The visitors did not need to be reigning monarchs to deserve music: the earl of Cumberland, for example, felt called on to send for musicians in 1612 when Lord

---

[27] For sources of all items in this paragraph referring to the Clifford, Kytson, Rutland, and Sidney families, and for many other illustrations of the role of professional musicians in the lives of the aristocracy see appendix, Entries Relating to Music, from Household Accounts. Notice particularly the account for the masque given by the earl of Cumberland in 1636 (Clifford accounts).

Armin, *A Nest of Ninnies*, ed. Collier, 9 (Elson, *Shakespeare in Music*, 35, uses this passage).

[28] Wilcox, *Exposition*, 69. Clifford: see appendix.

Wharton and "Sir Thomas his Lady" stopped at Londesborough. Richard Brathwaite, writing in *Some Rules and Orders for the Government of the House of an Earle*, 1621, his rather old-fashioned ideas of what ought to be, can hardly have been describing any contemporary English household when he included among the staff of an earl five musicians besides a trumpeter and a drummer, but it is not unlikely that musicians called in from York, Barton, or Grantham for great feasts were actually used much as he prescribed: "At great feasts, when the earl's service is going to the table, they are to play upon shagbut [sackbut], cornetts, shawms, and such other instruments going with wind. In meal times to play upon viols, violins, or other broken music. . . . At great feasts, or in time of great strangers" the drum is to sound at dinner time "till the ewer be ready to go up with the service, and then to give place to the musicians, who are to play on the instruments. . . ."[29]

Holidays, weddings, great guests, were not essential; anything would serve as reason for employing musicians: "1 December 1618. Item given this day in reward to two waits of Skipton, that were at Londesborough a week, and came to play to my Lord Clifford's horse races, so given them at their going away by my lord's commandment. six shillings." Or no excuse at all: "28 August 1612. Item given the same day in reward by my lord's commandment to the waits of York being seven in number who came to Londesborough and stayed all night and played in the great chamber after supper, thirteen shillings four pence." Rare music was sometimes planned long ahead of time. Sir Arthur Basset wrote to Sir Edward Stradling: ". . . I am hereby to request you to send unto me at any of my houses in Devonshire your servant Thomas Richards by the last day of this instant month, and to cause him to bring with him both his instruments, as well that which is stringed with wire strings, as his harp, both those that he had when he was last in Devon. I have given some commendations of the man and his instrument knowledge, but chiefly for the rareness of his instrument with wires, unto sundry of my good friends, namely to my cousin Sir Philip Sidney, who doth expect to have your man at Salisbury before the seventh of March next, where there will be an honorable assembly and receipt of many gentlemen of good calling. So hoping you will herein accomplish my request, do most heartily commend you to God's good keeping. From London this sixth of Feb-

[29] Belvoir: see appendix. Brathwaite, *Some Rules*, reprinted in *Miscellanea Antiqua Anglicana*, ed. Triphook, 3-4, 44.

ruary, 1583. Your very loving friend Arthur Basset." Perhaps this was the kind of party mentioned in a letter of about 1587: "You were expected yesterday. We had many lords and lordings at dinner, who spent all the day in music, and you might have done well to come among them. Here was Sir Harry Gray, Mr. Vavasour, and young Mr. Dudley, the great lord's son, men well known to you. . . ."[30]

Away from home, too, noblemen and gentlemen heard much music. Travelers frequently rewarded blind harpers, heard waits or other musicians while enjoying the wine and sugar served them by the mayors and burgesses of towns through which they passed, rewarded waits for waking them if they happened to stop overnight at an inn, and no doubt sometimes attended a musical service at a cathedral. Lieutenant Hammond of the military company in Norwich was wandering with his friends, uncertain of the way, in Lancashire, when "the melodious sound of a sweet cornett arrested [their] ears" and guided them to the house of Mr. Standish of Standish, the sheriff. The lieutenant happily recorded that at Newcastle "our host, a good fellow, and his daughter, an indifferent virginal player, somewhat refresh'd our weary limbs," and of the great caves near Bath: "Music doth sound, and re-echo, most sweetly, and melodiously in those hollow caverns, and passages, and we had a full trial thereof by a recorder. . . ."[31]

In London musical opportunities were almost unlimited: without special arrangement St. Paul's, Westminster abbey, the Chapel Royal, the King's Musick, the waits of London, and the theatre in season all had feasts for the ears of gentlemen. At one of the so-called private theatres, Blackfriars, where the boys of the Chapel Royal acted, "For a whole hour preceding the play," a foreigner wrote in 1602, "one listens to a delightful musical entertainment on organs, lutes, pandoras, mandoras, viols, and pipes, as on the present occasion, indeed, when a boy *cum voce tremula* sang so charmingly to the accompaniment of a bass-viol that unless possibly the nuns at Milan may have excelled him, we had not heard his equal on our journey." At the public theatres, more plebeian, initially at least, than the private theatres, trumpet blasts served instead of music before the prologue, but music sometimes filled the intermissions, came when called for by the dramatic situation during the acts, and followed the end of the plays. This

[30] Skipton and York waits: see appendix (Clifford). Basset's letter, *Sidneiana being a collection of fragments relative to Sir Philip Sidney* . . . , 81. Letter 1587? from W. Sterrell to Thomas Phelippes, cspd *1580-1625*, 231 (the passage is not in quotation marks in the *Calendar*).
[31] Hammond, *Relation 1634*, ed. Legg, 45, 31, 105.

postlude, about half an hour long, was described by a visitor in 1598 as "excellent music, variety of dances . . . ," and by the justices of the peace at Westminster sessions in 1612 as "certain lewd jigs, songs, and dances. . . ."[32]

Special events supplemented the regular fare. Noblemen, knights, gentlemen, and ladies were invited in June 1612 to attend an evening's entertainment "Prepared of an Italian, consort of strange music, consisting of nine instruments with other several instruments, musically concorded with Italian voices, very delectable. . . . Where also is pro-

---

[32] 1602: Diary of Frederic Gerschow, *Transactions*, Royal Historical Society, new series, VI (1892), 26, 28; the excerpt above is the translation of Wallace, *Children of the Chapel*, 107, except for the names of some of the instruments (*Orgeln, Lauten, Pandoren, Mandoren, Geigen, Pfeiffen*; *Geigen* could mean here any bowed instrument, and *Pfeiffen* probably flute or recorder). 1598: Hentzner, *Itinerary* (1629), 196, from Lawrence, *Elizabethan Playhouse*, 80-81. 1612: *Middlesex County Records*, II, 71; reference from Murray, *English Dramatic Companies*, I, 210.

Music was freely used in the early Elizabethan drama. Cowling, *Music on the Shakespearian Stage*, 17-18, gives the "Order of the Dumb-show before the First Act" of *Gorboduc*, by Norton and Sackville, produced by the gentlemen of the Inner Temple at Whitehall in 1562, as a typical example of the use of the "dumb-show" accompanied by music before acts to illustrate the plot. "First, the music of violins began to play, during which came in upon the stage six wild men . . ." bearing sticks bound together which they could not break until they were separated, an illustration of the moral exemplified in the play. In another early Elizabethan play, *Gammer Gurton's Needle*, "one finds definite allusion to the custom of playing music between the acts" (Lawrence, *Elizabethan Playhouse*, 76). See also "Early Elizabethan Stage Music," *Musical Antiquary*, I (1910), 30-40. Chambers, *Elizabethan Stage*, II, 542, note 1, states that Lawrence and Cowling "do not discriminate sufficiently the practice of the public theatres from that of the private theatres on the one hand and the early neo-classic court plays on the other. Here music is an integral part of the *intermedii* or dumb-shows. . . ." On the poetic and dramatic reasons (atmosphere, change of place and time, etc.) for the introduction of music into the plays see in particular Cowling; Evans, *Ben Jonson and Elizabethan Music*; and Lawrence; Noble, *Shakespeare's Use of Song*, may also be useful. The chief excuse for much of the music must have been its popularity with the spectators, of course: the point is sometimes forgotten.

Chambers, *Elizabethan Stage*, II, 554-557, summarizes the differences between the public and private theatres, and on p. 542 indicates his belief that use of music in the public theatre tended to grow.

For music in the theatre see also: Scott, "London's Earliest Public Concerts," *Musical Quarterly*, XXII (1936), 446 (further references); Dent, *Foundations of English Opera*; Lawrence, "Music in the Elizabethan Theatre," *Musical Quarterly*, VI (1920), 192-205; Lindsey, "The Music in Ben Jonson's Plays," *Modern Language Notes*, XLIV (1929), 86-92; Lindsey, "The Music of the Songs in Fletcher's Plays," *Studies in Philology*, XXI (1924), 325-355; Nierling, "The Music for Shakespeare," *Musical Quarterly*, XII (1926), 555-563; Welch, "Shakespeare—Musician," *Musical Quarterly*, VIII (1922), 510-527.

vided costly furniture . . . which are to be raffled [rifled], giving forty shillings apiece for three throws with three dice. . . . At Master Taylor's house, one of the king's majesty's servants, at Lincoln's Innfields. . . ." Colonel Hutchinson's widow recorded another delectable opportunity London afforded about 1636-1638: "The man [Charles Coleman, viol player in the King's Musick] being a skilful composer in music, the rest of the king's musicians often met at his house [in Richmond] to practice new airs and prepare them for the king; and divers of the gentlemen and ladies that were affected with music, came thither to hear; others that were not, took that pretense to entertain themselves with the company." And of course professional musicians could easily be secured. Phineas Pett recorded in his autobiography the story of a great outing he and about twenty others of Prince Henry's establishment took in 1612. When they had decided, while at Richmond, to go to Chatham with their wives "to be merry," Pett took them down from Greenwich in pinnaces, well supplied with food and wine for the day-long passage—five in the morning to six in the evening. On the first day Pett gave them a feast at his house; the second day they spent aboard "the great ship, the *Prince*, . . . and all their children's healths were drunk round with loud report of the ordnance, a noise of music attending us all the day. We took leave on board about ten of the clock at night, our music playing before us, and for our farewell there were twenty-five pieces of great ordnance discharged after the watch was set." More feasting, no doubt to music, followed on the next day; a sermon distinguished Sunday; rain, stopping them from their intended return on Monday, perhaps justified another day of feasting and music; and on Tuesday the holiday ended with the trip back up the river. Music, plentiful for those who wanted and could pay for it, may sometimes have been a little too plentiful. Dudley Carleton, traveling in Berkshire in October 1600 wrote to a friend: ". . . In our way from Witham hither, we met a company of mad wenches, whereof Mrs. Mary Wroughton and young Stafford were ringleaders, who traveled from house to house, and to some places where they were little known, attended with a concert of musicians, as if they had undertaken the like adventure as Kemp did from London to Norwich. They were at this house and missed us but half an hour." Little wonder if busy gentlemen felt no compulsion to spend their time learning or practicing music when it was as readily available for money as it was in 1600.[33]

[33] 1612: HMC *58, Bath Mss.*, ii, 61-62. Hutchinson, *Memoirs of the Life of*

"It Only Serveth"

When the whole scene is viewed, even thus cursorily, it appears that no class lacked music. Much of it all classes could enjoy in common; much of it only the upper classes could know and appreciate. Many in the upper classes, although seldom accomplished musicians themselves (even the code of the gentleman scarcely required this), could play and sing after a rough fashion; and some knew enough to want and to demand the best, on occasion, of the professional musicians they employed. Perhaps the upper classes made their greatest contribution to English music as admirers and critics of professional musicians and of composers.

Colonel Hutchinson, ed. Firth, 1, 80, 82. (I am indebted to Professor Elmer Beller of Princeton University for this passage.) Pett, *Autobiography*, ed. Perrin, 98-99. Carleton: CSPD *1598-1601*, 478.

EPILOGUE

EPILOGUE

"But what say I, Music? One of the seven Liberal Sciences? It is almost banished this Realm. If it were not, the Queen's Majesty did favor that excellent Science, Singing-men, and Choristers might go a begging, together with their Master the player on the Organs." The justness of John Bossewell's passing observation, written early in Elizabeth's reign in a book on armorial coats and crests, can be debated if it is closely construed, but it undoubtedly emphasizes properly the great importance of the sovereign in the history of music in English society. It is quite possible that without Elizabeth singing-men and choristers would have been swept out of the church establishment; and it is quite certain that Charles supported Laud in his efforts to raise the standards of performance in cathedrals throughout England. Certainly, if the sovereigns had not favored music, both ecclesiastical and secular, it might seem now that it had been banished the realm: the sovereigns were by far England's greatest patrons of music.[1]

The disparity between the positions of the sovereigns and of all other individual or corporate patrons, often illustrated in the preceding chapters, is reflected in the size of establishments maintained, the number of composers patronized, and perhaps most graphically in the wages paid. The following table (see over) may exaggerate the extremes, because the figures for the royal musicians include all regular income from the crown while those for the churchmen include only annual payments in cash, and for the waits only annual payments from town funds, without livery (York and Leicester figures are estimated minimum assessment collections). All of these musicians, royal, ecclesiastical and municipal, probably had additional income, with the extraneous income greatest relative to stipend, in the case of the waits.

In the Chapel Royal and the King's Musick the sovereigns supported most of the best musicians of England. The church employed most of the rest of the best musicians, private patrons, on terms not clearly revealed, other noted performers and composers, and the city of London a few more. More than wages, of course, account for the pre-eminence of the Chapel Royal and King's Musick.

Even begging, the alternative suggested by Bossewell, implies public support, and there was, of course, popular support for music in Elizabethan England, beyond that of such exceptional patrons as the Kytsons

[1] Bossewell, *Workes of Armorie* (1572), 3d book, folio 14. Hawkins, *History of Music*, cites this passage.

	WAITS			CHURCH		COURT	
	Various	Norwich	London	Laymen	Priests	C. Royal	K. Musick
c. 1475			£ 1.6.8				
c. 1524			3.6.8				
1536		£1.0.0	6.0.0				
1538		2.6.8					
1544						£ 29.13.1 ½	
1549		2.13.4					
c. 1550				£ 10.0.0 Windsor 8.0.0 York 6.13.4 Norwich	£ 13.6.8 Windsor 10.0.0 York		£ 46.10.10
1567	£ 2.0.0 Cambridge						
1568			8.0.0				
1570				8.0.0 Norwich			
1571	1.0.0* Nottingham		10.0.0				
1580	2.0.0 York						
1582			11.13.4				
1583	1.0.0* Ipswich 3.4.0 Leicester	3.0.0					
1604				8.13.4** to £ 12 Salisbury		40.0.0	46.10.10
1605			20.0.0				
1622	2.0.0 Cambridge						
1634				6.13.4** to £ 8 Bristol	12.0.0 Bristol		(Lanier: 272.5.0)
1635				10.0.0 Rochester	12.0.0 Rochester		

* Quarterage in addition. ** Pay increased from smaller to larger figure.

of Hengrave hall. As in all ages, most people enjoyed music of one kind or another; some of them, perhaps more than in many ages, learned to perform music for themselves, and many of these, neglecting to maintain their skill as they reached maturity but retaining a taste for advanced styles in performance and composition, became competent critics and enlightened if not munificent patrons; and a very large part of the population, of the lower as well as upper classes, helped support professional musicians of widely varying talent and training. Besides the handful of musicians at court, in cathedrals, and in private households, England supported thousands of waits and independent musicians, who at once educated and entertained their public, stimulated, by at least implicit competition, their superiors of the court and church, and formed a reserve pool from which new talent occasionally appeared for the court and church. Music in England rested on a broad foundation of a public that enjoyed music, even if not willing to pay much for it, and of an extensive class of professional musicians that could subsist if not flourish.

Nevertheless music and professional musicians were, on the whole, little more than tolerated. Persons who subscribed to Castiglione's views regarded musical training as important in the fashioning of a gentleman, but required moderation, and therefore usually mediocrity. Most professional musicians found themselves regarded with suspicion: they could be citizens or burgesses, but almost never important and honored citizens or burgesses. A few of them could subscribe themselves gentlemen and bachelor or doctor, but the appellations seldom indicated that they had a secure place in the upper strata of society. The men of the Chapel Royal were called gentlemen, and on the whole probably lived as gentlemen; the men of the King's Musick could afford to live as gentlemen, probably did, and probably thought of themselves as gentlemen. The swashbuckling behavior of some of them, as in 1629, when Nicholas Lanier and others of the king's servants quarreled with a man, beat him with their fists, and finally "went forth in a ruffling manner into Cornhill, flourishing their swords . . . ," suggests an assertive rather than assured state of mind. Sword-bearing and all, Lanier and his companions were still servants. So too were most of the composers who lived in private households. Some of them in their dedications indicate that their patrons had been as fathers to them; deep affection between masters and old family retainers makes servants no less subordinate. Hunsdon, master of the children in the Chapel Royal, and a few other musicians, had or won, by their service, wealth or university degrees, coats of arms and certified title to gentility, but they were exceptional, and it is doubtful that gentlemen of more conventional antecedents would have welcomed them as sons-in-law. Music, particularly by way of cathedral or Chapel Royal, thence university and church preferment, offered opportunity for advancement to a higher degree in society, but most professional musicians started and ended as menials, sometimes respected for their gifts and skill, usually only tolerated as long as they behaved circumspectly.[2]

The general social level of most professional musicians seems to have been lower middle class, if their status, and that of the families of non-musical occupations with which they had connections, was fairly closely related. In York three sons of John Sawhell, minstrel and citizen, became freemen during Mary's reign, each in a different occupation: tailor, glover, and goldsmith; sons of a grocer, a wright, a tailor, a porter, a laborer, and of two tapitors (tapissers), became musicians, while from musicians' families came a tailor, a tiler and a haberdasher, during Elizabeth's reign. The sons of a blacksmith, a joiner, and a saddler became musicians while from musicians' families came a tiler, a milner, a jerseyman, a tailor and a cordwainer in the reigns of James and Charles. As the records of the King's Musick and the registers of the freemen of York and other towns amply illustrate, however, most professional musicians followed a family tradition, son after father. Predominantly lower middle class, the profession can also correctly be described as without a real rank in society, partly because of the wide gulf between the position of the royal musicians and the poor musicians of country towns, but chiefly because musicians, required to behave correctly in the company of all ranks of society, conformed to the manners and dress of no single rank of society. All but the poorest and lowest musicians, and church musicians, had to be prepared in manner and dress to serve all comers, in inns as well as in the houses of the upper middle class, the gentry and nobility. The career of James Clifford (1622-1698), son of a cook, who became a chorister at Magdalen college, musician and cleric at St. Paul's, illustrates again the pathway to preferment which music could offer, just as the career of Orlando Gibbons, son of a wait, illustrates the connections, usually less patent, between various branches of the profession.[3]

[2] Nicholas Lanyer and others his majesty's servants: CSPD *1628-29*, 479 (that this Lanier was the master of the Musick is probable but not certain). Morley and another musician were sometimes designated gentlemen in parish registers; see A[rkwright], "Notes on the parish registers of St. Helen's, Bishopsgate, London," *Musical Antiquary*, I (1910), 44.

[3] *Register of the Freemen of the City of York*, ed. Collins, I, 274, 277 (Mary); II, 13-37 (Elizabeth); II, 51-84 (James and Charles). On Clifford see *Dictionary of National Biography*. In 1612-1613 Edmund Pollard, musician, second son of Thomas Pollard, husbandman, was admitted to the freedom of Leicester: *Register of the Freemen of Leicester*, ed. Hartopp, 107. In 1573 Nicholas Boniface, minstrel, and Anthony Boniface, mercer, both of Rye, gave bond for the appearance before the mayor of Anne Boniface: HMC *31, Rye Mss.*, 24. According to

Epilogue

Perhaps professional musicians in a sense constituted a little estate of their own, as journalists are said to. Certainly they formed a kind of hierarchy of their own, unrecognized but real, a system in fact but not theory, dependent at the bottom on the support of a wide public, dependent at the top on royal patronage. It is doubtful if the musicians of the court and cathedrals could have accomplished their great work if they had been the only accomplished musicians in England and if they had lacked interested and informed audiences; and still more doubtful that England would have had so great an age musically if the musical organizations of the court and church had not existed, and if musicians had had to depend on private and municipal patronage.

During the century before the civil wars, while the court establishments were growing to their fullest splendor and achieving their greatest triumphs, wandering minstrels transformed themselves into settled independent musicians and municipal waits, but, forerunners though they were of the professional musician of the twentieth century, neither they nor any institution were yet prepared to carry on the musical work of the church and court. The institutions which nourished England's musical greatness had developed gradually. When gradual change became impossible, when the monarch and his court and the church he led could no longer continue as music's greatest patrons, the long history of musical composition in England was interrupted, and the hierarchy which had made it possible was irreparably shattered.

Anthony à Wood, William Howes, born in or near Worcester, was "bred up among the musicians or waits in Worcester, afterwards petty-canon of Windsor ...," became a gentleman of the Chapel Royal after the Restoration and a member in ordinary of the king's "private music": Lives of the English Musicians, Bodleian Ms. 8568, Ms. Wood D.19(4), folio 70.

APPENDICES

APPENDIX A

APPOINTMENT OF LONDON WAITS

THIS appendix is designed primarily to present the history of the appointment of the waits of London and to show how the group expanded. The chronological arrangement, rather than a relatively meaningless alphabetical arrangement, has been chosen in order to facilitate determination of the membership at any selected time and to make possible the tracing of succession to places (see 1635 and 1637, Robert Herson, for example). Almost all names appear twice, first in the year of appointment, and then in year of retirement. In order to get all data given about any man, including references, the reader must look for the man's name under the years found in both the third and fourth columns; these dates are the keys to cross-references.

Abbreviations:

R32:16	Repertory, xxxii, folio 16
J10:16v	Journal, x, folio 16 verso
LB AB:152v	Letter Book AB, folio 152 verso
KM 45	*King's Musick*, ed. Lafontaine, page 45.

Year	Name	Year Apptd.	Year Retired		References
1442				Nine waits	LB K:206v
1475				Policy: six waits	J8:112
1495	John Wikes		1495	Awarded next vacancy in Philpot's Alms.	R1:12
1502	John Mychall, John Brown, William Pallyng, Nicholas Ryppes, John Wayles			Made free in city and in fellowship of minstrels.	J10:250v-251
1506	John Butson		c.1506	Pensioned in February.	R2:3
1518	William Blewet		1518	Dead by 23 Sep.	R3:235v
	John Fryth	1518		Blewet's place.	R3:235v
	John Ryppys		1518	Pensioned.	R3:237
1523				Six waits.	R6:56
1526				Sackbut bought.	R7:137
	William Cholmeley		1526	Retired.	R7:137
	John Warren	1526	(1571?)	Cholmeley's place.	R7:137
1548				Each wait can have two apprentices.	R11:481
1555	Richard Streache		1555	Pensioned.	R13i:255v
	Geoffrey Foster	1555	(1561)	Streache's place.	R13i:256v
				Sackbut bought.	R13ii:335
1557	Anthony Tyndall	1557	(1597)		R13ii:552v
1558	Williamson		1558	Negligent, resigns.	R14:63v
	Robert Howlett	1558	(1560)		R14:74v
1559	[Thomas] Bell	?	(1569)	Sells sackbut to city	R14:199v
1560	Robert Howlett	(1558)	1560	Resigns to serve queen	R14:346
	John Scryven	1560	(1565)	Apparently head wait 1561	R14:353v; (Sayle, *Lord Mayors' Pageants*, 40.)

· 247 ·

Year	Name	Year Apptd.	Year Retired		References
1561	Jeffrey Foster	(1555)	1561	Resigned	R14:448v
	Walter Lowman	1561	(1611)	Foster's place	R14:448v
				Set of viols bought	R14:509v, 514
1563	Robarte Strachie ["the elder"]	1563	(1616)		R15:286v
1565	John Screven	(1560)	1565	Deceased by 4 Sep.	R15:462v
	Thomas Comyn[gs]	1565	(1597)	Screven's place	R15:462v
1568				Six waits	R16:323v
				Set of recorders and six cornetts bought	R16:407
1569	Thomas Bell	[v. 1559]	1569	Pensioned	R16:484v
	John Baker	1569	(1582)	Bell's place	R16:484v
1570	Segar van Pilkam	1570	(1581)	Extra (seventh) man	R17:63
1571	Arthur Norton	1571	(1593)	Replacing Warren (1526)?	R17:239v
1576				"Certeyn newe Instruments" bought	R19:60v
1581				Two sackbuts bought	R20:170
	Seger van Pelchem	(1570)	1581	Leaves for continent; six waits again	R20:185
1582	John Baker	(1569)	1582	Dead by 15 Nov.	R20:376v
	Edward Blancq (also Blanck)	1582	(1594)	Baker's place	R20:376v
1583	Robert Baker	(1588)	(1594)	Apprentice to Anthony Tindall (1557-1597)	R20:453
1588	Robert Baker	1588	(1594)	Extra (seventh) man	R21:596
1593	Arthure Norton (called Morton	(1571)	1593	Resigned	R23:47v LB AB:152v)
	Thomas Carter	1593	(1616)	Norton's place	R23:47v
1594	Robert Baker	(1588)	1594	Resigns to serve queen; recorder player	R23:296 *KM* 45
	John Ballarde, yeoman	1594	(1601)	Baker's place (seventh?)	R23:296
	Edward Blanke	(1582)	1594	Resigned	R23:319v
	William Pryne	1594	(1613)	Blanke's place	R23:320v
1597	Anthony Tindall	(1557)	1597	Pensioned	R24:53v
	Thomas Comyngs	(1565)	1597	Pensioned	R24:53v
	John Robson	1597	(1613)	Place of one of above two	R24:54
	Stephen Thomas	1597	(1618)	Place of the other	R24:54
				Single, double, sackbuts and curtal bought	R24:95,145
1601	John Ballard	(1594)	1601	Dead by 8 Sep.	R25:274v
	Thomas Parkyns	1601	(1603?)	Ballard's place; wins contest in skill in all manner of musical instruments against Arthur Japon	R25:274v;271v
1603	Richard Ball	1603	(1622)		R26i:251v
1605				Seven (or more) waits	R27:66v-67
1611	Walter Lowman	(1561)	1611	Dead by 28 May; seventh place	R30:121
	Raph Strachime (Strachey)	1611		Lowman's place; reversion since 1605; served since about 1605	R30:121; R27:66v-67; R32:179v
1613	Edward Godfrey	1613	(1625)	Singer; an extra man	R31:44; R32:79, 109v
	Alphonso Ball	(1613?)	(1635)	Serving from about 1613	See notes 4 and 11, chapter two.

Appointment of London Waits

Year	Name	Year Apptd.	Year Retired		References
1613	Two boys	1613		Singers under Richard Ball	R31:175v
	John Robson	(1597)	1613	Dead by 25 Aug.	R31:150v
	John Sturt	1613	(1625)	Robson's place (one of the regular six places); lute	R31:150v; R39:86
	William Pynne [Pryne]	(1594)	1613	Dead by 23 May 1614, probably six months before	R31ii:336
1614	John Adsome	1614	(1640)	Pynne's place; served six months before appointment; flute, cornett, recorder	R31ii:336 KM 86, 92
1615				No more appointments to be made till only six waits	R32:109v
1616	Robert Strachey the elder	(1563)	1616	Pensioned	R32:247-247v
	Frauncis Park[er]	1616	(1641)	Strachey's place	R32:247-247v
	Thomas Carter	(1593)	1616	Dead by 26 Sep.	R32:356
	Arthur Carter	1616	(1631)	Son of Thomas; takes father's place jointly with Withall	R32:356
	Robert Withall	1616	(1625)	Trained under Richard Ball; shares place with Carter	R32:356
1618	Stephen Thomas	(1597)	1618	Dead by 16 June	R33:323v-324
	Robert Sammon	1618	(1619)	Thomas's place; Sammon, Carter and Withall to share wages; treble viol and wind instruments	R33:323v-324, 326; R-34:205
1619	Robert Salmon	(1618)	1619	Dead by 14 Sep.	R34:205-205v
	Robert Parker alias Baynes	1619	(1640)	Salmon's place; competed with Henry Field; especially good in wind instruments; double sackbut and "violen"; low tenor violin	R34:205-205v; R49: 331v-332; KM 76
	Henry Field	(1619) (1625)	(1641)	Serves without pay; treble "viollen"; wind	R39:86-86v
1620	Robert Tailor	1620	(1637)	Extra appointment; "orpheryon and base vyoll and poliphon"	R34:586
1622	Richard Ball (Balles)	(1603)	1622	Dead by 19 Nov.	R37:21; LB HH:199v
	John Wilson	1622	(1644?)	Ball's place	R37:21
1625	John Sturt	(1613)	1625	Dead by 27 Jan.	R39:86
	Thomas Sutton	1625		Sturt's place (one of the six) as lutanist; income to be shared with competitor, Henry Field	R39:86-86v
	Edward Godfreye	(1613)	1625	Dead by early Nov.	R40:2v
	John Olliver	1625	(1634)	Godfreye's place ("one of the six waits"); music and singing of the bass.	R40:2v
	[Robert] Withall	(1616)	1625	Dead by early Nov.	R40:2v-3

Year	Name	Year Apptd.	Year Retired		References
1625	Henry Field (Feilde)	1625	(1641)	Extra, evidently sharing places; serving since 1619	R40:2v-3, 16v, 383v; see above
1631	Arthur Carter	(1616)	1631	Dead by 22 March	R45:216v
	Ambrose Beeland	1631		Carter's place; "winde instrumentes and consorts"; violins in King's Musick	R45:216v; R47:358; *KM* 104
1634	John Oliver	(1625)	1634	Dead by 27 Feb.	R48:118v-119
	Alphonso Balls	1634	(1635)	Oliver's place; served since about 1613; lutes and voices in King's Musick	R48:272v-273; *KM* 59, 66; see above.
	Robert Herdson	(1635)	(1637)	Competed with Balls for voice place; may serve.	R48:118v-119, 272v-273
	son of John Adson			The wait breeding up a son to perfection in voice song and music for the city's service.	R48:435
1635	Alphonso Balls	(1634)	1635	Dead by 16 May	R49:200
	Robert Heardson	1635	(1637)	Balls's place; bass voice; service since 1634.	R49:200; see above
1637	Robert Herson	(1635)	1637	Dead by 17 Oct.	R51:347v
	Symon Ives	1637		Herson's place; song and music.	R51:347v
	Robert Strachey, John Adson, Thomas Sutten, Robert Parker, Henry Field, Mr Ives, Ambrose Beeland, Francis Parke, John Wilson.			City paying these nine waits Dec. 1637, Jan. 1638. Robert Strachey probably is the Raph Strachime appointed in 1611.	R52:47-47v, 53
1637	Robert Taylor	(1620)	1637	Dead by Nov.	R52:11v
	William Webb	1637		Taylor's place in song and music (extra).	R52:11v
1640	Robert Parker	(1619)	1640	Dead by 19 May; because of court service had John Strong serve for him often since before 1635, then latter's brother Edward.	R54:182; R49:331v-332; R52:254-254v
	Edward Strong	1640		Parker's place; served for him since before 1638, and given reversion then.	R54:182; R52:254-254v (see *KM*)
	John Adson	(1614)	1640	Dead by 7 July	R54:238v
	James Hinton	1640		Adson's place	R54:238v
1641	Francis Parker	(1616)	1641	Dead by 4 Feb.	R55:63v
	William Sanders	1641		Parker's place; in 1634 had long served for him, and then received reversion.	R55:63v; R48:434v-435 (see *KM*)
	Henry Feilde	(1625)	1641	Dead by 29 Oct.	R55:210
	Marmaduke Wright	1641		Feilde's place in competition with Robert Strong and Thomas Marks.	R55:210
1644	Ralph Street	(1611?)		On 12 Dec. their request	R57ii:27

Appointment of London Waits

Year	Name	Year Apptd.	Year Retired		References
1644	Thomas Sutton	(1625)		for payment of wages and liveries allowed. Ralph Street is probably the Raph Strachime appointed in 1611; see also 1637.	
	Ambrose Beeland	(1631)			
	William Sanders	(1641)			
	Edward Strong	(1640)			
	James Hinton	(1640)			
	Marmaduke Wright.	(1641)			
1645	William Webb	(1637)		On 29 April their request for back and further wages and liveries allowed. (With preceding, nine waits.)	R57ii:115v
	Simon Ives.	(1637)			

APPENDIX B

ENTRIES RELATING TO MUSIC, FROM HOUSEHOLD RECORDS

IN GLANCING at the following extracts, given in amplification of suggestions made in various chapters of this book, the reader should bear in mind that items selected from the accounts of many years are compressed into a few pages; the accounts should be examined a year at a time. The reader should also notice that the accounts from which these extracts are taken are carefully selected; no excerpts are given from those British Museum or privately owned manuscripts or from those publications of the Historical Manuscripts Commission in which there are few or no signs of musical activity. It is possible, nevertheless, that the families represented here were typical of the wealthier families that had a considerable interest in music. The original accounts do not necessarily reflect all household musical activity, nor do the reports of the Historical Manuscripts Commission necessarily mention all the items pertaining to music entered in the original accounts.

Extracts are given in the following order: Bertie, Cavendish, Chaloner, Cumberland, Howard of Naworth, Huntington, Kytson, North, Pelham, Rutland, Sidney, Spencer, and Willoughby. At the end appears a list of instruments made up from entries in miscellaneous papers, chiefly household inventories.

The general form, only, of the original entry, or of the entry as presented in a modern publication, is followed. An attempt is made to retain the original spelling in the case of proper names.

BERTIE ACCOUNTS

Richard Bertie (1517-1582) married Catherine, dowager duchess of Suffolk, in 1552, their daughter Susan was born in England in 1554, and their son Peregrine in Cleves in 1555. The family returned to England shortly after Queen Elizabeth's accession.

The items are taken from HMC 66, *Ancaster Mss.*, and the pages are indicated here by numbers in square brackets after the last item taken from each page.

January 1561: To Robert Lettis and Robart Balle of Godmanchester, musicians, 20s. March 1561: To the waits of Lincolne, the 12th day, 20d.[463] September 1561: To four musicians and a hobby horse which were at Beleawe at the marriage of Mr. Carro and Denman, 15s.10d.[464] December 1561: To a servant of my Lord Willowbies which offered to play and sing before my master and her grace, 20d. To two of my Lord Robart Dudleis men which came to play before them upon the drum and the fife, 6s. To my lord of Arrendalles players, 6s.8d. To the waits of London, 5s.[465]

January 1562: For a lute for Mr. Peregrine and Mistress Suzan, 46s.8d. [461] To divers noblemen's trumpeters to the number of ten, 20s. To the queen's trumpeters, 20s. To the queen's "violens," at new year's tide, 20s. To the earl of Warwyckes players, 7s.6d. March 1562: To Rooes when he mended Mr. Peregrine's lute, 10s.[466] April 1562: To the waits that played at her grace's lodging at the court, 20d. May 1562: To a morris dancer of Litle Bytam, 2s. July 1562: To the waits of Lyncolne in reward for playing, 3s.4d. To a juggler with his musicianer at Mr. Nautons marriage, 10s. September 1562: To my lord of Rutlandes man which played upon the lute, 6s.[467] To a bagpiper which played and sang before my master and her grace at Mr. Eirsbies, 3s.4d.[468]

CAVENDISH ACCOUNTS

William Cavendish was created earl of Devonshire in 1618. His son William, second earl, was born about 1591. The accounts refer chiefly to Chatsworth or Hardwicke, Derbyshire.

The items are taken from the manuscripts of the duke of Devonshire at Chatsworth. All but a few items are from Ms. 23; the folio numbers are indicated here by figures in square brackets after the last item taken from a folio. In the cases of the few items taken from Ms. 10A, "10A" is printed instead of the folio numbers within the square brackets.

Things bought at London and other payments by Travine: 20 January 1599: Given to fiddlers, 12d.[5v] 25 January: for strings and cotton for a case for Master William's viol, 1s.2d.[3v] 1 February: for strings for Master William's viol, 1s.[4] April: for a Latin primer and Besa his Testament for Master William, 5s.6d. . . . For two books of fish ponds and another pamphlet, 6d. . . . Talis and Bird and Yongs two sets of songs, 8s.[6v]

Trip from London, April 1599: at Lecester to the chamberlain, 12d., to the ostlers, 6d., to musicians, 6d.[8v]

August 1599: To Thomas Baines for a quarter teaching Master William to sing ended at midsummer last, 10s. To Hull of Mansfeld that he paid for carriage of three trunks from London and a lute . . . at three farthings a pound. Bestowed in ale of one D. . . . helped Fretwell to bring the little trunk and lute from Mansfeld. . . .[14]

Accounts, October 1599, for Sir William's expenses in London, 3 May-27 August 1599: To the queen's trumpeters by my master, 5s.[17] The 29th of May for three sets of song books, 16s. For a book entitled Historia memorabilia, 2s.4d.[17v] For a set of singing books, 3s.6d.[18] For a pamphlet of news from the Lowe Contries, 1d.[18v] For a set of singing books for Master William, 3s. . . . For a set of singing books, 1s.8d. . . . For a treble viol for Master William, £1.5.0.[19] (After August 11) for a box to put Master William's viol in, 20d. . . . Strings for the said viol, 2s.[19v] To Mr. Newcom's man for lute strings, 1s.[20] For singing books viz musica melodia divina olim pica harmonia celeste balleti petre Phelip inglishe (inglise?) madrige horatio vecchy music and for four quire of paper at 6d. the quire, 18s.8d. . . . Given to the book binder, 6d.[19v]

October 1599: To Thomas Banes by my master for teaching Master William and Mistress Francis to sing a quarter at Michaelmas last, £1.0.0.[23v] December 1599: My master his charges to London in Michaelmas term last . . . Nottingham diet, 23s., chamberlain, 12d., musicians, 6d.[21] December 1599: To Thomas Banes (music teacher; see August, above) by my master, 20s.[21v] (November 1599: wages for year ending at Christmas; about thirteen names, none identified as musicians; Banes not on list.)[26v] December 1599: For a latin book of fables and an Italian book, 2s.4d.[23v]

December 1599: Accounts for expenses of Sir William in London c. 29 October-28 November: To one that lent a lute for Lambert the frenchman to play on, 1s. Buttons and lace for the frenchman's cloak, 3s.2d. . . . The 29th of November to the frenchman's host, £3.0.0. (Just above "frenchmans hoste" almost illegible words have been inserted, which may be "half a yeres wages for . . .")[24]

To one that lent a lute for Lamberte the frenchman to play on, 1s. . . . Given to a broker for helping my master to Lambert, 10s. Buttons and lace for the frenchman's cloak, 3s.2d. (29 November, to Lambert's host in consideration of half a year's service "before hand," £3.0.0.)[10A]

December 1599, London: To Mr. Jenkinson for thirty-nine yards of red and green cloth for liveries at 11s. the yard, £21.9.0. For three yards more of the same cloth for the frenchman's livery, £1.13.0.[24v]

January 1600: New Year's gift to Thomas Banes, 5s. (Banes is not on the list of servants receiving wages and liveries; his payments come under foreign charges.)[10A] To Mr. Starken for Mr. Michaell Cavendishe his book of music for Master William, 4s.8d.[25]

March 1600: Sir William's expenses at Derby include: to the musicians at Derby, 12d. For a mutton given to the judges, 22s. To the sheriff a veal, 13s.6d.[26]

March 1600: To Thomas Banes for a quarter teaching Master William and Mistress Frauncis to sing, £1.0.0.[27] April 1600: A dozen of treble lute strings, 3s.6d.[29v]

London, June 1600: Singing books, 11s.[35v] For Stowes abridgment of chronicles and Morles songs of four parts, 3s.9d. (Twice, news from Flanders, 2d. each time.)[36]

July 1600: To Standish that my master gave to Thomas Banes for teaching Master William and Mistress Fraunces to sing a quarter ended at Midsummer, 20s. And that my master gave Master William for construing a piece of Livy, 10s.[34] September 1600: To Lambert (see above) which was paid him aforehand for his wages before his going away, 36s.[35] October 1600: To Mr. Starkey for two and a half dozen of small treble viol strings for Master

William at 4s. a dozen, 10s. (Starkey seems to be steward; he receives "coles" regularly.)[40]

December 1600, account for London, 22 September-6 October: To musicians, 6d. / my master by water to Westminster, 6d., 1s.[42v] To Mr. Norton for Hacklutes voyages, 22s. / a bible, 14s. / Camden, 7s., Terence, 2s., grammar, 2s. / Quintus Curtius, 2s.2d., Commens, 2s.10d., £2.12.0.[43] My master his going to a play at Powles, 18d. For a book entitled Hipollitus a Calibus, 15d. For a book of monuments (monumt.) in Westminster, 12d. To the poor, 3d.[43] For a book entitled Terence, 16d. (Other pamphlets, etc., including "art of setting corne," 3d.)[43] That my master adventures to the West Indians, £200.0.0.[45]

February 1601: To the East Indian Company for my master his increase of his adventure, £20.0.0.[48v] December 1600: To Banes for teaching Master William and Mistress Fraunces to sing the quarter ended at Christmas, £1.0.0.[41v] January 1601, "New Yeres tyde" gifts: To young Mr. Henry Cavendishe, 20s. Mr. Clarke, 5s., the butler and pantler, 5s., cooks, 15s. To Jo: Good, 5s., to Thomas Banes, 5s. Jo: Heyward, 5s. (Painter, porter, etc.)[46] March 1601: To Hallam which he gave by my master his commandment to Mr. Henry Cavendish musician, 2s. (Henry Cavendish may be a musician. Michael Cavendish, the composer, was a distant relative of Sir William Cavendish, apparently, and Henry may be a member of Michael's family; he does not seem to be of the direct family line of Sir William Cavendish.)[49] 30 March 1601 (Banes receives £1.0.0. for teaching Master William and Mistress Frances singing, for a quarter.)[49v]

January 1605, January 1606: (5s. reward to Banes each year.) January 1607: (Banes not on list of New Year's gift recipients.)

January 1606: Given by my lord to Mistress Frances for learning five lessons of the viol, 20s.

SIR THOMAS CHALONER ACCOUNTS

Sir Thomas Chaloner (1521-1565), the son of a London mercer, was educated at Oxford and Cambridge. He was known as a diplomat and poet.

The following are excerpts from Sir Thomas's private accounts, 1551-1556, written in his own hand. The folios in British Museum Lansdowne Ms. 824 are indicated in square brackets after the last item on a folio.

c. 1 December 1551: Paid to Appulton my man for stringing of lutes, 5s.[11v] Laid out at another time for lute strings and given as reward to Hewme the lute player, 10s. Paid to Point for the mending and tuning of my virginals, 13s.4d.

2 January 1552: Given to Hewme the lute player in reward . . . 10s.[12v] January 1552: Given to my wife upon Christmas day to play at cards, 10s. Paid to Point my servant for one quarters wages ended at Christmas, 20s.[13] Given to a frenchman that presented me a book of verses, 10s.[16] De-

livered to Apulton my servant upon his wages due at our Lady day next (1552). Given to him to buy lute strings, 8s.[18] (Given) to Jo: Rose for another viol to be made 29 October (1552) of the finest sort, 40s.[33v] Paid to Rose for mending of the little Venice lute of (hebens?), 10s. Paid to Rose 13 November (1552) for mending of other lutes and for a gross of strings, 24s.[34v] Given the 9th of December (1552) to Rose for new bellying of a lute, for stringing of two lutes and for other (percelles?), 30s.[36] (This item crossed out by same pen.): Given to a Fleming musician who teaches my daughter for song books Italian in four parts, 10s. (c. 24 December 1552.)[38]

January 1552: Paid for five set of books of Italian music, 17s.[40]

(c. 31 October 1553): Paid for the mending of a lute, 2s.[45] December: bought five dozen of "Mynyken" lute strings at 2s.8d. the dozen and one dozen "Katlyns" (lute strings), 14s.4d.[47]

(c. 1 September 1554): Item more than Brakenbury gave to the musicians et cetera, 22d.[52v] (The accounts imply that none of the persons named here was a professional musician in Sir Thomas Chaloner's regular pay; two of his servants may have played some instruments.)

EARL OF CUMBERLAND ACCOUNTS

Francis Clifford became the fourth earl of Cumberland after the death of his brother in 1605; the fifth earl, Henry (son of the fourth earl, 1591-1643) succeeded to the title on the death of his father in 1641, and died 1643. Lady Elizabeth Clifford, daughter of Henry, married Richard Boyle, earl of Cork and Burlington in 1634 at Skipton castle, Yorkshire. The estates were taken in 1643 by Anne Clifford, daughter of the third earl (countess of Dorset and Pembroke).

The following are excerpts from the Bolton manuscripts of the duke of Devonshire, now preserved at Chatsworth, Derbyshire. They relate principally to activity at the various northern castles of the Cliffords, including Brougham castle, Westmorland, Skipton castle, Yorkshire, Appleby castle, Westmorland, and Bolton castle, Yorkshire. The first number in the square brackets at the right indicates the number of the Bolton manuscript, the second number indicates the folio.

19 March 1611: Item given this day in reward to the musicians of Barton, being four in number who came hither and stayed one night, 5s. Item given the same day in reward by my lord's commandment to three men the waits of Richmond, 5s.[94:86] 8 April 1611: Item . . . in reward to Ned Trumpetter of Hull . . . who brought a letter . . . 5s.[94:86v] 24 April 1611: Item given in reward to a man and three boys that came to the gates and played there dwelling in Towston, 2s.[94:87v] 2 May 1611: Item given this day to George Masseter the instrument maker of York his boy that brought some things to Londsbrough for the music and it was by Mr. Stewardes direction, 6d.[94:88]

6 May 1611: Item paid this day to George Masseter the instrument maker of York for divers things done by him, and for a new "Citharen" and viol strings, and other instrument mending as appeared by his bill and it was in full payment of all the sum of £3.0.0[94:182] 6 June 1611: Item given in reward to fourteen players my lord of Darbies men, who played two plays here at Londsbrough the one after dinner and the other after supper by his lordship's own appointment, £3.0.0[94:89] 16 June 1611: Item given this day in reward to four men, the waits of Doncaster, who came to the gates and played there upon instruments and it was by my lord's commandment, 5s.[94:89v] 23 June 1611: Servants' wages: Item paid this day to George Mason in full payment of half a year's wages from Christmas last ending now at midsummer the sum of £3.6.8 (signed) George Maysonne (coachman received £2.10.0)[94:73v] 14 July 1611: Item given this day in reward by my lord's commandment to a blind harper that came to Londsbrough and played there, 2s.6d.[94:91] 29 August 1611: Item given this day in reward to three men the waits of Rotheram who came hither and played at the gates. And it was by my lord's own appointment, 2s.6d.[94:92v] 10 December 1611: Item paid to Roger Jackman of York for binding divers song books and other work done by George Mason his direction as by his note appeareth, 10s.[94:183] 29 December 1611: Item given this day in reward by my lord's and lady's commandment to two men and a woman that went about with puppet plays.[94:96a.v]

8 January 1612: Item paid this day to Stephen Grigges the musician of Barton which was given him in reward by my lord's appointment, for himself and four more for playing, and attending here this Christmas, £5.0.0.[94:96b] 31 January 1612: To a piper and another musician who played at the gates, 1s. 1 February 1612: Item given this day in reward by my lord's commandment to a blind man a harper, which was my lord Darbies man, and played here upon his harp, 2s.6d.[94:96b.v] 5 February 1612: To three men, waits of Rippon, who played at the gates, by my lord's command, 2s.[94:96b.v] 26 February 1612: Item paid this day, which was given by my lord's commandment to Stephen Grigges the musician of Barton, who was sent for hither to Londsbrough and his companions, and played here this Shrovetide and at my Lord Wharton his being here and Sir Thomas his lady . . . 20s.[94:96c.v] 11 March 1612: By my lord's command, to the waits of Bewley who played at the gates, 2s.6d., and to the four waits of Richmond, 3s.4d. 13 March 1612: To the queen's players who played after dinner, £2.0.0.[94:96d] 26 March 1612: Three men the waits of Leedes who played at the gates, 3s.4d. The thirteen players, lord of Darbies men, here two days and two nights, played four plays, £4.0.0.[94:96d.v] To four men the waits of Pomfrett who played at the gates . . . 3s.4d.[94:96e] 6 April 1612: Item paid this day to Arthur Wyatt which he laid out for viol strings, bought at York against my Lord Cliffordes coming, 7s., and for his own and his horses charges at York,

22d.[94:183v] 24 April 1612: four men, the waits of Carlile, for playing at the gates, 5s.[94:96e.v] 22 May 1612: three men, the waits of Lincolne for playing at the gates, 2s.6d.[94:96f.v] 7 July 1612: Item paid this day to George Mashrother the instrument maker of York, and sent by the cater upon account of work done by him since the last time he was paid as will appear by his bills, 40s.[94:183v] 19 July 1612: To sixteen players my Lady Elizabeth grace her servants who played a play after supper, 40s.[94:97b] 2 August 1612: Item paid this day by my lord's appointment to John Harrison of Rippon for a treble violin, which was bought of him by Mr. Holte, 30s.[94:184] 20 August 1612: Waits of Linne being four men . . . at the gates, 3s.4d.[94:97c.v] 28 August 1612: Item given the same day in reward by my lord's commandment to the waits of York being seven in number who came to Londsbrough and stayed all night and played in the great chamber after supper, 13s.4d.[94:97d] 23 September 1612: Queen's players who came but did not play, 13s.4d.[94:97e.v] 5 November (Gunpowder Plot anniversary) 1612: To the ringers who rang all day, 2s.6d.[94:97g] 9 December 1612: To eleven players, Lord Mounteagle's men, played two plays, £2.0.0.[94:97h] 19 December 1612: Item paid this day to George Mashrother of York instrument maker, in full payment of all his bills for mending instruments for my lord being now discharged by Mr. Stewards appointment, 38s.6d., as by his acquittance may appear . . .[94:185] 22 December 1612: Item delivered this day by my lord's appointment to Arthur Wyatt at his going to York, to buy viol strings, 6s.8d.[94:185]

13 January 1613: Stephen Grigges the musician of Barton and four others, for playing and attending at Londsbrough this Christmas, £5.0.0. Four men, the waits of —— (blank) played at the gates, 2s.[94:97j]

28 April 1614: Item paid this day to one Mr. Sperley for a bass viol bought of him, £2.0.0[95:240] 9 June 1614: To Mr. Sperley for an old treble viol, 20s., and for amending and stringing four other viols, with 12s. for a set of bows . . . 52s.[95:241] 14 July 1614: Item paid . . . to Mr. Symon which was to pay for a lute mending of my Lord Cliffordes, which my lord was pleased to pay for, 25s., and now to him to buy lute strings, 10s., in all, 35s. 15 July 1614: Item paid this day by my lord's commandment for amending a lute of Ned Cressettes the boy, and for a new case to it being sent by sea, 36s. Item paid the same day to Arthur Wyat, wherewith my lord did appoint him to buy viol strings and lute strings . . . 30s.[95:242] 16 July 1614: Item paid this day to Mr. Coperario by my lord's commandment for a "Lyro" viol and a case sent by sea to Londsbrough and bought of him by my lord, £7.0.0.[95:-242v]

22 May 1617: To Mr. George Mashrother of York, the instrument maker, for making seven bows and mending the viols that went to Skipton, 21s., and for his pains in coming to Londsbrough being sent for by my lord to mend instruments, 30s.[97:199v] 4 October 1617: To John Thornton and

... for carrying three viols to York to get them cut, 4s.[97:201] 19 November 1617: To George Mashrother of York for lute strings and viol strings and mending lutes, £6.0.0.[97:202]

1 December 1618: Item given this day in reward to two waits of Skipton, that were at Londsbrough a week, and came to play to my Lord Cliffordes horseraces, so given them at their going away by my lord's commandment, 6s.[98:130]

29 October 1632: (Bought at London) For strings for the harpsicon, 3s.[Ms. 169]

8 November 1633: Londsbrough castle. This day to George Masseter of York who was three days here with his man in tuning the organ and mending other instruments, £1.0.0. To his man, 1s.[172:166] 30 November 1633: Item bought at London five dozen violin strings for William Hudson, 14s.[172:166] Item bought then also, two masque books, 1s. Item paid Christopher Hetty for divers lute strings and other strings sent down to Mr. Karsden and William Hudson from London, £2.0.0. (Karsden and Hudson do not seem to appear in the wages part of the volume. Garden seeds are bought in London at this time.) [172:166v]

4 January 1634: Lord Derby's men who came to act a play, 13s.4d. 6 January 1634: Waits of York for their attendance this Christmas, £5.0.0.[172:77] 17 February 1634: This day given to certain players itinerants which acted before their lordships ... reward, £1.0.0. 14 March 1634: ... to musicians itinerants which played to my lady ... 2s.[172:77v] 26 July 1634: This day to certain French musicians and a singer, which were at my Lady Dungarvans marriage for their reward by his lordship's command, £6.0.0. (The marriage of Elizabeth Clifford.) The same day to the Music of Stamford for their reward and service done here at my Lady Dungarvans marriage nine weeks, £15.0.0. 28 July 1634: To my old lord to give to the Music of Stamford at their parting, 10s.[172:78] 8 November 1634: For bringing a harpsicon from London ... porters, 2s.[174:100v]

7 January 1635: For portage of an organ from my Lord Marshalls, 2s.[174:101] 28 January 1635: For a masque book, 6d.[174:132v] 27 March 1635: To William Hudson by his lordship's command for buying a new instrument, £4.0.0.[174:17]

Extraordinary Expenses, 1636:

First masque	To Paul for going to York for things for the masque	£0.4.6
	For six pair of gloves for the masquers	8.0
	For three dozen of ribboning of one sort	9.0
	For twenty-nine (?) yards of another	14.6
	...	
For the masque	For three sheets of pasteboard	9
	For tinfoil and diverse "cullers" for Henrick	12.7

[For the masque, continued]	For torches and wax candles	10.6
	. . .	
	For Paul's journey to York with horses for the Music of the City	10.0
	. . .	
	To Hugh Barrons and Moreby for bringing things to Skipton from York	2.6
	. . .	
	For a yard of calico	2.0
	For seven pair of pumps and shoes for the masquers	12.0
	To Thomas Bleasdell for "tayler" (?) work for Comus and his company	8.0
	To Thomas Moreby for the hire of four horses which the waits of York to . . . (?)	1.0.0
	To the waits of York for their attendance at masque	5.0.0
	To John Gerdler for himself	1.0.0
	To Adam Gerdler (an actor; see below)	1.0.0
	To the boys	10.0
	To the boy which danced	2.0
	. . .	
	To Mr. Henrick de Kesar for part of his charge and rewards in working the screen of the masque	3.0.0

[175:181-182]
. . .

15 April 1636: To Mr. Calvert of York upon account of eleven yards of gold tinsel fitting for scarfs for Comus and his company, £1.0.0.[175:182v]

28 February 1636: To a certain company of roguish players who presented A New Way to Pay Old Debts, for their reward, £1.0.0.[174:92v] To Adam Gerdler whom my lord sent for from York to act a part in The Knight of the Burning Pestle, 5s. To the Music of York when my Lord Digby was here at Skipton, £5.0.0.[174:92v]

January 1638: To Roger the piper his reward for attending here in Christmas . . . 10s.[Ms. 176] 8 December 1638: To Mr. John Ward of York for several sorts of strings for the musicians, 10s.6d.[177:190]

10 January 1639: To Roger the piper for his attendance all Christmas . . . 10s.[177:100v] To the waits of Kendall, 2s.[177:101] 20 September 1639: Waits of Kendall which offered to play to my lord, 1s.6d.[177:99] 12 October 1639: To the prince's trumpeters who sounded to his lordship and given a reward, 20s.[177:261v]

2 January 1640: To a company of Moulton players who were at Christmas two nights playing, 20s.[177:100] 12 January 1640 (Londsbrough): To the Music of York for their reward in attending all Christmas, £5.0.0.[177:266]

Household Records

Lord William Howard (1563-1640) of Naworth castle, Cumberland, was a commissioner for the border from 1618, and a scholar. He lived at Naworth from 1601 with his children and grandchildren.

The following excerpts (1612-1640) are from *Selections from the Household Books of Lord William Howard of Naworth Castle*, ed. George Ornsby; page numbers are indicated in square brackets after the last item from a page. According to the introduction (p. xliii), "There is not a trace of any instruction in music or singing, and no mention of the purchase of any kind of musical instrument. Dancing seems to have been the solitary accomplishment, with the exception of needlework and embroidery."

3 January 1612: Rewards: To John Trumpetor, 5s. 14 January: Reward: To three pipers at the gates, 3s. 15 January: To the waits at Carlyle, 2s.6d. 23 January: To Sir H. Curwen's three waits, 12d.[27] 21 March: To the waits of Pearoth, 2s. 25 March: To the waits of Rippon, 2s.6d. 31 March: To the waits of Carlyle, 2s. 26 April: To a piper at the gate, 6d. 9 May: To the waits of Doncaster, 3s.[28] 28 June: To J. Trumpeter, 5s. 13 July: To a musician sent from Mrs. Tayler, 20s.[29] 12 August: To Robert for teaching the gentlemen to dance, 40s.[30] 3 September: The waits of Wakefield, 2s.6d. . . . Jo. Trumpeter, 5s.[31]

1 August 1618: To three pipers at the gates, 2s.6d. 5 August: To three musicians at the gates, 2s.6d. 12 August: To the prince's players, 10s. 13 August: Carlile. Three consorts of musicians, 7s.6d.[87] 12 October: Carlile. To a piper that came out of Lankyshire, 2s.[88]

17 January 1619: Carlile. Musicians, 4s.6d. 22 January: To a juggler, 12d. 14 January: To a cornetter, 2s. 27 February: To three minstrels given by Mistress Mary, 18d. To two other, 12d. 13 March: To two pipers, 12d.[88] 28 April: To a piper, 2d. 20 June: To three musicians at the gate, 12d. 27 July: To the waits of Carlyle, 2s.6d. 31 July: To the musicians of Penreth, 2s.6d.[89] 23 July: To Mr. Heymore for teaching to dance, in part, 20s.[101]

31 October 1620: To the dancer, 20s. To the players, 10s.[130]

3 January 1621: To the fool of Brampton, 2s.6d. 16 February: To the prince's players, 10s. To a minstrel at the gates, "vij Marcij," 12d. . . . To the waits of Midlam, 12d. To the waits of Richmond, 12d. 24 April: To the waits of Carlyle, 12d.[131] 14 August: To two fiddlers at the gate, 12d. 31 August: To a company of players, 5s.[175] 12 November: To Mistress Mary to give unto two fiddlers, 2s.6d.[176]

6 April 1622: To three waits of Rippon, 2s. 22 April: To a harper, 6d.[177] 14 October: To a piper, 4d. To a cornetter, 2s.[192] 17 November: To the players of Penreth, 3s.

14 April 1623: To John Fidler for charges of burying his daughter Jane,

10s. 18 April: To a company of players at Coomcach, 5s. To the waits of Lancaster, 18d.[193]

8 December 1626: To the Scottish piper, 2s.6d. 30 December: To the piper of Brampton, 2s.6d.

8 January 1627: To the piper by my lady's command, 2s.6d.[236]

8 January 1630: To John Mulcaster, the piper, for playing at Nawarde this Christmas time, 15s. 5 March: To the pipers, the waits of Richmonde, 2s.6d. 15 April: To a company of musicians at my lord's lodgings at Arundell house (London), 5s.[262] 13 July: To a company of players, 5s. (probably Naworth) 13 August: To a company of fiddlers, 2s.6d.[263]

31 December 1633: To the prisoners at Carlile, 5s.

1 January 1634: To the piper by my lady upon New Year's day, 5s. 6 January: To John Mulcaster the piper for playing here all Christmas, 20s.[314] 4 March: To three pipers at Corbye, 18d. 7 March: To the waits of Darneton, 2s. 14 March: To three fiddlers, 2s. 17 March: To a company of pipers, 2s.6d.[315] 28 March: To two pipers, the waits of Durham, 2s. 1 April: To three several companies of musicians at the gate, by the porter, 5s.6d. To a poor woman, 4d. 21 May: To the waits of Penreth, 2s.[316] 11 June: To Michel Fidler at his marriage (from my lord), 10s. 17 June: To the waits of Durham, 5s. To a fiddler, 12d. 21 June: To a blind harper, by my lady's command, 5s. 24 June: To a soldier by my lady, 2s.[317] 22 August: To Mr. Robert Hymers for one month teaching Master William Howard and Mistress Elizabeth his sister to dance, 40s.[344]

ACCOUNTS OF THE EARLS OF HUNTINGTON

The third earl, Henry Hastings (1535-1595) was succeeded by George (1540-1604), who was succeeded by his grandson, Henry (1586-1643).

The following are from HMC 78, *Hastings Mss.*, i; pages are indicated by numbers in square brackets after the last item from a page.

(Wages of servants of third earl, c. 1595; evidently none of them were musicians.)[354]

(Inventory after death of third earl, 1596; no musical instruments at York.) [355-361]

21 November 1606: For a pair of Scotch "baggepipes" for the fool, 3s.4d. [363]

May day 1607: Given to my lord of Worcester's musicians, 5s.[364] 27 June: Given to your honor's musicians, 10s.[366]

29 January-1 February 1610, on trip from Donington to London: At Northampton, among rewards: To the musicians, 5s. Dunstable: To the musicians, 5s. St. Albans: To the musicians, 5s.[367] 15 February: Given to a company of "corniters," 3s.4d. 8 March: Given to him that teached you (fifth earl) to dance, £2.0.0. 22 March: Given to an Italian for playing the fool, £2.0.0. To the fiddlers, £1.0.0. 24 March: Given to a dancer that taught you

to dance, £2.0.0. 31 March: Given to Daniell the Irish harper, 30s.[368] 26 June: Given to a company of waits, 2s.6d. 1 August: Given to Sir John Harpar's musicians at Swerston, £1.0.0[369] 22 November: Given to a company of waits at the window, 3s.6d.[370]

Household expenses of Alice, countess of Derby, widow of Ferdinando, earl of Derby, while at Harefield, Middlesex: 7 August 1634: To Mr. Vaux for "harpsicall" strings, 18d.[376] 20 November: To Mr. Jones by my Lady Alice's appointment to pay for viol strings formerly sent, 10s. To him by her ladyship's appointment to buy viol strings now, 7s. 11 December: To Mr. Waldran for tuning a "harpsicall" and my lady's virginals, 16s.[376]

26 March 1635: To Mr. Jones, Mr. Allen, and Mr. Cotton to find their viols with strings til Michaelmas next, 20s.[377-378]

KYTSON ACCOUNTS

The following extracts from the household accounts of Thomas Kytson, of Hengrave, Suffolk, mentioned in chapter three and elsewhere above, are taken from Gage, *History and Antiquities of Hengrave in Suffolk*. Page numbers are indicated in square brackets after the last item from a page.

After 1 October 1572:[190] In reward to Johnson the musician at Hengrave, 10s. To my lord of Sussex's musicians, 5s. November: For ten yards "carsey" at 2s.1d. the yard, and 4d. over in all, given by my mistress to the musicians at Hengrave, 21s.2d.[191] In reward to Maude of Norwich for mending the virginals, 3s.3d.[192]

January 1573: In reward to the musicians at Brome, 3s. Among the officers there, 13s. To the housekeeper there, 12s.[195] March: In reward to the blind harper at Ware, 12d.[196] April: In reward among the waits of London for playing at my master his house there, 6s. In reward to Frith, the master of the dancing school, at my master his commandment, 2s. May: For stringing, tuning, and fretting my mistress's lute, 2s.6d. For passage by water, with the musicians, to "Mr. groom-porters" (Sir Thomas Cornwallis, cousin of Lady Kytson, groom-porter to the Queen) at Lewisham, 1s.6d.[197] To Mr. Arthur Halle's man for bringing a lute from his master to my mistress, 2s.6d.[198] June: To the musicians of Swanne Alley for many times playing with their instruments before my master and mistress, 6s.8d.[199] November: In reward to Richard Shawe for his pains at the marriages in the kitchen, 5s. For "nether stocks" for the singing boys, 3s. For silk facings and buttons for the boys' coats and jerkins, 3s.9d. For two girdles for them, 4d.[200] December: For two and a half dozen "mynekins," and two dozen "cattelins" for the viols, 7s.3d.

January 1574: For seven cornetts bought for the musicians, £4.0.0. In reward to Richarde Reede, one of the waits of Cambridge, for his attendance in Christmas time, 20s.[201] November: In reward to the Italian sent from Brome to teach my master, 10s. December: In reward to the musicians at Ware, 3s.[203] For an instrument called a curtall, 30s.[204]

January 1575: In reward to the musicians on New Year's morning, 40s. February: Paid to Robert, the musician, as so much by him paid for a "coople staffe" torches to light my mistress home on Candlemas night, supping at Mr. Townsend's, 2s.6d. February-March: For a trumpet, 40s. For a pair of virginals, 30s. In reward to six trumpeters at my master his commandment for sounding before his chamber on twelfth day, 10s.[204] April-May-June: To one Cosen for teaching the children of the virginals from Christmas until Easter, £3.0.0. In reward to Johnson, the musician, for his charge in "awayting" on my lord of Leycester at Kennelworth, 10s.[205] October-November: In reward to the morris dancers at my master his return into the country, 2s. For a song for my master and the ditty to the same, 2s.4d.[206]

LORD NORTH OF KIRTLING ACCOUNTS

These extracts are from the personal accounts (usually in his own hand) of Roger North, second Baron North of Kirtling, Cambridge (1530-1600).

The accounts are in British Museum Stowe Ms. 774 (two volumes bound in one), and concern the dates 1 January 1576-3 February 1582, and 1 April 1582-20 December 1589. Extracts have been published in *Archaeologia*, XIX (London, 1821), 283-301; readings have been compared in cases where items appear in *Archaeologia*. Folios in the manuscript are indicated here by numbers in square brackets after the last item taken from a folio.

1 January 1576: Given "Mistrells," 5s. Amongst my men, 5s.[5] 8-10 January: To minstrels, £3.0.0. To R. Giles man, 6s.8d.[5v] 16-17 January: Given my brother for his charges to London, 20s. . . . Play, 28s.4d. at dice[6] 19-21 February: Paid for two Italian books, 22s.[10v] 13-17 May: Given my lord of Essex players, 53s.4d.[16v] 1-2 June: Lost at "bowles," 10s. At chess, 2s.[17v] 6-7 June: Lost at "bowles," 11s.6d.[18] 2-3 July: Given . . . to the poor, 2s. . . . to my lord of Sussex minstrels, 5s.[20v] 3-4 September: Given . . . to piper, 12d.[24] 17-18 September: Given . . . to minstrels, 20s. To poor, 2s. [24v] 21 September: Servants wages . . . for this quarter include: Knolls, 20s., King, 10s., Knightley, 10s., Thomas Cooke, 25s. (maximum), Marow, 10s., "piper," 10s., "slawghterman," 10s. 2s.6d. (sic), Baker, 10s. ("Piper" is probably a proper name rather than an occupational designation, according to later entries.)[25]

1-2 April 1577: Fool . . . paid . . . "motley" for hose and coat and hose . . .[37] 13-16 May: Paid "piper" for "soom—" of lath nails bought at Roiston . . .[40v] 27-28 May: Given "piper," 2s. Given to a "travling Jacke" (?), 3s. To my "piper," 2s.6d. To the lackey, 12d.[41v] 25 June: Lost at play at Kenelworth, £50.0.0.[44v] 1-3 December: To my Lord Howard's players, 5s.[55v]

18-20 May 1578: To morris dancers, 2s.6d.[65v]

11-13 January 1579: Given . . . to minstrels, 2s. To player, 2s.6d. To poor, 2s.6d. . . . Lost at play, 9s.[85v] 17-29 June: London. To my Lord Lester's cooks for teaching the boy, 40s.[97] 28-30 September: To Lowdan's boy, 6d. . . . At the Faulcon, 2s. To the poor, 6s. To minstrel, 2s. (Cambridge)[105]

5-7 June 1580: Paid for books at London, 12s.[126]

(The names of "retainors longing to me the 7 of July 1589" include thirteen gentlemen, sixty-two yeomen, including "Rockeley Trompetor.") [II:3]

16-17 April 1582: Given to the trumpeter, 6s.8d.[II:5] 23 April-29 May: London. Paid for a new trumpet, 45s. and lent the trumpeter aforehand, 33s.4d. £3.18.4[II:6v] 24 June: Wages, midsummer quarter. Trumpetor, 20s. (Most get 10s. or less; many entries follow about him.)[II:9]

15 March 1583: Wages. (Trumpeter not on list.)[II:31] 2-4 June: To the Queen's players, 20s.[II:35v]

4 May 1587: Money laid out and spent from the 12 of April in my going to the Bathe and return which was the 4 of May . . . given to sundry as appears by particular bills as physicians, minstrels and others, £7.8.0. . . . [II:115v]

12-14 May 1588: Gave poor, 2s.10d. To Pratt's man, 10s. . . . Given the trumpeter, 20s. Given Prescot my "cornet," 40s. Given my brother, 40s. To sundry of my men, 26s. To sundry persons for presents, 7s.10d. £6.19.0. (Prescot may be a cornettist, or North's lieutenant.)[II:136v]

3-26 May 1589: London. For the book of martyrs, 40s. 8-9 August: To the poor, 5s. To musicians, 3s. . . .[II:164]

PELHAM ACCOUNTS

The following extracts are from the Pelham family (of Laughton, Sussex) accounts, now preserved in the British Museum, Additional Ms. 33,145. Folio numbers are indicated in square brackets at the end of the last line taken from a folio.

Summer 1632: Item paid the d(ancing?) Master Henley the dancer for teaching the children four weeks, £4.0.0.[53v]

25 March 1633: Item paid to Master Henly the dancer, £1.0.0.

25 March 1634: Item paid "her" for the dancer and writing man, £2.18.0. [73] 29 September: Item paid for Master Britten teaching the children the lute half a year (added:) Item for lute strings, £4.1.0. Item paid him for the new book (?), £4.0.0.[73v]

25 March 1635: (To Henley, the dancing master, £2.0.0.)[80] 29 September: Item paid for Jack's schooling and bill, £8.7.3. Item given Besses maid, 10s. Item given Besses lute master, 10s.[83v]

Candlemas term, 1635-1636: Item paid for Phills lute, £3.10.0.[86]

25 March 1636: Item paid my niece Mary for Phills master to sing and

the lute, £2.0.0.[87v] Item given to Jack at school, £2.0.0. Item given to his master, £1.0.0. Item given to Nan at Beddington, £10.0.0. Item paid Master Samon for Besses schooling and bill at her coming away "per" John Vine, £12.15.0. Item paid John Vine his charges that journey fetching Bess home, £5.0.0.[89]

25 March 1637: (Long account of charges for the children, including:) Item paid "Bonus bill" for Bess in Michaelmas term, £5.2.0. Item given her at London, £2.0.0. Item paid for a lute for her, £3.10.0. Item Master Blange his bill for Jacks, £2.0.0.[98]

25 March 1638: Item given to Phill to pay "hir" lute master, £2.0.0.[106v] 29 May: Item given to my cousin William Pelham at his going to Oxford this 29th of May for his commencement master, £14.0.0.[107]

c. 29 September 1640: Item paid the dancing master . . . £12.0.0. Item paid the writing master for Nan and Andrith (?), £3.4.0.[135v]

ACCOUNTS OF THE EARLS OF RUTLAND

Thomas Manners was created first earl in 1525. His son Henry (c. 1516-1563) succeeded him as second earl in 1543; Henry's brother married Dorothy, daughter of Sir George Vernon. The third earl, Edward (c. 1548-1587) was succeeded by his brother, John, who died in 1588. Roger, his son (1576-1612), became fifth earl, was succeeded by his son Francis (1578-1618), and by the cousin of Francis, John (1604-1679). The principal seat is Belvoir castle, Leicestershire.

The following excerpts are principally from HMC *24, Rutland Mss.,* iv; the page reference in this volume is indicated in square brackets after the last item from a page. A few quotations from letters are given, taken from the same, vol. i, and the page in this volume is identified by the small Roman numeral "i" preceding the page number.

January 1525: Item paid by my lord's command for the residue of a pair of virginals bought at my Lord Mountjoye's, 3s.4d.[266]

January 1531: New Year's gifts. Item to my lord's minstrels in reward, by my lord's command, to make them free of the company, 13s.4d. (London?)

(Probably 8 December 1530-1 December 1531): Juggler, 5s.; king's players, 6s.8d.; same juggler, 3s.8d.; earl of Sussex's minstrels, 3s.4d.; to the minstrels of the city of London, 3s.4d.; to Sir Henry Guldeforde's minstrels, 3s.4d.; to my "Lorde Marques of Execeter" minstrels, 5s.; to Sir Edward Nevelle's minstrels, 3s.4d.[270]

1532: Item delivered to my lord's minstrels for the time of Christmas, 20s.[275]

1536: Item in reward to the waits of Notyngham, by my lord's commandment, 7s.6d.[280] Item delivered to Mistress Tomesyne for a reward to the King's minstrels to teach my Lord Roos (courtesy title of eldest son of the earl of Rutland) to dance, 40s.[281] 24 June: Wages. (Average wage about

10s., e.g. gentlewomen waiters, yeoman ushers; chaplains, 50s. and 13s.4d. Minstrels are between porters and bakers, 10s. and 6s.8d.) The minstrels. Richard Pik, 10s. Thomas Tukman, 10s.[285]

1537: Item paid the 27th day of July for four viols bought at London, 53s.4d.[287]

August 1539: To Mr. Markham('s) minstrel, 3s.4d.; to Mr. Stapulton's minstrel, 2s.[292] Paid in reward to Doctor Lee's "shawmes and shag-boshes" (sackbuts) that played before my lord of Solfolke, by my lord's command, 3s.4d.[293] September. Item to Sir Henry Sacheverell('s) minstrel, by my lord's command, 2s. Item in reward to my Lord Lenard('s) minstrel . . . 20d. October: Item in reward to Mr. Gorge Pawlet bagpipe, 8d.[294] December: Item in reward, the 29th day of December, to a "drone" (bagpipe) that played and sang before the ladies, 7d.

January 1540: Item in reward to four players that played before the ladies of New Year's day, 20d. Item to four players that played before the ladies upon the twelfth evening, 2s.[295]

9 December 1539-22 December 1540: By the commandments of Lord Talbott and Lord Rose, to the wait players of York, 2s.[302]

September 1540: . . . to Doctor Lee's minstrels, the 9th day of September, 5s.[303] November-December (?) 1540: Given to Sir Henry Sycheverelles minstrels, 2s.6d. In reward to Sir John Markham's harper, 3s.4d. To a man to help to bring the viols between Croxton and Belwer, 2d.[304] 25 December: (Wages paid; list includes two minstrels.)[308]

21 February 1541: To Mr. Kyrkbe servant of Newarke for bringing the "regalles" (organ) hither against Christmas . . . 2s. Item paid, the same day, to Mr. Kyrkby, of Newark, for the loan of his regals all Christmas time, 5s. 9 April: To Richard Pyke for cord for the drum and skins for the head of the drum against the duke of Norfolke's coming to Belvoier, 3s.4d.[309] 11 July: To Richard Pyke for strings for the virginals and viols that he bought at London, 10s.[310] Rewards: Item given in reward, the first day of January, to two minstrels of Derbyshire which were servants to Mr. Bradbery, 8d.[312] 21 January: To a minstrel servant to Rowland Babyngton, "esquyer," 8d. (Payments for bull-baiting.)[313] 13 February: To the waits of Lyncolne, 2s. 18 February: To my lord of Cumberlande's minstrel, 2s. 16 March: To the regal maker for Nottingham for bringing a pair of regals against my lord's grace duke of Norfolke coming, 12d.[313] 1 April: Item given in reward, the first day of April, to Sir Gervys Clifton minstrel . . . 20d. 25 May: To three waits of Lynne, 2s. 20 July: To Mr. Babyngton minstrel, by the commandment of my lady, 12d. To my lord of Westmoreland servant that had a "daw(n)syng" bear, 3s.4d.[314] 15 September: To four minstrels of my lord's Matrevesse (Maltravers), by my lady's commandment, 20d.[315] 1541: First to my Lord Roose at the hunting of Hesillfurthe Cliffe for the finding of two hares, 16d.; at Mr. Markham at night to the min-

strel in reward there, 20d.; to the rest of Mr. Markham servants in reward, 5s.[317] 29 December: (three groups of players) to two minstrels of Mr. Sawage of Staffordshyre in reward, 12d.[321]

2 January 1542: To Mr. Jhon Dygby's minstrel of Kettelby in reward, 20d. 6 January: In reward to five players that came from Lencolne which played not before my lord, 2s. 8 January: To three minstrels of Nottengham in reward because they played not, 20d.[322] The same day in reward to six players of Derbbyshyre which played not, 20s. The same day to a juggler that "shoyd hes connyng in mackyng off a lyght for the banckyt," 20d. 9 January: To Sir Thomas Pyttes (probably a priest), by my lord's commandment, for singing all Christmas in the choir, 7s.6d.; more to a chorister that likewise sang in Christmas all the twelve days, 20d.—9s.2d. To Sir William Hwsse's minstrel in reward, 12d. 21 January: To Antony Halle in reward for his board four weeks when he was learning a play to play in Christmas, 7s.6d. 28 January: To Robert More, 2s. which he delivered in reward to a minstrel of my lord of Soffox's, 2s.[322] 13 April: To Mr. Pettes, the great priest of Grantam, in reward for being all Easter in my lord's chapel at Beywer, 5s. Item paid, the same day, in reward to a chorister for like time in my lord's chapel, 20d. Item paid the same day in reward to him that sung in my lord's chapel all the time of Easter with the great bass, 2s. c. 13 April: Item paid in reward to two minstrels, one of them Mr. Sachewerrelle's, the other my Lady Cockynge's, 2s. 24 April: To the waits of Leceser, 2s. To Sir Thomas Pettes, of Granttam (priest), and his chorister for singing in my lord's chapel at St. George's feast during three days, 2s. 27 April: To my Lord Cow(n)yers servants being minstrels, 2s. 30 April: To the waits of Leynckolne in reward, 20d.[323] 20 May: To Parson Pettes and his chorister for their pains taken in my lord's chapel the "Assenshon ewen" and the day following, 2s. 29 May: To my lord of Yorck minstrel, 2s. 3 June: To Parson Pettes of Grantam for serving in my lord's chapel at "Beywer Olly Thursday and all Wesson" week, 5s. 21 July: To Mr. Babenton's servant being a minstrel in reward by my lord's assignment, 12d. 23 July: To a minstrel of the king's, 3s.4d. (Bear wardens, twice; each 2s.)[324] 16 November 1541: For the regals £7.0.0.; more for the bringing of them from London to Beywer, 5s.— £7.5.0.[324] 11 March 1542: To Pycke for two dozen of lute strings called "menekyns," at 20d. the dozen, and ten dozen of "bressell" (Brussels) strings for the viols at 3d. the dozen, 5s.10d.[325]

(On the way from Belvoir to Parliament, 12 January 1542): Fodryngay. In reward to Sir Robert Kyrkham's minstrels for playing before my lord, . . . 3s.4d. Item given to diverse of the fellows in the college for playing a play before my lord, 6s.8d. To the children of the college for a forfeit of my lord's spurs, 8d.[326]

New Year's gifts, 1543: Given to Pyke, the minstrel, and his fellows, 3s.4d. 6 November 1542-29 October 1543: Given to my lord of Suffolk servant at

Belver, to the lord of "misrule" at Royston, and to diverse persons at London, £6.10.2.[339]

24 June 1549: (Wages; one chaplain, no minstrels, named.)[362-363]

Sir George Vernon's trip to London; at Derby, 26 January 1552: Item to the minstrels, 16d. Item for rewards, 22d.[571] Expenses of Sir George Vernon in London, February 1552: Item to my Lord Patchyte's minstrels, 12d.[573]

1 January 1553: To the trumpeter in reward for blowing a blast on New Year's day, 12d.[371] 9 January: Item to Mr. Dysney's minstrels, 20d. 12 January: Item to the waits of Doncaster, 2s. 20 January: Item given to my lord's players, 6s.8d. 20 March: Item . . . to the king's trumpeters, 20s.[372]

18 March 1558: Item given in reward to my lord's musicians, 40s. Item paid for two cornetts for my lady, 10s.[380] 1 January: Given to Weston for the teaching of Rycherd, my lady('s) page, to play on the lute, 10s.[381] 6 May: To Mr. Conyers, my Lord Roos schoolmaster, £3.3.4.[381] 28 June: To Mr. Frythe that teaches my lord's children to dance, 40s. (Reward). Given in reward to the master of fence that taught my Lord Roos and Mr. John Manners to play at weapons, 20s.[382] 26 April: Paid to Weston for teaching my lord's page to play on the lute, 10s.[383]

1 January 1559: To the Queen's trumpeters, 15s. To the musicians, 10s. 4 January: To Weston, lute player, 6s.8d. To Doctor Hill, 6s.8d. To Doctor Wendy, 19s. (etc.)[386]

5 February 1586: Roger Manners to the earl of Rutland, London: I have not forgotten Lady Elizabeth, but have a servant to play the virginals with her when Symons is away. I hope he will content you.[i:189] 26 May: Given in reward to my lord trumpeter . . . 40s.[388] 18 June: George Manners to his father John Manners of Haddon hall (husband of Dorothy Vernon M.), from Inner Temple Garden, London. Tells of his studies and exercise— dancing, tennis, running, leaping. Music apparently not included.[i:195-196]

3 August 1587: Edward Paston to the earl of Rutland. Recommends an organist from Norwich to teach the virginals to the earl's daughter.[i:223]

9 June 1588: Countess of Rutland to the countess of Bedford. Now that my daughter has recovered I commend her to you and resign all the power which I have over her. I beg you will form her in such course both for education and maintenance as you may think fit. . . . Her education has been barren hitherto, nor has she attained to anything except to play a little on the lute, which now, by her late discontinuance, she has almost forgotten. . . .[i:250]

Household expense at Winkburn, Nottinghamshire (a Rutland residence): 28 December 1590: To a musician and a piper at "towe" several times . . . 18d. 30 December: To the waits of Newarke . . . 3s.4d. 2 January 1591: To the waits of Donkester, being four of them . . . 3s. 17 January: To four musicians, being my Lord Welowbie men . . . 2s.[399] 19 January: Given to a harper and his man with him . . . 2s.[399] 15 March: To Sir Thomas Stanope his musicians, 3s.4d. 1 May: To the waits of Newarke . . . being five of them, 5s. 4 May: To three musicians . . . 2s.4d.[400] 25 May: To my Lord Comberland musicians . . . 3s.4d. 25 May: To Sir Thomas Stanope his musicians . . . 6s. (Illness at this time; baby?)[400]

11 May 1592: Thomas Screven, London, to Thomas Jegon, Winkburn. By the carrier of York you will receive a trunk for my lady . . . a latin book, and all the singing books you wrote for, save the duos, which cannot be gotten, for my Lady Elizabeth (the countess).[i:299]

16 March 1594: To the waits of Pomfrett, 2s.6d. 11 April: To Sir Henry Cavndyge (Cavendish) musicians, 3s.4d. 22 April: To the harper of Ednestowe, 12d. 6 June: To my Lord Wyllowbei's musicians of Kneathe, by my lady's commandment, 2s. 3 September: Unto my Lord Wyllobee's musicians being at Belvoire two days, by my lady's commandment, 40s.[407] 3 May: At Newarcke fair for three psalm books for my young masters, 3s.[408]

c. January 1599: (For my lord) Item for a "vyoll di gamba," bought *"per"* Payton, £4.0.0., and a case, 20s.—£5.0.0. c. February: (For my lord) Item . . . a music book, 10s. . . . French tennis balls, 4s. . . .[416] 29 August: To one that brought a harp from Uffington to Belvoir, 2s.6d.[426]

(Money disbursed for the Lady Fraunces Manners.) 24 April 1600: For a lute for her ladyship, £3.0.0.; a lute book, 3s.; a set of song books, 4s.6d.— Item then for three dozen of lute strings, 12s. 30 June: For a "violl di gamba," £4.0.0.; for a case, 20s., then sent to her.—£5.0.0.[432]

2 April 1602: To my lord of Northumberland his men playing upon cornetts, 5s.[437] 27 June: For a harp, £8.0.0. For a "violl di gamba," *"per"* Charles, £4.0.0.[438] 30 June: For the hire of a horse to carry down Rowland White, harper, 15s.[438] 2 March: To a musician that brought songs, 10s.[439] 25 September: Item given . . . to my Lord Willoughbye's musicians . . . 5s.[452]

28 June 1603: To Henygo Jones, a picture maker, £10.0.0.[446] 27 June: Item paid for my lord's supper and his company that night at Graves Ende, £6.12.0. Item to the musicians at Gravesend, 10s.[447] 20 July: Scarborough. To the musicians there, 5s. Given to the poor there, 10s.[449] 1603 (Huntington): Item paid for my lord's supper there one Saturday night, £6.10.0. (to the maids, 5s., chamberlains, 5s.) Item to the musicians, 20s. (To the poor, 5s.)[450] 1603 (at Warre at the Crowne): Item to the musicians, 10s.[450]

11 January 1608: To the waits of Grantham for playing at Belvoyer in Christmas, by his lordship's commandment, £3.0.0.[462]

8 January 1610: To Francklyn, musician, for himself and his men, playing at Belvoyer all Christmas, £5.0.0. (Also bear, bull.) 15 January: To my Lord Willoughbie's men for their music, by his lordship's appointment, 10s.[468]

7 January 1611: To the musicians, by his lordship's commandment, £3.6.8. 22 January: To Nynnyon Gibbion, trumpeter, his lordship's alms for one

half year, ended at Christmas last, 20s.[471] 7 September: To my Lord Wylloughbye's musicians, for playing at Bellvoyr when the strangers were there, 20s.[476]

7 January 1612: To the musicians for playing at Annesley in Christmas, all the twelve days, by my lord's commandment, £3.6.8.[477]

(For funeral of Roger, fifth earl.) 1612: Paid by the hands of Willyam Warren for charges at Bottesforrd, viz., getting of rushes against the funeral, charges also of the "quyer" of Southwell, for their "dyette," &c., £7.2.11.[480] 29 July: A reward to the choristers of Southwell, and others that did service in the parish church of Bottsford, in the county of Leicester, at the funeral of the noble Lord Roger . . . £20.0.0.[479] 10 August: Given to the waits of Lyncoln . . . £4.0.0. for playing at Bellvoyr when the king's majesty was there (to hunt), £4.0.0.[479]

7 January 1615: Unto Nichollas Francklyn, the musician, for music this Christmas . . . £6.13.4.[504]

(Costs of installation of the earl of Rutland in the Order of the Garter, Windsor.) 7 July 1616: For fees of the choir, £4.0.0. For fees of the king's trumpets . . . £6.0.0. To the king's musicians and companies, 40s. to either of them, £6.0.0.[509]

1617: Paid for lute strings for my Lady Katherin sent to Belvoire, 9s.6d. [511] 17 November: From my lord to his musicians that was my Lord Willobie's men, 10s. (reward). 20 December: To one John Blackbourne, of Nottingham, for mending my Lord Rosse's "citron" (cittern) and Mr. Markes his lute, 7s.[513]

8 January 1618: To my lord's musicians, for Christmas music *anno* 1617, by Mr. Jephson's directions from my lord, £6.13.4.[514]

c. June 1619: Paid to John Burrwood, organ maker, advanced him in part of payment for an organ to be by him made, the sum of £10.0.0.[516]

24 July 1620: To Hugh Bellerbye, of Grantham, carrier, for bringing down organ pipes, and other things. 31 July: To Mr. Burrall, organist, for work about the organs at Belvoire, £3.14.11. 9 January: London. Paid for making a lute and mending instruments for Andrew Markes, £2.13.0.[518]

(Charges at burial of Lord Roos, Westminster.) 7 March 1620: organist and singing men, £3.0.0.; choristers, 10s.[519]

c. March 1620: Paid to John Burrwood for making of an organ upon agreement for £55.0.0., whereof formerly paid £10.0.0, which was allowed in the last year's account, and now in full payment *per* "accquitance," £45.0.0. [519] 23 October: To the "musicq" . . . when the Lord Marquis Buckingham, Marcus Hambleton, Lord Crumbwell, and others were at Belvoir, 10s.[522]

8 January 1621: To George Moonne and the rest for Christmas music, 1620, by my lord's command, £6.13.4.[523] Musicians of Newarke—Paid by Wylliam Chappman, by my lady's command, 5s.[523]

25 June 1624: Paid to Ryley, the embroiderer, for badges for musicians, 36s.[526]

21 February 1623: To Edmound Eliott, Thomas Reay and William Baites, of the choir of Southwell, for service done at Bottsford at the funeral, £27.0.0.[528]

6 October 1637: To one Howett, a piper, who played here two days, 6s. 9 October: To the musicians of Grantham when my Lord and Lady Willowby were at Belvoior, £1.0.0.

7 January 1638: Paid to Grantham musicians for Christmas time at Belvoior ... £3.0.0. 28 March: Item given by my lords' command ... to Mr. Nowell's musicians, 6s.

7 May 1638: To Thomas Coates, of Stamford, organmaker, in part of payment of £6.13.4. for mending the organs in Belvoior chapel, £3.6.8. 17 August: Paid to Grantham musicians ... for playing then and once before, 11s. Paid to Grantham musicians, August the 32th (sic), 1638, by my lord's command, to Mr. Turfitt at the "Harle" and Countess of Westmorland being here for playing, £1.0.0. 3 September: To Edward Brock, the blind harper ... at his going away, £1.0.0. 17 September: To Grantham musicians ... at Lord Newbrooke's being here, 10s.[529]

1 April 1643: Item to Mounsier Sebastian, the dancing master, for one month ended the first of April, £3.0.0. Item paid to a man that made a case for my lord's viol, £1.0.0. c. April: Item paid to the "gittarman" that taught the Lady Francis for two months, and for her book, £4.2.6. Item paid the "gittarman" for mending an instrument for my Lady Frances, 7s. [532]

SIDNEY ACCOUNTS

These extracts refer to the families of Sir Henry Sidney (1529-1586), and of his son Sir Robert (1563-1626), later earl of Leicester. They are taken from HMC 77, *de l'Isle Mss.*, i, ii. Page numbers are indicated in square brackets after the last item from a page; all but the last two items are from volume one.

Accounts of Sir Henry as vice-treasurer in Ireland 1556-1559: A pair of virginals, £3.0.0.; mending and tuning, £1.0.0.; making of a lute and mending of another, 13s.; virginal strings, 2s.[381]

1566-1567: For one pair virginals, £4.0.0. Set of viols, £10.10.0 Strings, 16s.[242] 13 November 1567-1 March 1570: For the musicians, 19s.[244]

(Account for Sir Henry, Lord President of the Council in the Marches of Wales.) Michaelmas to Michaelmas, 1570-1571: The Allowance: Wages of servants in the household there as cooks, brewer, baker, "catur" and such like, for one whole year ended 25th March 1572, with £6.13.4. to the musicians in Christmas, £46.13.0. Liveries for the same servants, with 20s. for the musicians' liveries, and £8.0.0 for one hundred and eighty yards "fryes" sent to London, £26.1.0.[359]

c. September 1571: For a lute for Mistress Marye Sydney, my lord's daughter ... [256]

1573: Lute strings for Mistress Mary, 8s.[268]

1573-1574: Lute strings for Mistress Mary, 3s.[268]

(Payments for Robert Sydney and his sisters.) 1574: Given to the singers on May day, 1s. To minstrels on Midsummer day, 1s.[268]

(Expenses for Robert Sidney, at Oxford and elsewhere.) 1576: 21 April: To Richard Lant for his pains taken in teaching him to sing, 6s.8d.[269]

15 February 1579: To the musicians at Canterburie, 3s.[267]

(Rowland Whyte, at Penshurst, to Sir Robert.) 23 October 1595: Mistress Mary Sidney . . . is very forward in her learning, writing, and other exercises she is put to, as dancing and the virginals. . . .[ii:176]

(Rowland Whyte to Sir Robert Sidney, about his four children.) 9 February 1600: They are kept at their books, they dance, they sing, they play on the lute, and are carefully kept unto it.[ii:437]

ACCOUNTS OF THE SPENCERS OF ALTHORP

The following extracts, concerning the families of Sir John Spencer (died 1600) and of Sir Robert Spencer (died 1627; created Baron Spencer of Wormleighton in 1603), of Althorp, Northamptonshire, are taken from British Museum Additional Mss. 25,080, 25,081, and 25,082. Folio numbers are indicated in square brackets after the last item from a folio; items from the last two volumes of manuscripts are distinguished by small Roman numerals "i" and "ii" placed before the folio numbers.

1599?: Paid to the three minstrels which were accustomed to play at Christmas by your ladyship's command, 14s.6d.[4]

December-January 1599-1600: Given to the waits of Northampton, 5s.[12v]

6-13 December 1600: Paid to Chrysthopher the tuner of instruments, 13s. 4d.[113v] 13-20 December: Given to the Queen's man a harper, 5s.[116] 20-27 December: First paid to Christhopher the tuner of instruments, 5s. [119]

10-17 January 1601: Paid to the three minstrels for playing all Christmas, 14s.6d.[127] 7-14 February: Item paid unto the three minstrels for playing upon Candlemas day, 3s.[135v] 14-21 February: Given unto my Lord Mordyn's musicians by your ladyship's command, 10s.[137v] c. 7 November: First paid to the three minstrels for playing upon All Saints day, 3s.[222]

c. 9 January 1602: Given to Mr. Washington's man for bringing a "cople of capons," 12d. Paid to the three minstrels for playing all Christmas, 14s.6d. [242] c. 6 February: Paid to the three minstrels for playing upon Candlemas day, 3s.[251v] c. 6 November: Item t(o) the musicians for "Allholandaye," 3s.[i:42v]

c. 8 January 1603: Item paid to the musicians, 14s.6d.[i:61v] c. 22 January: Item for a quire of singing paper for my mistresses, 8d.[i:65v] c. 5 February: Item to the musicians, 3s.[i:68]

Before 24 December 1603: Item paid to the musicians, 10s.[i:145v]

c. 3 November 1604: Item paid to the musicians for Allhallows day, 3s.

Item paid to Streetes upon a bill for the dwarf for cotten and pockets and "bumbaste," 3s. Item for making his clothes, 7s. . . . .[i:232] Item for a pair of shoes for the dwarf, 10d. . . .[i:232v]

c. 12 January 1605: Item paid to the musicians, 15s.[i:254] c. 2 February: Item paid to the musicians, 3s.[i:261]

c. 26 January 1621: To young Hortopp two days laying up the timbers for the "shovelbord" table, 1s.[ii:4]

23 February 1622: To Blisse two days laying stones in the bowling alley, 2s.[ii:10]

WILLOUGHBY ACCOUNTS

The following extracts concern the youth and maturity of (Sir) Francis Willoughby and his sister, Margaret. They were children of Sir Henry Willoughby, who died in 1549 while they were young. The family seats were Middleton, Warwickshire, and Wollaton, Nottinghamshire; at the latter Sir Francis built a great hall.

The extracts are taken from HMC *69, Middleton Mss.*; page numbers are indicated here within square brackets after the last item taken from a page.

(Accounts for Francis and Margaret; occasionally Margaret writes the accounts; see pp. 406-407.) 1553: For a pair of virginals for me, 26s.8d. To Clarke for teaching me to play upon the virginals, for one month ended 27 May, 5s.; item to Mr. Horseley for another month ended 25 June, 5s.; item to him for the like another month ended 28 July, 5s. . . .[407]

1554: To the carrier of Tomworth for bringing up a pair of virginals from Myddelton, 16d. For stringing Master Fraunces his virginals "a newe" dressing them, 2s.8d. . . .

1555: To Mr. Horsseley to teach Fraunces Wylloughbye to play on the virginals, 2s.6d. Item to one that taught him to dance at several times, 4s.2d. [408] (Francis goes off to school in 1555.)[409] To Richard Bramley for teaching him (Francis) to sing, 5s.[411]

1556-1557 (for Mary): Item paid . . . for my nephew Fraunces . . . for paper for a song book for him, 12d.; item for a book binding for his songs, 10d.; for a Terence with diverse commentaries, 8s.; for a paper book for his lessons on the virginals, 15d. For the "Actes of the Appostelles" in meter to sing, 12d.[412] To Rycharde of Thaxsted for teaching him to play on the virginals and to sing, 2s.6d.[413] 1557: To Mr. Horseley for teaching him arithmetic and to play on the virginals, from the 27th of April until the 15th of May, viz., 18d. days at 16d. the week, 3s.4d. For the carriage of his virginals from Mr. Horseleyez to the Minorisse, 1d. Item for a paper book to write his songs that he learned on the virginals, 8d.

1558: (Francis goes to school at Cambridge.)[413] For mending his virginals, 12d.[414]

(Accounts for Francis Willoughby, as master of Wollaton, 1572 and after.)

10 November 1572: To the waits of Lychefyelde . . . in reward, by my master his commandment, 2s.[421] 12 November: In reward to my Lord Willoughbies (perhaps Peregrine Bertie, Lord Willoughby's) musicians, by my master his command, 8d.[422] December: To the waits of Nottingham for their quarter's wages ending at Christmas, 3s.4d.[423]

1 January 1573: In reward to the musicians for playing at my master his chamber door . . . 2s.[424] 3 February: To the two waits, 2s., for playing before my master[425] February (expenses of a journey; master and servant?): . . . at Lechefyeld for supper, fire, and wine, 13s.8d.; breakfast. . . , 5s.10d.; . . . to the waits there, 6d.; . . . at Stone . . . the waits there, 6d.; . . . at Darby . . . a fiddler there, 12d.; to the poor there, 3d. . . .[426-427] 2 June: Nottingham. In reward to the waits of Nottingham . . . 12d.[430] 12 September: To my Lord Willoughby his musicians . . . 2s.6d. 13 September: For the picture of my master, 10s. And for my mistress's picture, 20s.[432] 26 September: To Mr. Stanhopes waits . . . 2s. 24 October: To him for the carriage of the virginals and two pictures, 10s. To Roger that he paid for glass for the musicians chamber . . .[434] c. 26 November: To a virginal player by "th'andes" of B. Wedoson, 3s.4d.[436] c. 28 November: To the cater that he paid for the musician his horsemeat at Nottingham, his horse being tired, 4d. To the virginal player . . . , 5s. To Astell the virginal player . . . , 10s.[437] Wages paid at Christmas: My mistress, £13.6.8. . . . Johan Poker, 10s. . . . the coachman, 15s. . . . the musician, £5.0.0. . . .[439-440]

January 1574: To Edlin, the musician, for playing at my master his chamber door on New Year's day, 5s. To Arnolde fiddler . . . 6d. To three singers of Darby . . . 12d. To five players that did not play before my master, 2s.6d. To a harper . . . 6d.[440] To the waits of Lester . . . 2s.[441] To Blunt for nine weeks lodging the musicians, 3s. To Hugh Mercer that he gave to a harper, 6d.[441] To Mr. Stanhoppes waits . . . 2s. February: To five musicians that came with a play . . . 2s.[442] April: To Mr. Astell the virginal player, 10s. [444] May: To Tole for bringing a pair of virginals from London, 13s. 4d.[445] September: To John Edlin that he paid for six "knottes" of lute strings, 16d.[447] November: To Mr. Dynmock his musicians, 12d.[449] After Christmas 1574: To the waits of Nottingham . . . 12d. To five players of Darby . . . 2s. To a harper at the same time, 6d.[450] (Wages list for Christmas 1574, like the list of 1573; no musicians on the list, and no one received £5.0.0. pp. 449-450.)

February 1575: To the singing men of Derbie, by William Stokes, 12d.[451]

(The following are extracts from the collections of Cassandra Willoughby, 1702; they are necessarily less authentic than the preceding. There is, for example, no certainty about the position of the possessive apostrophe sign after "musitioners" in the fourth item below.): There is a friendly letter from Sir Matthew Arundell to Mr. Francis Willughby, which gives an account of some things which he had bought for him, and that he had sent him some songs, strings, and three books ... (London, the court; 1564?) [527] There is a letter from Lady Arundell which . . . tells her brother that she has made enquiry but could not yet hear of one that could play and sing, but she hopes she shall provide him one when she goes to London . . . (1575?) [528-529] There is in the library at Wollaton a letter written by Sir F(rancis) Willughby . . . to know if Mr. Creme can find him any treble lutes fit for his purpose. (1575) [536] A list of servants which did belong to Sir Francis Willughby and his lady, A.D. 1572, and their wages for a quarter of a year. (Last item): The "musitioners'" (possessive, plural) wages one quarter, £5.0.0. (Lady Cassandra modernized the list, and probably added the possessive sign. Compare the extract from the account of wages paid at Christmas 1573, given above.) [541-542]

INSTRUMENTS USED IN HOUSEHOLDS

(Items are not repeated from the preceding pages of this appendix.)

1 July 1555: Brussels. Earl of Devonshire to Mr. Thomas Gresham. Begs him to advance money to purchase "a scytheraine." (cittern?) [1]

24 April 1559: Appraisal of the goods of the late Sir Thomas Hilton of Hilton castle (Westmorland?). In the gallery. One bedstead, two feather beds ... one pair of old virginals, the hangings of painted clothes. . . . [2]

10 July 1561: Thomas Windebank to Cecil, from Paris. Mr. Thomas Cecil has no great taste for the lute, but likes the "cistern" (cittern?). [3]

1564-1565: For Thomas, earl of Northumberland (purchased): four little song books, 3s.6d., viol strings, virginal wire. [4]

1565: Inventory of goods of late Sir Ralph Hedworth, of Hawerton. A pair of virginals. [5]

1568: Inventory of the goods of the late Lady Hedworth (wife of the preceding) at Herington (Harrington, Cumberland?). One pair of virginals. [6]

1568-1569: Inventory of goods of Harald Marten, Cambridgeshire (farmer?). A pair of virginals. [7]

1569: Inventory of goods of Bartram Robson, of Durham (probably a clergyman; lived in a rented room). A pair of clavicords. [8]

1577: Inventory of goods of late Leonerde Temperleye, gentleman (retired soldier, farmer, northern England). Old "syttrone" and one broken "gyttrone" (cittern and gittern?). [9]

1579: Organ-harpsichord made for Sir Edward Hoby, of Bisham, Berkshire, and his wife. [10]

---

[1] CSPD *1547-80*, 68.

[2] *Wills and Inventories Illustrative of the History, Manners . . . of the Northern Counties of England* (Surtees Society, II), 181.

[3] CSPD *1547-80*, 179. [4] HMC 5, *Duke of Northumberland Mss.*, 226.

[5] *Wills and Inventories*, 227. [6] *ibid.*, 280-283.

[7] Registry of the University of Cambridge Ms., a collection of inventories.

[8] *Wills and Inventories*, 308. [9] *ibid.*, 420-423.

[10] James, *Early Keyboard Instruments*, 116.

1580: Inventory of goods of late Christopher Cooke, gentleman. Four "halbartts" . . . one great pair of virginals. . . .[11]

1581: Inventory of goods of late Cuthberte Ellyson, of Newcastell, Marchaunt. A pair of virginals.[12]

1583: Inventory of household furniture at Kenilworth of Robert Dudley, earl of Leicester. Instruments. An instrument of organs, regals, and virginals, covered with crimson velvet and garnished with gold lace. A fair pair of double virginals. A fair pair of double virginals, covered with black velvet. Two chests of instruments, the one with six "vialles," the other with five "violens" (Sir John Hubbard the five "violins," ut dicitr.). A case of flutes, "flewed" with silver, containing twelve pieces. Three bandoras in a case of leather. Three lutes in leather cases.[13]

1585-1586: For Thomas, earl of Northumberland. A theorbo, 40s.[14]

1586: Inventory of second earl of Bedford, Chenies, Devonshire. In a sitting room, a case of regals, a flute, virginals.[15]

1588: Sir George Chaworth to the countess of Rutland. I am without a pair of virginals and cannot as yet get any good. I shall be greatly beholden if you will sell or lend me an old pair which stand at Belvoir.[16]

1588-1589: Expenses of Lady Tresham of Rushton, Northamptonshire; other necessaries include lute strings, virginal wire, mending of musical instruments, paper and ink, and books for the children. . . .[17]

1594: Philip Gawdy to his brother about his friend Tom Forman: he wants nothing but a good cittern to his voice. . . .[18]

1595: Inventory of goods of the earl of Cumberland at Skipton castle, Barden, Appleby, Brougham castle and other places: no musical instruments (very detailed inventories).[19]

1596: Inventory of goods of Henry, earl of Huntington, at York. In the entry by the great chamber door . . . one pair of virginals sent to my lady.[20]

1597: Inventory of goods of late Thomas Tanckard, esquire, at Aldborough, Yorkshire, manor house. In Mrs. Beckwith parlor and the nursery. Item one standing bed . . . a trundle bed . . . two blankets, a pair of old virginals, a cushion. . . .[21]

1601: Inventory for the countess of Shrewsbury, at Chatsworth, Derbyshire. Middle "wardrop" (tapestries, cloth, towels, etc.), a pair of virginals (dishes, etc.). High gallery . . . an instrument with virginals. For the same, at Hardwicke: Long gallery. A pair of virginals.[22]

11 *Wills and Inventories*, 430.
12 *ibid.*, 434-437.
13 HMC 77, *de l'Isle Mss.*, i, 291.
14 HMC 5, *Duke of Northumberland Mss.*, 226.
15 Thomson, *Two Centuries of Family History*, 249.
16 HMC 24, *Rutland Mss.*, i, 261.
17 HMC 55 *Various* iii, *Clarke-Thornhill Mss.*, 48.
18 HMC 6, *Frere Mss.*, 522.
19 Mss. of duke of Devonshire, Bolton Mss.
20 Huntington Library Ms.
21 Sir Thomas Lawson-Tancred, *Records of a Yorkshire Manor*, 175-183.
22 Mss. of the duke of Devonshire.

1602: To Philip Gawdy's sister-in-law ... and first I will not discontent you with sending you two songs for the viol, that were given me from a very worthy musician at court not doubting but shortly to bring you some better store. ...[23]

1603: Inventory of Thomas Kytson's goods, Hengrave, Suffolk. In the chamber where the musicians play: one boarded chest ... with six viols. One boarded chest, with six "violenns." One case of recorders, in number seven. Four "cornutes," one being a "mute cornute." One great bass lute, and a "meane" lute. ... One treble lute, and a "meane" lute. ... One bandora, and a "sitherne" with a double case. Two sackbuts. ... Three "hoeboys," with a "curtall and a lysarden." Two flutes. ... One pair of little virginals. One wind instrument like a virginal. Two luting books (and many other books of music). One great pair of double virginals. One pair of great organs. In the dining chamber ... : Item, one pair of virginals, with irons ... chessboard. ... In the winter parlor ... : Item, a pair of virginals, with irons. In the chapel ... : Item, one pair of little organs, with a board which they stand on.[24]

1605: Inventory of goods of Thomas, Lord Arundell of Wardour, at Wardour castle: in the withdrawing parlor, a standing cupboard for the virginals.[25]

1605: Payment for a bass viol for family of Sir Alexander Temple.[26]

1605: Expenses of William Smith in his first quarter in Trinity college, Cambridge. For a viol, 50s.[27]

1609: Inventory of goods at Wollaton hall, Nottinghamshire (Willoughby). In the "Wardropp" ... Item, five instruments with cases. Item, a "tyller boe." Item, a white lute of bone ... (1550 inventory listed no musical instruments).[28]

1614: Expenses of Robert Wilton, sent to Cambridge at age of fifteen, included: Item paid for carrying his cittern thither ... 12d.[29]

1622: Inventory attached to will of Sir Henry Belassis "sometime of New-brough and now of the city of York, knight." Chapel. One table with falling leaves, one "forme," one pair of organs set upon a cupboard. ...[30]

1622: Inventory of goods (of Henry Jernegan?) at Cossey (Wales). In the wardrobe. Two irons to burn coal, a shovel for coal, a pair of virginals, a portmanteau of leather.[31]

1624: Inventory of goods of (Sir Thomas?) Fairfax. At Walton, Yorkshire. In the wardrobe ... a chest which Barbara keeps ... in the open press

---

[23] *Letters of Philip Gawdy of West Harling, Norfolk, 1579-1616*, ed. Jeayes, 123.
[24] Gage, *Hengrave*, 22-32. Compare Fellowes, *English Madrigal*, 12-13.
[25] Mathew, *Jacobean Age*, 33.   [26] Huntington Library Ms., Stowe accounts, 1603-1606.
[27] HMC *19, Townshend Mss.*, 13.   [28] HMC *69, Middleton Mss.*, 485-491 (474-485).
[29] Bennet, "Notes from a Norfolk Squire's Notebook," *Communications, Cambridge Antiquarian Society*, v (1884), 215.
[30] HMC *55 Various* ii, *Wombwell Mss.*, 112.   [31] HMC *13, Stewart Mss.*, 163-164.

a bass violin and the singing books. In your own chamber . . . an orpharion. . . . In the great chamber . . . a frame on which stands a pair of virginals. . . . At Gilling castle, Yorkshire. In the great chamber . . . a bill, a halbert, and a pair of "Rigalles." In the dining parlor . . . a viol chest. . . . In the wardrobe . . . a viol chest. . . . (Inventory of goods of Sir William Fairfax, 1595, included no instruments.)[32]

1631: Inventory of the goods of Robert, Viscount Kilmorey. In the great parlor. Three great maps . . . a pair of virginals on a frame. In the inner room. One bass viol, one lute, one orpharion, one bandora with a case, one iron to roast apples. . . .[33]

1633: Lodowick Bowyer, son of Sir John Bowyer of Herefordshire, played orpharion.[34]

1634: Sir Arthur Ingram, York, had an organ said to be worth five hundred pounds.[35]

1639: Account by the secretary of Secretary Windebank: freight of the virginals, £2.0.0.[36]

1637: Sir Henry Wotton wills his "Viol de Gamba" to Dr. Bargrave, dean of Canterbury.[37]

c. 1644 (?): Inventory of furniture left by Lord Cork at his house in York. One black box with a great viol in it . . . (on a similar list) diverse music books. . . .[38]

1644 (probably): At a house of the late earl of Cumberland. In the great hall . . . one pair of organs, one harpsicon. . . . In the gallery, one "shovell" board table, two trunks, one hundred and odd boards and planks, one viol chest with six stringed instruments. In the music room, (pictures, etc.). (1644, inventory of Appleby castle, no musical instruments.)[38]

1645: An inventory taken at Skipton castle of such goods is my lady Pembroke, May the 7th, 1645. In the billiard chamber, one table, one cupboard, one pair of harpsicalls, one little organ, one range. . . . In my lord's chamber . . . one chest of musical instruments. In the music room. Four pieces of gilt leather hangings, one range.[38]

1644: Inventory of the goods of the Countess-dowager Rivers, at an unnamed house. In the great chamber, a bandora and a case. . . . In the virginal coffer in the nursery, whereof my lady herself kept the keys. . . . In the nursery . . . a virginal box with lock and keys. . . .[39]

1648: Edward, Lord Herbert of Cherbury, willed his viols and lutes to the wife of his son, Richard (she was Mary, daughter of John, earl of Bridgwater).[40]

[32] "Inventories made for Sir William and Sir Thomas Fairfax . . . ," ed. Peacock, *Archaeologia*, XLVIII, pt. i (1884), 138-139, 149.   [33] HMC *13, Kilmorey Mss.*, 374.
[34] CSPD *1633-1634*, 215-216.   [35] Hammond, *Relation 1634*, ed. Legg, 21.
[36] CSPD *1638-1639*, 295.   [37] Walton, *Lives* (World's Classics), 147.
[38] Mss. of the duke of Devonshire, Bolton Mss.   [39] HMC *64, Verulam Mss.*, 36, 41, 49.
[40] Edward, Lord Herbert of Cherbury, *Autobiography*, ed. Lee, 160.

APPENDIX C

ENTRIES RELATING TO MUSIC, FROM MUNICIPAL RECORDS

DESIGNED mainly to illustrate and support part two on professional musicians in the provinces, and part five, "Amateurs of Music," this appendix includes selections from the records of Coventry, Nottingham, and York. As in Appendix B, the manuscript or published sources have been followed closely but not literally.

COVENTRY

Chamberlains' Accounts 1498-1574

(Preceding items taken from an accounting-year's accounts is given, in parentheses, the date of the closing or auditing of the account; the page number in the volume follows the date)

(October 1559; p. 248) waits' liveries 26s.8d. (October 1560; 252) the same. (October 1561; 253) waits for their wages 26s.8d. (October 1562; 254) To James Hewet for his part of the waits' liveries 8s.10d. (October 1563; 257) four waits for their wages 26s.8d. (Similar payments 1564, 1565) (October 1566; 262) the waits: James Hewett for his fee 6s.8d. Thomas Nicoles, Richard Stiff, Richard Sadeler, each the same. (Same amount paid yearly 1567-1571; accounts not itemized 1572; same amounts paid 1573, 1574) (pp. 265-279).

Chamberlains' and Wardens' Accounts 1574-1636

(Date and reference as above, with prefix of "c" or "w" according to whether the account is Chamberlains' or Wardens')

(w December 1574; pp. 1-3) to the four waits for their liveries and wages £4. Lord . . .'s players 3s.4d. (rewards for four more groups of players and four bearwards, amounts ranging from 3s.4d. to £2) Earl of Essex musicians 2s.6d. Earl of Leicester musicians 2s.6d. (w November 1575; 6-8) Four waits, liveries and wages, £4. Earl of Derby's bearward 10s. Lord of Hunsdonnes musicians 4s.4d. Earl of Essex jester 2s. Earl of Worcetters musicians 5s. Lord of Hunsdons musicians 12d. Earl of Leicesters players 26s.8d. Earl of Leicesters drumplayers and two of his flute players 5s. (three groups of players and bearward) Base pipe for the waits 7s. (c October 1575; 9) To the four waits 26s.8d. (c October 1576; 11) Wages of the four waits 26s.8d. (w November 1576; 12-13) Waits' wages £4. Earl of Worcester's players 6s.8d. Sir Foulke Grevile bearward, 10s. Earl of Essex's players, 10s. Earl of Essex's musicians, 2s.6d. (c October 1577; 15) To the four waits, 26s.8d. (w November 1577; 16-19) Earl of Leicester's bearward, 6s.8d. (three groups of players and three bearwards) Lord of Essex musicians, 2s.6d. Earl of Bath's players, 6s.8d. Earl of Bath's trumpeters, 3s.4d. (two groups of players) Four waits' wages, £4. (c October 1578; 22) Paid to four waits at Lammas their fee 6s.8d. apiece. (w November 1578; 25-27) Waits, £4. Lord Derby's players, 6s.8d. A stand for the mayor and mayoress at the play on the queen's holiday, 3s. Earl of Essex's players, 3s/ Earl of Worcester's players, 5s. Queen's bearward, 20s. Lord Vawse's bearward, 3s.4d. To the players at Mr. Oglianbys, 7s. Keeper of the queen's apes, 2s. Lord Dudley's musicians, 5s. Lord Hunsdon's musicians, 6s.8d. (payments for sermons occasionally). (three groups of players, two bearwards).

(1579 accounts similar, but no visiting musicians rewarded; pp. 31-33)

(c October 1580; 37) To the waits for this year past, 26s.8d. (w November 1580; 40-45) To the four waits due at Lammas £3.5.0. Given to noblemen's servants: earl of Worcester's players, 6s.8d. Lord Sandes bearward, 13s.4d. Lord Barkley's players, 6s.8d. Lady Essex musicians, 2s. Lord Barkley's bearward, 5s. (two groups of players and a bearward).

(1581 accounts similar; wardens pay the waits £4 again, and reward musicians of one nobleman and numerous bearwards and players; pp. 47-50)

(c October 1582; 64) Waits, 20s. (w November 1582; 67-78) To the three waits for their wages, £3. Constables at the two leets, 26s.8d. (six groups of players, two bearwards, all named for some nobleman). (c October 1583; 82) Waits, 26s.8d. (w November 1583; 85-89) And to the four waits viz. John Thomas, James Hewyt, Old Styffe, and Anthonye Styff for their wages this year last past every of them 20s. (six groups of players, three bearwards, and:) Lord Barkeles players and musicians, 13s.4d. Lord Dudles players and musicians, 6s.8d. Lord Hunsdons musicians, 6s.8d. Sir Thomas Stannopps musicians, 2s.6d. Mr. Nowells musicians, 3s.4d. (c October 1584; 104) Waits' wages 26s.8d. (w November 1584; 108-112) Waits, £4. (Six groups of players, three bearwards, and one lord's musicians rewarded, and:) Earl of Essex's musicians, 5s. Lord Hawardes musicians, 5s. Waits of Cambridge, 3s.4d. Waits of Chester, 5s. (c October 1585; 115) Waits' wages, 26s.8d. (w November 1585; 117-119) Waits, £4. Lord Chamberlain's musicians, 3s.4d. Earl of Leicester's players, 30s. And to our waits on the Leet day, 3s.4d. And to our waits at the old wardens account, 2s. Lord Shelfeldes players, 10s. John Wallans at a bearbaiting, 13s.4d. Sir George Hastings players, 10s. Lord Staffords players, 10s. Queen's bearward, 10s. Sir Thomas Darbies musician, 2s. Earl of Oxford's players, 13s.4d. Earl of Essex's musicians, 2s.6d. Lord Vawse bearward, 2s.6d. (c October 1586; 130) Waits' wages 26s.8d. (w November 1586; 133-135) (Wages and rewards as usual; the "men" of various lords and gentlemen are rewarded; and:) Sir Thomas Stanopps musicians, 12d. The Lord Chamberlain's musicians, 5s. Lord Dudley's musicians, 12d. Waits of Cambridge, 12d. Waits of Westminster, 6d. (c October 1587; 143) Waits' wages, 26s.8d. (w November 1587; 148-150) Waits' wages £4. Earl of Leicester's players last Lammas day, 30s. Earl of Sussex's players in September, 13s.4d. Queen's players in September 40s. Lord Admiral's players, 20s. And to the Lord Chamberlain's musicians that came with the judges at the assizes, 5s. Lord Shandos players, 10s. Lord of Leicester's players in July, 20s. Queen's players more in September, 20s. And to the waits of Leicester, 12d. (c October 1588; 160) Waits wages, 26s.8d. (w December 1588; 163-172) Waits, £4. (Seven groups of players, four bearwards including the bearward of this city, rewarded, and:) To Lake the Earl of Essex musician, 2s. A nobleman's musician, 3s.4d. Mr. Caudishe musicians, 3s.4d. (c October 1589; 176) Waits' wages, 26s.8d. (w November 1589; 179-182) Waits' wages, £4. Lord Stranges musicians, 3s.4d. Lord Chamberlain's musicians, 3s. Lord of Essex's musicians, 10s. To Lake the Earl of Essex's man, 2s. Queen's players, 20s. Wallans the bearward and his company, 13s.4d. Queen's players, 20s. (c October 1590; 191) Waits' wages, 26s.8d. (w December 1590; 194-198) And of £4 paid to Mr. Goldston for the waits of this city, £4. And of 20s. paid to old Stiffe late one of the waits by consent of this house, 20s. To players: Earl of Essex musicians, 2s. To the judges musicians at the two assizes, 6s.8d. Earl of Essex's players, 10s. Queen's players and the Turk, 40s. Lord Admiral's players, 20s. Earl of Worcester's players, 10s. Coventry players, 40s.

(1591 accounts similar, but fewer rewards, and none to visiting musicians indicated; pp. 204-213)

(1592 accounts similar, but more players rewarded, including a Mr. Dutton's, and the earl of Essex's musicians, who received 12d.; pp. 217-221)

(c October 1593; 226) Waits' wages, 26s.8d. (w November 1593; 229-231) And of £4 paid to Mr. Goldston in part of his wages for the waits, £4. Lord Admiral's players, 13s.4d. Lord Shandos players, 13s.4d. Queen's players, 40s. Earl of Pembroke's players, 30s. And to the tumbler that went on the ropes, 20s. Mr. Burnabies bearward, 5s. Paid for two wind instruments called curtalls that Mr. Goldston hath for the city, 33s.4d.

(1594: usual payments to waits; very few rewards, none to musicians; pp. 237-245)

(1595: usual payments to waits and usual number of rewards, including to earl of Essex musicians, 2s. and Lord Stafford's musicians, 12d.; pp. 252-260)

(c October 1596; 265) Waits' wages, 26s.8d. (w December 1596; 265-271) Mr. Goldston for the waits, £4. Earl of Huntington's bearward, 6s.8d. Lord Willoughbyes players, 10s. Queen's players, 10s. Sir Foulk Grevylls bearward, 10s. To the Morris dancers of Stonley, 3s.4d. Lord Darsies players, 6s.8d. Lord Ogles players, 10s. Queen's players, 40s. Earl of Derby's players, 10s. Lord Admiral's players, 10s. Queen's trumpeters and the earl of Essex's musicians, 4s.6d. Paid to certain men that carried armor on the queen's holiday at night 2s.1d. Wine, sugar, etc. at the parlor the same night. Paid to Thomas Massie for himself and the singers the same night, 20s.

(1597 accounts similar but without the queen's holiday; several groups of players and bearwards, a tumbler, and the earl of Essex's musicians, who received 5s.; pp. 281-289) (c October 1598; 294) Waits' wages, 26s.8d. (w December 1598; 300-305) Mr. Goldston's wife for the waits' wages, £4. Earl of Huntington's players, 10s. Earl of Essex's musicians, 5s. To the musicians of London, 5s. Lord Stafford's players, 6s. Earl of Derby's players, 10s. (and three other groups of players) Lord Willoughby's musicians, 3s.4d. Earl of Derby's players, 20s. (Accounts for many years mention payments to the poor, lame, etc., but this year seems to be the first mentioning persons with passports:) Given to vagrant persons that had passports from the 25 of April to the last of October, £4. Given to one Luce Lodge borne in this city and sent hither as a vagrant person to buy her apparel and to place her, 12s.

(1599 accounts similar, but no musicians rewarded; one that had "poppittes and camell" received 10s.; pp. 309-317)

(1600 similar, but with reward of 5s. to earl of Essex's musicians; pp. 323-333)

(c October 1601; 337) Waits' wages, 26s.8d. (w December 1601; 341-345) Waits' wages, £4. Sir ffulke Grivells bearward, 10s. Lord Dudley's players, 6s.8d; the same at another time, 3s.4d. Earl of Huntington's players, 10s. Queen's players, 30s. The musicians of Northampton, 2s.6d. Earl of Essex's musicians, 3s.4d. Earl of Derby's bearward, 3s.4d. Earl of Lincoln's players, 10s. Lord Mountegles players, 10s. Mr. Talbottes musicians, 18d. Earl of Worcester's players, 10s. Lord Evers players, 10s. Paid to Widdoe (widow?) Massam the virginal maker's wife to bring her to Basing stoke, 3s.4d.

(1602 accounts similar, with nine groups of players but no musicians rewarded, and 12d. given Mr. mayor at the parlor to see the "Babbon"; pp. 349-356)

(1603 and 1604 accounts similar, with many players and some bearwards rewarded but no musicians; pp. 358-377)

(1605 and 1606 accounts similar, but the number of groups of players declines to three in 1605 and to five in 1606; pp. 382-405)

(c October 1607; 415) Waits' wages, 26s.8d. (w November 1607; 419-425) Waits' wages, £4. Players: Queen's, 20s. Lord Shandies, 6s.8d. Lord Mount egles, 6s.8d. Lord Harford, 10s. Earl of Derby's, 10s. Lord Dudley's, 6s.8d. Lord Barkeleys, 20s. Lord Shandois, 10s. Paid to trumpeters and waits, 3s.4d.

(1608 and 1609 accounts similar, without payments to musicians except, as always heretofore, the city's own waits; pp. 434-457)

(c October 1610; 464) Waits' wages, 26s.8d. (w November 1610; 467-471) Waits' wages, £4. (four groups of players) Given to a company of musicians, 2s.6d. Paid for six yards of cloth for four liveries for the city's waits, £3. (c October 1611; 475) Waits' wages, 26s.8d. (w November 1611; 484-487) Waits' wages, £4. Four groups of players, together rewarded 2s.6d. Lord Evers president of Wales his musicians, 2s.

(Usual payments to the waits in 1612 accounts, with payments to four groups of players and a bearward; as in some other years the sexton of St. Michael's church received 6s.8d. for ringing six o'clock bell; pp. 497-509)

(c October 1613; 522) Waits' wages, 26s. 8d. (w November 1613; 526-532) Waits' wages, £4. Queen's players, 40s. Unto two of the company of the children of the Revels, 20s. Queen's or the Lady Elizabeth's players, £4. Given to the waits of Worster and the Lord Willoughby his men, 3s. Lord of Huntington his musicians, 5s. The Lord Compton his bearward, 5s. (c October 1614; 537) No payment to the waits. (w November 1614; 542-549) Waits' wages, £4. (Three groups of players rewarded) Earl of Worcestor's musicians, 2s.6d. To the waits for their pains at the Leet, 3s.6d. Lord Compton's bearward, 6s.8d.

[Council Book 1556-1641, p. 394; 14 August 1615: At this day it is agreed that Edward Man, Roger Newland, John Jelfes, John Hill, and William Holsworth, shall go to play with the waits about the city according to the ancient custom of the said city for which they are to have seven pounds by the year in money, and quarteridge also so that they play orderly as they should, out of which allowance they are to furnish themselves with comely and sufficient cloaks for the credit of the place, they are also to play at all solemn feasts, at Mr. mayor's command, and not to go forth of the city without licence obtained of the said Mr. mayor.]

(c October 1615; 557) No payment to the waits. (w November 1615; 568-575) No payment to the waits. (Trumpeters and players) Given to one Pendleton who brought his M[ajesty's?] letters patent to show art and skill as appeareth by a bill, 10s. The queen's players called the Revels, 40s.4d. Paid to the waits at Allhallows' dinner, 6s. Paid to the waits at another time, 5s. (c October 1616; 582) Waits' wages, 26s.8d. (w November 1616; 588-593) No wages paid to waits. To one that had king's warrant to show tricks with puppets, 3s.4d. To the Lord Willoughby's men, 2s. Lord Ivers trumpeters, 2s.6d. To the waits of Leicester the same day (30 March), 2s. To the waits of Nottingham the same day, 2s. To the waits of Sowtham as appeareth by the same bill, 12d. To the waits of Shrewsbury the same day, 2s. Given to the prince his players one quarter of the pound of refined sugar at the parlor and a quart of sack, 17d. To musicians, 12d. Earl of Shrewsbury's players, 5s. The duke and the lord treasurer's trumpeters, 5s. Waits of Shrewsbury, 2s.6d. Lord of Derby's bearward, 3s.4d. Lord Compton's bearward, 10s. Waits of Nottingham, 12d. Given to an Italian that thrust himself through the side to make experience of his oil, 20s. Prince' players, £3. Counsellors trumpeters, 10s. Waits of Lincoln, 2s. Palsgrave's players, 40s. Lady Elizabeth's players, 40s. Company of the Revels, 20s. Waits of Hereford, 2s. Lord of Derby's players 10s. Queen's players, 20s. Lord of Mounteagle's players, 10s. Given to the waits of this city, 2s. Queen's players, 40s. The fencers, 2s. Paid to John Launder and others which took pains in setting down and pricking the notes for the chimes in St. Michael's church, 2s.6d.

(1617 accounts much shorter; usual payment to waits by chamberlains, but not by wardens; three groups of players, the king's bearward, and trumpeters at the time when the mayor walked the wall, were rewarded; pp. 600-604)

(1618 accounts similar to 1617; chamberlains paid the waits and wardens did not; pp. 616-627)

(1619 accounts short; neither paid wages to the waits; few players; Lord of Worcestor's musician received 2s.; pp. 634-644)

(c October 1620; 654) No payment to waits. (w November 1620; 659-662) No payment to the waits. (Three groups of players and Starkey, the king's jester, rewarded) Musicians of Nottingham, 2s. (c October 1621; 668) No payment to waits. (w November 1621; 673-677) No wages to the waits. William Peadle and other players dancers upon ropes, 10s. To Martin Slathier one of the players of the late Queen Elizabeth, 5s. Lady Elizabeth's players, 22s. To Henry Walker and John Walker who brought the king's warrant to show works of art concerning the (castle of W?), 2s.6d. To the wait players of the Lady Grace, 3s. Wait players of Newark, 23d. Paid which was given to Gilbert Reason one of the prince's players who brought a commission wherein himself and others were named, 20s. King's sergeant trumpeter and ten more of king's trumpeters, £3.6.0. Wait players of Newark the same day, 2s. (w December 1622; 686-689) Lord Stanhopps trumpeters, 12d. Sir John Dancing (?) his wait players, 12d. Two several companies of wait players, 4s. Wait players of the earl of Northampton, 2s.6d. (One group of players and trumpeters of two noblemen) Lord Burghley's musicians, 12d.

(1623 accounts show no wages to waits, but have much longer list of rewards to players, trumpeters, companies of musicians, and waits, including waits of Maxfeild, musicians of Lichfield, waits of Lincoln, Derby, and Newark, and to the king's players for bringing up of "Bristow" youths in music; pp. 702-710)

(w November 1624; 726-730) Rewards to king's and prince's trumpeters, Lady Elizabeth's players. Given to Bartholomew Cloys being allowed by the master of the Revels for showing a musical organ with divers strange and rare motions, 5s. Four trumpeters of the Revels, 5s.

(1625 accounts still have no wages to waits, and wardens' accounts give very few rewards to entertainers; pp. 743-747)

(w November 1626: 754-758) Rewards to players "Nothing."

[Council Book 1556-1641, p. 554; 17 October 1627: the waits of this city shall have four marks per annum wages from this house and livery cloaks once in three years: so long time as they perform their duties to the approbation of this house.]

(c October 1627; 766) to the waits of this city for their wages for this year past, 53s.4d. (w November 1627; 771-776) King's players, 2s.6d. To the Revels, 2s. Paid to the said Gilbert Touckes (Tonckes) for dressing up gilding and enameling of four of the city's crests 13s.4d. and for eight yards

Appendix C

of eight penny broad ribbon to hang the crests about the wait players' necks 5s.4d. Paid for four cloaks for the wait players of this city . . . , £6.12.1. (c. October 1628; 787) Waits' wages, 53s.4d. (w November 1628, 791-795) High sheriffs trumpeters, 5s. and the Major Drummer of Ireland, 2s.6d. King's Revels, to Nicholas Hanson, one of that company, 5s. Paid for wine bread and beer for the fencers on Tuesday night the tenth of June last in rejoicing for the good success of the Parliament, 9s., and also paid, which was given to the Mr. of the Dancing horse, 3s. King's players, 10s. King's players, 5s. Sextons of St. Michael's and Trinity, being the night of rejoicing at the good proceedings of the Parliament the tenth of June last for ringing, 4s.2d. (c October 1629; 806) Waits' wages, 53s.4d. (w December 1629; 808-813) To strange wait players at several times, 7s.6d. To one Lacy who had a warrant to show feats of activity, 11s. For cloth and making up four cloaks for the wait players, £7.12.1. (c October 1630; 820) Wait players' wages, 53s.4d. (w December 1630; 822-829) Four trumpeters who had been at sea for the earl of Warwick who had loss by sea and had special certificate from divers noblemen in Ireland, 10s. William Vincent who came with the king's commission to show feats of activity and legerdemain, 5s. Given to Joseph More and others that was sworn servants to the king that they should not play, 20s. To one licenced to show a rare piece of work of the portraitures of the king of Bohemia his queen and children, 5s. Wait players of Derby, 2s. To Richard Tompson who had a commission to play the Worlds Wonder, 3s.4d. (c October 1631; 835) Waits' wages, 53s.4d. (w November 1631; 838-843) Musicians of the earl of Essex, 2s.6d. Waits of Ripon in Yorkshire, 2s. To another company of wait players called Worcester waits, 2s.6d. To another company of musicians, 16d. Waits of New Market, 2s. Waits of Derby, 2s.6d. Waits of Nottingham, 2s. King's trumpeters, 3s. Robert Kimpton (?) and John Carr, players of the Revels, 10s. Joseph More, John Townesend and other players to the Lady Elizabeth, 20s. Musicians of the earl of Rutland, 2s.

[Council Book 1556-1641, p. 607; 19 September 1632: The waits to have £4.10.0 a year henceforth, to be paid by the wardens only at Christmas and Michaelmas.]

(c October 1632; 851) Waits' wages, 53s.4d. (w December 1632; 854-859) Paid to William Costine, Thomas Hunter, Henry Fussell, with their assistants licenced to set forth and show an Italian motion with divers and sundry stories in it, 10s. Players of the Revels, 10s. Strange wait players at several times, 10s. (c October 1633; 869) No payment to the waits. (w December 1633; 873-879) Paid to the city's waitplayers for their whole year's wages, £4.10.0. Preston waits, 2s.6d. Shrewsbury waits, 2s.6d. Ripon waits, 2s. Halifax waits, 2s. Mr. Perry one of the king's players that came with a commission, 10s. Newark waits, 2s. Kendal waits, 2s. Italian motions, 10s. Nottingham waits, 2s.6d. Derby waits, 2s. To those that came with letters patent with the sight of the portraiture of Antwerp, 10s. To those with letters patent for roots, 6s.8d. Gold and silver and gilding and coloring the four crests for the city's waits, 20s. (w December 1634; 890-895) Waits' wages, £4.10.0. Queen's and other players, 5s. Prince's players, 40s. King's trumpeters, 40s. Waits of Ripon, 2s. Waits of Derby and Lincoln, 3s. Pay of constables to keep beggars and the like off the street during the day, £10.18.4.

[Council Book 1556-1641, p. 634; 4 March 1635: It is also farther agreed that whereas often heretofore the wait players of this city being the city's waits having been very troublesome unto this house as also at variance amongst themselves by their sundry differences (they are discharged) and farther that they shall bring in such instruments of music as they have of this city's.]

(w December 1635; 903-908) Paid to the city's wait players 45s. the 10th of April last in full discharge of their former wages they being from thenceforth utterly discharged, 45s. King's players who brought a commission from Sir Henry Harbert, £2.10.0. To Nottingham waits at two times, 3s.6d. Waits of Derby, 2s. Waits of Ripon, 1s. To William Daniell who brought a commission for the Revels, viz. for himself and sixteen more in June last, 10s.

Chamberlains' and Wardens' Accounts 1636-1711

(1636 accounts are similar, but without any payment to the city's former waits; players, visiting waits, and others, received rewards; pp. 3-9)

(w November 1637; 21-30) Players who came to the council house, 10s. William Daniell and others of the Revels, 10s. Feild the bearward, 2s.6d. The lord deputy's wait players, 2s.6d. Waits of Derby, 2s.6d. Waits of Ripon, 2s.6d. Waits of Nottingham, 3s. (Two shows, at different times) Waits of Nottingham, 18d. Paid given the sextons for ringing on the 17th of November being Queen Elizabeth's coronation day, 6s.6d.

(Accounts 1638-1640 are similar: bells continue to be rung in later years in memory of Queen Elizabeth Tudor; pp. 40-80)

NOTTINGHAM

(Stevenson, editing *Records of . . . Nottingham*, included a great deal of material of interest here, and some of what he prints in volume IV is abstracted here for the first several years selected. For the following years the original manuscript accounts of the chamberlains are used. Ordinary payments to Nottingham's own waits are omitted here. The accounting year was Michaelmas to Michaelmas.)

1568-1569

(*Records*, IV, 132-134; rearranged)

Rewards to waits: Derby, 12d. Leicester, 12d. Coventry, 8d. York, 12d. Grantham, 8d. Pomfret (Pontefract), 12d.

Other rewards: Mr. Stanhoppe minstrels, 8d. Sir Bryan Tuckes minstrels, 12d. Mr. Shurley's minstrels, 12d. Two minstrels and to them that did play with the hobby horse, 12d. Sir John Beron players, 3s.4d. Sir Richard Weyneman players, 2s. Lord Dakars minstrels, 16d. Sir John Cunstabyl minstrels, 12d. [Sir John Zouche musicians and Sir Thomas Kokyns, 12d. Chamberlains' accounts, Ms. 1611.] Earl of Sussex players, 6s.8d. Sir Humfray Wynfeld minstrels, 8d. Earl of Shrousbery bearward, 5s. Earl of Lesyter and Earl of Worster players, 20s. Mr. Stanhope minstrels, 12d. Sir Fraunces Smyth players, 2s. Lord Montegle bearward, 5s.

1571-1572

(*Records*, IV, 137-140; rearranged)

Rewards to waits: Wakefield, 8d. Derby, 12d. Newark, 8d. Ledes and Barton upon Humber, 10d. Leicester, 12d. Chesterfield, 6d. Ledes, 6d. [Oxford, 8d. Ms. 1612] Ratford, 4d. Newark, 6d. Grantham, 6d.

Other rewards: Sir Thomas Cockyn musicians, 8d. Lord Wylloughbe musicians, 16d. [Mr. Cokyn musicians, 12d. Ms. 1612] Earl of Shrosbery bearward, 6s.8d. Earl of Worster players, 6s.8d. Sir Richard Stapylton players, 3s.4d. Sir William Hollys musicians, 12d. (Sir William Holles of Houghton, Notts., grandfather of the first earl of Clare: Stevenson.) Mr. Forman minstrels, 4d. Mr. Pollyt musicians, 12d. Lord Mountegell bearward, 5s. [Lord of Hunsdons musicians, 15d. Mr. Cotton musicians, 8d. Ms. 1612]

1575-1576

[Ms. 1615]

9 December, earl of Lecyter and earl of Lyncolne musicians, 3s.4d. 24 December, Sir Thomas Stanhope musicians, 12d. 12 January, Sir Thomas Cockyn musicians, 8d. Same day, waits of Grantom, 8d. The Monday in Easter week at Saint Anne well unto three musicians there, 8d. 20 July, waits of Boston, 20d. 8 August, Lord Dyer and Justice Barom (?) a gallon of claret wine and a gallon of sack, 3s.4d. Same day, waits of Lesyter, 12d. Same day, waits of Neworke, 8d. 14 September, in wine and (?) to Mr. Jackeson that did make certain sermons at St. Mary's church, 18d. 20 September, Earl of Essex players, 6s.8d. "Gonners" that brought in May, 2s. Same day, dancers, 9s.

1576-1577

[Ms. 1616]

10 October, Heath the Jester, 2s. Lord Wyllowbe musicians, 2s. 30 October, waits of Boston and of Darbe, 12d. 12 November, Sir Edward Demackes musicians, 2s. 22 November, Earl of Lesyter musicians and earl of Lynkeolene musicians, 3s.4d. 18 December, waits of Shrowsberye, 12d. 6 January, waits of Lecyter, 12d. Same day, earl of Lecyter bearward, 6s.8d. 9 January, waits of Grantom, 12d. 11 January, waits of Boston, 12d. 13 January, waits of Newarke, 12d. 20 March, waits of Darbe, 12d. 22 April, Sir Thomas Stanhope

musicians, 6d. Same day, queen's bearward, 6s.8d. 2 May, earl of Darbye bearward, 5s. To certain of the earl of Rutland officers at Beyvar (Belvoir) when Mr. mayor and his brethren was there, 6s. 26 July, waits of Lencolne, 12d. 31 August, earl of Sussex players that play in the town hall, 13s.4d. 1 September, earl of Warwycke players, 10s. Same day, Lord Dudley musicians, 2s. Same day, Mr. Holmes, preacher, a bottle of wine and . . . sugar, 17d. 28 September, Sir Thomas Stanhope musicians, 12d.

1577-1578

[Ms. 1617]

13 October, earl of Warwycke musicians and players, 10s. 23 October, waits of Newark, 12d. 8 November, waits of Manchester, 12d. 10 November, Mr. Marcham musicians, 2s. Same time, Sir Thomas Venabylles musicians, 12d. 17 November, Sir Anthony Stryllay and my lady being at the castle (wine, etc.), 11s.4d. Same day, Mr. Sachaveryll musicians, 12d. 18 December, Sir Thomas Stanhope musicians, 16d. Same day, Mr. Powtryll musicians, 12d. 3 January, waits of Grantom, 12d. Same day, Mr. Bradlay musicians, 12d. 8 January to three minstrels beside Brystow, 12d. 19 January, earl of Woorster players, 5s. Same day, Sir Fraunces Wyllowbe a bottle of "muskedyne" and a bottle of claret wine, 3s. Same day, two musicians of Coventry, 10d. To two musicians at Myhell (Michael) Bonar house when Mr. mayor and his brethren did dine there when the fall (or falt?) was laid forth, 12d. 10 February, Sir William Hollys musicians, 12d. 28 February, Lord Wyllobe musicians, 16d. Same day, two musicians of Morhampton, 8d. 16 March, Lord Dudley musicians, 3s.4d. 4 April, earl of Essex musicians, 2s. 12 April, Lord Stafford musicians, 20d. To the youths that brought in May, 10s. 12 May, Mr. Few Wyllyams musicians, 2s. 30 May, waits of York, 20d. 1 June, Mr. Ratlyfe musicians, 6d. 20 July, Sir George Turpyn musicians, 12d. 23 September, Lord Mountegle musicians, 16d. 28 September, Lord Darsy musicians, 16d. John Lang and his fellow being musicians, 12d.

1578-1579

[Ms. 1618]

6 October (wine and sugar to the justices at the assizes), to the waits of Newark, 12d. 13 October, four musicians, 2s. 4 November, Sir Thomas Dawbye musicians, 12d. 5 November, Sir Fraunces Knowles musicians, 13s.4d. 10 November, waits of Darbe, 12d. 21 November, Mr. Fewe Wyllyams musicians, 16d. 4 December, four musicians, 16d. 7 December, Lord Straunge players, 6s.8d. 8 December, Mr. Tarrall musicians, 12d. 19 December, Lord Haworth players and musicians, 5s. 1 January, waits of Newark, 12d. 4 January, waits of Grantom, 12d. Same day, waits of Chasterfeld, 6d. 22 February, Sir Thomas Stanhope musicians, 12d. Same day, waits of Burton,

6d. 3 April, Lord Darsy musicians, 16d. Three musicians, 12d. 30 April, earl of Essex musicians, 2s. Item for all charge of bringing in of May and for eight pounds of gunpowder, 9s.4d. To the dancers at the same time, 8s. 23 May, earl of Darbe bearward, 10s. Same day, waits of Bostan, 12d. 25 May, Morden the bearward, 3s.4d. 7 June, waits of York, 12d. 9 June, players of Barton, 12d. 20 July, Mr. Beckingham the preacher, a bottle of wine, 8s. Same day, waits of Lynne, 16d. 23 September, William Hollys musicians, 12d. 12 September, queen's bearward, 6s.8d. 13 September, waits of York, 3s.4d. 16 September, four musicians, 20d.

(The accounts continue, like these, to contain many presents and rewards, and new towns and new persons appear from time to time. A few of the entries are particularly interesting: "to four musicians that played of waits," and "two poor men being minstrels," for example, from Ms. 1626, 1586-1587. The last full accounts are those for 1589-1590, given next. A fire early in the eighteenth century is said to have destroyed many of Nottingham's records; except for part of an account for 1591-1592 they skip from 1590 to 1614-1615.)

1589-1590

[Ms. 1630]

8 October, waits of Lytchfielde, 6d. 18 October, Sir Thomas Stanhops musicians, 6d. Lord of Sussex players, 6s.8d. Four musicians, 4d. Waits of Doncaster, 8d. Waits of Newarke, 4d. To our waits at the meeting of Mr. mayor and his brethren at John Veyryes, 12d. 30 March, waits of Coventry, 4d. Three poor Skotts men soldiers, 3d. Sir John Byron his musicianers, 6d. Two other poor soldiers, 2d. Four other musicians, 4d. Waits of Boston, 4d. Four musicians, 4d. 26 May, waits of York, 4d. Waits of Lytchfielde, 4d. 14 June, waits of Grantham, 6d. Waits of Pomfrett, 6d. 3 August, Mr. Clyffordes musicians of Lyncolneshire, 6d. Queen's players, 20s. Mr. Perpointes musicians, 6d. Sir Thomas Donkeys (or Doukeys) musicians of Yorkeshire, 4d.

(The contrast between the number of rewards given in even a partially destroyed account like that for 1591-1592, and those beginning in 1614 is striking; the accounts for two representative years follow, condensed as before.)

1616-1617

[Ms. 1633(a)]

The bearward on the sessions day, 3s.4d. The bearward on the sessions day after Christmas, 3s.4d. Players of the queen's Revels, 10s. The queen's players, 20s. The Prince's players, 10s. The queen's players belonging to the court, 10s. The Lady Elizabeth's players, 10s. Lord Stanhops bearward, 3s.4d. (no musicians or waits rewarded.)

[Ms. 1636]

The king's players of the chamber of Bristowe, 10s. The prince's players because they should not play in the town, 13s.4d. The late queen's players, 10s. The players of the king's Revels, 10s. The Princess Elizabeth's players, 10s. (no musicians or waits.)

YORK

York House Books

12 December 1571. A bill exhibited to my lord mayor by Arthur Hodgeson, one of the waits of this city was now read, requiring thereby that his honor would stand his good lord and friend concerning his apprentice that he might exercise with him and his other two fellows waits one of the four instruments belonging to this city and to have a coat etc. for the worship of this city and that it should not be hurtful to his other two fellows and that he would not claim any part of wages or customs within this city for his said apprentice and to be allowed of the city's charge for the said coat 6s.8d. (Book 24, folio 267; from transcript sent to me by the Reverend Angelo Raine, Hon. Archivist of the city of York.)

[Note: At first reading this seems to imply that apprentices could not ordinarily perform with the waits. It is more likely that what was special and required action of the city magistrates was use by an apprentice of one of the city instruments and for an apprentice to be given livery—the apprentice was to act in place of the fourth wait except for sharing returns. In December 1593 the waits requested a better allowance because, for one thing, they were "a man and a boy more than in former times." (Book 31, folio 45.) There were now five waits, and a fifth badge had been ordered in August 1593. The phrase may mean that by adding a fifth wait a fifth apprentice was also added, or it may mean that the group had grown to five men and a boy. In December 1598 the usual annual appropriation for waits' liveries added authorization for a yard of cloth for "their boy." (Book 31, folio 391 verso.) Here definitely is a special boy, distinct from apprentices the waits had. Apprentices were kept as a matter of course and without special compensation, whereas the keeping of a boy to sing treble would be an unusual expense deserving at least livery cloth in return. If this is the correct interpretation neither the 1593 nor the 1598 item rules out the possibility that in York the waits normally had their apprentices perform with them. In September 1602 one of the waits promised to provide "a sufficient boy against winter" (Book 32, folio 219); again a treble voice may have been desired.]

29 October 1572. Three men, including Richard Henryson, musician, had given recognizance to appear before the sessions court, had failed to appear, and so forfeited. (Book 25, folio 26 verso.)

2 September 1580. Richard Browne, minstrel, to be enfranchised for £6.13.4

to be paid in hand; upon payment thereof he is to have half of it returned to him. As long as he behaves well to remain enfranchised. (Book 27, folio 250.)

18 August 1602. Robert Sympson, musician, called into this court for walking abroad and playing music with company supposed to be disordered on Sunday night last is committed to ward there to remain until he deliver to my lord mayor a note of the names of all the persons who were abroad in his company the same night. (Book 32, folio 215.)

7 September 1608. Christopher Thompson, wait, who is contented to take Christopher Settle, a poor boy, to be his apprentice, is to be given 26s.8d. by the church wardens and overseers of St. Ellen's in Stonegate, and the boy is to have no more weekly relief. (Book 33, folio 131.)

26 October 1608. Richard Laverock, musicianer, contented to take John Yonge to be his apprentice, to have 13s.4d. out of the best stock of the parishes in Walmegate ward. (Book 33, folio 141.)

28 June 1611. Robert Paycock, musicianer who is a very poor man shall be licensed to keep an ale house or tipling house, putting in surety for good order. (Book 33, folio 252.)

7 July 1615. Robert Paycock, musician, who is to bind his son Francis Paycock apprentice unto James Simpson, tailor, shall have 13s.4d. from the stock of the parishes. (Book 34, folio 64 verso.)

22 October 1616. John Young, musician, who is to take Thomas Laverock as apprentice, is to have 13s.4d. from parish stock towards apparelling him. (Book 34, folio 102.)

4 December 1618. John Barton, occupation unnamed, brought before the mayor because the night before he had been playing on his instrument in the streets accompanied by some others; much disorder, windows broken, Barton drunk; remarks against the mayor, very offensively. To remain in prison until security had for his appearance before sessions. (Book 34, folio 157 verso.)

22 February 1619. Walter Paycock, son of Robert Paycock, who is to be bound apprentice to Symon Holmes, musician, for eight years, shall have 13s.4d. towards his clothing from the stocks of the parishes of this city. (Book 34, folio 165.)

8 February 1626. And now Symon Holmes, musician is committed to prison until he perform the order of the sessions in October last touching the nonpayment of 13s.4d. to Walter Paycocke, a poor boy his late apprentice (Book 35, folio 2 verso.)

22 October 1630. Thomas Girdler that hath been brought up as an apprentice with John Girdler his brother, one of this city's waits, being first admitted to the freedom of this city be admitted also to the place of the third wait. (Book 35, folio 90.)

APPENDIX D

TOWNS EMPLOYING WAITS

THIS list, compiled as a byproduct of general research on provincial musicians, is certainly not complete, but it suggests how very widely towns employed waits. The dates serve as a crude indication of the quantity of material which has turned up about the waits of each town. In cases where only two or three dates have been found, each date is separated by a comma; in cases where there are more than three dates, the first and last, separated by a dash, are given, except that if the series continues after 1660, 1660, or a date near it for which reference has been found, is used instead of the last date found. Where the data are particularly extensive an asterisk follows the second date. Where an item is taken from accounts kept for years that are not the modern calendar years, such as Michaelmas 1576 to Michaelmas 1577, the year the account ended is given here.

References to sources, for years named only, are included except when the towns, such as London, Norwich, and York, have been considered extensively in the text. In cases such as that of Ashbourne, where the reference is to the records of a different town, the correct implication is usually that the waits in question were rewarded in the latter town; sometimes the only record (found in the course of this study) of certain waits has been such notice of a reward given.

ABBREVIATIONS:

Coventry   Coventry Corp. Mss., Coventry Chamberlains' and Wardens' Accounts.

Devon   Mss. of the duke of Devonshire, Cumberland Mss.

Howard   *Selections from the Household Books of Lord William Howard of Naworth Castle,* ed. Ornsby.

Nott   Nottingham Corp. Mss., Nottingham Chamberlains' Accounts.

Stevenson   *Records of . . . Nottingham,* ed. Stevenson.

Ashbourne. 1586. Nott Book 1625.
Barnstaple. 1610. *Barnstaple Records,* ed. Chanter and Wainwright, II, 118.
Barton-upon-Humber. 1572. Stevenson, IV, 137; see note 10, chapter five, above.
Bath. 1587. Murray, *English Dramatic Companies,* II, 398.
Beverley. 1405-1662*. HMC *54, Beverley Mss.,* 158; *Beverley Borough Records,* ed. Dennett, 126-127.
Bewley. 1612, 1617. Devon, Bolton 94, folio 96d; Bolton 97, folio 103 verso.
Blyth. 1585, 1587. Nott Books 1624, 1627.
Boston. 1576-1592. Nott Books 1615-1631.
Bristol. 1563-1587. Murray, *English Dramatic Companies,* II, 380; Nott Book 1626.

Burton-on-Trent. 1579, 1585, 1587. Nott Books 1618, 1624, 1627.

Cambridge. 1484-1623*. *Annals of Cambridge*, ed. Cooper, I, 231, III, 147.

Canterbury. 1526?-1631*. Canterbury Corp. Mss., Bundle A54, Mss. 18 and 20; *Ancient Canterbury . . . Bunce*, 18.

Carlisle. 1612-1633. *Howard*, 27; *Some Municipal Records . . . Carlisle*, ed. Ferguson and Nanson, 286.

Chester. 1584-1634. Coventry 1574-1636, p. 112; Hammond, *Relation 1634*, ed. Legg, 48 (Chester had waits from Middle Ages to civil war).

Chesterfield. 1572-1589. Stevenson, IV, 139; Nott Book 1629.

Coventry. 1423-1635*.

Darneton. 1634. *Howard*, 315.

Derby. 1558-1639. Nott Book 1645; Coventry 1636-1711, p. 60.

Doncaster. 1554-1612. HMC 24, *Rutland Mss.*, iv, 372; *Howard*, 28.

Durham. 1634. *Howard*, 316, 317.

Gloucester. [c. 1590-1640.] Willcox, *Gloucestershire*, 232.

Grantham. 1558-1608. Nott Book 1645; HMC 24, *Rutland Mss.*, iv, 462.

Halifax. 1633. Coventry 1574-1636, p. 878.

Hereford. 1587, 1616. HMC *31, Hereford Corp. Mss.*, 337; Coventry 1574-1636, p. 592.

Hexham. 17th century. Webb, *English Local Government*, II, 199n.

Ipswich. 1538-1613*. Bacon, *Annalls of Ipswiche*, ed. Richardson, 212, 453.

Kendall. 1633, 1639, 1640. Coventry 1574-1636, p. 878; Devon, Bolton 177, folios 101, 99.

King's Lynn. 1646. Mann Mss., Norfolk Musicians, II, folio 33.

Lancaster. 1587, 1623. Nott Book 1626; *Howard*, 193.

Leeds. 1572-1612. Stephenson, IV, 137; Devon, Bolton 94, folio 96d verso.

Leeke. 1639, 1640. Coventry 1636-1711, pp. 60, 69.

Leicester. 1499-1668*.

Lichfield. 1574-1634. Nott Book 1613; Hammond, *Relation 1634*, ed. Legg, 59.

Lincoln. 1514-1636*. HMC 37, *Lincoln Corp. Mss.*, 25; Coventry 1636-1711, p. 8.

Liverpool. 1558-1600. *Liverpool Town Books*, ed. Twemlow, I, 79, II, 788.

London. 1442-1660*.

Loughborough. 1574. Nott Book 1613.

Lynn (King's Lynn?). 1541, 1579, 1612. HMC 24, *Rutland Mss.*, iv, 314; Nott Book 1618; Devon, Bolton 94, folio 97c verso.

Manchester. 1558-1669*.

Maxfield. 1623. Coventry 1574-1636, p. 709.

Midlam. 1621. *Howard*, 131.

Newark. 1571-1638. Stevenson, IV, 137; Coventry 1636-1711, p. 46.

Newcastle. 1639, 1640. Coventry 1636-1711, pp. 60, 69.

Newmarket. 1631. Coventry 1574-1636, p. 843.

Northampton. 1585-1600. Nott Book 1624; BM Ad.Ms. 25,080 (Spencer of Althorp), folio 12 verso.

Norwich. 1422-1660*.

Nottingham. 1463-1654*.

Oxford. 1573-1661*.

Penrith. 1612, 1619, 1634. *Howard*, 28, 89, 316.

Pontefract (Pomfret). 1569-1623. Stevenson, IV, 133; Coventry 1574-1636, p. 709.

Preston. 1633. Coventry 1574-1636, p. 878.

Retford. 1572, 1588, 1622. Stevenson, IV, 140; Nott Book 1627; Bridge, "Town Waits . . . ," *Proc. Mus. Assoc.*, 54th session (1928), 69.

Richmond. 1612, 1621, 1630. Devon, Bolton 94, folio 96d; *Howard*, 131, 262.

Ripley. 1581. Nott Book 1621.

Ripon. 1612-1637. Devon, Bolton 94, folio 96b verso; Coventry 1636-1711, p. 29.

Rochester. 1640. Burtt, "On the Archives of Rochester," *Archaeologia Cantiana*, VI (1866), 111-112.

Rotheram. 1585-1611. Nott Book 1624; Devon, Bolton 94, folio 92 verso.

St. Eedes (St. Ives?). 1585. Nott Book 1625.

Salford. 1600. *Portmote . . . Records of Salford*, ed. Mandley, I, 21.

Salisbury. 1540. 1572. HMC 55 *Various* iv, *Salisbury Corp. Mss.*, 220, 226.

Sheffield. 1566-1660. *Records of . . . Sheffield*, ed. Leader, 18, 173.

Shrewsbury. 1537-1633. HMC 47, *Shrewsbury Corp. Mss.*, 12; Coventry 1574-1636, p. 878.

Skipton. 1618. Devon, Bolton 98, folio 130.

Southampton. 1607-1620. *Assembly Books of Southampton*, ed. Horrocks, I, 43; HMC 18, *Southampton Corp. Mss.*, 28.

Sowtham. 1616. Coventry 1574-1636, p. 591.

Stone. 1573. HMC 69, *Middleton Mss.*, 426.

Wakefield. 1571, 1587, 1612. Stevenson, IV, 137; Nott Book 1626; *Howard*, 31.

Welby. 1592. Nott Book 1631.

Westchester. 1589. Nott Book 1629.

Westminster. 1586-1615. Nott Book 1625; Manchée, *Westminster City Fathers*, 85.

Wigan. 1588. Nott Book 1627.

Worcester. 1613, 1623, 1631. Coventry 1574-1636, pp. 529, 709, 842.

York. 1484-1640*.

APPENDIX E

THE KING'S MUSICK

THESE lists are designed to show in some detail the composition of the King's Musick at selected times, and something of the character of its growth. The years have been chosen both because they are significant in some way, and because the data available are fuller for them than for many years.

All of the warnings given in the related chapters—such as that the Musick undoubtedly expanded temporarily at coronations, and that some fee lists (including some used by Nagel) are unreliable—must be remembered here. These lists are not definitive: the printed sources used are not complete, or altogether correct as far as they go. In certain instances I have gone to the manuscripts themselves for fuller information, and I have compared, in many cases, the manuscripts used by Nagel, Lafontaine, and the editor of the lists in the *Musical Antiquary*, with their reports on them—in enough cases to satisfy myself that their reports are reasonably accurate and give correct impressions on the whole. Complete reexamination of the manuscripts would reveal some errors but would not change the story materially (the warrant dated 1622, October 11, in *KM*, 54, should be dated 1614, for example; PRO Ms. LC 5/115).

Dates given after the names of musicians are the inclusive years of their service in the King's Musick. The records used do not always show continuous service during periods indicated, and the periods probably were longer in some cases than I have indicated; the notes show the presence of such problems.

Abbreviations: *KM: King's Musick*, ed. Lafontaine. *MA*: "Lists . . . ," *Musical Antiquary*, I-IV (1909-1913). Nagel: *Annalen der englischen Hofmusik*, ed. Nagel. The notes follow the text.

1509[1]

Sackbuts and shawms of the privy chamber: Johannes, Guyllam Barrow, Edward John, Alexander Massu [i.e. Manseno[2]]

The. still shawms: John Chambre, marshal, Thomas Mayow, Thomas Spencer, John Abys, John Furneys, Richard Waren, Thomas Grenyng, Thomas Pegion

Minstrels: Hakenett de Lewys, Stephyn de Lalaunde, Bartram Brewer

Minstrels of the chamber: Buntanes [Bonitamps?], Barbram, Gyles [lute[3]], [Arthur (Dewes), lute[4]]

Tabrets with others: Marquesse Loreden, Janyn Marquesyn, Richard Anows

Fifteen or sixteen trumpets.

1518

Sackbuts: John van Herten (van Artain; 1516-31) John van Vincle (1516-31) Nicholas Forcivall (Clays de Forteville; 1516-40)[5]

Flute: John [de] Severnake (1518-58; also listed as rebec)[6]
Lutes: Gyles (1509-31)[7] Arthur Dewes (Master Arthur; 1509-38)[8]
Organist: Benet de Opicijs (1516-18)[9]
Harp: William More (1515-65)[10]
Organ- and instrument-maker: William Lewes (1514-48)[10]
Minstrels: Pety John Cokeren (1504-49)[11] Thomas Lewes (1517-20)[12] Christopher Cravila (Cravisa; 1518-20)[12] W. Kockyn (1517-18)[12] Josselon Percye (1517-18)[12]
Rebecs: Thomas Evans (1514 40)[12] John [de] Severnake (1518-58)[6]
Queen's minstrels: four received New Year's presents 1518-19, and one of them was Thomas Evans, rebec.[12]

1526[13]

Viols: Hans Hosenet[14] Hans Highorne (1526-49)
Sackbuts: Mark Anthony Petala, Venetian (1526-47) Pelegrine (1526-47) Nicholas Forcival (Clays de Forteville; 1516-40) John van Vincle (1516-31) Lewis van Wincle (1526-31) John van Herten (van Artain; 1516-31) John Antonia (John de Antonia; 1526-31) Ipolit de Salvator (1526-30) Aloisy de Blasia (1526) Fraunces de Salvator (1526)
Flute: John [de] Severnake (also listed as rebec) (1518-58)
Lutes: Gyles (1509-31) Arthur Dewes (Master Arthur; 1509-38) Philip van Welder (1526-53) Peter van Welder (1519-47)
Virginals: John Heywood (1520-53)
Harp: William More (1515-65)
Organ- and instrument-makers: John de John (1526-31) Gregory Estamproy (1526) William Lewes (1514-48)
Wait: Andrewe Newman (1526-40; in 1540, one of queen's three minstrels)
Minstrels: Pety John Cokeren (1504-49)[15] Hugh Woodhouse, sergeant of the minstrels (1526-47)[16]
Rebecs: Thomas Evans (1514-40; in 1540, one of queen's three minstrels) John Severnake (1518-58) John Pirot (1526-29)

1540

Viols: Hans Hosenet (1526-54)[17] Hans Highorne (1526-49)[17] Ambrose (Lupo) de Milano (1540-91)[18] Vincent de Venice (1540-47)[18] Albert de Venice (1540-59)[18] Romano da Milano (1540-41)[18] Alexander da Milano (1540-41)[18] (Joan) Maria da Cremona (1540-41)[18]
Sackbuts: Loyes de Jeronom (1531-49?)[19] Anthony Mary Galiardello (1539-73)[20] Nicholas Andrewe (1538-59)[21] Anthony Symonde (1538-47)[21] Nicholas Forcivall (1516-40)[21] Pelegrine (1526-47)[17] Mark Anthony Petala, Venetian (1526-47)[17]
Flutes: John [de] Severnake (also listed as rebec) (1518-58)[22] Guillam de

Vart (Duvett, Dufayt, Duwayt, Dufaite, Dovett, etc.; 1538-73)[23] Guillam de Trosse (de Trosshis, Trosses, Troche, etc.; 1538-62)[23] Nicholas Puvall (1539-47)[24]

Lutes: Philip van Welder (1526-53)[25] Peter van Welder (1519-59)[25] Alinxus de Basam (?)[26]

Virginals: John Heywood (1520-53)[27]

Harps: William More (1515-65)[27] Thomas Bowman (1529-40; one of queen's three minstrels)[28]

Organ- and instrument-makers: William Lewes (1514-48)[27] William Betton (1538-53)[29] Mighel Mercator (1529-41)[30]

Wait: Andrewe Newman (1526-40; one of queen's three minstrels)[27]

Welsh Minstrel: Robert Reynoldes (1537-49)[31]

Minstrels: Hugh Woodhouse (1526-47)[27] Pety John Cokeren (1504-49)[27] Anthony de Basson (de Basam, Bassanie, etc.; Venetian; 1538-73)[32] Jasper de Basam (de Basson, etc.; Venetian; 1540-77)[33] (John) Baptista de Basam (Bassanie, etc.; 1540-76)[33] John de Basam (Bassanie, etc.; 1540-70)[33]

Rebecs[27]: Thomas Evans (1514-40; one of queen's three minstrels) John Severnake (1518-58)

Prince Edward's Minstrels: three in 1538, and seven by 1547.[34]

·1547[35]

Viols: Hans Hosenet (1526-54)[36] Hans Highorne (1526-49)[36] Fraunces de Venice (1547-88) Marke Anthony Galyardo (1547-85) Ambrose (Lupo) de Milano (1540-91) George de Combre (Zorzi de Cremona; 1547-73) Vincent de Venice (1540-47) Albert de Venice (1540-59) (Thomas Browne, listed as singing-man in 1547, from 1554 is listed as a viol.)[37]

Sackbuts: Robert May (1547-77) Pelegrine (Pellegreine Symon; 1526-47)[38] Marke Anthony Petala (1526-47) Nicholas Andrewe (Nicholas Dandre; 1538-59) Anthony Symonde (Anthony Syma, 1538-47) Anthony Mary (Galiardello, Galyardo; 1539-73) (Loyes de Jeronom, Lewes; 1531-49)[36]

Flutes: John [de] Severnake (also listed as rebec) (1518-58)[36] Guillam de Trosse (1538-62)[36] Guillam de Vart (1538-73)[36] Nicholas Puvall (1539-47) Thomas Pagington (served Edward when he was prince; 1547-68)[39] Piero Guye (senior; 1547-1606)

Lutes: Peter van Wilder (1519-59)[40] Philip van Welder (1526-53)[41] (If Lewes is Augustine Bassani: 1540-1604)[42]

Singers: Arthur Kellyn (1547) William Browne (1547) Richard Atkinson (1547-54) John Temple (1547-54)

Singing-men and Children under Philips [of Chapel Royal; none of the following seem to have been in the Chapel:] Thomas Browne (1547-82)[37] Thomas Kent (1547-54) Thomas Bowde (1547-53) Thomas Lichefelde (1547) John Edmound (1547) George Pygge (1547) William Bradbury (1547) John Johnes (1547) Robert Mantell (1547)

Virginals: John Heywood (1520-53)[36]

Harps: William More (1515-65)[36] Bernerd de Pont (1547-55) Edwarde Lake (Lacke, Lak; served Edward when he was prince; 1547-58)[39]

Organ- and Instrument-makers: William Beton (1538-53)[36] William Lewes (1514-48)[43]

Songpricker: Robert Colson (1547-49)[44]

Bagpipe: Richard Woodwarde (Richard Edward; 1547-70)

Welsh Minstrel: Robert Reynoldes (1537-49)[36]

Musicians: (Alinso Bassani; included as lute above) John Bassano (Zuani Bassani; 1540-70) Anthony Bassano (1538-73) Jasper Bassano (Gespero Bassani; 1540-77) (John) Baptista (de) Bassano (Baptista Bassani; 1540-76) Hugh Pollard (also called minstrel; served Edward as prince; 1547-49)[39] Thomas Lye (also called minstrel; served Edward as prince; 1547-49)[39]

Minstrels: Hugh Wodhouse, marshal (Woodhouse; 1526-47) Robert Norman (1547) Hugh Grene (1547) Robert Strachon (1547) Thomas Pigen (1547) John Webbes (1547) Thomas Mayewe (1547) Pety John Cokeren (1504-49)[36]

Rebec: John de Severnacke (1518-58)[45]

1558[46]

Viol or Violin: Albert de Venice (1540-59) Fraunces de Venice (1547-88) George de Comy (Combre, de Cremonde, Cremona, etc.; 1547-73) Ambrose (Lupo) de Milano (1540-91) Marke Anthony (Galliardello; 1547-85) Paul Galliardello (1555-64) Innocent de Combe (de Comas, Coma, etc., alien; 1555-1603) Thomas Browne (viol; 1547-82)[47] Peter van Wilder (1519-59)[48]

Sackbuts: Nicholas Andrewe (1538-59)[40] Richard Welsh (1555-61)[49] Edward Devis (1555-61)[47] Anthony Mary Galliardello (1539-73) Robert May (1547-77) Nicholas Coteman (Cottman, Cockman; 1555-63) John Peacock (1555-65)

Flutes: John Severnake (1518-58)[47] Gilliam Trothes (de Trosse; 1538-62) Allen Robson (1547-68) Piero Guye (senior; 1547-1606) Thomas Packington (Pagington; 1547-86) Gilliam Duvete (de Vart, etc.; 1538-73) Jacobo Funyarde (alien; 1558-92)[50]

Lutes: Richard Pike (probably lute; 1553-68)[47] Augustine Bassani (1540?-1604)[51] Anthonie de Countie (Counter, de Choutye, de Chountie, etc.; 1552-80; also listed as virginalist)[52] Robert Woodward (1558-99)[47]

Virginals: Anthonie de Countie (also listed as lute)[52]

Harps: William More (1515-65) Edwarde Lake (1547-58)[47]

Instrument- and Regal-maker: William Treasorer (1552-60)[53]

Bagpipe: Richard Woodwarde (1547-70)[47]

Musicians[47]: Anthony (de) Bassano (1538-73) Baptista (de) Bassano (1540-

76) Jasper (de) Bassano (1540-77) John (de) Bassano (1540-70) Lodowicke Bassany (alien; 1558-92) Henry Vanwilder (1553?-1558). "Ordinary Musicians": Marten Kaynell, Thomas Elles, John Small, John White (all four, 1558 only)

Rebec: John de Severnake (1518-58)[54]

1570

See chapter eight, including note 15.

1590

Viols and violins[55]: Ambrose Lupo (de Milan; alien; 1540-91) Innocent de Come (alien; 1555-1603) Joseph Lupo (alien; 1563-1615) Petro Lupo (alien; 1567-1608) Seazer Galliardello (alien; 1585-1625) Thomas Lupo (senior; 1588-1627? perhaps another Thomas Lupo after 1619)[56]

Sackbuts: John Lanier (Lamer; alien; 1563-73, 1582-1616)[55] Marke Anthonio Basano (alien; 1565-99)[55] Raphe Grene (1565-99)[56] Samuel Garshe (1590-1628)[57] (Andrea Bassano?)[58]

Flutes[55]: Piero Gye (alien; 1547-1606) James Funier (Funyarde; alien; 1558-92) Nicolas Lamer (Lanier; alien; 1561-1615 or 1618) Gomer van Osterwerke (alien; 1570-92) James Harden (alien; 1575-1626)

Recorders: Andrea Bassano (alien; 1590-1626)[58] Jerome Bassano (alien; 1590-1631)[59] Edward Bassano (alien; 1590-1607)[59] Arthur Bassano (alien; 1590-1607)[59]

Lutes[56]: Augustine Bassano (1540?-1604; alien)[60] Robert Woodward (1558-99) John Johnson (1579-94) Mathias Mason (1579-1609) Robert Hales (1583-1616) Walter Piers (Pears, Peirce, etc.; 1589-1604)

Instrument-makers: Edmonde Schetz (1587-1601)[56] Andrea Bassano (listed also as recorder; alien; 1590-1626)[58]

Musicians: Lodowicke Bassano (alien; 1558-92)[55] William Demano (Damon; alien; 1581-94)[55] Richard Greaves (1590-97?)[61]

1603[62]

Viols and Violins: Innocent Comen (de Come; 1555-1603)[63] Anthonie Comie (1603-29)[63] (George Eastland, 1603)[63] Joseph Lupo (1563-1615) Peter Lupo (1567-1608) Cesar Galliardello (1585-1625) Thomas Luppo senior (1588-1627?) William Warren (1594-1611) Thomas Luppo junior (1598-1642; possibly two men) Alfonso Ferrabosco II (1602-27; senior) Rowlande Rubbidge (1602-20)[64]

"Hoboies and Sagbuttes": John Lanier (1563-73, 1582-1616) Samuel Garshe (1590-1628) Henry Troches (1597-1607) John Snowsman (1599-1641) Henry Porter (1603-17) Thomas Mason (1603-26) Jerome Lanier (1603-42)

Flutes: Piero Guy (senior; 1547-1606) Nicholas Lanier (senior; 1561-1615 or 1618) James Hardinge (Harden; 1575-1626) Innocent Lanier (1592-1625)

Peter Edney (1597?-1607) John Phelps (Phelpas; c. 1602-15)[65] Andrea Lanier (c. 1602-42)[66] Anthony Bassano (1603, 1624-40; perhaps two men) Petro Guy, junior (1603, 1625-41)

Recorders: Anthony Bassano (also listed as flute; 1603, 1624-40)[67] Augustine Bassano (1540?-1604)[68] Jerome Bassano (1590-1631) Andrea Bassano (1590-1626)[69] Arthur Bassano (1590-1607) Edward Bassano (1590-1607) Robert Baker (senior; 1594-1637) Alfonso Lanier (1594-1613)

[Cornetts: Andrea Lanier (also listed as flute; c. 1602-42)[66] Anthony Bassano (also listed as flute; 1603, 1624-40)[67] Jerome Lanier (also listed as hautboy and sackbut; 1603-42)][70]

Lutes: Augustine Bassano (also listed as recorder; 1540?-1604)[68] Walter Peirce (1589-1604) Robert Hales (1583-1616) Mathias Mason (1579-1609)

Harp: Gormock McDermott (c. 1602-18)[71]

Instrument-maker: Andrea Bassano (1590-1626; also listed as recorder)[69] Robert Henlake (1603-10)[64]

Musicians: Thomas Cordall ("Lutes and others"; 1603)

1612[72]

Viols and Violins: Joseph Lupo (1563-1615) Caesar Galliardetto (1585-1625) Thomas Lupo senior (1588-1627?) Thomas Lupo junior (1598-1642) Rowland Rubish (Rubbidge; 1602-20) Alfonso Ferrabosco II (senior; 1602-27) Anthonie Comie (1603-29) Jeromye Hearne (1607-15) Daniell Farraunt (1607-42) Alexander Chessam (1608-25) Horatio Lupo (1611-26) Thomas Warren (1611-42)

Sackbuts and Hautboys: John Lanier (1563-73, 1582-1616) Samuel Garshe (1590-1628) John Snowsman (1599-1641) Henry Porter (1603-17) Thomas Mason (1603-26) Jerome Lanier (1603-42)[73] Clement Lanier (1604-42)

Flutes: Nicholas Lanier senior (1561-1615 or 1618) James Harden (1575-1626) Innocent Lanier (1592-1625) John Phelps (c. 1602-15)[74] Anthony Bassano (1603, 1624-40)[74] Petro Guy junior (1603, 1625-41)[75]

Recorders: Andrea Bassano (1590-1626)[76] Jerome Bassano (1590-1631)[77] Robert Baker senior (1594-1637)[77] Alfonso Lanier (1594-1613)[78] Anthony Bassano (1603, 1624-40)[79] Clement Lanier (1604-42)[80]

[Cornetts: Andrea Lanier (c. 1602-42)[74] Jerome Lanier (1603-42)[73] Anthony Bassano (1603, 1624-40)[79] Clement Lanier (1604-42)[80]]

Lutes: Robert Hales (1583-1616) Robert Johnson (composer; 1604-33) Philip Rosseter (composer; 1604-23) John Dowland (composer; 1611-25) Simon Merson (1609-17) [John Coperario? composer. 1612? 1625-26][81]

Harp: Gormock McDermott (c. 1602-18)[74]

Instrument-makers, Keepers: Andrea Bassano (1590-1626) Edward Norgate (1611-42)[82] Thomas Meller (1612-17)[83] Thomas Hamlyn (1612)[84]

Queen Anne's Musicians: Five Dutch, four French musicians, Mr. Daniell,

Mr. Littleboy, Buckan, Oliver, Isaake,[85] John Maria Lugario (Italian; 1607-23)

Musicians of Henry, Prince of Wales[86]: Alfonso Ferrabosco, instructor in the art of music to the prince (listed above as viol or violin)[87] Walter Quinn, teacher of music for the prince[88] Dr. John Bull (composer, organist, virginalist) Robert Johnson (lute, above) Thomas Lupo (violin, above) John Mynors, Jonas Wrench (of the lutes and voices, 1625) Thomas Day (singer) John Sturte, Valentine Sawyer, Thomas Cutting (famous lutanist) Thomas Ford (composer; of lutes and voices, 1625) John Ashby, Edward Wormall (of the lutes and voices, 1625) Sig. Angelo (probably Angelo Notary, composer, of the lutes and voices, 1625)

Musicians of Prince Charles: (John Coperario taught him viol da gamba)[81] John Bewchesney, singing teacher, Frenchman[89] Norman Lister, musician to Prince Charles[88]

1618[90]

Viols and Violins: Cesar Galliardello (1585-1625) Thomas Lupo senior (1588-1627?) Thomas Lupo junior (1598-1642) Rowland Rubbidge (1602-20) Alfonso Ferrabosco II (senior; 1602-27) Anthony Comy (1603-29) Daniel Farrant (1607-42) Alexander Chessham (1608-25) Horatio Lupo (1611-26) Thomas Warren (1611-42) John Frende (1614-42) John Woodington (1616?-42)[91] Norman Lesley (1616-21)

Hautboys and Sackbuts: Jerome Lanier (1603-42)[92] Clement Lanier (1604-42) Samuel Garshe (1590-1628)[93] John Snowsman (1599-1641) Thomas Mason (1603-26) Richard Blagrave (1616-41)

Flutes: James Harden (1575-1626) Innocent Lanier (1592-1625) Andrea Lanier (c. 1602-42)[94] Anthony Bassano (1603-40)[95] Petro Guy junior (1603-41)[96] Nicholas Guy (1615-29)[97]

Recorder: Andrea Bassano (1590-1626)[98] Jerome Bassano (1590-1631)[93] Robert Baker senior (1594-1637)[98] Anthony Bassano (1603-40)[95] Clement Lanier (1604-42)[99] John Hussey (1613-28)[100]

[Cornetts: Jerome Lanier, Andrea Lanier, Anthony Bassano, Clement Lanier][99]

Lutes: Robert Johnson (1604-33) Philip Rosseter (1604-23) John Dowland (1611-25) Nicholas Lanier II (1615-42) Timothie Collins (1617-42) [John Coperario? (1612?-26)][99] [Adam Vallett?][101]

Harps[102]: Gormock McDermott (c. 1602-18) Philip Squire (1618-40?) (Lewis Evans, boy being educated on Irish harp and other instruments by Philip Squire)

Instrument-makers: Andrea Bassano (1590-1626)[98] Edward Norgate (1611-42)[99]

Queen Anne's Musicians[108]: John Maria Lugario (1607-23) Lewes Richard (Richart; French) Camille Provoste (French) John Chauntred (French)

Claud Oliver (French) Peter de la Mare (French) Christopher Harwood, tuner of instruments, Jehan Savage, William Le Graund, Daniel Hayes, William Treshey, Gilbert Johnson.

Musicians of Charles, Prince of Wales: John Coperario[99] (Nicholas Lanier II, lute, £200; Thomas Ford, of the lutes and voices, £120; Robert Johnson, lute, £60; Thomas Day, singer, £64; Alfonso Ferrabosco II, senior, instructor to the prince "in the art of musique,"[104] viol and violin, £40; Thomas Lupo junior, violin, £40; John Lawrence, lutes and voices, £40; John Kelly, lute, £40; John Coggeshall, lute, £40; Robert Taylor, lutes and voices [viol?], £40; Richard Deering, lutes and voices [virginals], £40; John Drew, lutes and voices, £40; John Lanier II, lutes and voices, £40; Edward Wormall, lutes and voices, £40; Angello Notary, lutes and voices, £40; Jonas Wrench, lutes and voices, £40; Alphonso Bales, lutes and voices, £20; Robert Marsh, lutes and voices, £20)[105]

1625

Viols and Violins: Cesar Galliardetto (1585-1625)[106] Thomas Lupo the younger (1598-1642)[107] Alfonso Ferrabosco II (1602-27)[108] Anthonie Comie (1603-29)[106] Daniel Farraunt (1607-42)[109] Alexander Chessam (1608-25)[106] Horatio Lupo (1611-26)[106] Thomas Warren (1611-42)[106] John Friende (viol[110]; 1614-42)[109] John Woodington (1616?-42)[111] Adam Vallett (Adrian Valet[110]; 1617?[111]-25)[106] John Heydon (1619-38)[106] Leonard Mell (1620-40)[106] John Hopper (John Hooper[106]; 1621-42)[110] Davis Mell (1625-42)[106] Richard Dorlin (Richard Dorncy senior; 1625-42)[106] Robert Major (Roger Mayer, viol[110]; 1625)[109] James Johnson (1625-39; succeeds Chessam in November)[107] Harding (1625)[110] Robert Taylor (1625-37)[112] (Thomas Lupo the elder?)[113]

Composer for the Violins: Thomas Lupo the elder[113]

Composer of Music to the King: John Coperario[114]

Hautboys and Sackbuts: Samuel Garshe (1590-1628)[106] John Snowsman (1599-1641)[106] Thomas Mason (1603-26)[106] Jerome Lanier (1603-42)[106] Clement Lanier (1604-42)[106] Richard Blagrave (1616-41)[100] James Troches (1625)[115] Edward Harding (1625-26)[115] Henry Bassano (1625-42)[106] Robert Baker junior (1625-41)[106] Andrea Bassano (1590-1626)[110]

Flutes: James Harden (1575-1626)[107] Innocent Lanier (1592-1625)[108] Andrea Lanier (c. 1602-42)[106] Anthony Bassano (1603, 1624-40)[116] Petro Guy junior (1603-41)[106] Nicholas Guy (1615-29)[106] Thomas Mell (1620-40)[117] William Noke (1624-31)[115] William Gregory (1625-42)[118] Henry Ferrabosco (succeeding Innocent Lanier; 1625-42)[119]

Recorders: Andrea Bassano (1590-1626)[120] Jerome Bassano (1590-1631)[115] Robert Baker senior (1594-1637)[115] Anthony Bassano (1603-1640)[121] Clement Lanier (1604-42)[122] John Hussey (1613-28)[115] William Noke (1624-31)[123] Robert Baker junior (1625-41)[124]

[Cornett: Andrea Lanier, Anthony Bassano, Clement Lanier, Jerome Lanier.[125] Robert Baker junior[124] Henry Ferrabosco[119]]

Lutes and Voices: [Lutes] Robert Johnson (1604-33)[109] John Dowland (1611-25)[109] Nicholas Lanier II (1615-42)[109] Timothy Collins (1617-42)[109] Maurice Webster (1623-37)[109] John Coggeshall (Coxall[108]; 1625-42)[110] Adam Vallett?[111]

[probably Lutes] John Lanier II (1625-42)[126] John Lawrence (1625-35)[110] John Kelly (1626?-42)[127]

[probably Voices] John Daniel (1625)[126] Thomas Ford (1612-42)[126] Alfonso Bales (1625-35)[126] John Ballard (1625)[126] Charles Coleman (1625-42?; violist)[109] Thomas Day (1612-42)[110] John Drew (1625-42)[126] Robert Marsh (1625-31)[126] Angelo Notary (1625-42)[126] Edward Wormall (1612-42)[126] Jonas Wrench (1612-26)[126] John Coperario (listed above as composer; 1622?-1626)[126]

Virginals with Lutes and Voices: Richard Deering (1625-30)[128]

Virginals: Orlando Gibbons (1619-25)[107] Thomas Warwick (succeeds Gibbons as virginalist and as musician in ordinary; two stipends; 1625-42)[107]

Harper: Philip Squire (1618-40)[129]

Instrument-makers: Andrea Bassano (1590-1626)[107] Edward Norgate (1611-42)[110]

Musicians: Robert Bourman (1625)[108] Abraham Coates (1625)[108] Francis Cozens (1625)[109] James Graye (1625)[108] Thomas Hassard (1625)[108] Gilbert Johnson (1618-25)[108] Norman Lesley (1625)[108] Sebastian Lopier (1625)[108]

Queen Henrietta Maria's Musicians: about twelve Frenchmen and three singing-boys. The men included three of the Frenchmen formerly in Queen Anne's service, and Nicholas du Vall, later sworn into the king's music for lutes and voices.[130]

1635[131]

Viols and Violins: Daniel Farrant (1607-42; £46 a year, i.e. 20d. a day and £16.2.6 a year for livery)[132] Thomas Warren (1611-42; £46)[133] John Friend (1614-42; £46)[134] John Woodington (1616?-42)[135] John Heydon (1619-38; £46)[133] Leonard Mell (1620-40; £46)[133] John Hopper (1621-42; £46)[133] Davis Mell (1625-42)[133] Richard Dorney (1625-42; £20, £10)[136] James Johnson (1625-39; £46)[133] Robert Taylor (1625-37; £40, £20)[137] Thomas Lupo junior (1598-1642; £46 and £40 annuity granted by Charles as Prince of Wales)[138] Nicholas Piccart (1627-42; £46)[133] Alfonso Ferrabosco III (junior; 1627-42)[139] Robert Parker (1628-40)[140] Theophilus Lupo (1628-42; £40 [and livery £16.2.6][141] £20 arrears) Robert Tomkins (1633-40; £46.10.10, £23.5.5) Francis de la France (1635-38; £50)[142] Stephen Nau (1627-42)[143]

Composer of Music for the Violins: Stephen Nau (1627-42; £200, £100)[143]

Hautboys and Sackbuts: John Snowsman (1599-1641; £46) Jerome Lanier (1603-42; £46.10.10, £23.5.5 arrears, £24.6.8, £12.3.4 arrears, and with son William Lanier, £46.10.10, £23.5.5 arrears) Clement Lanier (1604-42; £46.10.10, £23.5.5) Richard Blagrave (1616-41; £46)[133] Henry Bassano 1625-42; £46.10.10, £11.12.8½ arrears, and £46.10.10 with same arrears) (John Friend: see viols) John Mason (1626-40; £46.10.10, £23.5.5) William Lanier (1626-41; with his father Jerome, £46.10.10, £23.5.5) (Robert Parker, double sackbut: see viols) Edward Bassano (1628-38; £46.10.10, £34.18.1½) Christopher Bell (1628-40; £60.2.6, £30.1.3) John Strong[144]

Flutes: Andrea Lanier (1602-42; £67.9.2, £33.14.7, and £60, £30 arrears) Petro Guy junior (1603-41; £40.9.2, £20.4.7) Thomas Mell (1620-40; £46.10.10, £23.5.5) Henry Ferrabosco (1625-42; £40, £20 arrears, and £40, £20 arrears; also of the voices) William Gregory (1625-42; £46)[133] (Alfonso Ferrabosco: see viols) John Ferrabosco (1630-42)[145] John Adson (1633-40; £46.10.10, £23.5.5)

Instructor in Flute and Cornett: Andrea Lanier (for keeping and educating two boys, £59.13.4 a year)[146]

Recorders: Robert Baker (senior; 1594-1637; £66.2.6, £33.1.3) Anthony Bassano (1603-40; £58.14.2, £14.17.0½) (Clement Lanier: see sackbuts, and 1625 lists) Robert Baker junior (1625-41)[147] (John Adson: see flutes)[148]

Cornetts: Jerome Lanier: see hautboys[149] Andrea Lanier: see flutes[149] Anthony Bassano: see recorders[150] Clement Lanier: see sackbuts[149] Robert Baker junior: see recorders[149] Henry Ferrabosco: see flutes[149] Alfonso Ferrabosco junior: see viols[149] John Adson: see flutes[148]

Master of the Musick: Nicholas Lanier II (1615-42; £200, £100)[151]

Lutes and Voices: [lutes] Nicholas Lanier II[151] Tymothie Collins (1617-42; £40 and livery £16.2.6)[152] Maurice Webster (1623-37?)[153] John Coggeshall (1625-42; £40, £20) Nicholas Duvall (1633-42; £60, £30)[154] Anthony Roberts (1625-42; £40, £20) Robert Dowland (1626-41)[155] Henry Lawes (1631-42; £20, £15) Lewis Evans (1633-42)[156] William Lawes (1635-42; £40, £20)[157]

[probably lutes] John Lanier II (1625-42; £40, £10) John Lawrence (1625-35; died, replaced by William Lawes)[158] John Kelly (1626-42; £40, £10)

[probably voices] Thomas Ford (1612-42)[159] Alfonso Bales (1625-35; £20)[160] Charles Coleman[161] Thomas Day (1612-42)[162] John Drew (1625-42; £40, £20) Angelo Notary (1625-42; £40, £20) Edward Wormall (1612-42; £40, £20) (Henry Ferrabosco: see flutes) John Wilson (1635-42, in room of Bales)[163]

Teacher of Two Singing Boys: (Thomas Day: see voices, above)

Virginals with Voices: Giles Tomkins (1630-42; £40, £20)

Virginals: Thomas Warwick (1625-42; £46 and £40)[164]

Harps: Philip Squire (1618-40; £46.10.10, £23.5.5) John de Flelle (1629-41)[165]

Instrument-makers: Edward Norgate (1611-42; £60)[166] Thomas Cradock 1626-35; £20)[167]

Musicians: John Foxe (1635-36; £40)[168] Gottschelike Barr (1635; £100)[169]

Queen's Musicians: probably about as in 1625 and 1640.

1640

See chapter eight, including note 17.

1. *KM*, 2-4, except for material in square brackets.

2. According to Nagel, 7, Alexander Manseno, sackbut, received thirty shillings for his month's pay in May 1509.

3. According to Nagel, 8, Master Giles, lute, received forty shillings pay in July 1509.

4. According to Nagel, 8, Master Arthur, lute, was mentioned at Michaelmas 1509; he is probably to be identified with the Arthur Dewes, of whom last mention is made in 1538, apparently.

5. All appointed in April 1516: Nagel, 13. Most of the terminal dates given are the first and last records available when the players were serving. The three sackbuts above are noted as serving on several subsequent dates, e.g. 1528 (*MA*, IV, 180).

6. Appointed as rebec in October 1518 at 16d. per day: Nagel, 14. On several subsequent dates he was named as rebec, e.g. 1547, 1552 (*MA*, IV, 55, 58), and also as flute, e.g. 1547, 1558 (*KM*, 8, 12).

7. Named on many dates, e.g. 1509 (*KM*, 3; *MA*, IV, 178) and 1531 (*MA*, IV, 183).

8. In 1518 listed in Nagel, 14.

9. Appointed on 1 March 1516 to wait upon the king in his chamber at 33s.4d. a month, and record of his service survives through April 1518: Nagel, 13-14.

10. In 1518 listed in Nagel, 14.

11. Named on many dates, e.g. 1504 (*KM*, 2) and 1549 (*MA*, IV, 57).

12. Listed in 1518 in Nagel, 14-15.

13. From Nagel, 16, except for the minstrels, for whom see notes 15 and 16. Philip van Welder is not listed as lute, but Philip Welter is as minstrel. Nagel remarks that the list is probably not complete.

14. There are records of his service in various years from 1526 to 1554; he may have served before and after these dates. Similarly, the other dates given are incomplete.

15. Not named in 1526 lists, but in 1504 (*KM*, 2), 1509-11, 1549 (*MA*, IV, 178-179, 57), etc.

16. *KM*, 5, 8. There seem always to have been three minstrels belonging to the queen, as there were in 1540; see Nagel, 20. Princess Mary had three minstrels in 1525 and 1533: *Privy Purse Expenses of the Princess Mary*, ed. Madden, 250, 13.

17. Named on many dates, e.g. 1526 and 1547: Nagel, 16, 22.

18. Appointed on 1 May 1540 with wage of one shilling a day: Nagel, 20.

19. Loyes de Jeronom, just arrived (probably from Italy via Southampton) in 1531: *Privy Purse Expences of Henry the Eighth*, ed. Nicolas, 165, 170, 174. Perhaps this musician is represented by Lewes in 1549: *MA*, IV, 57.

20. A Venetian; named on many dates, e.g. 1539, at 16d. a day wages (Nagel, 20) and 1547 (*KM*, 6).

21. Andrewe and Symonde had each received 8d. a day wages, which were increased to 16d. a day in September 1540, by grant to them of the 16d. a day wages of Vorcifal who had just died: Nagel, 21.

22. See note 6, above.

23. Listed on many dates. In February 1538 they each received 53s.4d. for a month's wages; in 1552 they are listed as musician stranger at thirty-eight pounds a year each: Nagel, 18 and BM Arundel Ms. 97, folio 3; *MA*, IV, 58.

24. Appointed in November 1539 (Nagel, 20); among several 1547 listings are livery allowances in *KM*, 6, 8.

25. Among several listings are those of 1531 and 1547: *MA*, IV, 183, 55.

26. Alinxus de Basam, one of five brothers, was granted 2s.4d. a day wages on 14 April 1540 (Nagel, 20); Lewes de Basson appears where Alinxus should be in list of 1541 (Nagel, 21); and Augustine Bassanie seems to fill the same shoes in 1552 (*MA*, IV, 58). Augustine continues to 1604.

27. See 1526 list, above.

28. Nagel, 20.

29. Serving in 1538 at five pounds a quarter (Nagel, 19, and BM Arundel Ms. 97, folios 26 verso, 39), 1547 (*MA*, IV, 56), and other years.

30. Serving in 1529 at £22.10.0 a year (*MA*, IV, 180, 181); he does not appear on the account of payments on Lady-day 1541 (Nagel, 21).

31. Appointed minstrel on 4 August 1537 at £3.6.8 (Nagel, 18); in 1547 and 1549 this Welsh minstrel received his half-year's wages at this rate at Michaelmas (*MA*, IV, 56, 57).

32. Appointed instrument-maker on 30 October 1538, at one shilling a day to be paid quarterly (Nagel, 19); from 1541 on (Arundel Ms. 97, folio 164 verso) he is called invariably minstrel or musician, and not instrument-maker.

33. Grant of pension of fifty pounds a year each, and 2s.4d. a day wages to John, and 1s.8d. a day wages to the other two: Nagel, 20.

34. *Privy Purse Expenses of the Princess Mary*, ed. Madden, 56; *MA*, IV, 56, 57.

35. *KM*, 5-8, unless other references are given.

36. See 1540 list, above.

37. Listed as singing-man (or child) in *KM*, 7, 8; appointed viol in 1554 (*KM*, 9) and so listed until 1582 (there are a few exceptions, but he is never called a singing-man again).

38. Nagel, 22.

39. *KM*, 7; *MA*, IV, 57 (at one shilling a day).

40. *MA*, IV, 55 (at thirty shillings a month).

41. *MA*, IV, 55 (at 66s.8d. a month).

42. See 1540 lists, above. This doubtful identity is only possible. Lewes is listed in *KM*, 6, and Alinso Bassani in the same, p. 8.

43. *MA*, IV, 56.

44. *MA*, IV, 56, 57 (music copyist).

45. See 1518 lists, above.

46. *MA*, I, 57, unless other references are given.

47. *KM*, 12-13.

48. Listed as lute until 1547; in 1547 he is also listed as viol (*KM*, 6, 8); in 1555 as viol (*KM*, 9); in 1558 as viol, twice (*KM*, 12); and in 1559 as flute, probably by mistake (PRO Ms. SP 12/8, No. 10). Nagel, 24, includes him as a lute in Queen Mary's establishment.

49. Listed in 1557 in *KM*, 10, and in 1559 in a list of those in arrears in paying a subsidy, PRO Ms. SP 12/8, No. 10.

50. *KM*, 13; *MA*, I, 58, appointed to receive pay from 30 November 1558 at 1s.8d. a day.

51. *KM*, 11, listed as musician; listed as lute 1594-1604 (*MA*, II, 115-118, 174-176), as recorder in 1603 (*KM*, 45), and was succeeded by a sackbut player, Clement Lanier (*MA*, II, 177).

52. Listed as virginalist in 1552 at £30.8.4. a year (1s.8d. a day) (*MA*, IV, 58), as serving Queen Mary (Nagel, 24); listed as lutanist from 1555 (*KM*, 9, 10, 12, 17 etc.); 1564 on in *MA*, I, 60.

53. Listed in 1552 at ten pounds a year in *MA*, IV, 58, and in 1560 in *KM*, 14.

54. See 1518 lists, above. *KM*, 12.

55. *Returns of Aliens*, ed. Kirk, ii, 427. Indenture of second payment of first subsidy granted in 1589 and assessed on the queen's household; the musicians of the chamber are classed as "musicions," "Violens," "Sagbotes," and "Flutes." They are also listed elsewhere for 1590, including usually *MA*, II, 53-54.

56. *MA*, II, 53-54.

57. Nagel, 32.

58. Listed as a musician in subsidy list, 1590 (see note 55, above) and 1590-92 and 1597 (Nagel, 32-33); as recorder in 1603 (*KM*, 45), as sackbut in 1625 (Nagel, 40); and Henry Bassano was admitted as musician in the wind instruments in 1626 in his place (*KM*, 62). He is also listed in 1603 and other years as an instrument-maker (*MA*, II, 175, etc.).

59. Listed as musicians in subsidy list of 1590 (see note 55, above) and for 1590-92 and 1597 in Nagel, 32-33; various other records list them as musicians, but in 1603 they are given as recorders (*KM*, 45). Jerome Bassano is also listed as recorder in 1625 (*KM*, 57; Nagel, 40) and 1628 (*KM*, 65). The records do not seem to show how long after 1607 Edward and Arthur Bassano served, if at all.

60. Listed as musician on subsidy list of 1590 (see note 55, above); see also 1558 lists, above.

61. Nagel, 32, 34.

62. *KM*, 44-46, unless other references are given.

63. Innocent de Comye is given for 1603 in *MA*, II, 175. According to this record, he was

succeeded by his son Anthonie Comie at twenty pence a day and livery; the son appears in *KM*, 45. According to CSPD *1580-1625*, 377, Innocent Come was succeeded by George Eastland; this is the only reference, apparently, to Eastland in this connection, and probably is incorrect.

64. *MA*, II, 175.

65. Jo. Phelps is named on a list of fees granted probably late in Elizabeth's reign (Nagel, 35); he received £70.17.6 a year. John Phelpas is on a list of musicians serving 1607 (Nagel, 37) and his place of musician was granted to a flutist and one other person in 1615 (CSPD *1611-18*, 299) from which it is possible to surmise that he was a flutist.

66. He was a son of Nicholas Lanier senior and was named on the list of fees granted in Elizabeth's reign (Nagel, 35). He received £17.9.2 a year according to this. In 1612 he was granted a place of musician on the flute for life (CSPD *1611-18*, 138). Later he received grants for training boys in flute and cornett (1626: *KM*, 61, etc.) and bought cornetts (1630: *KM*, 75, etc.); he may have played both cornett and flute.

67. Listed as flute above, from *KM*, 45, but the same man, probably, in 1625 (Nagel, 40) and 1628 (*KM*, 65) is listed as recorder. Besides these instruments he probably played cornett, because he received warrant for money spent for purchasing three of them in 1631 (*KM*, 75).

68. *KM*, 45. Also listed as lute; see lists for 1558, above.

69. *KM*, 45. Also listed as instrument-maker; see lists for 1590, above.

70. Although usually listed as a sackbut it may be that he also played cornett, because in 1633 six cornetts were purchased for him and five others: *KM*, 83.

71. Named in a list of fees granted probably late in Elizabeth's reign (Nagel, 35). He received £46.10.10 a year. He was serving as musician in 1607 (Nagel, 37) and his successor, Philip Squires, probably a harper, was appointed in 1618 (CSPD *1611-18*, 559), from which it is probable that McDermott was a harper.

72. *MA*, II, 239-240, unless other references are given.

73. Serving in various years 1603 (*KM*, 45), 1605 and 1607 (Nagel, 36-37), 1621 (HMC *3, de la Warr Mss.*, 301), 1625 (*KM*, 56-57; Nagel, 40), and more regularly to 1642. He is also listed here as a cornett because one was bought for him in 1633 (*KM*, 83).

74. See lists for 1603, above.

75. Given mourning livery in 1603 (*KM*, 45) he next appears in the records in 1625 when he was listed as a musician in "The Chamber of our late Sovereign Lord King James" (*KM*, 57); another list in 1625 called him flutist (Nagel, 40), and in 1628 he was again called flutist (*KM*, 66). There are various subsequent records of him. He was probably continuously in royal service from before 1603 to after 1641, but appearing regularly on some set of accounts no longer available or unused as yet; many musicians must have been on similar accounts.

76. Also listed as instrument-maker; see lists for 1590, above.

77. Listed in many entries but not regularly on any series of accounts available to me. Between 1607 (Nagel, 37) and 1625 (*KM*, 57) his name does not appear, but it is clear that he was serving.

78. Like Jerome Bassano and Baker, Alfonso Lanier is not on any regular series of accounts I have seen. He does not appear between 1607 (Nagel, 37) and 1613 when his successor, John Hussey, was appointed (CSPD *1611-18*, 210).

79. Also listed as flute and cornett (see 1603 lists, above). Although he does not appear on lists between 1603 and 1624 it is probable that he was serving during that time.

80. Also listed as sackbut, above. In 1625 he was listed as a recorder (Nagel, 40), and as of the wind instruments (*KM*, 57). A cornett was bought for him in 1633: *KM*, 83.

81. Coperario, alias Cooper, was rewarded with twenty pounds in 1613 for his services for a masque in 1612 (*Issues of the Exchequer*, ed. Devon, 164-165), which suggests that he may have been in the royal service at that time. He taught Prince Charles the viol da gamba, according to Hawkins, *History*, 566, and may have been in the royal service in 1612 for this purpose if for no other. On 12 May 1625 "Coperario's music" had been a group in the court musical establishment for three years, according to a note of a petition passing through Sir John Coke, master of requests (HMC 23, *Cowper Mss.*, 195). There are subsequent records of his regular services to the court.

82. Granted office of tuner of the king's virginals, organs, etc., with Andrea Bassano, in 1611 (CSPD *1611-18*, 93), he was listed as keeper of the organs in 1625 (Nagel, 40) and is regularly listed thereafter.

83. Given as keeper of instruments by Nagel, 38. In 1617 he was paid for strings and other necessities which he had provided for Prince Henry in 1612, according to *Issues of the Exchequer*, ed. Devon, 196-197.

84. Given as organ-maker by Nagel, 38.

85. So listed in *KM*, 50. Mr. Daniell was probably John Daniel, composer, who was among the "lutes and voices" in 1625 (Nagel, 40, and *KM*, 59); it could be that Daniell Farrant, the noted violist, or Daniel Hayes (see 1618) was meant.

According to a warrant for patents for annuities for four musicians (which later records show to be the queen's) the four Frenchmen and their annuities were: Lewis Richart, £155; Camille Prevost, £130; Claude Olivier, £100; Peter de la Mare, £115 (1612: HMC *1, Bromley-Davenport Mss.*, 79).

The names of twelve of the musicians are given in 1618, below.

86. Hawkins, *History*, 566, from Birch, *Life of Henry*, unless other references are given.

87. According to accounts of arrears, 1619, in HMC *3, de la Warr Mss.*, 310.

88. *KM*, 50.

89. *Issues of the Exchequer*, ed. Devon, 142 (writ for payment of forty pounds, 28 July 1611).

90. *MA*, III, 57-58, unless other references are given.

91. On 12 May 1625 Woodington petitioned his master, King Charles, saying that he had been musician to King James for six years and musician "to his majesty [King Charles as prince?] in Coperario's music for three years" (HMC *23, Cowper Mss.*, 195).

92. Listed on many dates but not in 1618, although he was undoubtedly in service then. 1607: Nagel, 37. 1621: HMC *3, de la Warr Mss.*, 301. See also 1612 lists above for reasons for listing as recorder and cornett.

93. Years for which records are available include 1607 (Nagel, 37) and 1625 (*KM*, 57; Nagel, 40).

94. *KM*, 52. Also listed as cornett; see 1603 lists, above.

95. Although not listed between 1603 (*KM*, 45) and 1624 (CSPD *1623-25*, 346) he was probably serving in the meantime. He is also listed as cornett by inference from his purchase of three cornetts in 1631 (*KM*, 75), and as recorder because he is so listed in 1625 (Nagel, 40) and 1628 (*KM*, 65).

96. Listed in 1603 (*KM*, 45), 1625 (*KM*, 57; Nagel, 40), and subsequently.

97. Listed in 1615 (CSPD *1611-18*, 299), 1621 (HMC *3, de la Warr Mss.*, 301), and subsequently.

98. Also listed as instrument-maker; see 1590 lists, above.

99. See 1612 lists, above.

100. Listed in 1613 (CSPD *1611-18*, 210), 1625 (of late king's chamber; *KM*, 57; Nagel, 40), 1628 (*KM*, 65).

101. The Adam Vallett received into the king's service in 1617 as a lute at sixty pounds a year until he should be admitted in ordinary (*Issues of the Exchequer*, ed. Devon, 213) seems to be the same man listed as violin in 1625 (*KM*, 57) and the *Adrian* Valet also listed as violin in 1625 (Nagel, 40).

102. McDermott, listed in Nagel, 35, as musician c. 1602, at £46.10.10, was serving in 1607 (Nagel, 37), and succeeded by Philip Squire in 1618 (CSPD *1611-18*, 559) from which it may be inferred that McDermott played the same instruments as Squire. In 1618 Squire was appointed to teach Lewis Evans on the Irish harp and other instruments for thirty pounds a year (*Issues of the Exchequer*, ed. Devon, 234). Evans is listed as lute in ordinary 1633-42. Squire was listed as "of the consort" and as harper in 1625, and as of "the lutes and voices" in 1628.

103. *KM*, 52, except for Lugario (*MA*, III, 57-58). See "Huygens," *Grove*.

104. *KM*, 63.

105. These musicians, from Nicholas Lanier on, may not have been in the service of the prince in 1618; in 1626 Nagel (41) says that they were given a "Garantie folgender Jahrgelder . . . hatte Karl als Prinz von Wales zugesagt." CSPD *1625-26*, 372, gives the list, and in the same, p. 145, there is an abstract of a warrant, 1625, for nine hundred forty-four pounds a year for annuities granted by the king, when Prince of Wales, to his musicians. The amounts as given by Nagel add up to nine hundred sixty-four pounds. Whether it was Thomas Lupo junior or senior Nagel does not state. The instruments specified above are given from records concerning the musicians' other services.

106. *KM*, 57-58. A list headed "The chamber of our late sovereign lord King James."

107. *MA*, III, 114-115.

108. *KM*, 59. List headed "The chamber of King Charles." Alfonso Ferrabosco is listed as viol in Nagel, 40.

109. *KM*, 58. List headed "The consort" of the chamber of the late King James. See note 161.

110. Nagel, 40.

111. See 1618 lists, above.

112. Nagel, 40; of "the lutes and voices." In the London waits he played orpharion, bass viol, and poliphon (see Appendix A, above) and his successor was to be sworn a musician for the "viols and voices" (*KM*, 95).

113. Probably the Thomas Lupo senior who was listed as violin 1588-1619, but not certainly; there seem to have been three Thomas Lupos. Thomas Lupo, sometimes called the elder, was appointed "composer for our violins" in 1621 (*KM*, 53) and was paid as such forty marks a year with £16.2.6 a year for livery from 1621 until his death in 1627 (*MA*, III, 110-115, 171; *KM*, 54), and was exempted from subsidy payment in 1625 (Nagel, 40). That the composer can be identified with the violinist is suggested by the appointment of Theophilus Lupo in room of his father Thomas Lupo, deceased, as violinist, in 1628 (*KM*, 65); the coincidence of dates suggests that Thomas Lupo the elder continued to hold a violin place along with a new appointment as composer, from 1621 to 1627.

114. In 1626 Alfonso Ferrabosco (II; viol; 1602-27) succeeded the late John Coperario (of the lutes and voices, teacher of Charles as prince on the viol da gamba), according to CSPD *1625-26*, 569.

115. *KM*, 57-58, chamber of late sovereign; Nagel, 40.

116. Listed as recorder in 1625 (Nagel, 40) but as flute in 1603 (*KM*, 45). Perhaps two men. Also listed as cornett, below; see 1618 lists.

117. Listed as flute, succeeding Peter Edney, in 1620 (Nagel, 38) and as of the windy instruments of the late king's chamber, 1625 (*KM*, 57). He may be the same man who served Prince Henry as keeper of instruments, 1612 (Thomas Meller).

118. *KM*, 57-58, chamber of late sovereign; *MA*, III, 114-115.

119. *MA*, III, 124. Also listed as cornett because one was bought for him in 1633: *KM*, 83.

120. Listed as sackbut, above, and instrument-maker, below; in 1603 he was listed as recorder (*KM*, 45).

121. Nagel, 40. He was listed as flute in 1603, and is listed as cornett below (see 1618 lists).

122. Nagel, 40. Also listed as sackbut above, and cornett below; see 1618 lists.

123. Listed as flute above (Nagel, 40) as of the windy instruments of late king's chamber, 1625 (*KM*, 57), and as recorder, 1628 (*KM*, 65).

124. Recorder: Nagel, 40. Listed as hautboy and sackbut above (these instruments, 1628: *KM*, 66) and as cornett below because one was bought for him in 1633 (*KM*, 83).

125. See 1612 lists, above.

126. *KM*, 108, chamber of King Charles; Nagel, 40.

127. Although the earliest listing found for Kelly is 1626, the fact that he received an annuity of forty pounds a year granted to him by Charles as Prince of Wales argues that Kelly was in royal service in 1625 or before: *KM*, 61, 62; see 1618 lists, above.

128. Listed as of the lutes and voices in 1625 (Nagel, 40) and 1628 (*KM*, 66) and as a musician for the virginals with the voices in ordinary in 1630 when he was replaced by Giles Tomkins (*KM*, 71).

129. *KM*, 58, consort of the chamber of the late king; Nagel, 40.

130. One list in *KM*, 59, from lord chamberlain's accounts, vol. 557, has mostly the same names as PRO Ms. SP16/3, folio 112 verso. There are some differences; if all the essentially different names are counted, there were fifteen or sixteen musicians at this time, all French, apparently.

131. Unless there is a footnote reference, the name, the yearly fees received (written first) and the arrears due on 3 November 1635 come from PRO Ms. SP16/301, No. 9, folio 25-25 verso.

132. *MA*, III, 176. Pay indicated in 1607 (*MA*, II, 235). Most of the musicians recorded in *MA* are not on the PRO list, evidently because of different paying offices.

133. *MA*, III, 176. Pay from these same lists (in a few cases learned from pay of predecessor).

134. Listed in *MA*, III, 176, as sackbut, probably by mistake. Pay given in the same, p. 54.

135. Listed in many years although not 1635. 1633, livery at £16.2.6; 1638, £12 for a Cremona violin: *KM*, 84, 99.

136. This pay, from the PRO manuscript, does not seem to be all that he received; see two items in *KM*, 70.

137. The £40 and arrears due, from the PRO manuscript. Perhaps this was a separate fee from the £40 annuity granted by Charles when he was Prince of Wales, or perhaps the annuity was Taylor's only income from the court.

138. £40 annuity recorded in CSPD *1625-26*, 372; and pay given in *MA*, II, 235: 20d. a day and £16.2.6. a year.

139. He held several places in room of his late father, but just what is in question. According to *KM*, 63, he held a viol's place and a place in the wind instruments, 1627; subsequently he was listed both as viol and flute, and received two liveries a year (1635, violin: *MA*, III, 176). According to CSPD *1628-29*, 44, he also enjoyed an annuity of £50 granted by Charles as Prince of Wales to A. Ferrabosco II as Charles's instructor in music. The PRO manuscript gives him only once at £50 a year, £25 arrears (probably the annuity). He may have had three places, together worth well over £100 a year.

140. Evidently he held two places, as viol at £46 a year (*MA*, III, 172-176, 229-231) and as double sackbut (*KM*, 66, 97, 100, 105). It is probably for the latter post that the £46.10.10 with arrears of £23.5.5. was listed in the PRO manuscript.

141. *KM*, 65.

142. Sworn in ordinary June 1635, with pay to start on next vacancy; granted pay of £50 a year from privy purse, during pleasure, July 1635: *KM*, 91, 92.

143. Stephen, Estienne, Nau, Nan, Naw, etc. seems to have held two posts, one as violin (*KM*, 64, 76, etc.) and as composer (1628, warrant for pay at 40 marks a year in place of late Thomas Lupo, with livery: *KM*, 64, and *MA*, III, 171-176, 228-231). In the PRO manuscript his pay is given as £200 a year.

144. To serve in place and absence of John Snowsman; sworn in ordinary 1634, but apparently without pay: *KM*, 97. Pay started in room of Snowsman in 1641: *MA*, III, 232.

145. Listed for many years: see *KM*, 75, 76, 78, 81, 82, 86, and following. Although he received liveries, his pay is not given.

146. Listed as flute and cornett also. He received pay, according to the records, for keeping and training two boys for the royal service in 1626, 1628, 1630, 1631, 1633, 1637, 1638, 1640, 1641—presumably every year: *KM*, 61, 67, 74, 75, and following.

147. Robert Baker junior is not recorded in 1635 (if it is assumed that the Robert Baker listed in the PRO manuscript was his father). He is listed in 1625 as of the windy instruments (*KM*, 57) and as recorder (Nagel, 40); as of the hautboys and sackbuts in 1628 (*KM*, 66); a cornett was bought for him in 1633 (*KM*, 83); and he was sworn a musician for the wind instruments in place of his late father in 1637 (*KM*, 96). What he was paid before then is in question.

148. He was paid for a treble cornett and a treble recorder in 1636: *KM*, 92.

149. A cornett was bought for him in 1633: *KM*, 83.

150. He was paid for three mute cornetts in 1631: *KM*, 75.

151. The two hundred pound annuity, listed in the 1635 PRO manuscript and elsewhere, was granted by Charles as Prince of Wales, according to CSPD *1625-26*, 145, 372. He also held a place as lutanist; in 1633, for example, he received a livery as master, and another as lutanist: *KM*, 85. His pay as lutanist was £40 a year and livery: *MA*, III, 229. He also sang: *KM*, 58.

152. On Michaelmas 1636 he was also paid arrears for half a year ended Lady-day 1628, and in 1638 arrears for the half year ended at Michaelmas 1628: *MA*, III, 176, 229.

153. His successor received £40 a year and livery according to *MA*, III, 229, but only 20d. a day, or about £30 a year, and livery, according to a warrant to the treasurer of the chamber: CSPD *1635-36*, 356.

154. Also one of Queen Henrietta Maria's musicians (double liveries: CSPD *1633-34*, 446). According to the patent for his wages, 1633, twenty of the sixty pounds were for lute strings: *KM*, 87. Similarly other musicians received various large amounts for strings, above their salaries.

155. His pay was £40 a year and livery according to *MA*, III, 229, but only 20d. a day and livery according to Nagel, 41.

156. His pay was £40 a year and livery according to *MA*, III, 229, but only 20d. a day and livery according to *KM*, 87. He was evidently the person trained in Irish harp and other instruments from 1618.

157. According to the PRO manuscript. Apparently he received livery payments in addition: 1637, 1640, KM, 99, 105, and following.

158. KM, 91. He held a £40 annuity granted by Charles as Prince of Wales: CSPD *1625-26*, 145, 372.

159. According to the PRO manuscript his fee was £80, £40 in arrears. According to CSPD *1625-26*, 145, 372, he had an annuity of £120 granted by Charles as Prince of Wales. The records show that he received liveries nearly every year: KM, 61, 70, 75, 78, and following.

160. The PRO manuscript has £20 as his fee, and under arrears "obijt"; he was dead by May 1635, and replaced by John Wilson. According to CSPD *1625-26*, 145, 372, he had an annuity of £20 granted by Charles as Prince of Wales.

161. He was of "the consort" of the late king's chamber in 1625, and of the lutes and voices in 1628: KM, 58, 66. Perhaps he served until 1642, although the entries at the Restoration suggest new appointment: KM, 114, 119, and following. He is mentioned in chapter nine, above.

162. According to the PRO manuscript he received £64, with arrears of £32, and £40, with arrears of £20. He was granted an annuity of £64 by Charles as Prince of Wales (CSPD *1625-26*, 145, 372) and £40 a year for keeping and teaching two singing-boys from 1626 (KM, 61, 64, 73, and following). He also received livery payments: KM, 75, 105-107, and following.

163. Warrant for such liveries for life as enjoyed by Bales, and £20 a year: KM, 91. Nearly all the musicians in the PRO manuscript received liveries, at £16.2.6 a year, in addition to the fees indicated: KM.

164. MA, III, 176. Paid for two places held by his predecessor Orlando Gibbons, from 1625.

165. KM, 70, 79, 91, 98, 111.

166. MA, III, 172, 176. He also received various amounts for materials used, and other expenses: KM, 68, 70, and following.

167. Granted in 1626 for oversight and tuning of the king's organs at St. James's and Whitehall privy lodgings: CSPD *1625-26*, 566. The wording of the grant implies that he had been royal organ-maker before 1626. The next and last reference to him is in PRO Ms. SP 16/290, No. 85, payment of £20 in 1635.

168. CSPD *1635*, 122. He was granted an act of denization in 1636: CSPD *1635-36*, 220. No other references to him seem to be available, except for the appointment of a successor to him, in the voices, at the Restoration: KM, 118.

169. CSPD *1635*, 122.

BIBLIOGRAPHY

Since it is provided chiefly to help readers identify the abbreviated titles given in the footnotes, this list has been restricted as a rule to manuscripts and books cited above. Even here long titles are frequently abbreviated: a bibliography, complete in every respect, of manuscripts and books dealing in some way with the subject of the present book would by itself fill a large volume. Brief comment on principal sources and secondary works appears in footnotes above, and particularly at the beginning of parts and chapters.

A. Manuscripts, grouped alphabetically according to collection (Bodleian, British Museum, etc.)

B. Books published before 1701 (original editions) (page 320).

C. Published Documents (including CSPD, HMC, town records, modern editions of books originally published before 1701; alphabetically by author, place, or institution, as appropriate) (page 336).

D. Works written and printed after 1700 (page 347).

MANUSCRIPTS

Bodleian Library, Oxford:

Ballad commending music, c. 1550. *Ashmolean Ms. 48.*

Bradwell Accounts, 1631-1635. *Bodleian Ms. Top. Oxon. e. 185.*

Buckingham, duchess of, accounts, 1629-1634. *Bodleian Ms. Eng. misc. c. 208.*

Eltham, Statutes of (1526). *Laud Ms. P. 597.*

Gyles, Indenture between N. Gyles and dean and canons of Windsor, 1595. *Ashmolean Ms. 1125.*

Household accounts of a lady, London, 1594-1596 [copy]. *Malone 44.*

Livery companies of London, Lists of members, c. 1650. *Rawlinson D. 24.*

Musicians appointed at court, 1554. *Tanner 90.*

North, Diary of Sir John, 1575. *Bodleian Ms. Add. C. 193.*

North, Household accounts of Lady, 1588-1589. *Bodleian Ms. Add. C. 193.*

Notebook of a Cambridge physician, 1594. *Rawlinson D. 213.*

Smyth, Private account book of John Smyth of Nibley, steward of the manor of Berkeley: 1601-1618. *Bodleian Ms. Eng. misc. e. 6.*

Speech made in the music Schools, Oxford, at the Act, 1640, by Richard West. *Tanner 88.*

Wood, Anthony à, "Lives of English Musicians." *Wood D. 19 (4).*

British Museum:

Beverley, The orders of the Ancient Company or Fraternity of Mynstralls in Beverley. *Lansdowne Ms. 896,* folios 153-156 verso.

Caryll family, Household accounts of the, 1615ff. *Ad. Mss. 28,240-28,242, 28,250.*

Chaloner, Private account book of Sir Thomas Chaloner, 1551-1556. *Lansdowne Ms. 824.*

Company of musicians, London, records, 1661-1679. *Harleian Ms. 1911.*

Cromwell, Household accounts of the family of Cromwell of Ramsey, Huntingtonshire, 1546-1672. *Ad. Mss. 33,460-33,461.*

Dover, Churchwardens' accounts for St. Mary's church, 1536-1558. *Egerton Ms. 1912.*

Estrange, Extracts from accounts of Sir Thomas L'Estrange, 1519-1589. *Ad. Ms. 27,449.*

Gawdy, Household accounts of B. and F. Gawdy, 1570-1576, 1582-1586, 1626-1639. *Ad. Mss. 27,398-27,399.*

Harington, Sir John, miscellaneous papers of. *Ad. Ms. 27,632.*

Ipswich, Churchwardens' accounts of St. Peter's church, 1563-1664. *Ad. Ms. 25,344.*

Kinge, Hugh, "To all true preachers." *Harleian Ms. 2019,* folios 8-5 (reversed).

Norris Papers, vols. III and IV (Lancashire, c. 1553-1629). *Ad. Mss. 36,926-36,927.*

North, Accounts of Roger North, second baron North, of Kirtling, Cambridgeshire, 1575-1589. *Stowe Ms. 744.* [Extracts printed in *Archaeologia,* XIX (1821), 283-301.]

Norton, Sir Richard, Letterbook, 1625-1640. *Ad. Ms. 21,922.*

Oxenden family, accounts, seventeenth century. *Ad. Mss. 28,006-28,008.*

Pelham, Accounts of Pelham family of Laughton, Sussex, 1620-1642. *Ad. Mss. 33,143-33,147.*

"The praise of musick the profite and delight it bringeth to man & other the creatures of God And the necessarye use of it in the service & Christian Churche of God." *Royal Ms. 18Bxix.*

Ravenscroft, A treatise of music by Thomas Ravenscroft. *Ad. Ms. 19,758.*

Royal Household accounts, 1538-1541. *Arundel Ms. 97.*

Royal Household accounts, 1547. *Lansdowne Ms. 2.*

Royal Household accounts, 1574. *Harleian Ms. 589.*

Spencer, Household accounts of the family of Spencer of Althorp and Wormleighton, 1599-1647. *Ad. Ms. 25,080-25,083.*

Stuart, Correspondence between Lady Arabella and Prince Henry, 1607. *Harleian Ms. 6986,* folios 74, 76. 78.

Cambridge, University Library:

Mountgomerye, John. "A booke contayning the manner and orrder of a watche to be used in the cittie of london up on the even of sainct John bapptiste and sainct peter as in tyme past hathe binne acustumedd." [1585] *Ms. Ll. IV. 4.*

School exercises in the art of music, 1634. *Ms. Dd. III. 17.*

Survey of the sciences (seventeenth century). *Ms. Dd. X. 30.*

Bibliography

Cambridge, Registry of the University:
A collection of the inventories of the effects of members deceased within the
precincts of the University, 1560-1729.

Canterbury Corporation:
Ordinance of Minstrels Company, c. 1526. Bundle A54, Mss. 18 and 20.
Chamberlains' Accounts, Book 12, 1558-1568. [Actually 1557-1568.]
Chamberlains' Accounts, Book 14, 1577-1587.
Chamberlains' Accounts, Book 15, 1587-1592.
Chamberlains' Accounts, Book 16, 1592-1602.
Chamberlains' Accounts, Book 17, 1602-1610.
Chamberlains' Accounts, Book 18, 1610-1620.
Burmote Minutes, 1542-1578.
Burmote Minutes, 1578-1602.

Coventry Corporation:
Chamberlains' and Wardens' Accounts, A7 (a) 14 Henry VII-16 Elizabeth.
Chamberlains' and Wardens' Accounts   (b) 17 Elizabeth-11 Charles I.
Chamberlains' and Wardens' Accounts   (c) 12 Charles I-9 Anne.
Council Books, A14 (a) 3 and 4 Philip and Mary-16 Charles I.

Cumberland, Earl of: see below, under *Devonshire.*

Devonshire, Mss. of the Duke of Devonshire, at Chatsworth, Derbyshire:
Inventory for the Countess of Shrewsbury, Chatsworth, 1601.
Inventory for the Countess of Shrewsbury, Hardwicke, 1601.
Cavendish, Account book for Sir William Cavendish, 1597-1601. *Hardwicke
Ms. 10A.*
Cavendish, Account book for Sir William Cavendish, 1599-1607. *Hardwicke
Ms. 23.*

*Devonshire, Mss. of the Duke of Devonshire, at Chatsworth: Manuscripts
related to the family of the Earl of Cumberland:*
Inventory of goods at Skipton castle, 1595, and elsewhere. *Bolton Mss.*
"The charge of a Journaie from Bickerton to London . . . 1620. . . ." *Bolton
Mss.*
Accounts for the Earl of Cumberland, 1610-1613. *Bolton Ms. 94.*
Accounts for the Earl of Cumberland, 1614. *Bolton Ms. 95.*
Accounts for the Earl of Cumberland, 1617. *Bolton Ms. 97.*
Accounts for the Earl of Cumberland, 1632. *Bolton Ms. 169.*
Accounts for the Earl of Cumberland, 1633-1634. *Bolton Ms. 172.*
Accounts for the Earl of Cumberland, 1634-1635. *Bolton Ms. 174.*
"Disbursed in his Lordshipps Jorny into Iireland by the way of Scotland
begonn at Skipton. . . ." 1635. *Bolton Mss.*
Accounts for the Earl of Cumberland, 1638. *Bolton Ms. 176.*
Accounts for the Earl of Cumberland, 1638-1639. *Bolton Ms. 177.*

Bibliography

"Checkrole" of the Earl of Cumberland's house at the Piazzo in Covent Garden, London, 1 January 1642. *Bolton Ms. 91.*

Inventory of furniture of Lord Cork, left at his house in York, c. 1644. *Bolton Mss.*

Inventory of the goods of the late Earl of Cumberland, Skipton castle, 23 January 1644 [1645?]. *Bolton Mss.*

"A note of goods left att Skipton for the Countesse of Pembroke" [c. 1645?]. *Bolton Mss.*

"An Inventory taken at Skipton Castle of such goods which is my lady Pembrooke May the 7th 1645." *Bolton Mss.*

Huntington Library, San Marino, California:
Henry earl of Huntington, inventory of goods of, York, 1596.

Henry earl of Huntington, inventory of goods of, Donington Park, 1633.

The same, 1635.

John Lord Lumley, catalogue of the library of, 1610. [Photostatic copy of *Ms. 0.4.38* of Trinity College, Cambridge.]

Temple family accounts, 1580-1628. *Stowe Mss.*

London Corporation:
Journals of the Proceedings of the Common Council of the City of London, 1416ff., and index.

Letter Books of the City of London, 1275ff., and index.

Liber legum, 1342-1590 [Sixteenth century calendar of acts of the common council of the city of London].

Repertories of the Court of Aldermen of the City of London, 1495ff., and index.

Setting the Watch. 1585. [See above, *Cambridge, University Library Mss.*]

Newark-on-Trent Corporation:
Corporation Minutes, sixteenth and seventeenth centuries. [Temporarily in the custody of Guy Parsloe, Esq., secretary of the Institute of Historical Research, London, 1939; Mr. Parsloe pointed out a useful passage on folio 80 verso.]

Norwich Central Public Library:
Mss. notes on music and musicians, chiefly in East Anglia, made by the late Arthur Henry Mann, 25 volumes. [Used principally:]

    I.   Norfolk musical events.

    II.   Norfolk musicians.

    III.   Norwich Cathedral Musical Events.

    VIII-IX. Norwich Musical Events.

    X-XIII. Norwich Musicians.

      [Derived in part from original manuscripts, e.g. cathedral and city archives, in part from secondary works.]

Bibliography

Nottingham Corporation:
Chamberlains' Accounts 1557-1645. Books 1610-1647.

Public Record Office, London:
Chapel Royal, Mss. related to the.
SP 12/163, No. 88. SP 38/5, No. 7. SP 38/7, No. 42. SP 16/154, No. 75.
LC 2/4, LC 5/37, LC 5/38, LC 5/115, LC 5/180, LC 9/90, LC 9/254.
Company of Musicians, Westminster, Mss. related to the. *Patent Roll C. 66.-2692. SP 38/17, No. 74*.
Disorders committed by royal musicians, papers related to the. SP 12/173, No. 25. SP 12/181, No. 48.
Gutstring-makers, petition to the king, and exhibitions, 1637. SP 16/373, No. 80, i-v.
King's Musick, Accounts and other Mss. related to the. SP 15/4, No. 27. *Declared Accounts of the Audit Office, Bundle 380, Rolls 1, 2; Bundle 381, Rolls 6-10; Bundle 382, Roll 11; Bundle 390, Rolls 52-54*. SP 12/8, No. 10. SP 12/47, No. 83. SP 16/54, No. 19. SP 16/222, No. 4. SP 16/229, No. 66. SP 16/229, No. 67. SP 16/259, Nos. 1, 87. SP 16/290, Nos. 31, 85. SP 16/301, No. 9. SP 16/313, No. 34. SP 16/474, No. 2. LC 2/4 (5), LC 5/38, LC 5/50, LC 5/51, LC 5/115, LC 5/179, LC 9/254.
Lecture on music at Oxford in 1608, letter about. SP 14/35, No. 17.
Queen Henrietta Maria's musicians, papers concerning. SP 16/3, Nos. 112, 113. SP 16/132, No. 49. SP 16/474, No. 3.
Visitation of churches in Buckinghamshire in 1637, notes taken during. SP 16/366, No. 79.
Westminster, aliens lodging in, lists of. SP 16/56, No. 71. SP 16/300, No. 75.

Trinity College, Cambridge, Library:
Ayres to be sunge to the lute and base vyole. Newly composed by George Handford. Dedicated to Prince Henry. 1609. R. 16. 29. 645.

Warren, Mss. of Cuthbert Leicester-Warren, Esq., J.P., at Tabley House, Cheshire:
A manuscript volume marked "Music," by Sir Peter Leycester of Tabley house; early and middle seventeenth century; includes lessons for the lyro-viol and a treatise, "Prolegomena historica de musica."
A manuscript book of notes on music, made by Sir Peter Leycester in the Bodleian library.

York Corporation:
Minstrels' Ordinance 1561. Ms. Book 20A (also known as B/Y), folios 222-223 verso.
Minstrels' Ordinance 1578. Ms. Book 22, folios 142 verso-143 verso.
House Books, 1st Series, Books 25-35.

Bibliography

WORKS PUBLISHED BEFORE 1701

Adson, John. *Courtly masking ayres for violins, consorts and cornets.* London, 1611.

Agrippa, Henry Cornelius. *Of the vanitie and uncertaintie of artes and sciences,* translated by Ja[mes] San[ford]. London, 1569.

Alison, Richard. *An howres recreation in musicke, apt for instruments and voyces. Framed for the delight of gentlemen and others which are wel affected to that qualitie, all for the most part with two trebles, necessarie for such as teach in private families, with a prayer for the long preservation of the King and his posteritie.* London, 1606.

Alison, Richard. *The psalmes of David in meter, the plaine song beeing the common tunne to be sung and plaide upon the lute, orpharyon.* London, 1599.

Alsted, Johann Heinrich. *Templum musicum: or, the musical synopsis, of the learned and famous Johannes-Henricus-Alstedius, being a compendium of the rudiments both of the mathematical and practical part of musick: of which subject not any book is extant in our English tongue,* trans. John Birchensha. London, 1664.

Amner, John. *Sacred hymnes of 3. 4. 5. and 6. parts for voyces & vyols.* London, 1615.

Attey, John. *The first booke of ayres of foure parts, with tableture for the lute: so made, that all the parts may be plaide together with the lute, or one voyce with the lute and base-vyoll.* London, 1622.

Batchelors Delight, The, being a pleasant new song. London [seventeenth century].

Bacon, Francis. *Sylva Sylvarum or a naturall history in ten centuries.* London, 1627.

Barley, William. *A new booke of tabliture, containing sundrie easie and familiar instructions, shewing howe to attaine to the knowledge, to guide and dispose thy hand to play on sundry instruments, as the lute, orpharion, and bandora: Together with divers new lessons to each of these instruments. Wherunto is added an introduction to prickesong, and certaine familiar rules of descant, with other necessarie tables plainely shewing the true use of the scale or gamut, and also how to set any lesson higher or lower at your pleasure. Collected together out of the best authors professing the practise of these instruments.* London, 1596, for William Barley [who may be the author].

Barlow, William. *Psalmes and hymnes of praier and thanksgiving.* [n.p.], 1613.

Barnard, John [ed.]. *The first booke of selected church musick, consisting of services and anthems, such as are now used in the cathedrall, and collegiat churches of this kingdome. Never before printed. Whereby such bookes as were heretofore with much difficulty and charges, transcribed for the use of the quire, are now to the saving of much labour and expence, publisht for the generall good of all such as shall desire them either for publick or private exercise. Collected out of divers approved authors.* London, 1641.

Bartlet, John. *A booke of ayres with a triplicitie of musicke, whereof the first part is for the lute or orpharion, and the viole de gambo, and 4. partes to sing, the second part is for 2. trebles to sing to the lute and viole, the third part is for the lute and one voyce, and the viole de gambo.* London, 1606.

Bateson, Thomas. *The second set of madrigales to 3. 4. 5. and 6. parts: Apt for viols and voyces.* London, 1618.

Bathe, William. *A brief introduction to the skill of song: concerning the practise.* London, [1584?].

Bernard, Richard. *Davids musick, or psalmes of that royall prophet, once the sweete singer of that Israel: unfolded logically, expounded paraphrastically, and then followeth a more particular explanation of the words, with manifold doctrines and uses briefly observed out of the same.* London, 1616.

Bevin, Elway. *A briefe and short introduction of the art of musicke, to teach how to make discant, of all proportions that are in use: very necessary for all such as are desirous to attaine to knowledge in the art; and may by practice, if they can sing, soone be able to compose three, foure, and five parts: and also to compose all sorts of canons that are usuall, by these directions of two or three parts in one, upon the plain-song.* London, 1631.

Bossewell, John. *Workes of armorie, devyded into three bookes, entituled, the concordes of armorie, the armorie of honor, and coates and creastes.* London, 1572.

Brathwaite, Richard. *The English gentleman: containing sundry excellent rules or exquisite observations, tending to direction of every gentleman, of selecter ranke and qualitie; how to demeane or accommodate himselfe in the manage of publike or private affaires.* London, 1630.

Braithwaite, William. *His Majesties gracious grant to William Braithwaite for the sole printing and publishing musicke, his way.* [London? c. 1636.]

Braithwaite, William [ed.] *Siren coelestis centum harmoniarum, duarum, trium & quatuor vocum. Quam nova vite principibus etiam necdum vulgatis auctoribus legit, pro temporum dierumq; festorum diversitate concinnavit, & organis item accommodavit, & in lucem dedit, Georgius Victorinus Monachij. Eandum, methodo docendi, et discendi musicam longè facillima, Augustissimi Caroli magnae britaniae monarchae, illustri diplomate roborata & stabilita, Willihelmus Bray-Thwaitus anglus,*

*aeterni Evangelij minister, adeòq; humano generi, communicavit, &
commendavit.* London, 1638.

Brice, Thomas. *Against filthy writing and such like delighting.* London [no
date. Heber Collection of Elizabethan Ballads, Huntington Library].

Buck, George. *The third universitie of England. Or a treatise of the foundations of all the colledges, auncient schooles of priviledge, and of houses
of learning, and liberall arts, within and about the most famous cittie of
London. With a briefe report of the sciences, arts, and faculties therein
professed, studied, and practised. Together with the blazon of the armes,
and ensignes thereunto belonging. Gathered faithfully out of the best
histories, chronicles, records, and archives.* London, 1615 [with Edmund
Howe's first edition of Stow, *Annales,* London, 1615].

Burdet, Ro. *The refuge of a sinner. Wherein are briefly declared the chiefest
poinctes of true salvation.* London, 1565 [Heber Collection of Elizabethan
Ballads].

Bushell, Thomas. *The severall speeches and songs, at the presentment of Mr.
Bushells rock to the queenes . . . majesty. Aug. 23 1636.* Oxford, 1636.

Butler, Charles. *The principles of musik, in singing and setting: with the
two-fold use therof, [Ecclesiasticall and Civil.]* London, 1636.

Byll, Thomas. *A Godly song, entituled, a farewell to the world.* London,
[1630?].

Byrd, William, and Thomas Tallis. *Cantiones, quae ab argumento sacrae
vocantur, quinque et sex partium.* London, 1575.

Byrd, William. *A gratification unto Master Case.* London, [1586?].

Byrd, William. *Psalmes, sonets, and songs of sadnes and pietie, made into
musicke of five parts: whereof, some of them going abroade among
divers, in untrue coppies, are heere truely corrected, and th'other being
songs very rare and newly composed, are heere published, for the recreation of all such as delight in musicke.* London, 1588.

Byrd, William. *Psalms, songs, and sonnets: some solemne, others joyfull,
framed to the life of the words: fit for voyces or viols of 3. 4. 5. and 6.
parts.* London, 1611.

Byrd, William. *Songs of sundrie natures, some of gravitie, and others of
mirth, fit for all companies and voyces. Lately made and composed into
musicke of 3. 4. 5. and 6. parts: and published for the delight of all
such as take pleasure in the exercise of that art.* London, 1589.

Campion, Thomas. *A new way of making fowre parts in Counter-point, by
a most familiar, and infallible rule. Secondly, a necessary discourse of
keyes, and their proper closes. Thirdly, the allowed passages of all con-
cords perfect, or imperfect, are declared. Also by way of preface, the
nature of the scale is expressed, with a briefe method teaching to sing.*
London, [1610 or 1620?].

Campion, Thomas. *The description of a maske, presented before the kinges majestie at Whitehall, on twelfth night last, in honour of Lord Hayes, and his bride, daughter and heire to the honourable the Lord Dennye, their marriage having been the same day at court solemnized. To this by occasion other small poemes are adjoyned.* London, 1614.

Campion, Thomas. *A relation of the late royall entertainment given by the right honorable the Lord Knowles, at Cawsome-house neere Redding: to our most gracious Queene Anne, in her progresse toward the Bathe, upon the seven and eight and twentie dayes of Aprill. 1613. Whereunto is annexed the description, speeches, and songs of the lords musque, presented in the banquetting-house on the mariage night of the high and mightie, count palatine, and the royally descended the Ladie Elizabeth.* London, 1613.

Campion, Thomas. *The description of a maske: presented in the banqueting roome at Whitehall, on Saint Stephens night last, at the mariage of the right honourable the earle of Somerset: And the right noble the Lady Frances Howard. Whereunto are annexed divers choyse ayres composed for this maske that may be sung with a single voyce to the lute or base-viall.* London, 1614.

Campion, Thomas. *Songs of mourning: bewailing the untimely death of Prince Henry.* London, 1613.

Campion, Thomas. *The third and fourth booke of ayres: composed by Thomas Campian. So as they may be expressed by one voyce, with a violl, lute, or orpharion.* London [1612].

Campion, Thomas. *Two bookes of ayres. The first contayning divine and morall songs: The second light conceits of lovers. To be sung to the lute and viols, in two, three and foure parts: or by one voyce to an instrument.* London, [1610].

Carleton, Richard. *Madrigals to five voyces.* London, 1601.

Case, John. *Apologia musices tam vocalis quam instrumentalis et mixtae.* Oxford, 1588.

[Case, John.] *The praise of musicke: wherein besides the antiquitie, dignitie, delectation, & use thereof in civill matters, is also declared the sober and lawful use of the same in the congregation and church of God.* Oxford, 1586.

Cavendish, Michaell. *14. Ayres in tabletorie to the lute expressed with two voyces and the base violl or the voice & lute only. 6. more to 4. voyces.* London, 1598.

Child, William. *The first set of psalmes of III voyces fitt for private chappells or other private meetings with a continuall base either for the organ or theorbo newly composed after the Italian way.* London, 1639.

Churchyard, Thomas. *A discourse of the queenes majesties entertainment in Suffolk and Norffolk: with a description of many things then presently seene.* London, [1579?].

Cleaver, Robert. *A godlye form of householde government: for the ordering of private families, according to the direction of Gods word.* London, 1598.

Coperario, John. *Funeral teares for the death of the right honorable the Earl of Devonshire. Figured in seaven songes, whereof six are so set forth that the wordes may be exprest by a treble voice alone to the lute and base viole, or else that the meane part may bee added, if any shall affect more fulnesse of parts. The seaventh is made in forme of a dialogue, and can not be sung without two voyces.* London, 1606.

Coperario, John. *Songs of mourning: bewailing the untimely death of Prince Henry. And set forth to bee sung with one voyce to the lute, or violl.* London, 1613.

Corkine, William. *Ayres, to sing and play to the lute and basse violl; with pavins, galliards, almaines, and corantos for the lyra violl.* London, 1610.

Corkine, William. *The second booke of ayres, some, to sing and play to the base-violl alone: others, to be sung to the lute and base violl.* London, 1612.

Cosyn, John. *Musike of six, and five partes. Made upon the common tunes used in singing of the psalmes.* London, 1585.

Cotton, John. *Singing of psalmes a gospel-ordinance. Or a treatise, wherein are handled these foure particulars.* London, 1647.

Croce, Giovanni. *Musica sacra: to sixe voyces. Composed in the Italian tongue. Newly Englished.* London, 1608.

Damon, William. *The former booke of the musicke of M. William Damon, late one of her majesties musitions: conteining all the tunes of Davids psalmes, as they are ordinarily soung in the church: most excellently by him composed into 4. parts. In which sett the tenor singeth the church tune. Published for the recreation of such as delight in musicke.* London, 1591.

Damon, William. *The psalmes of David in English meter with notes of foure partes set unto them, by Guilielmo Daman, for John Bull, to the use of the godly Christians for recreatyng themselves, in stede of fond and unseemely ballades.* London, 1579.

Davison, Francis. *A poeticall rapsodie, containing: diverse sonnets, odes, elegies, madrigals, epigrams, pastorals, eglogues, with other poems, both in rime and measured verse.* London, 1611.

Day, John [printer]. *Certaine notes set forth in foure and three parts to be song at the morning communion, and evening praier, very necessarie for the church of Christe to be frequented and used: & unto them added divers godly praiers & psalmes in the like forme to the honor & praise of God.* London, 1560.

Dekker, Thomas. *Troia-nova triumphans. London triumphing, or, the solemne, magnificent, and memorable receiving of . . . Sir John Swiner-*

ton knight, into the citty of London, after his returne from taking the oath of maioralty at Westminster . . . 29. of October, 1612. London, 1612.

Desainliens, Claudius. *Campo di fior or else the flourie field of foure languages of M. Claudius Desainliens, alias Holiband: For the furtherance of the learners of the Latine, French, English, but chieflie of the Italian tongue.* London, 1583.

Desainliens, Claudius. *The French Littelton. A most easie, perfect, and absolute way to learne the Frenche tongue.* London, 1566.

Desainliens, Claudius. *The French schoolemaister, wherin is most plainlie shewed, the true and most perfect way of pronouncinge of the Frenche tongue, without any helpe of maister or teacher.* London, 1573.

Descartes, René. *Renatus Des-Cartes excellent compendium of musick: with necessary and judicious animadversions thereupon. By a person of honour.* London, 1653.

Dowland, John. *The first booke of songes or ayres of foure parts with tableture for the lute: So made that all the partes together, or either of them severally may be song to the lute, orpherion or viol de gambo. Also an invention by the sayd author for two to playe upon one lute.* London, 1597.

Dowland, John. *Lacrimae, or seaven tears figured in seaven passionate pavans, with divers other pavans, galiards, and almands, set forth for the lute, viols, or violons, in five parts.* London, [1605?].

Dowland, John. *A pilgrimes solace, wherein is contained musicall harmonie of 3. 4. and 5. parts, to be sung and plaid with the lute and viols.* London, 1612.

Dowland, John. *The second booke of songs or ayres, of 2. 4. and 5. parts: with tableture for the lute or orpherion, with the violl de gamba.* London, 1600.

Dowland, John. *The third and last booke of songs or aires. Newly composed to sing to the lute, orpharion, or viols, and a dialogue for a base and meane lute with five voices to sing thereto.* London, 1603.

Dowland, Robert [ed.]. *A musicall banquet. Furnished with varietie of delicious ayres, collected out of the best authors in English, French, Spanish and Italian.* London, 1610.

Dowland, Robert [ed.]. *Varietie of lute-lessons: Viz. fantasies, pavins, galliards, almaines, corantoes, and volts: Selected out of the best approved authors, as well beyond the seas as of our owne country. Whereunto is annexed certaine observations belonging to lute-playing: by John Baptisto Besardo of Visonti. Also a short treatise thereunto appertayning: by John Dowland batcheler of musicke.* London, 1610.

[Drayton, Michael]. *The harmonie of the church. Containing the spirituall songes and holy hymnes, of godly men, patriarkes . . . now (newlie) reduced into sundrie kinds of English meeter: meete to be read or sung for the solace and comfort of the godly.* By M. D. London, 1591.

Dugdale, Gilbert. *The time triumphant, declaring . . . the arival of our soveraigne . . . James into England.* London, 1604.

[Earle, John, Bishop]. *Micro-cosmographie. Or, a peece of the world discovered; in essayes and characters.* London (1628), 1633 (sixth edition).

East, Michael. *The fift set of bookes, wherein are songs full of spirit and delight, so composed in 3. parts, that they are as apt for vyols as voyces.* London, 1618.

East, Michael. *The fourth set of bookes, wherein are anthemes for versus and chorus, madrigals, and songs of other kindes, to 4. 5. and 6. parts: apt for viols and voyces.* London, 1618.

East, Michael. *Madrigals to 3. 4. and 5. parts: apt for viols and voices.* London, 1604.

Est [East], Michaell. *The second set of madrigales to 3. 4. and 5. parts: apt for viols and voices.* London, 1606.

East, Michael. *The seventh set of bookes, wherein are duos for two base viols, so composed, though there be but two parts in the eye, yet there is often three or foure in the eare. Also fancies of 3. parts for two treble viols, and a base violl: so made, as they must be plaied and not sung. Lastly, ayerie fancies of 4. parts, that may be as well sung as plaid.* London, 1638.

East, Michael. *The sixt set of bookes, wherein are anthemes for versus and chorus, of 5. and 6. parts: apt for violls and voyces.* London, 1624.

Easte, Michaell. *The third set of bookes: wherein are pastorals, anthemes, neopolitanes, fancies, and madrigales, to 5. and 6. parts: apt both for viols and voyces.* London, 1610.

Edwardes, Roger. *A boke of very godly psalmes and prayers, dedicated to the Lady Letice Vicountesse of Hereforde.* London, 1570.

Eglesfield, James. *A heavenly hymne to the King of Heaven. Presented in a sermon.* London, 1640.

Erondell, Peter. *The French garden: for English ladyes and gentlewomen to walke in. Or a summer dayes labour. Being an instruction for the attayning unto the knowledge of the French tongue: wherein for the practise thereof, are framed thirteene dialogues in French and English, concerning divers matters from the rising in the morning till bed-time.* London, 1605.

Euclid. *The elements of geometrie of the most auncient philosopher Euclide of Megara. Faithfully (now first) translated . . . by H. Billingsley . . . with a very fruitfull preface made by M. I. Dee, specifying the chiefe mathematical sciences, what they are, and whereunto commodious: where, also, are disclosed certaine new secrets mathematicall and mechanicall, untill these our daies, greatly missed.* London, [1570?].

Bibliography

Farmer, John. *Divers and sundrie waies of two parts in one, to the number of fortie, upon one playn song. . . .* London, 1591.

Fenner, Dudley. *A short and profitable treatise of lawfull and unlawfull recreations, and of the right use and abuse of those that are lawefull.* Middleburgh, 1587.

Ferrabosco, Alfonso. *Lessons for 1. 2. and 3. viols.* London, 1609.

Filmer, Edward [ed.]. *French court-aires with their ditties Englished. Of foure and five parts. Together with that of the lute.* London, 1629.

Forde, Thomas. *Musicke of sundrie kindes, set forth in two bookes. The first whereof are, aries for 4. voices to the lute, orphorion, or basse-viol, with a dialogue for two voices, and two basse viols in parts, tunde the lute way. The second are pavens, galiards, almaines, toies, jigges, thumpes and such like, for two basse-viols, the lieraway, so made as the greatest number may serve to play alone, very easie to be performde.* London, 1607.

G., B. *The joyfull receyving of the queenes most excellent majestie into . . . Norwich.* London, 1578.

Gibbons, Orlando. *Fantazies of three parts.* London [1606].

Gibbons, Orlando. *The first set of madrigals and mottets of 5. parts: apt for viols and voyces.* London, 1612.

Gibbons, Orlando. *Parthenia, or the maydenhead of the first musicke that ever was printed for the virginalls. Compsed by the three famous masters: William Byrd, Dr. John Bull, & Orlando Gibbons, Gentilmen of his majesties most illustrious chappell. Dedicated to all the maisters and lovers of musick.* London, [1611?].

Glanville, Bartholomew de. *Batman upon Bartholome, his booke de proprietatibus rerum, newly corrected, enlarged and amended: with such additions as are requisite, unto every severall booke: Taken foorth of the most approved authors, the like heretofore not translated in English.* London, 1582.

Glanville, Bartholomew de. *Bertholomeus de proprietatibus rerum* [Translated by John of Trevisa]. London, 1535.

Gosson, Stephen. *The schoole of abuse.* London, 1579.

Greaves, Thomas. *Songes of sundrie kindes; first aires to be sung to the lute, and base violl. Next, songs of sadnesse, for the viols and voyce. Lastly, madrigalles for five voyces.* London, 1604.

Hacket, John. *Scrinia reserata: a memorial offer'd to the great deservings of John Williams.* London, 1693.

Hilton, John. *Ayres, or fa la's for three voyces.* London, 1627.

Holborne, Anthony. *The cittharn schoole, by Antony Holborne gentleman, and servant to her most excellent majestie. Hereunto are added sixe short aers Neapolitan like to three voices without the instrument: done by his brother William Holborne.* London, 1597.

Bibliography

Holborne, Anthony. *Pavans, galliards, almaines, and other short aeires both grave, and light, in five parts, for viols, violins, or other musicall winde instruments.* London, 1599.

Hume, Tobias. *Captaine Humes poeticall musicke. Principally made for two basse-viols, yet so contrived, that it may be plaied 8. severall waies upon sundry instruments with much facilitie. 1. The first way or musicke is for one bass-viole to play alone in parts, which standeth alwaies on the right side of this booke. 2. The second musicke is for two basse-viols to play together. 3. The third musicke, for three basse-viols to play together. 4. The fourth musicke, for two tenor viols and a basse-viole. 5. The fift musicke, for two orpherions and a basse-viole. 6. The sixt musicke, for two orpherions and a basse-viole. 7. The seventh musicke, to use the voyce to some of these musicks, but especially to the three basse-viols, or to the two orpherions with one basse-viole to play the ground. 8. The eight and last musicke, is consorting all these instruments together with the virginals, or rather with a winde instrument and the voice.* London, 1607.

Hume, Tobias. *The first part of ayres, French, Pollish, and others together, some in tabliture, and some in pricke-song: with pavines, galliards, and almaines for the viole de gambo alone, and other musicall conceits for two base viols, expressing five parts, with pleasant reportes one from the other, and for two leero viols, and also for the leero viole with two treble viols, or two with one treble. Lastly for the leero viole to play alone, and some songes to bee sung to the viole, with the lute, or better with the viole alone. Also an invention for two to play upon one viole.* London, 1605.

Hunnis, William. *Seven sobs of a sorrowfull soule for sinne. Comprehending those seven psalmes of the princelie prophet David, commonlie called poenitentiall: framed into a forme of familiar praiers, and reduced into meeter by William Hunnis, one of the gentlemen of hir majesties honourable chapell, and maister to the children of the same. Whereunto are also annexed his handfull of honisuckles; the poore widowes mite; a dialog between Christ and a sinner; divers godlie and pithie ditties, with a Christian confession of and to the Trinitie; newlie printed and augmented.* London, 1583.

Izacke, Richard. *Remarkable antiquities of the city of Exeter.* London, 1681.

Johnson, Richard. *A crown garland of goulden roses gathered out of Englands royall garden. Being the lives and strange fortunes of many great personages of this land. Set forth in many pleasant new songes and sonetts never before imprinted.* London, 1612.

Jones, Inigo, and Sir William Davenant. *Britannia triumphans. A masque.* London, 1637.

Jones, Inigo. *The temple of love. A masque. Presented by the queenes majesty, and her ladies, at White hall on Shrove-Tuesday, 1634.* London, 1634.

Jones, Robert. *The first booke of songes & ayres of foure parts with tableture for the lute. So made that all the parts together, or either of them severally may be song to the lute, orpherian or viol de gambo.* London, 1600.

Jones, Robert. *The first set of madrigals of 3. 4. 5. 6. 7. 8. parts, for viols and voices, or for voices alone; or as you please.* London, 1607.

Jones, Robert. *A musicall dreame or the fourth booke of ayres, the first part is for the lute, two voyces, and the viole de gambo; the second part is for the lute, the viole and four voices to sing: the third part is for one voice alone, or to the lute, the basse viole, or to both if you please, whereof, two are Italian ayres.* London, 1609.

Jones, Robert. *The second booke of songs and ayres, set out to the lute, the base violl the playne way, or the base by the tableture after the leero fashion.* London. 1601.

Jones, Robert. *Ultimum vale, with a triplicity of musicke, whereof the first part is for the lute, the voyce, and the viole de gambo. The 2. part is for the lute, the viole, and foure partes to sing. The third part is for two trebles, to sing either to the lute, or the viole or to both, if any please.* London, 1608.

Jonson, Ben. *Lovers made men. A masque presented in the house of the right honorable the Lord Haye, by divers of noble qualitie, his friends. For the entertaynment of Monsieur Le Baron de Tour, extraordinarie ambassador for the French king. On Saterday the 22. of February, 1617.* London, 1617.

Jonson, Ben. *The masque of augures.* London, 1621.

Jonson, Ben. *The masque of the gypsies.* London, 1640.

Kemp, William. *Kemps nine daies wonder, performed in a daunce from London to Norwich. Containing the pleasure, paines and kinde entertainment of William Kemp between London and that citty in his late morrice.* London, 1600.

Kirbye, George. *The first set of English madrigalls, to 4. 5. & 6. voyces.* London, 1597.

Kynaston, Sir Francis. *Corona minervae. A masque.* London, 1635.

Lasso, Orlando di. *Novae aliquot et ante hac non ita usitatae ad duas voces cantiones suavissimae, omnibus musicis summè utiles: nec non tyronibus quàm ejus artis peritioribus summopere inservientes.* London, 1598.

Lasso, Orlando di. *Recueil du Mellange d'Orlande de Lassus, contenant plusieurs chansons, tant en vers Latins qu'en ryme Francoyse, a quatre, & cinq parties.* London, 1570.

Lawes, Henry. *Choice psalms put into musick, for three voices. The most of which may properly enough be sung by any three, with a thorough* base. *Compos'd by Henry and William Lawes, brothers; and servants to his majestie. With divers elegies, set in musick by sev'rall friends, upon the death of William Lawes. At the end of the thorough base are added nine canons of three and foure voices, made by William Lawes.* London, 1648.

Leighton, Sir William. *Teares or lamentations of a sorrowfull soule.* London, 1613.

Leighton, Sir William. *The teares or lamentacions of a sorrowfull soule: composed with musical ayres and songs, both for voyces and divers instruments. And all psalmes that consist of so many feete as the fiftieth psalme, will goe to the foure partes for consort.* London, 1614.

Leighton, Sir William. *Vertue triumphant, or a lively description of the foure vertues cardinall.* London, 1603.

Lenton, Francis. *The Innes of Court anagrammatist; or the masquers masqued in anagrammes.* London, 1634.

[LeRoy, Adrien] *A briefe and easye instrution to learne the tableture to conducte and dispose thy hande unto the lute Englished by J. Alford Londenor.* London, 1568.

LeRoy, Adrien. *A briefe and plaine instruction to set all musicke of eight divers tunes in tableture for the lute. With a briefe instruction how to play on the lute by tablature, to conduct and dispose thy hand unto the lute, with certaine easie lessons for that purpose. And also a third booke containing divers new excellent tunes. All first written in French by Adrian LeRoy, and now translated into English by F. Ke. Gentelman.* London, 1574.

Lodge, Thomas. [A reply to Stephen Gosson's *Schoole of abuse*] London [1579-1580?].

L[owe], E[dward]. *A short direction for the performance of cathedrall service. Published for the information of such persons, as are ignorant of it, and shall be call'd to officiate in cathedrall, or collegiate churches, where it hath formerly been in use.* Oxford, 1661.

Luminalia, or the festivall of light. Personated in a masque at court, by the queenes majestie, and her ladies. On Shrovetuesday Night, 1637. London, 1637.

Mace, Thomas. *Musick's monument; or a remembrancer of the best practical musick, both divine, and civil, that has ever been known, to have been in the world. Divided into three parts. The first part, shews a necessity of singing psalms well, in parochial churches, or not to sing at all; . . . with an assurance of a perpetual national-quire; and also shewing, how cathedral musick, may be much improved, and refined. The second part, treats of the noble lute. . . . In the third part, the generous viol . . . with some curious observations . . . concerning it, and musick in general.* London, 1676.

Marbeck, John. *A booke of notes and common places, with their expositions, collected and gathered out of the workes of divers singular writers, and brought alphabetically into order.* London, 1581.

The maske of flowers. Presented by the gentlemen of Graies-Inne, at the court of White-hall, in the banquetting house upon twelfe night, 1613. Being the last of the solemnities and magnificences which were performed at the marriage of the right honourable the earle of Somerset, and the Lady Francis daughter of the earle of Suffolke, Lord Chamberlaine. London, 1614.

Mason, George, and John Earsden. *The ayres that were sung and played, at Brougham Castle in Westmerland, in the kings entertainment: Given by the right honourable the earle of Cumberland, and his right noble sonne the lord Clifford.* London, 1618.

Maynard, John. *The XII. wonders of the world: set and composed for the violl de gambo, the lute, and the voyce to sing the verse, all three joyntly, and none severall: also lessons for the lute and base violl to play alone: with some lessons to play lyra-wayes alone, or if you will, to fill up the parts, with another violl set lute-way.* London, 1611.

Middleton, Thomas, and William Rowley. *A courtly masque; or the device called, the world tost at tennis.* London, 1620.

Middleton, Thomas. *The Inner-Temple masque. Or masque of heroes.* London, 1619.

Millington, Thomas. *The true narration of the entertainment of his royall majestie, from the time of his departure from Edenbrough; till his receiving at London.* London, 1603.

Morley, Thomas [ed.]. *Canzonets, or little short songs to foure voyces: celected out of the best and approved Italian authors.* London, 1597.

Morley, Thomas. *Canzonets, or little short songs to three voyces.* London, 1593.

Morley, Thomas. *The first booke of balletts to five voyces.* London, 1595.

Morley, Thomas [ed.]. *The first booke of consort lessons, made by divers exquisite authors for six instruments to play together, the treble lute, the pandora, the cittern, the base-violl, the flute & treble-violl. Newly set forth at the coast & charges of a gentleman, for his private pleasure, and for divers others his frendes which delight in musicke.* London, 1599.

Morley, Thomas [ed.]. *Madrigals to five voyces. Celected out of the best approved Italian authors.* London, 1598.

Morley, Thomas. *Madrigals to foure voices published by Thomas Morley. Now newly imprinted with some songs added by the author.* 2nd edn., London, 1600.

Morley, Thomas. *A plaine and easie introduction to practicall musicke, set downe in forme of a dialogue: devided into three partes, the first teacheth to sing with all things necessary for the knowledge of prickt-song. The second treateth of descante and to sing two parts in one upon a plainsong or ground, with other things necessary for a descanter. The third and last part entreateth of composition of three, foure, five or more parts with many profitable rules to that effect. With new songs of, 2. 3. 4. and .5 parts.* London, 1597.

Morley, Thomas [ed.]. *Madrigales. The triumphes of Oriana, to 5. and 6. voices.* London, 1601.

Morley, Thomas. *Il primo libro delle ballette a cinque voci.* London, 1595.

A Mournefull dittie, entituled Elizabeths losse, together with a welcome for King James. London, 1603? [Heber Collection of Elizabethan Ballads].

Munday, Anthony. *A banquet of daintie conceits. Furnished with verie delicate and choyse inventions, to delight their mindes, who take pleasure in musique, and there-withall to sing sweete ditties either to the lute, bandora, virginalles or anie other instrument. Published at the desire of bothe honorable and worshipfull personages, who have had copies of divers of the ditties heerein contained.* London, 1588.

[Munday, Anthony?] *A second and third blast of retrait from plaies and theaters: . . . Set forth by Anglo-phile Eutheo.* London, 1580.

Mundy, John. *Songs and psalmes composed into 3. 4. and 5. parts, for the use and delight of all such as either love or learne musicke.* London, 1594.

Nabbes, Thomas, *Playes, maskes, epigrams, elegies, and epithalamiums. Collected into one volume.* London, 1639.

Naile, Robert. *A relation of the royall, magnificent, and sumptuous entertainement, given to the high, and mighty princesse, Queene Anne, at the renowned citie of Bristoll, by the mayor, sheriffes, and aldermen thereof; in the moneth of June last past, 1613. Together with the oration, gifts, triumphes, water-combats, and other showes there made.* London, 1613.

Nenna, Sir John Baptista. *Nennio, or a treatise of nobility.* London, 1595.

Nixon, Anthony. *Londons dove: or a memoriall of the life and death of Maister Robert Dove, citizen and marchant-taylor of London.* London, 1612.

Northbrooke, John. *Spiritus est vicarius Christi in terra. A treatise wherein dicing, dauncing, vaine plaies or enterludes with other idle pastimes, &c. commonly used on the Sabboth day, are reprooved, by the authoritie of the worde of God and auncient writers. Made dialoguewise.* London, 1579.

Notari, Angelo. *Prime musiche nuove à una, due, et tre voci, per cantare con la tiorba, et altri strumenti, novamente poste in luce.* London, [1613?].

The Organs funerall or the quiristers lamentation for the abolishment of superstition and superstitious ceremonies. In a dialogicall discourse be-

tween a quirister and an organist, An. Dom. 1642. London, 1642 [Thomason Tracts, British Museum].

Ornithoparcus, Andreas. *Andres Ornithoparcus his micrologus, or introduction; containing the art of singing. Digested into foure bookes. Not only profitable, but also necessary for all that are studious of musicke. Also the dimension and perfect use of the monochord, according to Guido Aretinus. By John Douland.* London, 1609.

The Pathway to musicke, contayning sundrie familiar and easie rules for the readie and true understanding of the scale, or gamma-ut: wherein is exactlie shewed by plaine deffinitions, the principles of this arte, brieflie laide open by way of questions and answers, for the better instruction of the learner. Whereunto is annexed a treatise of descant, & certaine tables, which doth teach how to remove any song higher, or lower from one key to another, never heretofore published. London, 1596.

Peacham, Henry. *The compleat gentleman. Fashioning him absolute in the most necessary & commendable qualities concerning minde or bodie that may be required in a noble gentleman.* London, 1622.

Peacham, Henry. *The truth of our times: revealed out of one mans experience, by way of essay.* London, 1638.

Peacham, Henry. *The worth of a peny: or a caution to keep money. With the causes of scarcity and misery of the want hereof in these hard and mercilesse times: And also how to save it in our diet, apparell, recreations, &c. And also what honest courses men in want may take to live.* London, 1641.

Peerson, Martin. *Mottects or grave chamber musique. Containing songs of five parts of severall sorts, some ful, and some verse and chorus. But all fit for voyces and vials, with an organ part; which for want of organs, may be performed on virginals, base-lute, bandora, or Irish harpe. Also, a mourning song of sixe parts for the death of the late right honorable Sir Fulke Grevil, knight of the honourable order of the Bath, Lord Brooke . . . Composed according to the rules of art.* London, 1630.

Peerson, Martin. *Private musicke, or the first booke of ayres and dialogues: contayning songs of 4. 5. and 6. parts, of severall sorts, and being verse and chorus, is fit for voyces and viols. And for want of viols, they may be performed to either the virginall or lute, where the proficient can play upon the ground, or for a shift to the base viol alone.* London, 1620.

Pilkington, Francis. *The first booke of songs or ayres of 4. parts: with tableture for the lute or orpherion, with the violl de gamba.* London, 1605.

Ravenscroft, Thomas. *A breife discourse of the true (but neglected) use of charact'ring the degrees by their perfection, imperfection, and diminution in measurable musicke, against the common practise and custome of these times. Examples whereof are exprest in the harmony of 4. voyces, concerning the pleasure of 5. usuall recreations. 1 hunting, 2 hawking, 3 dauncing 4 drinking 5 enamouring.* London, 1614.

Ravenscroft, Thomas [ed.]. *Deuteromelia; or the second part of musicks melodie, or melodius musicke of pleasant roundelaies; K. H. mirth, or freemens songs. And such delightfull catches. Qui canere potest canat. Catch, that catch can.* London, 1609.

Ravenscroft, Thomas [ed.]. *Melismata. Musicall phansies, fitting the court, citie and countrey humours. To 3. 4. and 5. voyces.* London, 1611.

Ravenscroft, Thomas [ed.]. *Pammelia. Musicks miscellanie, or mixed varietie of pleasant roundelayes, and delightfull catches, of 3. 4. 5. 6. 7. 8. 9. 10. parts in one. None so ordinarie as musicall, none so musical, as not to all, very pleasing and acceptable.* London, 1609.

Robinson, Thomas. *New citharen lessons, with perfect tunings of the same, from foure course of strings to fourteene course, even to trie the sharpest teeth of envie, with lessons of all sortes, and methodicall instructions for all professors and practitioners of the citharen.* London, 1609.

Robinson, Thomas. *The schoole of musicke: wherein is taught, the perfect method of true fingering of the lute, pandora, orpharion and viol de gamba; with most infallible generall rules, both easie and delightfull. Also, a method, how you may be your owne instructer for prick-song, by the help of your lute, without any other teacher: with lessons of all sorts, for your further and better instruction.* London, 1603.

Rosseter, Philip. *A booke of ayres, set foorth to be song to the lute, orpherian, and base violl.* London, 1601.

Rosseter, Philip [ed.]. *Lessons for consort: made by sundry excellent authors, and set to sixe severall instruments: namely, the treble lute, treble violl, base violl, bandora, citterne, and the flute.* London, 1609.

The Royall passage of her majesty from the tower of London, to her palace of White-hall, with all the speaches and devices, both of the pageants and otherwise, together with her majesties severall answers. London, 1604.

[Sandys, Sir Edwin] and Robert Tailour. *Sacred hymns. Consisting of fifti select psalms of David and others, paraphrastically turned into English verse. And by Robert Tailour set to be sung in five parts, as also to the viole, and lute or orph-arion. Published for the use of such as delight in the exercise of musick in hir original honour.* London, 1615.

Segar, W. *Honor military, and civill, contained in foure bookes.* London, 1602.

Slatyer, William. *Psalmes, or songs of sion: turned into the language, and set to the tunes of a strange land. By W. S. intended for Christmas carols, and fitted to divers of the most noted and common, but solemne tunes, every where in this land familiarly used and knowne.* London, before 1635.

A new booke of Tabliture, containing sundrie easie and familiar instructions, shewing howe to attaine to the knowledge, to guide and dispose thy hand to play on sundry instruments, as the lute, orpharion, and bandora: together with divers new lessons to each of these instruments. Whereunto is added an introduction to prickesong, and certaine familiar rules of descant, with other necessarie tables plainely shewing the true use of the scale or gamut, and also how to set any lesson higher or lower at your pleasure. Collected together out of the best authors professing the practise of these instruments. London, 1596.

Tomkins, Thomas. *Songs of 3. 4. 5. and 6. parts.* London, 1622?.

Vautor, Thomas. *The first set: being songs of divers ayres and natures, of five and sixe parts: apt for vyols and voyces.* London, 1619.

Vives, Joannes Ludovicus. *A very frutefull and pleasant boke called the instruction of a Christian woman made fyrst in Laten and dedicated unto the quenes good grace by the right famous clerke mayster Lewes Vives and turned out of Laten into Englysshe by Rycharde Hyrd, whiche bok who so redeth diligently shal have knowlege of many thynges wherin he shal take great pleasure and specially women shall take great commodyte and frute towarde the encrease of vertue & good maners.* London, [2nd edition, 1540?].

Ward, John. *The first set of English madrigals to 3. 4. 5. and 6. parts: apt both for viols and voyces. With a mourning song in memory of Prince Henry.* London, 1613.

Watson, Thomas. *The first sett, of Italian madrigalls Englished, not to the sense of the originall dittie, but after the affection of the noate. There are also heere inserted two excellent madrigalls of Master William Byrds, composed after the Italian vaine, at the request of the sayd Thomas Watson.* London, 1590.

Weelkes, Thomas. *Balletts and madrigals to five voyces, with one to 6. voyces.* London, 1598.

Weelkes, Thomas. *Madrigals of 5. and 6. parts, apt for the viols and voices.* London, 1600.

Weelkes, Thomas. *Madrigals to 3. 4. 5. & 6. voyces.* London, 1597.

Weelkes, Thomas. *Madrigals of 6. parts, apt for the viols and voices.* London, 1600.

Whythorne, Thomas. [*Cantus, bassus,*] *of duos, or songs for two voices composed and made by Thomas Whythorne Gent. Of the which, some be playne and easie to be sung, or played on musicall instruments, & be made for yong beginners of both those sorts. And the rest of these duos be made and set foorth for those that be more perfect in singing or playing as aforesaid, all the which be devided into three parts, that is to say: The first, which doth begin at the first song, are made for a man and a childe to sing, or otherwise for voices or instruments of musicke, that be of the like compasse or distance in sound. The second, which doth begin at the XXIII. song, are made for two children to sing. Also they be aptly made for two treble cornets to play or sound: or otherwise for voices or musicall instruments, that be of the lyke compasse or distance in sound. And the third part which doth begin at the XXXVIII. song, (being all canons of two parts in one) be of divers compasses or distances, and therefore are to be used with voices or instruments of musicke accordingly.* London, 1590.

Wilbye, John. *The first set of English madrigals to 3. 4. 5. and 6. voices.* London, 1598.

Wilbye, John. *The second set of madrigales to 3. 4. 5. and 6. parts, apt both for voyals and voyces.* London, 1609.

W[ilcox], T[homas]. *An exposition uppon the booke of the Canticles, otherwise called Schelomons song. Published for the edification of the church of God.* London, 1585.

Wither, George [and Orlando Gibbons]. *The hymnes and songs of the church; divided into two parts. The first part comprehends the canonicall hymnes.* London, [1623?].

Wright, James. *Historia Histrionica.* London, 1699.

Wright, Nicholas. *A commendation of musicke, and a confutation of them which disprayse it.* London, [1563?].

Yonge, Nicholas [ed.]. *Musica transalpina. Madrigales translated of foure, five and sixe partes, chosen out of divers excellent authors, with the first and second part of La Verginella, made by Maister Byrd, upon two stanza's of Ariosto, and brought to speake English with the rest.* London, 1588.

Yonge, Nicholas. *Musica transalpina. Cantus. [Altus, etc.] The second booke of madrigalles to 5. & 6. voices: translated out of sundrie Italian authors & newly published by Nicolas Yonge.* London, 1597.

Youll, Henry. *Canzonets to three voyces.* London, 1608.

PUBLISHED DOCUMENTS

Aliens. *Letters of Denization and acts of naturalization for aliens in England, 1509-1603,* ed. William Page. Huguenot Society, vol. 8. Lymington, 1893.

Aliens. *Returns of Aliens dwelling in the city and suburbs of London . . . Henry VIII to . . . James I,* ed. R. E. G. Kirk and E. F. Kirk. Huguenot Society, vol. 10. London, 1900-1908.

Anglicanism: the thought and practice of the Church of England, Illustrated from the Religious Literature of the 17th century, ed. Paul Elmer More and Frank L. Cross. Milwaukee, 1935.

Bibliography

Armin, Robert. *A nest of ninnies*, London, 1608. In *Fools and Jesters: with a reprint of Robert Armin's Nest of Ninnies* [ed. J.P.C.], London, 1842.

Ascham, Roger. *The Scholemaster*. London, 1570, ed. Edward Arber. London, 1870.

Ascham, Roger. *Toxophilus*. London, 1545, ed. Edward Arber. London, 1869.

Bacon, *Annalls of Ipswiche*, see Ipswich.

Barnstaple Records, Reprint of the, ed. J. R. Chanter and Thomas Wainwright. Barnstaple, 1900.

Beaumont and Fletcher, Songs and Lyrics from the Plays of, ed. Hugh McDonald, with contemporary musical settings ed. E. H. Fellowes. London, 1928.

Beverley Borough Records, 1575-1821, ed. J. Dennett. Yorkshire Archaeological Society, Record Series, vol. 84. Wakefield, 1933.

Braithwaite, Richard. "Some rules and orders for the government of the house of an earle," in *Miscellanea Antiqua Anglicana*, ed. Robert Triphook, i, i. London, 1816.

Brereton, Sir William. *Journal, 1635*, ed. J.C. Hodgson. Surtees Society, vol. 124. London, 1915.

Bristol: *The Annals of Bristol in the Seventeenth Century*, ed. John Latimer. Bristol, 1900.

Calendar: see *State Papers*.

Cambridge, Annals of, ed. C. H. Cooper. Cambridge, 1842-1908.

Cambridge Borough Documents, ed. W. M. Palmer. vol. 1. Cambridge, 1931.

Canterbury, Ancient. The records of Alderman Bunce. Republished from the *Kentish Gazette*, 1800-1801. Canterbury, 1924.

Carlisle, Some municipal records of the city of, ed. R. S. Furguson and W. Nanson. Cumberland and Westmorland Antiquarian and Archaeological Society. Extra Series, vol. 4. Carlisle, 1887.

Casa, Giovanni della. *A renaissance Courtesy-Book/ Galateo of Manners & Behaviours*, ed. J. E. Spingarn. Boston, 1914.

Castiglione, Baldassare. *The Book of the Courtier from the Italian of Count Baldassare Castiglione done into English by Sir Thomas Hoby anno 1561*, ed. Walter Raleigh. London, 1900.

Chamberlain, John, The Letters of, ed. N. E. McClure. American Philosophical Society, *Memoirs* xii, pts. i, ii. Philadelphia, 1939.

Chapel Royal. *The Old Cheque-Book, or Book of Remembrance of the Chapel Royal*, ed. E. F. Rimbault. Camden Society, 2d Series, vol. 3. London, 1872.

Chapel Royal: Harold N. Hillebrand, "The Early History of the Chapel Royal," in *Modern Philology*, xviii (1921), 233-268.

Chester: *Quarter Sessions Records with Other Records of the Justices of the Peace for the County Palatine of Chester, 1559-1760*, ed. J. H. E. Bennett and J. C. Dewhurst. Record Society for the publication of original documents relating to Lancashire and Cheshire, vol. 94. Chester, 1940.

Cholmley, Sir Hugh. *Memoirs of Sir Hugh Cholmley addressed to his two sons.* London, 1787.

Cleland, James. *The Institution of a young noble man.* Oxford, 1607. Scholars' Facsimiles and Reprints: Vol. 1, Introduction and text; introduction by Max Molyneux. New York, 1948.

Clifford, Anne. *The Diary of the Lady Anne Clifford,* ed. V. Sackville-West. London, 1923.

Commons Debates 1621, ed. W. Notestein, F. H. Relf, H. Simpson. New Haven, 1935.

Commons. *Debates in the House of Commons in 1625,* ed. S. R. Gardiner. Camden Society, 2d Series, vol. 6. London, 1873.

Commons Debates for 1629, ed. W. Notestein and F. H. Relf. Minneapolis, 1921.

Commons. *Journals of the House of Commons,* 1547ff.

Coventry Leet Book: or Mayor's Register, containing the records of the City Court Leet or View of Frank pledge, A.D. 1420-1555, ed. M. D. Harris. *Early English Text Society,* vols. 134, 135, 138, 146. London, 1907-1913.

Coventry. *Two Coventry Corpus Christi Plays,* ed. Hardin Craig. *Early English Text Society,* vol. 87. London, 1901.

Cranmer, Thomas. *The Remains of Thomas Cranmer, D.D. Archbishop of Canterbury,* ed. Henry Jenkyns. Oxford, 1833.

Derby. *Household Books of Edward and Henry, Earls of Derby,* ed. F. R. Raines. Chetham Society, vol. 31. Manchester, 1853.

Desiderata Curiosa: or, a collection of divers scarce and curious pieces relating chiefly to matters of English history, ed. Francis Peck. London, 1732.

Devereux Papers, Richard Broughton's, 1575-1601, ed. H. E. Maldon. Camden Society, *Miscellany,* vol. 13. London, 1924.

D'Ewes, Simonds. *The Journal of Sir Simonds D'Ewes from the beginning of the Long Parliament to the opening of the trial of the earl of Strafford,* ed. W. Notestein. New Haven, 1923.

Dramatic Companies: *John T. Murray, English dramatic companies 1558-1642.* London, 1910.

Durham. *The Statutes of the Cathedral Church of Durham, with other documents relating to its foundation and endowment by King Henry the Eighth and Queen Mary,* ed. A. H. Thompson. Surtees Society, vol. 143. London, 1929.

Elizabeth. *Household Expenses of the Princess Elizabeth during her residence at Hatfield, Oct. 1, 1551 to Sept. 30, 1552,* ed. P. C. S. Smythe, Viscount Strangford. Camden Society, *Miscellany,* vol. 2. London, 1853.

Bibliography

Elizabeth of York. *Privy Purse Expenses of Elizabeth of York* [and] *Wardrobe accounts of Edward the Fourth*, ed. N. H. Nicolas. London, 1830.

England as Seen by Foreigners in the Days of Elizabeth and James the First. Comprising translations of the journals of the two dukes of Wirtemberg in 1592 and 1610; both illustrative of Shakespeare, ed. William B. Rye. London, 1865.

English Madrigal School, ed. E. H. Fellowes. London, 1913-1924.

English School of Lutenist Song Writers, ed. E. H. Fellowes. London, 1920ff.

Exchequer: *Issues of the Exchequer; being payments made out of His Majesty's revenue during the reign of King James I*, ed. Frederick Devon. London, 1836.

Fairfax. "Inventories Made for Sir William and Sir Thomas Fairfax, Knights, of Walton, and of Gilling Castle, Yorkshire, in the Sixteenth and Seventeenth Centuries," ed. Edward Peacock, in *Archaelogia*, vol. 48, i (1884), 121-126.

Foedera, Conventiones, litterae et cujuscunque generis acta publica inter reges Angliae et alios quosvis imperatores, reges, pontifices, principes, vel communitates, ed. Thomas Rymer and George Holmes. 3d edn., The Hague, 1739-1745.

Fortescue Papers, ed. S. R. Gardiner. Camden Society, 2d Series, vol. 1. London, 1871.

Gawdy. *Letters of Philip Gawdy of West Harling, Norfolk, and of London to various members of his family, 1579-1616*, ed. Isaac H. Jeayes. London, 1906.

Gilbert, Sir Humphrey. "Queene Elizabethes Achademy" in *Early English Treatises and Poems on Education, Precedence and Manners in Olden Time*, ed. F. J. Furnivall and others. Early English Text Society, Extra Series, vol. 8, pp. 1-12. London, 1869.

Goodman, Godfrey. *The court of James the First*, ed. J. S. Brewer. London, 1839.

Hammond. *A Relation of a Short Survey of Twenty-six Counties observed in a seven weeks journey begun on August 11, 1634 by a captain, a lieutenant, and an ancient. All three of the military company in Norwich*, ed. L. G. Wickham Legg. London, 1904.

Hammond. *A Relation of a Short Survey of the western counties made by a lieutenant of the military company in Norwich in 1635*, ed. L. G. Wickham Legg. Camden Society, *Miscellany*, vol. 16. London, 1936.

Hardy, Sir Thomas Duffus. *Syllabus (in English) of the Documents Relating to England and Other Kingdoms Contained in the Collection Known as "Rymer's Foedera."* London, 1869-1885.

Harrison, William. *An historicall description of the iland of Britaine.* London, 1577, 1587, in Raphael Holinshed, *Chronicles of England, Scotland, and Ireland*, ed. Henry Ellis, London, 1807-1808.

Bibliography

Hayward, Sir John. *Annals of the First Four Years of the Reign of Queen Elizabeth*, ed. John Bruce. Camden Society, vol. 7, 1840.

Henry VIII. *Calendar of Letters and Papers of the Reign of Henry VIII, preserved in the Public Record Office, the British Museum, and elsewhere in England*, ed. J. S. Brewer and others. London, 1862ff.

Henry VIII. *The Privy Purse Expences of King Henry the Eighth from November MDXXIX to December MDXXXII*, ed. Nicholas H. Nicolas. London, 1827.

Herbert. Edward Lord Herbert of Cherbury. *Autobiography*, ed. Sidney Lee, 2d edn., London, 1906.

Hertford County Records. Notes and extracts from the sessions rolls 1581 to 1698, ed. W. J. Hardy, vol. 1. Hertford, 1905.

Hertford. "Private Purse Accounts of the Marquis of Hertford, Michaelmas 1641-2," ed. F. C. Morgan, in *The Antiquaries Journal*, vol. 25 (1945), 12-42.

Hillebrand: see Chapel Royal.

Historical Manuscripts Commission, *Reports*. London, 1870ff.

Listed alphabetically by name of owner of manuscripts at time reports were made. If the volume is not known by the name of the owner, a short title is then given. The date is year of publication of the report, and the number in square brackets refers to the numbering system suggested by the commission in its *Guide to the Reports, part one, Topographical*, pp. 1-14; these numbers are those used in footnotes throughout the present volume (e.g. HMC 24). The least useful volumes are omitted here.

Alexander, W. Cleverly, in *Various Collections*, III, 259-264 (1904) [55, iii].

Ancaster, earl of. Thirteenth report, app. vi, 203-261 (1893) [32].

Ancaster, earl of. (1907) [66].

Bath, marquis of. (1904-1908) [58, i-iii].

Beccles, Suffolk, corporation of. *Various Collections*, VII, 70-79 (1914) [55, vii].

Bertie: see Ancaster.

Beverley, Yorkshire, corporation of. (1900) [54].

Braye, Lord. Tenth report, app. vi, 104-252 (1887) [15].

Bridgewater Trust Office, Walkden, Lancashire, Mss. at the. Eleventh report, app. vii, 126-167 (1888) [22].

Bridgnorth, corporation of. Tenth report, app. iv, 424-437 (1885) [13].

Buccleuch and Queensberry, duke of. (1899-1926) [45, i-iii].

Burford, Oxfordshire, corporation of. *Various Collections*, I, 29-64 (1901) [55, i].

Canterbury, corporation of. Ninth report, app. i, 129-177 (1883) [8, i].

Canterbury, dean and chapter of. Ninth report, app. i, 72-129 (1883) [8, i].

Carlisle, corporation of. Ninth report, app. i, 197-203 (1883) [8, i].

Cheddar, Somersetshire, parish of. Third report, app., 329-331 (1872) [2].

Chester, corporation of. Eighth report, app., 355-403 (1881) [7].

Cholmondeley, Reginald. Fifth report, app., 333-360 (1876) [4].

Coventry, corporation of. Fifteenth report, app. x, 101-160 (1899) [47].

Cowper, Earl. Twelfth report, app. i-iii (1888-1889) [23, i-iii].

Davenport, W. Bromley. Second report, app., 78-81 (1871) [1].

Downshire, marquess of. (1924-1940) [75, i-iv].

Dudley: see Isle.

Dunwich, Suffolk, late corporation of. *Various Collections*, vii, 80-113 (1914) [55, vii].

Essex, custos rotulorum and justices of the peace of the county. Tenth report, app. iv, 466-513 (1885) [13].

Exeter, city of. (1916) [73].

Faversham, Kent, corporation of. Sixth report, app., 500-511 (1877) [5].

Frere, George Edward. Seventh report, app., 518-537 (1879) [6].

Gell, Henry Chandos-Pole-. Ninth report, app. ii, 384-403 (1884) [8, ii].

Gloucester, corporation of. Twelfth report, app. ix, 400-529 (1891) [27].

Gloucester, diocese of. *Various Collections*, vii, 44-69 (1914) [55, vii].

Graham, Sir Frederick U. Sixth report, app., 319-322 (1877) [5].

Gurney, John Henry. Twelfth report, app. ix, 116-164 (1891) [27].

Hastings, Reginald Rawdon. (1928-1934) [78].

Hereford, corporation of. Thirteenth report, app. iv, 283-353 (1892) [31].

Hood, Sir Alexander Acland-. Sixth report, app., 344-352 (1877) [5].

Hopkinson, Francis. Third report, app., 261-267 (1872) [2].

Ipswich, corporation of. Ninth report, app. i, 222-262 (1883) [8, i].

Isle, Lord de l'Isle and Dudley. Third report, app., 227-233 (1872) [2].

Isle, Lord de l'Isle and Dudley (1925-1934) [77, i-ii].

Jervoise, F. H. T. *Various Collections*, iv, 140-174 (1907) [55, iv].

Kenyon, Lord. Fourteenth report, app. iv (1894) [35].

Kilmorey, earl of. Tenth report, app. iv, 358-374 (1885) [13].

Laud, Archbishop William, papers relating to his visitations, 1634. In report on the manuscripts of the House of Lords. Fourth report, app., 124-159 (1874) [3].

Leconfield, Lord. Sixth report, app., 287-319 (1877) [5].

Leicester, corporation of. Eighth report, app., 403-441 (1881) [7].

Lincoln, corporation of. Fourteenth report, app. viii, 1-120 (1895) [37].

Lloyd, S. Zachary. Tenth report, app. iv, 444-450 (1885) [13].

Lords, House of. Fourth report, app. i, 1-170 (1874) [3].

Magdalene college, Cambridge. Fifth report, app., 481-484 (1876) [4].

Mar and Kellie, earl of. (1930) [60, ii].

Middleton, Lord. (1911) [69].

Molyneux, William More. Seventh report, app., 596-681 (1879) [6].

Montagu of Beaulieu, Lord. (1900) [53].

Northumberland, duke of. Sixth report, app., 221-233 (1877) [5].

Pepys Manuscripts preserved at Magdalene college, Cambridge (1911) [70].

Plymouth, corporation of. Ninth report, app. i, 262-285 (1883) [8, i].

Plymouth, corporation of. Tenth report, app. iv, 536-560 (1885) [13].

Portland, duke of. (1894) [29, iii].

Rutland, duke of. Twelfth report, app. iv (1888) [24, i].

Rutland, duke of. (1905) [24, iv].

Rye, corporation of. Fifth report, app., 488-516 (1876) [4].

Rye, corporation of. Thirteenth report, app. iv, 1-246 (1892) [31].

Salisbury, corporation of. *Various Collections*, iv, 191-254 (1907) [55, iv].

Salisbury, dean and chapter of. *Various Collections*, i, 338-388 (1901) [55, i].

Salisbury, marquess of. (1883ff.) [9].

Savile, Augustus William. Eleventh report, app. vii, 119-126 (1888) [22].

Shrewsbury, corporation of. Fifteenth report, app. x, 1-65 (1899) [47].

Southampton, corporation of. Eleventh report, app. iii, 1-144 (1887) [18].

Stewart, Captain James. Tenth report, app. iv, 59-146 (1885) [13].

Tabley, Lord de. First report, app. 46-50 (1870) [1].

Thetford, Norfolk, corporation of. *Various Collections*, vii, 119-152 (1914) [55, vii].

Thornhill, Tresham papers of T. B. Clarke-. *Various Collections*, iii, 1-154 (1904) [55, iii].

Townshend, Marquess. Eleventh report, app. iv (1888) [19].

Verulam, earl of. (1906) [64].

Wadham college, Oxford. Fifth report, app., 479-481 (1876) [4].

Warr, Earl de la. Fourth report, app., 276-317 (1874) [3].

Wells, dean and chapter of. Tenth report, app. iii (1885) [12].

Willoughby of Wollaton: see Middleton.

Wiltshire, Records of quarter sessions. *Various Collections*, i, 67-176 (1901) [55, i].

Wombwell, Sir George. *Various Collections*, ii, 1-226 (1903) [55, ii].

Worcester, Records of the county of. *Various Collections*, i, 282-326 (1901) [55, i].

Yarmouth, corporation of Great. Ninth report, app. i, 299-324 (1883) [8, i].

Hoby, Lady Margaret. *Diary (1599-1605)*, ed. Dorothy M. Meads. London, 1930.

Bibliography

Holles, Gervase. *Memorials of the Holles Family 1493-1656*, ed. A. C. Wood. Camden Society, 3d Series, vol. 55. London, 1937.

Household: *A collection of ordinances and regulations for the government of the royal household . . . Edward III to William and Mary.* Society of Antiquaries, London, 1790.

Howard. *Selections from the household books of Lord William Howard of Naworth castle,* ed. George Ornsby. Surtees Society, vol. 68. London, 1878.

Ipswich: *The Annalls of Ipswiche,* ed. Nathaniell Bacon, 1654. Ed. William H. Richardson, Ipswich, 1884.

King's Musick. A transcript of records relating to music and musicians 1460-1700, ed. Henry Cart de Lafontaine. London, 1909.

King's Musick: *Annalen der englischen hofmusik von der zeit Heinrichs VIII. bis zum tode Karls I,* ed. Wilibald Nagel. *Supplement to Monatsheften für Musikgeschichte, XXVI.* Leipzig, 1894.

King's Musick: "Lists of the King's Musicians," *Musical Antiquary,* IV (1913), 55-58, 178-183.

King's Musick: "Lists of the King's Musicians from the Audit Office declared accounts," *Musical Antiquary,* I (1910), 56-61, 119-124, 182-187, 249-253, II (1911), 51-55, 114-118, 174-178, 235-240, III (1912), 54-58, 110-115, 171-176, 229-234.

Lancashire Quarter Sessions Records, vol. 1, ed. James Tait. Chetham Society, New Series, vol. 77. Manchester, 1917.

Leicester: William Kelly, *Notices illustrative of the drama, and other popular amusements . . . extracted from the chamberlains' accounts . . . of Leicester.* London, 1865.

Leicester: *Records of the borough of Leicester . . . 1103-1603,* ed. Mary Bateson; *1603-1688,* ed. Helen Stocks and W. H. Stevenson. London, 1899, 1901; Cambridge, 1905, 1923.

Leicester: *Register of the Freemen of Leicester, 1196-1770,* ed. Henry Hartopp. Leicester, 1927.

Leicester: Inventory of the goods of Robert Dudley, earl of Leicester, 1588-1590, ed. C. L. Kingsford, *Archaeologia,* LXXIII (1923), 28-51.

Lincoln: *Episcopal records in the time of Thomas Cooper,* ed. C. W. Foster. Lincoln Record Society, vol. 2. Lincoln, 1912.

Lincoln: *The state of the church in the reigns of Elizabeth and James I as illustrated by documents relating to the diocese of Lincoln.* Vol. 1, ed. C. W. Foster. Lincoln Record Society, vol. 23. Lincoln, 1926.

Liverpool Town Books. Proceedings of the assemblies 1550-1862, ed. J. A. Twemlow. Liverpool, 1918, 1935.

London: *Analytical index to the series of records known as the remembrancia. Preserved among the archives of the city of London. A.D. 1579-1664,* ed. W. H. and H. C. Overall. London, 1878.

Bibliography

London: *Register of the Freemen of the City of London in the Reigns of Henry VIII and Edward VI*, ed. Charles Welch. London, 1908.

Machyn, Henry. *The Diary of Henry Machyn, Citizen and Merchant-Taylor of London from A.D. 1550 to A.D. 1563*, ed. John G. Nichols. Camden Society, vol. 42. London, 1848.

Maisse, André Hurault de. *A Journal of all that was Accomplished by Monsieur de Maisse, Ambassador in England from Henry IV to Queen Elizabeth Anno Domini 1597*, translated and ed. G. B. Harrison and R. A. Jones. London, 1931.

Manchester: *The court leet records of the manor of Manchester from the year 1552 to the year 1686 . . .*, ed. J. P. Earwaker. Manchester, 1884ff.

Manningham. *Diary of John Manningham of the Middle Temple, and of Bradbourne, Kent, barrister-at-law. 1602-1603*, ed. John Bruce. Camden Society, vol. 91. London, 1868.

Mary. *Privy Purse Expenses of the Princess Mary, daughter of King Henry the Eighth, afterwards Queen Mary*, ed. Frederick Madden. London, 1831.

Melville, Sir James. *Memoirs*, ed. A. F. Steuart. London, 1929.

Mercers: *Acts of Court of the Mercers' Company 1453-1527*, ed. Laetitia Lyell and Frank D. Watney. Cambridge, 1936.

Merchant Adventurers: *Extracts from the records of the Merchant Adventurers of Newcastle-upon-Tyne*, ed. F. W. Dendy. Surtees Society, vols. 93, 101. London, 1895, 1899.

Merchant Taylors: *Memorials of the Guild of Merchant Taylors of the fraternity of St. John*, ed. Charles M. Clode. London, 1875.

Middlesex County Records, ed. John C. Jeaffreson. Middlesex County Records Society, vols. 1-3. London, 1886-1888.

Middlesex: *County of Middlesex Calendar to the sessions records*, ed. William Le Hardy. New Series. London, 1935ff.

Mulcaster, Richard. *Elementarie*. London, 1582. Ed. E. T. Campagnac. Oxford, 1925.

Mulcaster, Richard. *Positions*. London, 1581. Ed. Robert H. Quick. London, 1888.

Musicians. *Handbook of the Worshipful Company of Musicians* [preface by Clifford B. Edgar]. 3d edn., London, 1915.

Musicians. City of London Livery Companies' Commission, *Report and Appendix*. Vol. 3. London, 1884. (Parliament, Sessional papers; *Reports from Commissioners*, vol. 39, part 3. 1884.)
[On pp. 593-599, report on Musicians' Company of London prints 1604 charter, and bylaws, but with some inaccuracy. Refers to second report of Commission on Municipal Corporations, Sessional Papers, 1837, vol. 25, pp. 241-242. This report throws a little light on the condition of the company in the 1830s, but not much on the earlier period.]

Newcastle, Margaret, duchess of. *The life of the duke of Newcastle*. Everyman's Library, London, 1916.

"Northumberland Household Book" in *Antiquarian Repertory*, ed. Thomas Percy, IV, 9-344. London, 1810.

Norwich, The records of the city of, ed. William Hudson and John C. Tingey. Norwich, 1906, 1910.

Nottingham, Records of the borough of, ed. W. H. Stevenson, James Raine, W. T. Baker. London, 1882ff.

Oxford council acts, 1583-1626; 1626-1665, ed. H. E. Salter; H. E. Salter and M. G. Hobson. Oxford Historical Society, vol. 87, 95. Oxford, 1928, 1933.

Oxford: *Selections from the records of the city of Oxford . . . from Henry VIII to Elizabeth*, ed. William H. Turner. Oxford, 1880.

Oxford: *Reminiscences of Oxford by Oxford Men, 1559-1850*, ed. Lilian M. Quiller Couch. Oxford Historical Society, vol. 22. Oxford, 1892.

Oxinden Letters. Being the correspondence of Henry Oxinden of Barham and his circle, ed. Dorothy Gardiner. London, 1933.

Patent Rolls: *Calendar of Patent Rolls preserved in the Public Record Office*, vol. 5 (1446-1509) and following volumes. London, 1909ff.

Peeris, William. *The Musicall Proverbis in the Garet at the New Lodge in the Parke of Lekingfelde*, ed. Philip Wilson. London, 1924.

Percy, Henry, Ninth earl of Northumberland. *Advice to his Son*, ed. G. B. Harrison. London, 1930.

Perlin, Stephen. "Description of England and Scotland by a French Ecclesiastic in the Sixteenth Century" in *Antiquarian Repertory*, ed. Thomas Percy, IV, 501-520. London, 1810.

Pett, Phineas. *Autobiography*, ed. W. G. Perrin. Navy Records Society, London, 1918.

Puttenham, George. *The Arte of English Poesie*, ed. Gladys D. Willcock and Alice Walker. Cambridge, 1936.

Reading. *Diary of the Corporation of Reading (1431-1654)*, ed. J. M. Guilding. London, 1892-1896.

Salford: *The portmote or court leet records of the borough or town and royal manor of Salford from the year 1597 to the year 1669 inclusive*, ed. J. G. de T. Mandley. Chetham Society, New Series, vols. 46, 48. Manchester, 1902.

Serre: "History of the Entry of Mary de Medicis, the Queen Mother of France, into England, anno 1638. Translated from the French of the Sieur de la Serre, Historiographer of France, published anno 1639," in *Antiquarian Repertory*, ed. Thomas Percy, IV, 520-548. London, 1810.

Sheffield, The Records of the Burgery of, ed. John D. Leader. London, 1897.

Sidney: *Sidneiana: being a collection of fragments relative to Sir Philip Sidney Knt. and his immediate connections*, ed. S. Lichfield. London, 1837.

Bibliography

Skinners: *Records of the Skinners of London. Edward I to James I*, ed. John J. Lambert. London, 1934.

Somerset, Quarter session records for the county of, ed. E. H. Bates Harbin. Somerset Record Society. London, 1907-1912.

Southampton: *The assembly books of Southampton, 1602-16*, ed. J. W. Horrocks. Southampton Record Society. Southampton, 1917-1925.

Staffordshire quarter sessions rolls, ed. S. A. H. Burne, William Salt. Archaeological Society. Kendal, 1931-1940.

State Papers: *Calendar of Letters and State Papers relating to English affairs . . . Simancas*, vol. 4 (1587-1603). London, 1899.

State Papers: *Calendar of State Papers, Domestic Series* [1547-1641]. London, 1856ff.

State Papers: *Calendar of State Papers and Manuscripts Relating to English Affairs . . . Venice*. London, 1864ff.

Stationers: *Records of the Court of the Stationers' Company 1576 to 1602 from Register B*, ed. W. W. Greg and E. Boswell. Bibliographical Society, London, 1930.

Statutes of the Realm, ed. A. Luders, T. E. Tomlins, J. Raithby and others. London, 1810-1828.

Stow, John. *A Survey of London*, London, 1603. Ed. Charles L. Kingsford. Oxford, 1908.

Stubbes, Phillip. *The Anatomie of Abuses: contayning a discoverie, or briefe summarie, of such notable vices . . .*, London, 1583. Ed. J. P. C. London, 1870.

Tudor and Stuart Proclamations 1485-1714, ed. Robert Steele and the earl of Crawford. Oxford, 1910.

Tudor Economic Documents being select documents illustrating the economic and social history of Tudor England, ed. R. H. Tawney and Eileen Power. London, 1924.

Visitation Articles and Injunctions of the Period of the Reformation, ed. Walter H. Frere. Alcuin Club, vols. 14-16. London, 1910.

Visitation Articles and Injunctions, 1575-1582, 1583-1603, ed. W. P. M. Kennedy, pts. ii and iii of: W. P. M. Kennedy, *Elizabethan Episcopal Administration. An essay in sociology and politics*. Alcuin Club, vols. 25, 27. London, 1924.

Visitation articles: see HMC, Laud.

Walton, Izaak. *The lives of John Donne, Sir Henry Wotton, Richard Hooker, George Herbert and Robert Sanderson*. The World's Classics, Oxford, 1927.

Wills and inventories illustrative of the history, manners . . . of the northern counties of England from the eleventh century downwards. Part I, ed. James Raine. Surtees Society, vol. 2. London, 1835.

Winchester: *The Statutes Governing the Cathedral Church of Winchester*

Given by King Charles I, ed. Arthur W. Goodman and William H. Hutton. Oxford, 1925.

York Civic Records, ed. Angelo Raine. Yorkshire Archaeological Society, Record Series, vols. 98, 103, 106, 108, 110, 112, 115. Wakefield, York, London, 1939-1950.

York Plays. The plays performed by the crafts or mysteries of York on the day of Corpus Christi in the 14th, 15th, and 16th centuries, ed. Lucy Toulmin Smith. Oxford, 1885.

York. *Register of the Freemen of the City of York from the City Records*, ed. Francis Collins. Surtees Society, vols. 96, 102. Durham, 1897, 1899.

York: *Tudor parish documents of the diocese of York*, ed. J. S. Purvis. Cambridge, 1948.

Yorkshire: *Quarter Sessions Records*, ed. J. C. Atkinson. North Riding Record Society, vols. 1-4. London, 1884-1886.

Yorkshire: *Records of a Yorkshire Manor*, ed. Sir T. Lawson-Tancred. London, 1937.

WORKS WRITTEN AND PRINTED AFTER 1700

Abraham, Gerald. *A hundred years of music*. London, 1938.

Allen, Edward Heron-. *De Fidiculis bibliographia: being an attempt towards a bibliography of the violin and all other instruments played with a bow in ancient and modern times*. London, 1890-1894.

Anderton, H. Orsmond. *Early English Music*. London, 1920.

Andrews, Hilda. "Elizabethan keyboard music: my Ladye Nevells book 1591," *Musical Quarterly*, XVI (1930), 59-71.

Anthon, Carl. "Some aspects of the social status of Italian musicians during the sixteenth century," *Journal of renaissance and baroque music*, I (1946), 111-123, 222-234.

Apel, Willi. *Harvard dictionary of music*. Cambridge, Massachusetts, 1944.

Arkwright, G. E. P. "Elizabethan choirboy plays and their music," *Proceedings of the Musical Association*, 40th session (1914), 117-138.

Arkwright, G. E. P. "An English pupil of Monteverdi," *Musical Antiquary*, IV (1913), 236-257.

Arkwright, G. E. P. "Note on the instrumental accompaniment of church music in the sixteenth and early seventeenth centuries," in John Milton, *Six Anthems*, ed. Arkwright. *Old English Edition*, No. 12. London, 1900, 13-21.

Arkwright, G. E. P. "Notes on the Ferrabosco family," *Musical Antiquary*, III (1912), 220-228, IV (1913), 42-54.

A[rkwright], G. E. P. "Notes on the parish registers of St. Helen's, Bishopsgate, London," *Musical Antiquary*, I (1910), 41-44.

Atkins, Sir Ivor A. *The early occupants of the office of organist and master of the choristers of the Cathedral Church of Christ and the Blessed Virgin Mary, Worcester.* London, 1918.

Aydelotte, Frank. *Elizabethan rogues and vagabonds.* Oxford, 1913.

Baldwin, Thomas Whitfield. *The organization and personnel of the Shakespearean company.* Princeton, 1927.

Bannister, Arthur Thomas. *The Cathedral Church of Hereford. Its history and constitution.* London, 1924.

Barker, Ernest, ed. *The character of England.* Oxford, 1947.

Barrett, William A. *English church composers.* London, 1894.

Barrett, William A. "Music in cathedrals," *Proceedings of the Musical Association,* 3d session (1877), 84-98.

Bennet, E. K. "Notes from a Norfolk squire's notebook," *Communications, Cambridge Antiquarian Society,* v (1884), 201-224.

Bent, J. Theodore. "Master Dallam's mission," *The Antiquary,* xviii (1888), 5-10, 55-59.

Bentley, Gerald E. *The Jacobean and Caroline stage.* Oxford, 1941.

Bessaraboff, Nicholas. *Ancient European Musical Instruments: an organological study of the instruments in . . . the Museum of Fine Arts, Boston.* Cambridge, Massachusetts, 1941.

Birch, Thomas. *The life of Henry Prince of Wales, eldest son of King James I. Compiled chiefly from his own papers, and other manuscripts, never before published.* London, 1760.

Blom, Eric. Review of Paul H. Lang, "Music in western civilization," in *Music and Letters,* xxiv (1943), 54-59.

Boas, Frederick S. *Christopher Marlowe.* Oxford, 1940.

Boas, Frederick S. *Shakespeare and the universities.* Oxford, 1923.

Bontoux, Germaine. *La chanson en Angleterre au temps d'Elisabeth.* London, 1936.

Boyd, Morrison. *Elizabethan music and musical criticism.* Philadelphia, 1940.

Brenet, Michel. "Deux comptes de la Chapelle-musique des rois de France," *Sammelbände der internationalen musikgesellschaft,* vi (1905), 1-31.

Brennecke, Ernest, Jr. "A day at Christ Church, 1573," *Music and Letters,* xix (1938), 22-35.

Brennecke, Ernest, Jr. *John Milton the elder and his music.* New York, 1938.

Bridge, Sir Frederick. "A seventeenth century view of musical education," *Proceedings of the Musical Association,* 27th session (1901), 121-130.

Bridge, Sir Frederick. *Shakespearean music in the plays and early operas.* London, 1923.

Bridge, Joseph C. "The Chester 'Recorders,'" *Proceedings of the Musical Association,* 27th session (1901), 109-120.

Bridge, Joseph C. "Town waits and their tunes," *Proceedings of the Musical Association,* 54th session (1928), 63-92.

Bridges, Robert. "English Chanting," *Musical Antiquary,* ii (1911), 125-141.

Bibliography

Brown, Cornelius. *A history of Newark on Trent*. Newark, 1907.

Brown, John Howard. *Elizabethan schooldays. An account of the English grammar schools in the second half of the sixteenth century*. Oxford, 1933.

Bukofzer, Manfred F. *Music in the baroque era from Monteverdi to Bach*. New York, 1947.

Bumpus, John S. *A history of English cathedral music 1549-1889*. London, 1910(?).

Bumpus, John S. *The organists and composers of St. Paul's Cathedral*. London, 1891.

Burgon, John W. *The life and times of Sir Thomas Gresham*. London, 1839.

Burney, Charles. *A general history of music from the earliest ages to the present period*. London, 1776-1789.

Burtt, Joseph. "On the archives of Rochester," *Archaeologia Cantiana*, VI (1866), 111-112.

Byrne, Muriel St. C. *Elizabethan life in town and country*. 2d edition, London, 1934.

Byrne, Muriel St. C. and Gladys Scott Thomson. *"My Lords's Books." The library of Francis, second earl of Bedford in 1584*. London, 1931(?).

Chambers, E. K. *The Elizabethan stage*. Oxford, 1923.

Chambers, E. K. *The mediaeval stage*. Oxford, 1903.

Chambers, E. K. *Sir Henry Lee. An Elizabethan Portrait*. Oxford, 1936.

Chambers, E. K. *William Shakespeare*. Oxford, 1930.

"A chapel royal anthem book of 1635," *Musical Antiquary*, II (1911), 108-113.

Chappell, William. *Old English popular music. A new edition . . .* , ed. H. Ellis Wooldridge. London, 1893.

Christie, James. *Parish clerks. Some account of parish clerks . . . of the ancient fraternity . . . of S. Nicholas*. London, 1893.

Clode, Charles M. *The early history of the guild of Merchant Taylors . . . London*. London, 1888.

Colles, H. C. "Some musical instruction books of the seventeenth century," *Proceedings of the Musical Association*, 55th session (1929), 31-50.

Corner, G. R. Talk on a contract for making a pair of organs for the church of Allhallows, Barking, 1519, reported in *Proceedings of the evening meetings of the London and Middlesex and Surrey Archaeological Societies*, 1862, pp. 86-91.

Cowling, G. H. *Music on the Shakespearian Stage*. Cambridge, 1913.

Cummings, W. H. "Organ accompaniments in England in the sixteenth and seventeenth centuries," *Proceedings of the Musical Association*, 26th session (1900), 193-211.

Dart, R. Thurston. "Morley's consort lessons of 1599," *Proceedings of the Musical Association*, 74th session (1948), 1-9.

Davey, Henry. *History of English Music*. 2d edition, London, 1921.

Bibliography

Dent, Edward J. *Foundations of English Opera.* Cambridge, 1928.

Dent, Edward J. "The Laudi Spirituali in the 16th and 17th centuries," *Proceedings of the Musical Association,* 43d session (1917), 63-95.

Dickinson, Edward. *Music in the history of the western church.* New York, 1903.

Dickson, W. E. *A catalogue of ancient choral services and anthems preserved among the manuscript scores and part-books in the cathedral church of Ely.* Cambridge, 1861.

Dietz, Frederick C. *English public finance, 1558-1641.* New York, 1932.

Dixon, Richard W. *History of the Church of England, from the abolition of the Roman jurisdiction.* Oxford, 1895-1903.

Dodge, Janet. "Lute music of the XVIth and XVIIth centuries," *Proceedings of the Musical Association,* 34th session (1908), 123-153.

Dolmetsch, Arnold. *Interpretation of the music of the XVIIth and XVIIIth centuries revealed by contemporary evidence.* London, 1915.

"Robert Douland's Musicall Banquet, 1610," *Musical Antiquary,* i (1910), 45-55.

Dowling, Margaret. "The printing of John Dowland's *Second booke of songs or ayres,*" *The Library,* 4th series, xii (1932), 365-380.

Dunlop, Olive Jocelyn. *English apprenticeship and child labour. A history.* London, 1912.

Dunlop, Olive Jocelyn. "Some aspects of early English apprenticeship," *Transactions of the Royal Historical Society,* 3d series, v (1911), 193-208.

"Early Elizabethan stage music," *Musical Antiquary,* i (1910), 30-40.

E., F. G. "A famous choir school. St. George's Chapel, Windsor," *Musical Times,* xliv (1903), 166-169.

Eggar, Katherine E. "The seventeenth Earl of Oxford as musician, poet and controller of the queen's revels," *Proceedings of the Musical Association,* 61st session (1935), 39-60.

Einstein, Alfred. "The English madrigal and 'Musica Transalpina,'" *Music and Letters,* xxv (1944), 66-77, xxvii (1946), 273-274.

Elson, Louis Charles. *Shakespeare in music; a collation of the chief musical allusions in the plays of Shakespeare, with an attempt at their explanation and derivation, together with much of the original music.* Boston, 1900 (1914).

Erlebach, Rupert. "William Lawes and his string music," *Proceedings of the Musical Association,* 59th session (1933), 103-119.

Esdaile, Katharine A. *English Church Monuments 1510 to 1840.* London, 1946.

Evans, Willa M. *Ben Jonson and Elizabethan Music.* Lancaster, 1929.

Fellowes, Edmund Horace. *English cathedral music from Edward VI to Edward VII.* 3d edn., London, 1946.

Fellowes, E. H. *English madrigal.* London, 1925.

Bibliography

Fellowes, E. H. *The English madrigal composers.* Oxford, 1921.

Fellowes, E. H. "John Wilbye," *Proceedings of the Musical Association,* 41st session (1915), 55-86.

Fellowes, E. H. "Misprints and errors," *Music and Letters,* XVII (1936), 371-373.

Fellowes, E. H. *Organists and masters of the choristers of St. George's Chapel in Windsor Castle.* London, 1939(?).

Fellowes, E. H. "Orlando Gibbons, 1583-1625," *Proceedings of the Musical Association,* 51st session (1925), 39-56.

Fellowes, E. H. *Orlando Gibbons. A short account of his life and work.* Oxford, 1925.

Fellowes, E. H. "The songs of Dowland," *Proceedings of the Musical Association,* 56th session (1930), 1-26.

Fellowes, E. H. "Thomas Weelkes," *Proceedings of the Musical Association,* 42d session (1916), 117-143.

Fellowes, E. H. *William Byrd.* London, 1936.

Firth, C. H. *The House of Lords during the Civil War.* London, 1910.

Fitzgibbon, H. Macaulay. "Instruments and their music in the Elizabethan drama," *Musical Quarterly,* XVII (1931), 319-329.

Flood, W. H. G. "Master Sebastian of Paul's," *Musical Antiquary,* III (1912), 149-157.

Flood, W. H. G. "Queen Mary's Chapel Royal," *English Historical Review,* XXXIII (1918), 83-89.

Förster, Max. "Shakespeare-musik," *Germanisch-Romanische Monatsschrift,* XVI (1928), 298-304.

Foss, Hubert J. [ed.]. *The heritage of music.* Oxford, 1928-1934.

Fox, Evelyn. "The diary of an Elizabethan gentlewoman," *Transactions of the Royal Historical Society,* 3d series, II (1908), 153-174.

Frere, W. H. *The English Church in the reigns of Elizabeth and James I. (1558-1625).* London, 1904.

Gage, John. *History and antiquities of Hengrave, in Suffolk.* London, 1822.

Galpin, Francis W. *Old English instruments of music. Their history and character.* 3d edn., London, 1932.

Galpin, Francis W. "The sackbut, its evolution and history," *Proceedings of the Musical Association,* 33d session (1907), 1-25.

Gladding, Bessie A. "Music as a social force during the English Commonwealth and Restoration," *Musical Quarterly,* XV (1929), 506-521.

Glyn, M. H. *About Elizabethan virginal music and its composers.* 2d edn., London, 1934.

Glyn, M. H. "The National School of Virginal Music in Elizabethan Times," *Proceedings of the Musical Association,* 43d session (1917), 29-50.

Gordon, Philip. "The Morley-Shakespeare myth," *Music and Letters,* XXVIII (1947), 121-125.

Graves, Thornton S. "The 'Act Time' in Elizabethan theatres," *Studies in Philology*, XII (1915), 103-134.

Green, Valentine. *The history and antiquities of the city and suburbs of Worcester*. London, 1796.

Gross, Charles. *The Gild Merchant*. Oxford, 1890.

Grout, Donald J. *A short history of opera*. New York, 1947.

Grove's dictionary of music and musicians, ed. H. C. Colles. 3d edn., New York, (1927) 1935. *Supplementary Volume*. New York, 1940.

Hadland, F. A. "The waits," *Musical News. A weekly journal of music*, XLIX (1915), 106-107, 125-126, 149-150, 177-178, 198-200, 214-215.

Hall, Hubert. *Society in the Elizabethan Age*. 4th edn., London, 1901.

Hamilton, A. H. A. *Quarter sessions from Queen Elizabeth to Queen Anne . . . (chiefly of the county of Devon.)* London, 1878.

Hammerich, Angul. "Musical relations between England and Denmark in the seventeenth century," *Sammelbände der internationalen musikgesellschaft*, XIII (1912), 114-119.

Harris, Clement A. "Church choirs in history," *Music and Letters*, XVII (1936), 210-217.

Harris, David G. T. "Musical education in Tudor times (1485-1603)," *Proceedings of the Musical Association*, 65th session (1939), 109-139.

Hawkins, Sir John. *A general history of the science and practise of music*. (London, 1776) 3d edn., London, 1875.

Hayes, Gerald. *King's music: an anthology. With an essay by Sir H. Walford Davies*. London, 1937.

Hayes, Gerald. *Musical instruments and their music 1500-1750*. London, 1928, 1930.

Helm, Everett B. "Italian traits in the English madrigal," *The Music Review*, VII (1946), 26-34.

Henderson, A. M. "Old English keyboard music (Byrd to Arne)," *Proceedings of the Musical Association*, 64th session (1938), 85-95.

Henry, Leigh. *Dr. John Bull, 1562-1628*. London, 1937.

Herford, C. H. and Percy Simpson. *Ben Jonson*. Oxford, 1925ff. Vols. 1 and 2, *The Man and his work*.

Hillebrand, Harold N. "The early history of the Chapel Royal," *Modern Philology*, XVIII (1921), 251-268.

Hope, R. C. "Notes on the Minstrels' Pillar, St. Mary's church, Beverley," *Transactions of the East Riding Antiquarian Society*, III (1895), 67-68.

Hope, R. C. "Notes on the musical instruments on the labels of the arches in the nave of Beverley Minster," *Transactions of the East Riding Antiquarian Society*, III (1895), 63-66.

Hough, John. "The historical significance of the counter-tenor," *Proceedings of the Musical Association*, 64th session (1938), 1-24.

Hughes, Charles W. "Richard Deering's Fancies for viols," *Musical Quarterly*, xxvii (1941), 38-46.

Hymns ancient and modern for use in the services of the church. With accompanying tunes. Historical edition with notes on the origins of both hymns and tunes and a general historical introduction [ed. W. H. Frere]. London, 1909.

James, Philip. "Early keyboard instruments," *Proceedings of the Musical Association*, 57th session (1931), 23-39.

James, Philip. *Early keyboard instruments from their beginnings to the year 1820.* London, 1930.

Jebb, John. "Catalogue of ancient choir-books at S. Peter's College, Cambridge," *Ecclesiologist*, xx (1859), 163-178, 242-254.

Jebb, John. *The choral service of the United Church of England and Ireland.* London, 1843.

Johnson, A. H. *The history of the worshipful company of the drapers of London: preceded by an introduction on London and her gilds up to the close of the XVth century.* Oxford, 1914-1922.

Jones, Paul Van Brunt. *The household of a Tudor nobleman.* Cedar Rapids, 1918.

Judd, P. "The songs of John Danyel," *Music and Letters*, xvii (1936), 118-123.

Judges, A. V. *The Elizabethan Underworld.* London, 1930.

Kastendiek, Miles Merwin. *England's musical poet, Thomas Campion.* New York, 1938.

Kelso, Ruth. *The doctrine of the English gentleman in the sixteenth century. With a bibliographical list of treatises on the gentleman and related subjects published in Europe to 1625.* Urbana, 1929.

Kennedy, W. P. M. *Elizabethan Episcopal Administration. An essay in sociology and politics.* Alcuin Club, vol. 25. London, 1924.

Kerr, Jessica M. "Mary Harvey—the Lady Dering," *Music and Letters*, xxv (1944), 23-33.

Kidson, Frank. *British Music Publishers, Printers and Engravers: . . . from Queen Elizabeth's reign to George the Fourth's, with select bibliographical lists of musical works printed and published within that period.* London, 1900.

Knappen, M. M. *Tudor puritanism. A chapter in the history of idealism.* Chicago, 1939.

Knights, L. C. *Drama & society in the age of Jonson.* London, 1937.

Kramer, Stella. *The English Craft Gilds and the Government.* New York, 1905.

Kramer, Stella. *The English Craft Gilds.* New York, 1927.

Kristeller, Paul O. "Music and learning in the early Italian Renaissance," *Journal of renaissance and baroque music*, i (1947), 255-274.

Bibliography

Lafontaine, H. Cart de. "The King's Musick," *Proceedings of the Musical Association*, 36th session (1910), 29-45.

Lambert, J. Malet. *Two thousand years of Gild Life*. Hull, 1891.

Langwill, Lyndesay G. "The bassoon: its origin and evolution," *Proceedings of the Musical Association*, 66th session, 1940, 1-21.

Lawrence, W. J. "Music in the Elizabethan Theatre," *Musical Quarterly*, VI (1920), 192-205.

Lawrence, W. J. *The Elizabethan Playhouse and other studies*. Philadelphia, 1912.

Lawrence, W. J. "William Treasorer," *Musical Antiquary*, III (1912), 103-106.

Leach, Arthur F. *English schools at the Reformation, 1546-48*. Westminster, 1896.

Lennard, Reginald, ed. *Englishmen at rest and play*. Oxford, 1931.

Leonard, E. M. *The early history of English poor relief*. Cambridge, 1900.

Ley, Henry G. "The music of the English church," *History*, New Series XVII (1932), 193-200.

Leycester, Sir Peter. *Historical antiquities of Cheshire*. London, 1673. See Ormerod, below.

Liljegren, S. B. *The fall of the monasteries and the social changes in England leading up to the Great Revolution*. Lund, 1923.

Lindsey, Edwin S. "The music in Ben Jonson's plays," *Modern Language Notes*, XLIV (1929), 86-92.

Lindsey, Edwin S. "The music of the songs in Fletcher's plays," *Studies in Philology*, XXI (1924), 325-355.

Lipson, E. *The economic history of England*. Vol. 1, 7th edn., 1937; vols. 2, 3, 2d edn., 1934. London.

Livi, Giovanni. "The Ferrabosco Family," *Musical Antiquary*, IV (1913), 121-142.

Lyon, John. *History of the town and port of Dover and Dover castle, with some account of the Cinque Ports*. Dover, 1813-1814.

Macdermott, Kenneth H. *Sussex church music in the past*. 2d edn., Chichester, 1923.

Maitland, S. R. "Archbishop Whitgift's college pupils," *The British magazine and monthly register of religious and ecclesiastical information*, XXXII (1847), 361-379, 508-528, 650-656, XXXIII (1848), 17-31, 185-195, 444-463.

Man, John. *The history and antiquities . . . of the borough of Reading*. Reading, 1816.

Manchée, W. H. *The Westminster City Fathers (the Burgess Court of Westminster) 1585-1901*. London, 1924.

Manly, J. M. "The children of the Chapel Royal and their masters," in *Cambridge History of English Literature*, ed. A. W. Ward and A. R. Waller, Cambridge, 1908ff., vol. 6, 279-292.

Bibliography

Mathew, David. *The Jacobean Age.* London, 1938.

McCabe, William H. "Music and dance on a 17th-century college stage," *Musical Quarterly,* xxiv (1938), 313-322.

Mee, John H. *The oldest music room in Europe. A record of eighteenth century enterprise at Oxford.* London, 1911.

Mees, Arthur. *Choirs and choral music.* New York, 1901.

Mellers, Wilfred. *Music and society.* London, 1946.

Meyer, Ernst H. *English chamber music.* London, 1946.

Meyer, Ernst H. "Form in the instrumental music of the seventeenth century," *Proceedings of the Musical Association,* 65th session (1939), 45-61.

Meyer, Ernst H. "The 'In Nomine' and the birth of polyphonic instrumental style in England," *Music and Letters,* xvii (1936), 25-36.

Meyer, Ernst H. *Die mehrstimmige Spielmusik des 17. Jahrhunderts in Nord- und Mitteleuropa. Mit einem Verzeichnis der deutschen Kammer- und Orchestermusikwerke des 17. Jahrhunderts.* Kassel, 1934.

Mildmay, H. A. St. John. *A brief memoir of the Mildmay Family.* London, 1913.

Millard, James Elwin. *Historical notices of the office of Choristers.* London, 1848.

Miller, Hugh M. "John Bull's organ works," *Music and Letters,* xxviii (1947), 25-35.

Miller, Hugh M. "Sixteenth-century English Faburden compositions for keyboard," *Musical Quarterly,* xxvi (1940), 50-64.

Miller, Hugh M. "Pretty wayes: for young beginners to looke on," *Musical Quarterly,* xxxiii (1947), 543-556.

Monk, W. H. "The cultivation of church music," *Proceedings of the Musical Association,* 8th session (1882), 29-58.

Murray, John Tucker. *English dramatic companies, 1558-1642.* London, 1910.

Music. A monthly magazine devoted to the art, science, technic and literature of music. Chicago, 1891-1902.

The Musician. London, 1905-1906.

The Musician. London, 1919-1921.

Nagel, Wilibald. "Die Entwickelung der Musik in England," *Die Musik,* v (1903), 35-45.

Nagel, Wilibald. *Geschichte des Musik in England.* Strassburg, 1894-1897.

Naylor, E. W. "Music and Shakespeare," *Musical Antiquary,* i (1910), 129-148.

Naylor, E. W. *Shakespeare and music.* 2d edn., London, 1931.

Naylor, E. W. "Three seventeenth century poet-parsons and music," *Proceedings of the Musical Association,* 54th session (1928), 93-113.

Neale, John Ernest. *Queen Elizabeth.* London, 1934.

Newton, Richard. "English lute music of the Golden Age," *Proceedings of the Musical Association,* 65th session (1939), 63-90.

Nicholls, George. *A history of the English poor law.* London, 1854.

Nichols, John. *History and antiquities of the county of Leicester.* London, 1795-1811.

Nichols, John. *The progresses, processions, and magnificent festivities of King James the First.* London, 1828.

Nichols, John. *The progresses and public processions of Queen Elizabeth.* 2d edn., London, 1823.

Nicholson, Sydney. *Quires and places where they sing.* London, 1932.

Nicholson, Sir Sydney H. "The choirboy and his place in English music," *Proceedings of the Musical Association,* 70th session (1944), 53-74.

Nicoll, Allardyce. *Stuart masques and the renaissance stage.* New York, 1938.

Nierling, J. "The music for Shakespeare," *Musical Quarterly,* XII (1926), 555-563.

Noble, Richmond S. H. *Shakespeare's use of song.* London, 1923.

"Notes on organs and organ-builders," *Musical Antiquary,* IV (1913), 98-102.

Oliver, George. *History and antiquities of the town and minster of Beverley.* Beverley, 1829.

O'Neill, Norman. "Music to stage plays in England," *Sammelbände der internationalen musikgesellschaft,* XIII (1912), 321-328.

Onions, C. T., ed. *Shakespeare's England.* Oxford, 1916.

Ormerod, George. *History of the county palatine and city of Chester . . . incorporated with a republication of King's Vale Royal and Leycester's Cheshire Antiquities,* 2d edn., ed. Thomas Helsby, London, 1882.

Ouseley, Sir Frederick Gore. "Considerations on the history of ecclesiastical music of western Europe," *Proceedings of the Musical Association,* 2d session (1876), 30-47.

Palmer, R. Liddesdale. *English social history in the making. The Tudor Revolution.* London, 1934.

Pattison, Bruce. "Literature and music in the age of Shakespeare," *Proceedings of the Musical Association,* 60th session (1934), 67-86.

Pattison, Bruce. *Music and poetry of the English renaissance.* London, 1948.

Pattison, Bruce. "The roundelay in the August ecloque of *The Shepheardes Calender,*" *The Review of English Studies,* IX (1933), 54-55.

Pattison, Bruce. "Sir Philip Sydney and music," *Music and Letters,* XV (1934), 75-81.

Pearce, E. H. *Annals of Christ's Hospital.* London, 1901.

Perkins, Jocelyn. *The crowning of the sovereign of Great Britain and the dominions overseas.* London, 1937.

Perkins, Jocelyn. *The organs and bells of Westminster Abbey.* London, 1937.

Pfatteicher, Carl F. *John Redford, organist and almoner of St. Paul's Cathedral in the reign of Henry VIII. With special reference to his organ compositions.* Kassel, 1934.

Bibliography

Phillips, C. Henry. *The singing church*. London, 1946.

Pickel, Margaret B. *Charles I as patron of poetry and drama*. London, 1936.

Poulson, George. *Beverlac; or, the antiquities and history of the town of Beverley*. London, 1829.

Prideaux, Sir Walter Sherburne. *Memorials of the Goldsmiths' Company being gleanings from their records between the years 1335 and 1815*. London, 1896(?).

Pulver, Jeffrey. *A biographical dictionary of old English music*. London, 1927.

Pulver, Jeffrey. *A dictionary of old English music and musical instruments*. London, 1923.

Pulver, Jeffrey. "Viols in England," *Proceedings of the Musical Association*, 47th session (1920), 1-21.

Ravn, V. C. "English instrumentalists at the Danish court in the time of Shakespeare," *Sammelbände der internationalen musikgesellschaft*, VII (1905), 550-563.

Reyher, Paul. *Les masques Anglais. Etude sur les ballets et la vie de court en Angleterre (1512-1640)*. Paris, 1909.

Ribton-Turner, C. J. *A history of vagrants and vagrancy and beggars and begging*. London, 1887.

Rimbault, Edward F. *The early English organ builders and their works from the fifteenth century to the period of the great rebellion*. London, 1864(?).

Robertson, Dora H. *Sarum Close. A history of the life and education of the cathedral choristers for 700 years*. London, 1938.

Roper, E. S. "Music in the English Chapels Royal c. 1135-Present Day," *Proceedings of the Musical Association*, 54th session (1928), 19-34.

Rowse, A. L. *The England of Elizabeth: The structure of society*. New York, 1951.

Rowse, Alfred L., and G. B. Harrison. *Queen Elizabeth and her subjects*. London, 1935.

Sachs, Curt. *The history of musical instruments*. New York, 1940.

Sachs, Curt. *World history of the dance*, translated by Bessie Schönberg. New York, 1937.

Salzman, L. F. *England in Tudor times: An account of its social life and industries*. London, 1926.

Sayle, R. T. D. *Lord Mayors' pageants of the Merchant Taylors' Company in the 15th, 16th and 17th centuries*. London, 1931.

Schelling, Felix E. *The Queen's progress and other Elizabethan sketches*. Boston, 1904.

Scholes, Percy A. "The musicians' company: a curious question," *The Monthly Musical Record*, LXII (1932), 195-196.

Scholes, Percy A. *Oxford companion to music*. London, 1938.

Scholes, Percy A. *The puritans and music in England and New England. A contribution to the cultural history of two nations*. London, 1934.

Scholes, Percy A. "The purpose behind Shakespeare's use of music," *Proceedings of the Musical Association*, 43d session (1917), 1-16.

Schramm, Percy E. *A history of the English coronation*, translated by L. G. Wickham Legg. Oxford, 1937.

Scott, Charles Kennedy. *Madrigal singing*. 2d edn., London, 1931.

Scott, Hugh Arthur. "London's earliest public concerts," *Musical Quarterly*, XXII (1936), 446-457.

Sellers, Maud. "The city of York in the sixteenth century," *English Historical Review*, IX (1894), 275-304.

Sharp, Thomas. *A dissertation on the pageants or dramatic mysteries anciently performed at Coventry*. Coventry, 1825.

Shaw, G. Bernard. "The reminiscences of a quinquagenarian," *Proceedings of the Musical Association*, 37th session (1911), 17-27.

Shore, S. Royle. "The vocal accompaniment of Plainchant," *Proceedings of the Musical Association*, 61st session (1935), 105-125.

Smart, John S. "The Italian singer in Milton's sonnets," *Musical Antiquary*, IV (1913), 91-97.

Social England, ed. H. D. Traill and J. S. Mann. 2d edn., London, 1902.

Southgate, T. L. and others. *English music [1604 to 1904] being the lectures given at the music loan exhibition of the worshipful company of musicians, held at Fishmongers' Hall, London Bridge, June-July, 1904*. 2d edn., London, 1911.

S[quire], W. B. "John Dowland," *Musical Times*, XXXVII (1896), 792-794, XXXVIII (1897), 92-93.

Stainer, J. F. R. "The middle temple masque," *Musical Times*, XLVII (1906), 21-24.

Stainer, Sir John. "On the musical introductions found in certain metrical psalters," *Proceedings of the Musical Association*, 27th session (1901), 1-50.

Stanier, R. S. *Magdalen school. A history of Magdalen college school, Oxford*. Oxford Historical Society, New Series, vol. 3. Oxford, 1940.

Steele, Mary Susan. *Plays and masques at court during the reigns of Elizabeth, James and Charles*. New Haven, 1926.

Steele, Robert. *The earliest English music printing; a description and bibliography of English printed music to the close of the sixteenth century*. London, 1903.

Stephen, George Arthur. *The waits of the city of Norwich, through four centuries to 1790*. Norwich, 1933.

Stopes, Charlotte C. "Mary's Chapel Royal and her coronation play," *The Athenaeum*, No. 4063, 9 September 1905, 346-347.

Stopes, Charlotte C. "William Hunnis and the revels of the Chapel Royal," *Materialien zur kunde des älteren Englischen dramas*, ed. W. Bang, vol. 29, Louvain, 1910.

Stopes, Charlotte C. "William Hunnis, the dramatist," *The Athenaeum*, No. 3779, 31 March 1900, 410-412.

Stowe, A. R. M. *English grammar schools in the reign of Queen Elizabeth*. New York, 1908.

Straeten, E. Van der. *The history of the violin*. London, 1933.

Sullivan, Mary. *Court masques of James I. Their influence on Shakespeare and the public theatres*. New York, 1913.

Symonds, E. M. "The diary of John Greene," *English Historical Review*, XLIII (1928), 385-394, 598-604.

Tanner, Thomas and James Nasmith. *Notitia Monastica*. London, 1787.

Terry, Charles Sanford. *Bach, a biography*. London, 1928.

Terry, Sir Richard. "Calvin's first psalter," *Proceedings of the Musical Association*, 57th session (1931), 1-21.

Terry, R. R. "John Merbecke (1523?-1585)," *Proceedings of the Musical Association*, 45th session (1919), 75-96.

Thewlis, George A. "Oxford and the Gibbons Family," *Music and Letters*, XXI (1940), 31-33.

Thompson, James. *History of Leicester from the time of the Romans to the end of the seventeenth century*. Leicester, 1849.

Thomson, Gladys Scott. *Two centuries of family history. A study in social development*. London, 1930.

Thorp, Margaret Farrand. "Shakespeare and the fine arts," *Publications of the Modern Language Association*, XLVI (1931), 672-693.

Trevor-Roper, H. R. *Archbishop Laud 1573-1645*. London, 1940.

Trotter, Eleanor. *Seventeenth century life in the country parish, with special reference to local government*. Cambridge, 1919.

Turberville, Arthur S. *A history of Welbeck abbey and its owners*. Vol. 1, 1539-1755. London, 1938.

Unwin, George. *Gilds and companies of London*. 3d edn., London, 1938.

Unwin, George. *Industrial organization in the sixteenth and seventeenth centuries*. Oxford, 1904.

Victoria history of the counties of England, by William Page and others. Westminster, 1900ff.

Walker, Ernest. *A history of music in England*. London, 1924 (1907).

Wallace, Charles W. *The children of the chapel at Blackfriars 1597-1603*. University Studies of the University of Nebraska, vol. 8, 103-321. Lincoln, Nebraska, 1908.

Warlock, P. *The English Ayre*. London, 1926.

Watson, Foster. *The English grammar schools to 1660: their curriculum and practice*. Cambridge, 1908.

Webb, Sidney and Beatrice. *English local government from the revolution to the municipal corporations act*. London, 1906-1929.

Weekes, Walter P. "Presidential address [on the history of music]," *Annual*

Bibliography

Reports and Transactions of the Plymouth Institution and Devon and Cornwall Natural History Society, XVII, i (1925), 3-23.

Weigall, Rachel. "An Elizabethan gentlewoman," *Quarterly Review*, CCXV (1911), 119-138.

Welch, Charles. *History of the Cutlers' Company of London*. London, 1916, 1923.

Welch, Charles. *History of the Worshipful Company of Pewterers of the city of London based upon their own records*. London, 1902.

Welch, Christopher. *Six lectures on the recorder and other flutes in relation to literature*. London, 1911.

Welch, R. D. "Shakespeare—Musician," *Musical Quarterly*, VIII (1922), 510-527.

Wells, Henry W. *Elizabethan and Jacobean Playwrights*. New York, 1939.

Welsford, Enid. *The court masque*. Cambridge, 1927.

West, John E. *Cathedral organists past and present*. London, 1899.

West, John E. "Old English organ music," *Proceedings of the Musical Association*, 37th session (1911), 1-16.

West, John E. "Old English organ music," *Sammelbände der internationalen musikgesellschaft*, XII (1911), 213-221.

West, Violet Sackville-. *Knole and the Sackvilles*. London, 1922.

Westrup, J. A. "Domestic music under the Stuarts," *Proceedings of the Musical Association*, 68th session (1942), 19-53.

Westrup, J. A. "Foreign musicians in Stuart England," *Musical Quarterly*, XXVII (1941), 70-89.

Westrup, J. A. "William Byrd (1543-1623)," *Music and Letters*, XXIV (1943), 125-130.

Whitaker, Wilfred B. *Sunday in Tudor and Stuart Times*. London, 1933.

Whitley, William T. *Congregational hymn singing*. London, 1933.

Whittaker, W. Gillies. "Byrd's Great Service," *Musical Quarterly*, XXVII (1941), 474-490.

Willcox, William B. *Gloucestershire. A study in local government 1590-1640*. New Haven, 1940.

Williams, Charles F. Abdy. *A short historical account of the degrees in music at Oxford and Cambridge*. London, 1893.

Williamson, George Charles. *George, Third Earl of Cumberland (1558-1605). His life and his voyages. A study from original documents*. Cambridge, 1920.

Williamson, George Charles. *Lady Anne Clifford, Countess of Dorset, Pembroke, and Montgomery, 1590-1676: Her life, letters, and work*. London, 1922.

Wilson, Elkin C. *Prince Henry and English Literature*. Ithaca, 1946.

Wilson, F. P. "The English jest-books of the sixteenth and early seventeenth centuries," *Huntington Library Quarterly*, II (1939), 121-138.

Bibliography

Wodderspoon, John. *Memorials of the ancient town of Ipswich*. Ipswich, 1850.

Wolf, Johannes. "Early English musical theorists from 1200 to the death of Henry Purcell," *Musical Quarterly*, xxv (1939), 420-429.

Wolf, Johannes. "English influence in the evolution of music," *Sammelbände der internationalen musikgesellschaft*, xiii (1912), 33-39.

Woodward, G. R. "The Genevan psalter of 1562; set in four-part harmony by Claude Goudimel in 1565," *Proceedings of the Musical Association*, 44th session (1918), 167-192.

Wright, Louis. *Middle-class culture in Elizabethan England*. Chapel Hill, 1935.

Young, Percy. "The Royal Music," *Music and Letters*, xviii (1937), 119-127.

INDEX AND GLOSSARY

The names of the less familiar musical terms are listed alphabetically in the index and briefly described or distinguished there (see reference works such as Grove, Pulver, Scholes). Only more important references are given.

Abraham, Gerald, xiv

actors: laws against vagabondage, 56-58; licenses to travel, 56, 57; nominally retained, 65-66; play nights at court, 188

Adeon, John, 44, 45n, 51, 185

alien musicians: attracted to King's Musick, 177, 195; in London, 63

Alison, Richard, 60

almoner, 136, 146

Anne of Denmark, Queen (wife of James I), 149, 179, 180, 189

anthems: 148; verse, 150; books of, 156n

Anthony, Saint, 9

apprentices: functions of institution, 16-17, 21; general custom and law governing, 122; in Beverley, 117; in households of aristocracy, 68-70; in London, Company of Musicians of, 16-25; age, 24-25; examination, 18; formal requirements, 24-25; freedom of company and city, 23; life, 17; masterpiece not required, 19; musical training, 18; number of, 21, 22, 23; professional lore, 17-18; term of indentures, 21; transfer of, 24; in York, 111-112; in non-musical occupations, 202-203

ARCHLUTE: Bass of the lute family, with extra bass strings at the side. See plates.

Armada, defeat of, 80

Ascham, Roger, 212-214

Attey, John, 59

Bach, J. S., 195

Bacon: Edward, 61n; Sir Francis, 52; Sir Nicholas, 49

bagpipe: 178, 183, 202; Lincolnshire bagpipe, 234; rustic musician called, 128; waits use, 85

baitings, bear, bull, 206

BANDORA: Plucked, wire-strung, instrument, providing bass for a consort, also called pandora. 52, 193

barbers and surgeons, fellowship of in Canterbury, minstrels and waits assigned to, 114

barbershops, 203

Barnstaple, waits' wages in, 93

Bartlet, John, 61n, 70

Barton, independent musicians of, 120n, 233

Bassano family: 178, 182; Andrew, 42, 43n; Anthony, 184, 185; Arthur, 42, 43n; Augustine, 184; Baptista, 184; Edward, 181; Henry, 185; Jasper, 184; Jerome, 42, 43n; John, 184; Lodovico, 184; Mark Anthony, 184; see also Appendix E, 296-313

Bateson, Thomas, 60

Bath: caves near, 236; organ built, 155; waits at Southampton, 107

Bedern, residence of vicars choral of York, 138

beef breakfasts, York waits play at, 81

Bertie Household Accounts, 252-253

Beverley: Minstrels' Pillar, St. Mary's, 116; waits' chains and badges, 90

Fraternity of minstrels of: claims jurisdiction over area between Trent and Tweed rivers, 116; reserves monopolies in, 117; apprenticeship, 117; limits teaching, 117; restricts villagers, 127

Blackfriars Theatre, music at, 236

Blancq (Blanck, Blancks), Edward, 43n, 44

Brathwaite, Richard, 215, 217-218, 235

brideales (briales), 125, 206

Bridgewater, earl of, 59-60, 64, 64n; see also Ellesmere, Lord

Bristol: parish churches, 155, 156; population, 109

Cathedral choir: choristers, 142; deprived of "house of commons," 138; organist-master of choristers, 142; pay, 137; size reduced to increase pay, 137; some singing-men also parish clerks or organists resulting in abandonment of singing at certain services, 139, 151-152; voices reported indifferent, 152; wealthy singing-man also epistoler, 147-148

Waits: rental allowance, 99; at Nottingham, 105; at Southampton, 107

brotherhoods (brotherhedis), 28

Buckingham, marquis and duke of, 42, 61, 63

Bull, John, 149, 163, 164, 174, 223n

Byrd, William, 148, 150, 163, 166, 191

Cambridge: colleges, 135, 172-173, 194; waits visit Coventry, 107; wages of waits, 93

Campion, Thomas, 192

Canterbury: Chapel Royal gentlemen from, 194; fellowship of minstrels, 114-115; minstrels put into fellowship of barbers and surgeons, 114

Cathedral choir: choristers, 141, 145; cornetts and sackbuts with, 149; master of children, 141; pay, 137; size maintained by employing low-salaried substitutes, 135-136

Waits: celebrate holidays, welcome celebrities, play at official dinners, 80, 81; dispute number of boys, 84; livery, 89; num-